BLOOD
ROYAL

Also by Hugh Bicheno

Battle Royal

BLOOD ROYAL

THE WARS OF THE ROSES: 1462–1485

HUGH BICHENO

PEGASUS BOOKS
NEW YORK LONDON

Blood Royal

Pegasus Books Ltd
148 West 37th Street, 13th Floor
New York, NY 10018

Copyright © 2017 by Hugh Bicheno

First Pegasus Books hardcover edition June 2017

ISBN: 978-1-68177-428-2

10 9 8 7 6 5 4 3 2 1

Printed in the United States of America
Distributed by W. W. Norton & Company, Inc.

For
JACK and ISABELLA
SEBASTIAN and RUAN

My Heart's Delight

CONTENTS

List of Maps 1–32 · x

List of Tables · xi

Protagonists and Marriages · xii

Maps 1–4 · xxvi

Princes of the Blood Family Tree · xxx

House of York Family Tree · xxxii

House of Neville Family Tree · xxxiv

House of Woodville Family Tree · xxxvi

Preface · xxxviii

Chronology of the events of *Battle Royal* · xl

Prologue · Legitimacy · 1

I · Edward · 10

II · Warwick · 20

III · Louis · 30

IV · Elizabeth · 42

V · Henchmen · 53

VI · Clarence · 64

VII · Edward · 76

VIII · Warwick · 84

IX · Kingship · 93

X · Treason · 102

XI · *Coup d'état* · 111

XII · Showdown · 122

XIII · Biter Bit · 132

XIV · Noises Off · 144

XV · Out of the Ashes · 152

XVI · Bloodless Victory · 161

XVII · The Arrival · 170

XVIII · Epic of Arms · 181

XIX · Crush the Seed · 191

XX · Gloucester · 202

XXI · Elizabeth · 212

XXII · Edward · 221

XXIII · Dishonour · 230

XXIV · Septic Siblings · 241

XXV · Money Matters · 250

XXVI · The Marches · 260

XXVII · Daggers in Men's Smiles · 272

XXVIII · Naked Villainy · 282

XXIX · Nemesis · 293

XXX · Hearts and Minds · 304

XXXI · Opening Moves · 313

XXXII · Endgame · 323

XXXIII · Checkmate · 334

Epilogue · Somewhat Musing · 346

Appendix A · 352
English Peerage 1462–85, by seniority

Appendix B · 360
Archbishops and Bishops 1462–85

Appendix C · 362
Chief Office Holders 1462–85

Appendix D · 363
Titles, Lands, Honours and Offices of
Richard 'The Kingmaker' Neville

Appendix E · 365
1475 Expedition: Indentures

Appendix F · 369
Titulus Regius

Further Reading · 375

Acknowledgements · 382

Image Credits · 382

Index · 383

MAPS

1. Historic Counties and Regions of England and Wales · xxiii
2. Archdioceses and Dioceses of England and Wales · xxiv
3. Ancient Roads, Rivers and Battlefields · xxv
4. Great North Road and Western Spur · xxvi
5. Sieges & Battles in the North-East, 1462–4 · 16
6. Kingdom of France 1461 · 32
7. Burgundian Lands 1461 · 33
8. Wales and the Marches · 56
9. Principal Estates of the Crown and Leading Magnates, c. 1455 · 66
10. Redistribution of Estates, c. 1468 · 67
11. East Riding, Yorkshire · 109
12. Edgcote Campaign, 1469 · 116
13. Battle of Edgcote · 124
14. Losecote Campaign, 1470 · 138
15. The Channel, 1470 · 162
16. Edward's Itinerary, 1470–71 · 171
17. Barnet Campaign, 1471 · 176
18. Battle of Barnet, 15 April 1471 · 186
19. The Channel, 1471 · 192
20. Tewkesbury Campaign, 1471 · 195
21. Battle of Tewkesbury, 4 May 1471 · 197
22. Richard's North, 1471–75 · 205
23. Edward IV's Expedition, 1475 · 233
24. Prince Edward's Council · 263
25. Scots Border Campaign, 1480–82 · 267
26. Richard III's Progress, 1483 · 295
27. Henry Tudor's Invasion, August 1485: Converging Armies · 327

28. Henry Tudor's Invasion, August 1485: Advance to
Contact · 327

29. Battle of Bosworth, 22 August 1485: Close Approach,
Phase 1 · 335

30. Battle of Bosworth, 22 August 1485: Close Approach,
Phase 2 · 335

31. Advance to Contact · 338

32. Death Ride · 339

TABLES

Neville and Woodville Marriages · 49

Chronology of the 1469 Edgcote Campaign · 117

Chronology of the 1470 Losecote Campaign · 139

Chronology of the 1471 Barnet Campaign · 177

Named in *The Ballad of Bosworth Field* · 330

PROTAGONISTS AND MARRIAGES

d: died of natural causes   k: killed in battle   x: executed or murdered

Angus, Earl of – see Douglas, Black and Red.

Anjou, Marguerite d' (d.1482), Henry VI's queen, mother of Edward of Westminster and heroic leader of the Lancastrians.

Anjou, René d' (d.1480), Duke of. Failed claimant to kingdoms of Naples and Aragon, indifferent father of Marguerite.

Arundel, Earl of – see FitzAlan, William.

Audley, Lord – see Tuchet, John.

Austria, Archduke Maximilian of (d.1519), heir of Emperor Frederick III of Habsburg, married Duchess Marie of Burgundy.

Beauchamp, Anne (d.1492), Countess of Warwick by right, married the Kingmaker.

Beaufort, Edmund (k.1471), styled Duke of Somerset, Henry's younger brother.

Beaufort, Henry (x.1464), Duke of Somerset. Devoted Lancastrian.

Beaufort, John (k.1471), styled Marquess of Dorset. Henry's youngest brother.

Beaufort, Margaret (d.1509), married (1) Edmund Tudor, Earl of Richmond, by whom mother of Henry VII; (2) Henry Stafford; (3) Thomas, Baron Stanley.

Beaujeu, Anne of (d.1522), eldest daughter of Louis XI, regent for Charles VIII.

Beaumont, William (d.1507), Viscount. Unjustly attainted Lancastrian.

Bedford, Duchess/Duke of – see Luxembourg, Jacquetta de/ Neville, George.

Bellingham, Henry (d.1484), one of the last Lancastrian knights to submit.

Bergavenny, Lord – see Neville, Edward.

Berkeley, William (d.1492), Lord Berkeley/Earl of Nottingham. Victor over Viscount Lisle at Nibley Green.

Berners, Lord – see Bourchier, John.

Berry, Charles (d.1472), Duke of. Troublesome younger brother of Louis XI.

Blount, Walter (d.1474), Lord Mountjoy. Married widow of 1st Duke of Buckingham.

Bonville, Cecily (d.1529), Baroness Bonville and Harington by right. Wealthiest heiress in England, married Thomas Grey, Marquess of Dorset.

Booth, Laurence (d.1480), Prince-Bishop of Durham, Lord Chancellor and Archbishop of York.

Booth, William (d.1464), Archbishop of York, older half-brother of Laurence.

Boteler, Lady Eleanor (d.1467), née Talbot, mistress of Edward IV.

Boteler, Ralph (d.1473), Yorkist, father-in-law of Lady Eleanor.

Bourchier, Edward (d.1539), Lord FitzWarin.

Bourchier, Eleanor (d.1474), dowager Duchess of Norfolk, Henry's sister.

Bourchier, Henry (d.1483), Viscount Bourchier, Earl of Essex, Lord Treasurer, uncle of Edward IV by marriage.

Bourchier, Humphrey (k.1471), Lord Cromwell, Henry's son.

Bourchier, Humphrey (k.1471), son of Lord Berners.

Bourchier, John (d.1474), Lord Berners, Henry's brother.

Bourchier, John (d.1495), Lord Ferrers of Groby by marriage, Henry's son.

Bourchier, John (d.1539), Lord FitzWarin. Youthful supporter of Henry Tudor.

Bourchier, Thomas (d.1486), Cardinal Archbishop of Canterbury, Henry's younger brother.

Bourchier, William (d.1470), Lord FitzWarin by marriage, Henry's brother.

Bourchier, William (d.1480), Viscount Bourchier, Henry's heir, married Anne Woodville. Their son inherited the earldom of Essex.

Bracher, William (x.1485), Yeoman of the Crown. He betrayed his comrades.

Brackenbury, Robert (k.1485), Gloucester retainer, Constable of the Tower of London.

Bray, Reginald (d.1503), Confidential courier of Lady Margaret Beaufort, built Henry VII Chapel, Westminster Abbey.

Bresse, Phillipe of (d.1497), Prince of Savoy. Bitter enemy of Louis XI.

Brézé, Pierre de (k.1465), Seneschal of Normandy, devoted supporter of Marguerite d'Anjou.

Brittany, Frañsez (d.1488), Duke of. Erratic supporter of the Lancastrian cause.

Brooke, John (d.1512), Lord Cobham. Devoted Yorkist.

Brugge, Lodewijk van (d.1492), lord of Gruuthuse, made Earl of Winchester for helping Edward IV recover the throne.

Buckingham, Duke of – see Stafford, Henry.

Burgh, Thomas (d.1496), lord of Gainsborough, Edward IV's Master of the Horse.

Burgundy, Anthony (d.1504), Grand Bastard of, half-brother of Charles 'the Bold's'.

Burgundy, Charles 'the Bold' (k.1477), Duke of, previously Count of Charolais, married (2) Margaret of York.

Burgundy, Marie (d.1482), Duchess of, only child of Charles 'the Bold', married Archduke Maximilian of Austria.

Burgundy, Philippe (d.1467), Duke of, married Isabella of Portugal, John of Gaunt's granddaughter.

Butler, John (d.1478), Earl of Ormond in Ireland.

Castille – see Isabella.

Catesby, William (x.1485), betrayer of Lord Hastings, close confederate of Richard III.

Chandée, Philibert de, lord of Montfalcon, future Marshal of France. Commanded Henry Tudor's vanguard and rewarded with the earldom of Bristol.

Charolais, Count of – see Burgundy, Charles 'the Bold', Duke of.

Chastellain, Georges (d.1475), Chronicler, secretary to Pierre de Brézé, courtier of Charles 'the Bold'.

Clapham, John (x.1470), Midlands esquire of the body to the Kingmaker.

Clarence, George (x.1478), Duke of. Treacherous younger brother of Edward IV; married Isabel Neville, the Kingmaker's elder daughter.

Cobham, Lord – see Brooke, John.

Commynes, Philippe de (d.1511), Chronicler, councillor to Charles 'the Bold' and Louis XI.

Conyers, John (d.1489), steward of Middleham for the Kingmaker and Richard of Gloucester.

Cooke, Thomas (d.1478), London draper and alderman, Lord Mayor in 1462. Persecuted by Edward IV.

Corbet, Richard (d.1493), Shropshire knight, fought for Henry Tudor.

Courtenay of Bocconoc, Hugh (x.1471), cousin of the Earls of Devon. Lancastrian, son Edward fought for Henry Tudor and made Earl of Devon.

Courtenay of Powderham, brothers William, Walter and Humphrey. Opponents of their cousins the Earls of Devon, members of Clarence's affinity.

Courtenay, Elizabeth (d.1493), widow of James Luttrell and Humphrey Tuchet, both killed fighting for Lancaster, godmother to Clarence's son.

Courtenay, Henry (x.1469), heir to the attainted earldom of Devon. Judicially murdered.

Courtenay, John (k.1471), restored as Earl of Devon in 1470.

Courtenay, Peter (d.1492), Bishop of Exeter. Fought for Henry Tudor.

Cromwell, Baron – see Bourchier, Humphrey.

Crowland Continuator, Invaluable anonymous clerical chronicler.

Dacre, Humphrey (d.1485), heir to attainted Dacre of the North barony, restored 1473.

Daubeney, Giles (d.1508), leading 1483 rebel, later Lord Daubeney.

Devereux, Walter (k.1485), Lord Ferrers of Chartley by marriage, brother-in-law of William Herbert. Lifelong Yorkist, supporter of Richard III.

Devon, Earl of – see Stafford of Southwyck, Humphrey and Courtenay, John.

Dorset, Marquess of – see Beaufort, John and Grey, Thomas.

Douglas, Archibald 'Bell the Cat' (d.1513), Red Earl of Angus.

Douglas, George (d.1463), Red Earl of Angus.

Douglas, James (d.1488), last Black Earl of Angus.

Dudley, Lord – see Sutton, John.

Duras, Gaillard (d.1481), lord of. Narbonnais exile, loyal Yorkist, Governor of Calais.

Dynham, John (d.1501), Lord, comrade-in-arms of Edward IV, Lord Treasurer.

Edward IV (d.1483), King of England, son of Cecily Neville, married Elizabeth Woodville.

Edward V (x.1483), briefly King of England.

Edward of Middleham (d.1484), Prince of Wales, Richard III's son.

Edward of Westminster (k.1471), Prince of Wales, Henry VI's son, married Anne Neville.

Essex, Earl of – see Bourchier, Henry.

Exeter, Duke of – see Holland, Henry.

Fauconberg, Bastard of – see Neville, Thomas.

Fauconberg, Lord – see Neville, William.

Ferrers of Chartley, Lord – see Devereux, Walter.

Ferrers of Groby, Elizabeth (d.1483), Baroness by right, mother of Elizabeth Woodville's first husband John Grey, married (2) John Bourchier.

Fiennes, William (k.1471), Lord Saye and Sele.

FitzAlan, Thomas (d.1524), Lord Maltravers, married Margaret Woodville.

FitzAlan, William (d.1487), Earl of Arundel, married the Kingmaker's sister Joan.

FitzHugh, Henry (d.1472), Lord, Kingmaker retainer, married his sister Anne.

Fitzwarin, Lord – see Bourchier, William and John.

Fogge, John (d.1490), household treasurer for Henry VI and Edward IV. Fought for Henry Tudor.

Fortescue, Dr John (d.1480), jurist, Marguerite d'Anjou's chancellor in exile.

Fortescue, John (d.1515), Hertfordshire knight, esquire of the body to Edward IV.

Frederick III (d.1493), first Habsburg Holy Roman Emperor.

Fulford, Thomas (d.1490). Lancastrian West Country knight and outstandingly persistent troublemaker.

Gates, Geoffrey (d.1477), Marshal of Calais for the Kingmaker.

Gloucester, John of, illegitimate son of Richard III.

Gloucester, Richard, Duke of – see Richard III.

Grey of Codnor, Henry (d.1496), Lord. Disputatious Midlands magnate.

Grey of Powys, John (d.1497), created baron in 1482, a title claimed by his attainted father but not previously confirmed.

Grey of Ruthyn, Henry (d.1490), Lord, later Earl of Kent. Eldest son married Eleanor Woodville, second son married Anne Woodville, widow of William, Viscount Bourchier.

Grey, Edward (d.1504), Viscount Lisle by marriage, Queen Elizabeth's brother-in-law from her first marriage. Richard III supporter.

Grey, Richard (x.1483), younger son of Elizabeth Woodville's first marriage, member of the Prince of Wales's Council.

Grey, Ralph (x.1464), Northumberland Yorkist turncoat.

Grey, Thomas (d.1501), Marquess of Dorset, elder son of Elizabeth Woodville's first marriage, married (1) Anne Holland, daughter of Anne of York; (2) Cecily Bonville.

Grey, William (d.1478), Bishop of Ely. papal appointee, Yorkist.

Greystoke, Ralph (d.1487), Lord, Kingmaker retainer, married Henry FitzHugh's sister.

Gruuthuse, lord of – see Brugge, Lodewijk van.

Guelders, Mary of (d.1463), married James II of Scotland, regent mother of James III.

Hall, Edward (d.1547), Tudor chronicler.

Harcourt, Robert (x.1470), Midlands Kingmaker retainer.

Harrington, James (k.1485?), Gloucester retainer, feuded with Lord Stanley.

Hastings, Richard (d.1503), Lord Welles by marriage, son of William.

Hastings, William (x.1483), Lord, Edward IV's intimate friend and Lord Chamberlain. Mortal enemy of the Woodvilles, married the Kingmaker's sister Katherine.

Haute, Richard (d.1487), comptroller of the Prince of Wales's household, married Earl Rivers's sister Elizabeth.

Henry VI (x.1471), King of England, married Marguerite d'Anjou.

Henry VII (d.1509), King of England, married Elizabeth of York.

Herbert of Raglan, William (x.1469), Lord Herbert, later Earl of Pembroke. Held Wales for Edward IV, half-brother of the Vaughan brothers, married sister of Walter Devereux.

Herbert, Richard (x.1469), younger brother of the elder William.

Herbert, Walter (d.1507), younger brother of the younger William. Fought for Henry Tudor.

Herbert, William (d.1491), Lord Dunster/Earl of Pembroke/Earl of Huntingdon, married (1) Mary Woodville; (2) Katherine, bastard daughter of Richard III.

Hervey, Nicholas (x.1471), Bristol City Recorder, Lancastrian.

Hildyard, Robert (d.1485), rebel 'Robin of Holderness'.

Holland, Henry (x.1475), Duke of Exeter, divorced husband of Edward IV's sister Anne of York.

Howard, John (k.1485), Lord, later Duke of Norfolk. Henchman of Edward IV, key player in Richard III's *coup d'état* and right-hand man.

Hungerford, Robert (x.1464), Lord Hungerford and Moleyns. die-hard Lancastrian.

Hungerford, Thomas (x.1469), heir to the attainted barony.

Hungerford, Walter (d.1540), fought for Henry Tudor, barony restored.

Isabella (d.1504), Queen of Castille by right, rejected by Edward IV.

James III (k.1488), King of Scotland, kidnapped by his nobles in 1480.

Kendall, John (k.1485), Richard III's private secretary.

Kennedy, James (d.1465), Bishop of St Andrews. Opponent of regent Mary of Guelders.

Kent, Earl of – see Neville, William and Grey of Ruthyn, Edmund.

Kingmaker – see Richard Neville.

Landais, Pierre (x.1485), chief minister to Duke Frañsez of Brittany.

Langstrother, John (x.1471), Prior of St John's Hospital. Kingmaker henchman.

Latimer, Lord – see Neville, George.

Lincoln, Earl of – see Pole, John de la.

Louis XI 'the Universal Spider' (d.1483), King of France.

Lovell, Francis (d.1488?), Lord and Viscount Lovell. Lifelong friend of Richard III.

Lumley, Thomas (d.1485), Lord. Neville then Richard of Gloucester retainer, died before Bosworth.

Luttrell family, attainted Somerset Lancastrian family, fought for Henry Tudor, restored.

Luxembourg, Jacques de (d.1487), lord of Richebourg, brother of Jacquetta.

Luxembourg, Jacquetta de (d.1472), Duchess of Bedford, Countess Rivers, Woodville matriarch.

Luxembourg, Louis de (x.1475), Count of Saint-Pol, brother of Jacquetta. Perpetual schemer.

Mackerell, Dr Ralph, Jurist, colleague of John Morton, diehard Lancastrian.

Maletta, Alberico (d.1466), Milanese ambassador to Louis XI.

Maltravers, Lord – see FitzAlan, Thomas.

Mancini, Dominic, Observed and reported the events of 1483 in London for the French court.

Maredudd, Rhys ap (d.1510), Denbigh uplands clan chief, fought for Henry Tudor.

Markham, Dr John (d.1479), Chief Justice who defied Edward IV.

Milan, Duke of – see Sforza, Francesco and Galeazzo Maria.

Moleyns, Lord – see Hungerford, Robert.

Montgomery, Thomas (d.1495), diplomat for Edward IV, fought for Henry Tudor.

More, Thomas (x.1535), Author of the Tudor 'black legend' of Richard III.

Morton, Dr John (d.1500), councillor to Marguerite d'Anjou in exile, made Bishop of Ely by Edward IV. Bitter opponent of Richard III.

Mountjoy, Lord – see Blount, Walter.

Mowbray, Anne (d.1481), Countess of Norfolk, married Richard, Duke of York.

Mowbray, John (d.1476), Duke of Norfolk, married Elizabeth Talbot.

Neville, Anne (d.1485), the Kingmaker's younger daughter, married (1) Edward of Westminster; (2) Richard, Duke of Gloucester; later Richard III.

Neville, Cecily (d.1495), dowager Duchess of York, the Kingmaker's aunt, matriarch of the Yorkist dynasty.

Neville, Edward (d.1476), Lord Bergavenny by marriage, dispossessed by his nephew the Kingmaker.

Neville, George (d.1469), Lord Latimer by marriage, the Kingmaker's uncle and ward.

Neville, George (d.1476), Bishop of Exeter, Archbishop of York, the Kingmaker's brother.

Neville, George (d.1483), Duke of Bedford, deprived 1478, son of John Neville.

Neville, Isabel (d.1476), the Kingmaker's elder daughter, married George, Duke of Clarence.

Neville, John (k.1471), Lord Montagu, Earl of Northumberland, Marquess Montagu, the Kingmaker's brother.

Neville, Katherine (d.1484?), the Kingmaker's aunt, much remarried dowager Duchess of Norfolk.

Neville, Katherine (d.1504), the Kingmaker's sister, married (1) William Bonville, Baron Harington of Aldingham; (2) William, Lord Hastings.

Neville, Ralph (d.1499), Lord, later Earl of Westmorland, Gloucester retainer.

Neville, Richard 'the Kingmaker' (k.1471), Earl of Warwick by marriage and Earl of Salisbury.

Neville, Thomas 'Bastard of Fauconberg' (x.1471), illegitimate son of William Neville.

Neville, William (d.1463), Lord Fauconberg by marriage, Earl of Kent, the Kingmaker's uncle.

Noreys, William (d.1506), Lancastrian knight reconciled with Edward IV, fought for Henry Tudor.

Norfolk, Duke of – see Mowbray, John and Howard, John.

Northumberland, Earl of – see Neville, John and Percy, Henry.

Ogle, Robert (k.1469), Lord. Northumberland Neville retainer and rebel 'Robin of Redesdale'.

Oxford, Earl of – see Vere, John.

Parr of Kendal, William (d.1483), Lord. Westmorland Neville retainer, later Edward IV's household comptroller.

Paston, John, father (d.1466) and two namesake sons (d.1479, 1509), East Anglian gentry whose letters and papers are an invaluable source for the period 1422–1509.

Pembroke, Earl of – see Tudor, Jasper and Herbert, William.

Percy of Scoton, Robert (k.1485), Lifelong Yorkist, Gloucester retainer.

Percy, Henry (x.1489), attainted Earl of Northumberland, restored 1470. Gloucester retainer.

Percy, Ralph (x.1464), uncle of Henry. Die-hard Lancastrian.

Pole, John de la (d.1492), Duke of Suffolk (restored 1463), married Edward IV's sister Elizabeth.

Pole, John de la (k.1487), Earl of Lincoln, married daughter of Thomas FitzAlan.

Portugal, Isabella of (d.1471), Duchess of Burgundy.

Ratcliffe, Richard (k.1485), Richard III's right-hand man in the North.

Richard (k.1459), Duke of York, married Cecily Neville, patriarch of the Yorkist dynasty.

Richard (x.1483), Duke of York, Edward IV's second son, married Anne Mowbray.

Richard III (k.1485), King of England, Duke of Gloucester, married Anne Neville, the Kingmaker's younger daughter.

Richmond, Countess/Earl of – see Beaufort, Margaret / Tudor, Henry.

Rivers, Earl – see Woodville, Richard, Anthony and Richard.

Robin of Holderness – see Hildyard, Robert.

Robin of Redesdale – see Ogle, Robert.

Roos, Edmund (d.1504), exiled heir to attainted barony, restored 1485.

Roos, Thomas (x.1464), Lord. Die-hard Lancastrian.

Russell, John (d.1494), Bishop of Lincoln, Edward IV's Lord Privy Seal, Richard III's Lord Chancellor.

Saint-Pol, Count of – see Luxembourg, Louis de.

Salisbury, Earl of – see Neville, Richard.

Salkeld, Richard (d.1501), Cumberland Neville retainer, Constable of Carlisle.

Savage, John (d.1492), Yorkist, Stanley retainer, fought for Henry Tudor.

Savoy, Bona of (d.1503), princess of Savoy, rejected by Edward IV, married Galeazzo Maria Sforza.

Saye and Sele, Lord – see Fiennes, William.

Scales, Lord – see Woodville, Anthony.

Scrope of Bolton, John (d.1498), Lord. Yorkshire Neville retainer, married sister of Henry FitzHugh.

Scrope of Masham, Thomas (d.1475), Lord. Yorkshire Neville retainer.

Scrope of Masham, Thomas (d.1493), Lord. Yorkshire Neville retainer.

Sforza, Francesco (d.1466), Duke of Milan.

Sforza, Galeazzo Maria (x.1476), Duke of Milan.

Shaw, Dr Ralph (d.1484), renowned preacher, brother of the Lord Mayor of London.

Shore, Jane (d.1527?), Edward IV's last mistress.

Shrewsbury, Earl of – see Talbot, John and George.

Somerset, Duke of – see Beaufort, Henry.

St Leger, Thomas (x.1483), second husband of Anne of York.

Stafford of Grafton, Humphrey (x.1486), Die-hard supporter of Richard III.

Stafford of Southwyck (previously Hooke), Humphrey (x.1469), Lord, later Earl of Devon. Edward IV's comrade-in-arms and later his regime lock on the West Country.

Stafford, Henry (k.1471), uncle of the Duke of Buckingham, married Margaret Beaufort.

Stafford, Henry (x.1483), Duke of Buckingham. Key player in Richard of Gloucester's *coup d'état* who rebelled against him two months later, married Katherine Woodville.

Stafford, John (d.1473), Earl of Wiltshire, uncle of the Duke of Buckingham.

Stanley, George (d.1503), Lord Strange by marriage to niece of Elizabeth Woodville. Their son inherited the earldom of Derby.

Stanley, Thomas (d.1504), Lord, later Earl of Derby, married (1) the Kingmaker's sister Eleanor; (2) Margaret Beaufort. Key player in Henry Tudor's *coup d'état*.

Stanley, William (x.1495), younger brother of Thomas. North Wales March magnate and member of the Prince of Wales's Council, fought for Edward IV in 1461 and 1471 and for Henry Tudor in 1485.

Stewart, Bernard (d.1508), Seigneur d'Aubigny and commander of the *Garde Écossaise* who fought for Henry Tudor.

Stillington, Richard (d.1491), Bishop of Bath and Wells, Lord Chancellor to Edward IV. Instrumental in Richard III's *coup d'état*.

Sudeley, Lord – see Boteler, Ralph.

Suffolk, Duke of – see Pole, John de la.

Sutton, John (d.1487), Lord Dudley. Close friend of Henry VI, changed sides after being wounded at Blore Heath.

Sutton, William (d.1483), Bishop of Durham, son of John. Fought for Edward IV.

Tailboys, William (x.1464). East Midlands and Northumberland lord, Lancastrian thug.

Talbot, George (d.1538), Earl of Shrewsbury, Richard III's ward.

Talbot, Gilbert (d.1517), granduncle of George, leader of Talbot affinity for Henry Tudor.

Talbot, John (d.1473), Earl of Shrewsbury. Cautious Lancastrian.

Talbot, Thomas (k.1470), Viscount Lisle. Killed by Lord Berkeley at Nibley Green.

Thomas, Morgan and David ap, two eldest of three Lancastrian brothers.

Thomas, Rhys ap (d.1525), youngest of the Thomas brothers. Fought for Henry Tudor.

Tiptoft, John (x.1470), Earl of Worcester. Fierce supporter of Edward IV.

Tresham, Thomas (x.1471), Speaker of the Commons, Lancastrian.

Tuchet, John (d.1490), Lord Audley. Father killed fighting for Lancaster at Blore Heath; comrade-in-arms of Edward IV.

Tuddenham, Thomas (x.1462). East Midlands lord, Lancastrian thug.

Tudor, Henry – see Henry VII.

Tudor, Jasper (d.1495), attainted Earl of Pembroke restored 1485, Henry's uncle and companion in exile.

Tunstall, Richard (d.1492), twice-attainted Lancastrian knight, served Edward IV as an ambassador, made a garter knight by Richard III and a privy counsellor by Henry VII.

Tyrell, James (x.1502), Richard III's esquire of the body, entrusted with confidential tasks.

Vaughan, Roger of Tretower (x.1470), half-brother of William Herbert. Beheaded by Jasper Tudor.

Vaughan, Thomas of Hergest (k.1469), half-brother of William Herbert.

Vaughan, Thomas of Monmouth (x.1483), no relation to the others, Edward IV's household treasurer and member of the Prince of Wales's Council.

Vaughan, Thomas of Tretower (k.1486?), son of Roger. Probably killed leading rebellion against Henry VII.

Vere, John (d.1513), attainted Earl of Oxford restored 1485, married the Kingmaker's sister Margaret.

Vergil, Polydore (d.1555), Tudor historian.

Warkworth, John (d.1500), author of one of the best sources for the early years of Edward IV's reign.

Warwick, Countess/Earl of – see Beauchamp, Anne/ Neville, Richard.

Welles, Richard (x.1470), attainted Lord restored 1468, attainted again 1470, also Lord Willoughby by marriage.

Welles, Robert (x.1470), son of Richard.

Wenlock, John (k.1471), Lord, Kingmaker retainer and Lieutenant of Calais.

Woodville, Anne (d.1489), daughter of Richard and Jacquetta, mother of future Earls of Essex and of Kent.

Woodville, Anthony (x.1483), Lord Scales by marriage, Earl Rivers, eldest son of Richard and Jacquetta, head of the Prince of Wales's Council.

Woodville, Catherine (d.1497), daughter of Richard and Jacquetta, married (1) Henry Stafford, Duke of Buckingham, and mother of his heir; (2) Jasper Tudor.

Woodville, Edward (k.1488), son of Richard and Jacquetta. Fought for Henry Tudor.

Woodville, Eleanor (d.1512), daughter of Richard and Jacquetta, married Anthony, eldest son of Edmund Grey of Ruthyn.

Woodville, Elizabeth, daughter of Richard and Jacquetta, married (1) John Grey of Groby; (2) Edward IV.

Woodville, Jacquetta (d.1509), daughter of Richard and Jacquetta, married John, Lord Strange of Knockyn. Their daughter Baroness Strange by right married George Stanley.

Woodville, Joan (d.1462), sister of Richard, married Richard Haute.

Woodville, John (x.1469), son of Richard and Jacquetta, married dowager Duchess of Norfolk.

Woodville, Lionel (d.1484), Bishop of Salisbury, son of Richard and Jacquetta.

Woodville, Margaret (d.1490), daughter of Richard and Jacquetta, married Thomas FitzAlan, Lord Maltravers, mother of future Earl of Arundel.

Woodville, Mary (d.1481), daughter of Richard and Jacquetta, married William Herbert, Lord Dunster, Earl of Pembroke and Earl of Huntingdon, mother of his sole heiress.

Woodville, Richard (x.1469), Lord and Earl Rivers, married Jacquetta de Luxembourg. Woodville patriarch.

Woodville, Richard (d.1491), Earl Rivers, son of Richard and Jacquetta.

Worcester, Earl of – see Tiptoft, John.

Worcester, William of (d.1482?), author of *Annales Rerum Anglicarum*, an occasionally useful source for the period up to 1468.

York, Anne of (d.1476), Edward IV's older sister, married and divorced Henry Holland, then married her lover Thomas St Leger.

York, Cecily of (d.1507), third daughter of Edward IV, betrothed to the future James IV of Scotland, married to one of his retainers by Richard III.

York, Duke of – either Richard, Yorkist dynasty patriarch, or his namesake grandson.

York, Elizabeth of (d.1503), Edward IV's second sister, married John de la Pole, Duke of Suffolk, mother of his namesake heir, Earl of Lincoln.

York, Elizabeth of (d.1503), eldest daughter of Edward IV, married Henry VII.

York, Margaret of (d.1503), Edward IV's youngest sister, married Duke Charles of Burgundy.

Zouche, John (d.1526), Lord, strong supporter of Richard III, attainted 1485, restored 1495.

1. HISTORIC COUNTIES AND REGIONS OF ENGLAND & WALES

SCOTLAND

THE MARCHES

SMALL COUNTIES

A   Anglesey
B   Bedfordshire
H   Huntingdonshire
Hx Hexhamshire
I   Isle of Ely
M   Middlesex
R   Rutland
Rch Richmondshire

Edinburgh

Northumberland

Cumberland

Hx

Durham

Westmorland   Rch

Isle of Man

North

Riding

THE NORTH   East

West   Yorkshire   Riding

Riding   York

Lancashire

A

Caernarvon

Flint

Denbigh

Cheshire

Derbyshire

Nottinghamshire

Lincolnshire

Merioneth

WALES

THE MARCHES

Montgomery

Shropshire

Staffordshire

MIDLANDS

Leicestershire   R

I

Norfolk

EAST   Norwich

Radnor

Cardigan

Warwickshire

Cambridgeshire

ANGLIA

H

Pembroke

Carmarthen

Brecknock

Herefordshire

Worcestershire

Northamptonshire

B

Suffolk

Glamorgan

Monmouth

Gloucestershire

Oxfordshire

Buckinghamshire

Hertfordshire

Essex

HOME

M

London

Bristol

SOUTH

Wiltshire

Berkshire

COUNTIES

Somerset

WEST

Surrey

Kent

Hampshire

Sussex

WEST COUNTRY

Exeter

Dorset

Devon

Cornwall

Isle of Wight

© Hugh Bicheno

xxvi

2. ARCHDIOCESES
AND DIOCESES OF
ENGLAND & WALES

See also Appendix B
Archbishops and Bishops
1440–62

SCOTLAND

Carlisle

Durham

YORK

Bangor

Chester

Lincoln

St Asaph

Lichfield

Hereford

Coventry

Ely

Norwich

St David's

Worcester

Dorchester

London

Llandaff

Bath

Salisbury

Rochester

CANTERBURY

Wells

Winchester

Chichester

Exeter

© Hugh Bicheno

4. GREAT NORTH ROAD AND WESTERN SPUR
(greatly simplified)

0   25   50   75

miles

Edinburgh Dunbar

Berwick

SCOTLAND

Belford

Alnwick

Newcastle

Durham

Darlington

Richmond

Middleham

Northallerton

Skipton

York

Tadcaster

Halifax

Ferrybridge

Doncaster

Rotherham

Retford

Newark

Nottingham

Grantham

Stamford

Oakham

Kettering

Huntingdon

St Neots

Bedford

Baldock

Royston

St Albans

Ware

Barnet

London

© Hugh Bicheno

PRINCES OF THE BLOOD

Edward III = Philippa d'Hainault
(1312–77)   (d.1369)

Edward, = Joan	Lionel = Elizabeth	1. Blanche = John of = 3. Kath
the Black Countess	of Antwerp, Burgh	of Lancaster Gaunt Swyn
Prince of Kent	Duke of	*Hous*
	Clarence	*Beau*

Richard II   Philippa = Edmund   Henry IV
(1367–1400)   Countess   Mortimer   (1367–1413)
                     of Ulster   3rd Earl
                                 of March   Henry V
                                                   (1387–1422)

                                                   Henry VI
                                                   (1421–71)

Elizabeth = Henry 'Hotspur'   Roger Mortimer = Alianore
Mortimer   Percy   4th Earl of   Holland
                                  March

                        Anne Mortimer = Richard of Conisburg
                                        3rd Earl of Cambridg
                                        House of York

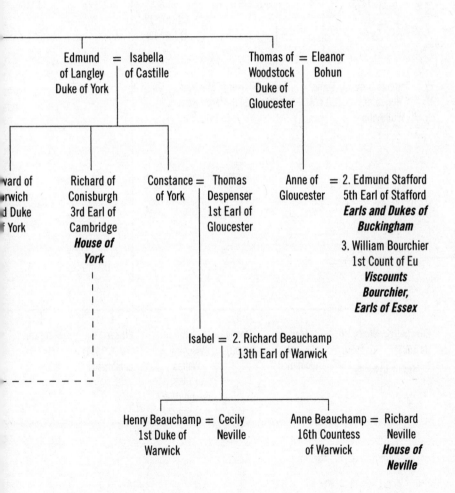

Edmund = Isabella
of Langley   of Castille
Duke of York

Thomas of = Eleanor
Woodstock   Bohun
Duke of
Gloucester

·vard of
·rwich
·d Duke
· York

Richard of
Conisburgh
3rd Earl of
Cambridge
*House of
York*

Constance = Thomas
of York   Despenser
             1st Earl of
             Gloucester

Anne of = 2. Edmund Stafford
Gloucester   5th Earl of Stafford
             *Earls and Dukes of
             Buckingham*

          3. William Bourchier
             1st Count of Eu
             *Viscounts
             Bourchier,
             Earls of Essex*

Isabel = 2. Richard Beauchamp
          13th Earl of Warwick

Henry Beauchamp = Cecily
1st Duke of   Neville
Warwick

Anne Beauchamp = Richard
16th Countess   Neville
of Warwick   *House of
                 Neville*

xxxi

HOUSE OF YORK

k. = killed in battle   x. = executed

1. Henry Holland = Anne = 2. Thomas
Duke of Exeter   (d.1476)   St Leger
(k.1475)   (x.1483)

Edward = Elizabeth
Earl of March   Woodville
later   (d.1492)
Edward IV
(1442–83)

Edmund
Earl of Rutland
(d.1460)

Thomas Grey = Anne   Anne = George Manners
House of (d.1474) (d.1526) 11th Baron Roos
Woodville   (d.1513)

Elizabeth = **Henry VII**   Mary   Cecily = John   **Edward V**   Margaret
(d.1503)   (d.1509)   (d.1482) (d.1507) Viscount   (1470–k. 1483)   (1472)
                                                Welles   unmarried
Tudor Dynasty   unmarried   (d.1498)
                                                no surviving
                                                issue

[1] Margaret's eldest son Henry, Baron Montagu, was executed 1539 and his young son was imprisoned until his death *c.*1542. Her second son Cardinal Reginald Pole was Archbishop of Canterbury under Queen Mary. Margaret was beatified in 1889.

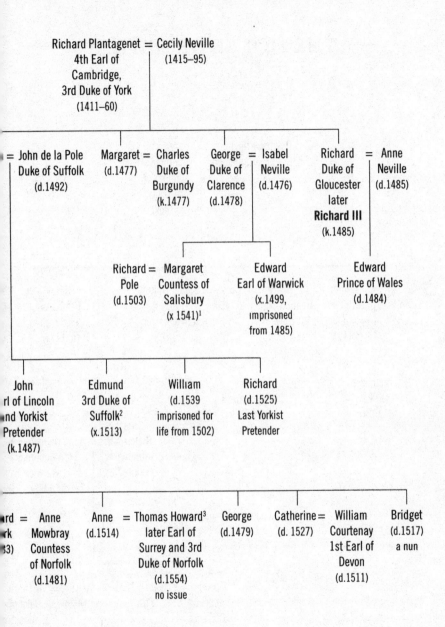

Richard Plantagenet = Cecily Neville
4th Earl of   (1415–95)
Cambridge,
3rd Duke of York
(1411–60)

= John de la Pole   Margaret = Charles   George = Isabel   Richard = Anne
  Duke of Suffolk   (d.1477)   Duke of   Duke of Neville   Duke of   Neville
  (d.1492)   Burgundy   Clarence (d.1476)   Gloucester (d.1485)
                                (k.1477)   (d.1478)   later
                                                                 Richard III
                                                                 (k.1485)

                     Richard = Margaret   Edward   Edward
                     Pole   Countess of   Earl of Warwick   Prince of Wales
                     (d.1503) Salisbury   (x.1499,   (d.1484)
                               (x 1541)[1]   imprisoned
                                                 from 1485)

John   Edmund   William   Richard
rl of Lincoln   3rd Duke of   (d.1539   (d.1525)
nd Yorkist   Suffolk[2]   imprisoned for   Last Yorkist
Pretender   (x.1513)   life from 1502) Pretender
(k.1487)

rd = Anne   Anne = Thomas Howard[3]   George   Catherine = William   Bridget
k   Mowbray   (d.1514) later Earl of   (d.1479)   (d. 1527)   Courtenay   (d.1517)
3)   Countess   Surrey and 3rd   1st Earl of a nun
     of Norfolk   Duke of Norfolk   Devon
     (d.1481)   (d.1554)   (d.1511)
                          no issue

[2] Edmund was demoted to earl in 1493 and deprived of the earldom in 1504.
[3] Howard was uncle to Anne Boleyn and Catherine Howard, Henry VIII's second
and fifth wives, both executed.

THE HOUSE OF NEVILLE

k. = killed in battle   x. = executed

Richard Neville = Alice
5th Earl of Salisbury | Montacute
(d.1460) | Countess of
Salisbury
(d.1462)

Joan = William   1. Henry = Cecily = 2. John Tiptoft   Henry = Alice
(d.1462) | 16th Earl   Beauchamp | (d.1450) | 1st Earl   5th Baron | (d.15
of Arundel   1st Duke of   of Worcester   FitzHugh
(d.1487)   Warwick   (x.1470)   (d.1472)
(d.1446)

Thomas,   Anne   Richard
17th Earl   15th Countess   6th Baron
(d.1524)   of Warwick
(d.1448)

Richard 'the = Anne Beauchamp
Kingmaker' | 16th Countess
(k.1471) | of Warwick
(d.1492)

George = Isabel   Anne = Richard
Duke of | (d.1476)   (d.1485) | Duke of
Clarence   Gloucester
House   **House**
of York   **of York**

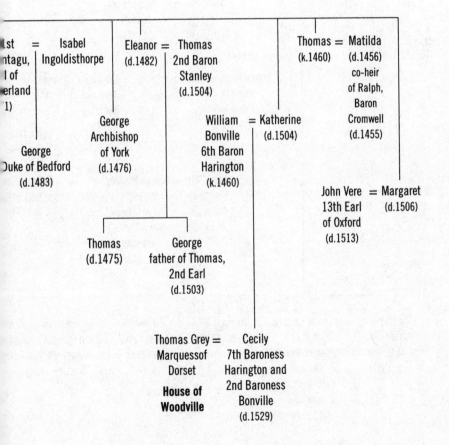

st = Isabel
ntagu, Ingoldisthorpe
l of
erland
1)

George
Duke of Bedford
(d.1483)

Eleanor = Thomas
(d.1482)   2nd Baron
            Stanley
            (d.1504)

George
Archbishop
of York
(d.1476)

William = Katherine
Bonville   (d.1504)
6th Baron
Harington
(k.1460)

Thomas = Matilda
(k.1460)   (d.1456)
           co-heir
           of Ralph,
           Baron
           Cromwell
           (d.1455)

John Vere = Margaret
13th Earl   (d.1506)
of Oxford
(d.1513)

Thomas
(d.1475)

George
father of Thomas,
2nd Earl
(d.1503)

Thomas Grey = Cecily
Marquess of   7th Baroness
Dorset   Harington and
House of 2nd Baroness
Woodville Bonville
              (d.1529)

——THE HOUSE OF WOODVILLE——

k. = killed in battle   x. = executed

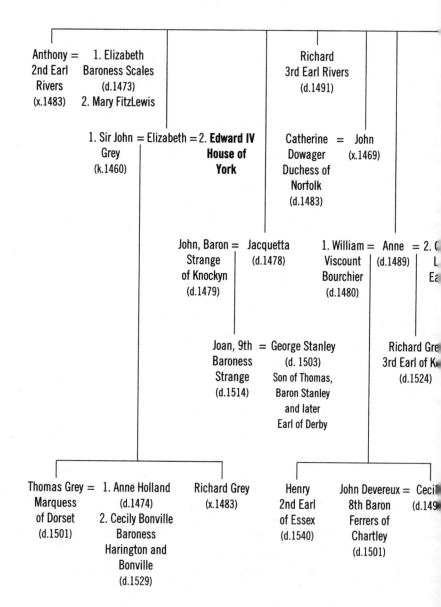

Anthony =   1. Elizabeth
2nd Earl   Baroness Scales
Rivers   (d.1473)
(x.1483)   2. Mary FitzLewis

Richard
3rd Earl Rivers
(d.1491)

1. Sir John = Elizabeth = 2. **Edward IV**
Grey   **House of**
(k.1460)   **York**

Catherine = John
Dowager   (x.1469)
Duchess of
Norfolk
(d.1483)

John, Baron = Jacquetta
Strange   (d.1478)
of Knockyn
(d.1479)

1. William = Anne = 2. C
Viscount   (d.1489)   L
Bourchier   Ea
(d.1480)

Joan, 9th = George Stanley
Baroness   (d. 1503)
Strange   Son of Thomas,
(d.1514)   Baron Stanley
            and later
            Earl of Derby

Richard Gre
3rd Earl of K
(d.1524)

Thomas Grey = 1. Anne Holland
Marquess   (d.1474)
of Dorset   2. Cecily Bonville
(d.1501)   Baroness
               Harington and
                 Bonville
                 (d.1529)

Richard Grey
(x.1483)

Henry
2nd Earl
of Essex
(d.1540)

John Devereux = Ceci
8th Baron   (d.149
Ferrers of
Chartley
(d.1501)

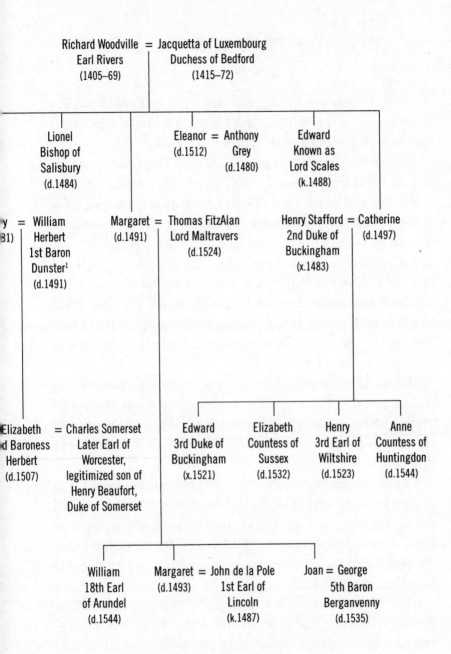

Richard Woodville = Jacquetta of Luxembourg
Earl Rivers   Duchess of Bedford
(1405–69)   (1415–72)

Lionel   Eleanor = Anthony   Edward
Bishop of   (d.1512)   Grey   Known as
Salisbury   (d.1480)   Lord Scales
(d.1484)   (k.1488)

y = William   Margaret = Thomas FitzAlan   Henry Stafford = Catherine
31)   Herbert   (d.1491)   Lord Maltravers   2nd Duke of   (d.1497)
      1st Baron   (d.1524)   Buckingham
      Dunster¹   (x.1483)
      (d.1491)

Elizabeth = Charles Somerset   Edward   Elizabeth   Henry   Anne
d Baroness   Later Earl of   3rd Duke of   Countess of   3rd Earl of   Countess of
Herbert   Worcester,   Buckingham   Sussex   Wiltshire   Huntingdon
(d.1507)   legitimized son of (x.1521)   (d.1532)   (d.1523)   (d.1544)
             Henry Beaufort,
             Duke of Somerset

William   Margaret = John de la Pole   Joan = George
18th Earl   (d.1493)   1st Earl of   5th Baron
of Arundel   Lincoln   Berganvenny
(d.1544)   (k.1487)   (d.1535)

¹Eldest son of Lord William Herbert, 1st Earl of Pembroke. William Jr. surrendered the earldom of Pembroke in 1479 when made Earl of Huntingdon.

PREFACE

Blood Royal takes up the saga first developed in *Battle Royal*. For those arriving at the story with this volume, a short list of the major events in the preceding book follows these notes.

The first three appendices list English peers (A), senior clergy (B) and the Lords Treasurer and Lords Chancellor (C). Genealogy practically defined the earlier period and family trees of the leading noble house are still handy reference tools, but after 1462 the focus shifts towards individuals like Richard 'The Kingmaker' Neville (D).

For simplicity's sake I have omitted the French participle 'de' from all English family names, while retaining 'de la' as more distinctive. I have retained the 'de' for French names only when stated in full (thus Pierre de Brézé), while anglicizing their titles. I have also omitted the prefix 'Sir' because just about every non-noble in this narrative was a knight.

The pound sterling (£), the mark, and the *livre tournois* were not coins, but units of account. The mark was two-thirds of a pound sterling and the *livre tournois* about 6.6 = £1. The French gold crown or *écu* was a coin nominally worth about 4 shillings (one fifth of £1).

To provide the modern standard of living equivalence given in [square brackets] after the sums in contemporary units, I averaged the figures from MeasuringWorth.com at ten-yearly intervals to arrive at a rough and ready rate of £1 = £636 for the period 1430–85. Had I used the 'economic status' equivalence instead, it would have been £1 = £18,166.

None of the contemporary or near-contemporary accounts are entirely dependable, and some are misleading. When even an accurate factual narrative is elusive, character and motive are almost entirely speculative. Modern facial reconstruction techniques can put flesh on skulls, but only imagination and empathy can suggest what went on inside them.

Their way of life was very different, but they were driven by the same appetites and passions as we. Although the religious dimension cannot be dismissed, we are on safer ground in assuming that the main driver of our story was the dedication of all who lived above the subsistence level to the pursuit of sex, money and, above all, power.

CHRONOLOGY OF *BATTLE ROYAL*

1437   Henry VI assumes personal kingship, aged 16. Strongly influenced by William de la Pole, Earl of Suffolk (made marquess in 1444 and duke in 1448).

1445   Henry marries 15-year-old Marguerite d'Anjou, cedes occupied Maine and northern Anjou to her father.

1449–50 French drive the English out of occupied Normandy.

1450   Jack Cade's rebellion. Suffolk impeached, murdered.

1451   French conquer duchy of Aquitaine, held by the English since 1154. Briefly recovered in late 1452, lost permanently in 1453.

1452   Richard, Duke of York, makes an armed demonstration against the king's favourites and is humiliated.

1453   Henry becomes catatonic. Recovers Christmas 1454.

1454   York named Protector with the support of powerful Richard Neville, Earl of Salisbury, and his no less powerful namesake son, Earl of Warwick.

1455   **First Battle of St Albans.** York and the Nevilles kill the king's favourite, Edmund Beaufort, Duke of Somerset, and his supporters Henry Percy, Earl of Northumberland and John, Baron Clifford.

1456–7 Queen Marguerite emerges as the leader of the Lancastrians.

1459   Yorkists plan a rebellion. Salisbury destroys the Queen's army at **Blore Heath**. Henry leads a large army against them and they flee into exile after a bloodless confrontation at **Ludford Bridge**. York and his son Edmund go to Ireland, the Nevilles and York's eldest son Edward to Calais.

1460   Prolonged struggle for Calais between Warwick and Henry Beaufort, Duke of Somerset, Edmund's son, won by Warwick.

1460   Warwick and Edward return to England, defeat the Lancastrians at **Northampton**, capture the king. York returns from Ireland expecting to be made king, but is double-crossed by Warwick and only named heir apparent. On 30 December York and Salisbury defeated and killed at Wakefield.

1461   Marguerite's army marches south, defeats Warwick at **Second Battle of St Albans** and recovers the king. Two weeks earlier Edward routed an army led by Jasper Tudor, Earl of Pembroke, at **Mortimer's Cross** on the Welsh border.

Marguerite cannot advance on London, occupied by Edward, who is proclaimed king. Edward and Warwick march north and on 29 March fight three battles ending with their overwhelming victory at **Towton**.

LEGITIMACY

HENRY VI'S CAUSE SHOULD HAVE BEEN IRRECOVERABLE after the crushing defeat of his followers at the Battle of Towton on Palm Sunday 1461. Even before that blood-bath, the Lancastrians had lost the support of the Church and the mercantile class, in particular the vital Calais-based Merchants of the Staple: all had swung solidly behind Edward IV, the Yorkist usurper. Yet a hard core of Lancastrians fought on and lost every-thing, though they could have retained their lives, titles and property by making peace with the new order.

What motivated them? It was certainly not devotion to dispir-iting Henry VI, or even to charismatic Marguerite d'Anjou, his admirable queen. The modern mind finds it difficult to compre-hend their motives because the concepts of shame and honour play a reduced role in our society. Most of us are Sir John Falstaff's children:

> Well, 'tis no matter; honour pricks me on. Yea, but how if honour prick me off when I come on? How then? Can honour set-to a leg? No. Or an arm? No. Or take away the grief of a wound? No. Honour hath no skill in surgery, then? No. What is honour? A word. What is in that word 'honour'? What is that 'honour'? Air. A trim reckoning! Who hath it? He that died o' Wednesday. Doth he feel it? No. Doth he hear it? No. 'Tis insensible then?

Yea, to the dead. But will it not live with the living? No. Why?
Detraction will not suffer it. Therefore I'll none of it. Honour is
a mere scutcheon.

It may seem absurd to suggest that honour played a life-defining
role among men who schemed incessantly against each other, stole
by force when they could not subvert the law to their advantage,
and regularly broke the most sacred oaths. Yet it did, and provides
the key to understanding why the new Yorkist dynasty was insecure
and ultimately unsuccessful.

There was no shame in surrendering to a worthy opponent. For
example Robert, Lord Hungerford, was captured by the French in
1453 and fully accepted his obligation to pay a ruinous ransom to
obtain his release. The same rules did not apply during the Wars of
the Roses for several reasons, chief among them personal hatreds.
Thus when leading Yorkist Richard Neville, Earl of Salisbury, surrendered on terms at Wakefield, he was butchered in cold blood even
though he had surely promised his captors an enormous ransom.

Denied the prospect of ransom, common soldiers had little incentive to take prisoners. The expensive armour and distinctive tabards
that once advertised that their wearers were worth taking alive were
now just desirable spoils of war to be stripped from their corpses.
In some instances commanders may have promised their troops a
financial reward for the capture of named opponents, but usually
because they wished to inflict a more ignominious fate.

That some still surrendered was probably the result of combat
exhaustion – also the reason why the hand-to-hand fighting phase
of battles was relatively short. Towton marked the nadir, with no
mercy shown even to the humble conscripts who made up the vast
majority of armies. We dwell on the blood feuds of lords because
their doings are known – but desire for revenge also seared the souls
of the sons of slaughtered men whose names were not recorded.

As in the aftermath of any civil war, the victors were faced with
the imperative need to reverse the pitiless polarization that had been

necessary to prevail. This proved particularly difficult for Edward IV and his principal supporter, the Earl of Salisbury's namesake heir Richard Neville, Earl of Warwick, because the Lancastrians regarded them as unworthy opponents. It was the reason why some Lancastrians refused to accept the verdict of Towton, and why the war dragged on intermittently for another generation.

Was the Yorkist cause dishonourable? Well – yes. The Lancastrian Henry IV seized the throne in 1399 because his cousin Richard II, the legitimate king, expropriated Henry's inheritance from his father, John of Gaunt. That was an invitation to a trial of strength, which the king lost. Richard of York had no such justification to rebel against Henry VI, whose only offence (other than chronic weakness) was a cautious refusal to hand over the administration of his kingdom to a haughty cousin with as good or better right by blood to the throne.

The issue of blood right became crucial after York was killed at Wakefield on 30 December 1460, because there were good reasons to believe that Edward, his heir, was not his son. He did not resemble Richard in any way: parents of slight build and average height do not engender burly sons 7–8 inches taller than they. Richard conspicuously slighted Edward in favour of his second son, Edmund, who was also killed at Wakefield, while contrary to the medieval norm Edward made no great effort to honour the memory of his supposed father until several years after the question of his true parentage nearly cost him the throne.

Not for nothing is the word 'legitimacy' employed to describe a government's legal and moral right to rule. The suspicion that Edward's mother, Cecily née Neville, was an adulteress and he a bastard was more damaging to his authority than the evident fact that he had usurped an anointed king. In 1469–70 it was whispered to discredit him by Warwick (her nephew) and Edward's brother George, Duke of Clarence. Thirteen years later, until he concocted an alternative to spare his mother's blushes, it was also the legal premise that Richard, her youngest son, thought to advance when he seized the throne from Edward's namesake heir.

Added to which, Edward was barely 19 years old when he became king in 1461 and, regardless of his precocious brilliance as a battlefield commander, he undoubtedly owed the throne to the machinations of his 38-year-old cousin Warwick. It was Warwick who made Calais a Yorkist stronghold, won over the Company of the Staple and persuaded Pope Pius II's legate Francesco Coppini to back the Yorkist cause with the full might of the Church, and Warwick who commanded the loyalty of the ever-rebellious men of Kent.

Like his father, Warwick owed his eminence to favour shown him by Henry VI, built up further by Queen Marguerite's desperate effort to turn him into the Lancastrian regime's strongman in the later 1450s. This made him a greater traitor than Edward in Lancastrian eyes, compounded to loathing when he engineered the battlefield treachery that precipitated the rout and slaughter of Lancastrian nobles at Northampton in 1460.*

In addition to the intense hatred the Nevilles of Middleham had earned by their insatiable avarice, Warwick's devouring ambition also made him an uncertain prop for the new regime. He was like an Italian Renaissance warlord miscast in late medieval England. Despite being showered with offices and with lands taken from the defeated Lancastrians, he calls to mind King Louie's song in Disney's version of *The Jungle Book*:

> I've reached the top and had to stop
> And that's what's bothering me

In 1463 Bishop Kennedy, regent for King James III of Scotland, wrote that Warwick was 'governor of the realm of England'. A year later the Governor of Abbeville in Picardy wrote to King Louis XI of France, 'in England they have but two rulers – M. de Warwick and

---

*Also for a similar selective massacre after the First Battle of St Albans in 1455.

another whose name I have forgotten'. Warwick has been known as the 'Kingmaker' ever since Shakespeare put these words in the mouth of Marguerite in *Henry VI, Part 3*:

> Peace! Impudent and shameless Warwick, peace;
> Proud setter up and puller down of kings;

The encounter with Marguerite crowned a series of acts of the blackest treachery, whose aim was to achieve for Warwick the status Bishop Kennedy incorrectly attributed to him, and which Warwick thought he deserved. This appears to have been his sole motivation – he said he felt dishonoured by Edward, who not only did not make him a duke but also rubbed salt in the wound by refusing permission for his brother Clarence, at the time next in line to the throne, to marry one of Warwick's daughters.

Clarence is a very modern figure. He was driven by an overpowering sense of entitlement, a now common condition that was limited to princes of the blood in the late Middle Ages. Favourable circumstances he did nothing to shape spared him the reality checks that normally correct adolescent whininess and self-absorption, until at last he pushed his luck too far.

Warwick did not seek power because he believed, as Richard of York did, that he would be a more just and competent ruler, but because his pride would settle for nothing less. It also blinded him to his own shortcomings. While he fully possessed the *furbizia* (unscrupulous cunning) indispensable to contemporary Italian princes, it was Edward's great good fortune that in the military sphere Warwick's cleverness took the form of over-elaboration.

Behind Warwick was Edward's contemporary Louis XI, the greatest of the Valois kings, who was to *furbizia* what the Grand Canyon is to valleys. He was a man who lived only for power, and cared nothing for luxury or any other of its secondary rewards. His father expelled the English from Normandy and Aquitaine, but it was Louis – despite a near-fatal stumble in 1465 over his own hubris – who achieved the more difficult task of forging a nation from the semi-autonomous feudal fragments he inherited.

Edward's reign coincided with Louis XI's almost exactly. Although nineteen years older, Louis became king five months later than Edward and died five months after him. Even their male heirs were born five months apart. All the major political upheavals of Edward's reign were influenced, when not initiated, by Louis. The Hundred Years War between England and France did not officially end until the Treaty of Picquigny in 1475, when Edward and his closest associates were bought off with pensions.

Given the enormous disparity in wealth and population between the two kingdoms, Edward could only aspire to be more than an inconvenience to Louis by combining with Burgundy and Brittany. Conversely, Louis did not have to invest very much to stir the pot across the Channel because the English supplied the ingredients and the heat themselves, while the Scots generally required only modest financial inducement to cause trouble.

These, then, were the main structural elements of discord with which Edward had to wrestle throughout his reign. It was an era of personal kingship and although he was a more 'hands-on' monarch than his hapless predecessor, maintaining order in England and Wales was like trying to herd cats. He had neither the income nor the inclination to create a national bureaucracy, and for regional government had to depend on established local magnates, or endow others to make them first among equals, and hope they would repay him with loyalty.

Unlike the norm under Henry VI, the interests of Edward's inner circle seldom diverged significantly from his own. Outstanding among them were William Herbert, effectively his viceroy in Wales, and William Hastings, his closest friend and chamberlain, who controlled access to the king throughout his reign. Hastings' even-handedness was widely commented and his only enemies appear to have been Edward's queen and her family.

Thanks to unique rights of property ownership and inheritance, women played a more important role in the history of England than they did elsewhere. The recent work of female authors has shed much-needed light on the role of women during the Wars of the Roses. Unfortunately most of it is necessarily speculative, as no narratives by women survive and they seldom feature in chronicles written by men. When they do 'intrude' into the male narrative, it is as active players in moments of crisis; but, obviously, if they had the power to affect events at such moments, their influence in normal times must have been considerable.

If one could choose a single item that would do most to illuminate this poorly documented period, it would be a diary or memoir written by Jacquetta de Luxembourg. Married at 17 to the Duke of Bedford, Henry VI's elder uncle and next in line to the throne, she was widowed at 19 and two years later married handsome Richard Woodville without obtaining the legally required royal licence. Anthony, their first child, was born rather less than nine months later, and thirteen more children testified to her robustness and their abiding passion.

Jacquetta became a confidante of Queen Marguerite and secured the advancement of her husband in the Lancastrian hierarchy. She also accompanied her husband – by now Baron Rivers – to Calais in a vain effort first to deny and later to wrest it away from Warwick. Her standing as the second most senior lady at court under Henry VI (after Marguerite) and, until he started his own family, Edward IV (after his mother) undoubtedly facilitated the reconciliation between her husband and the new king soon after Towton.

There can be no doubt that Jacquetta had a great deal to do with the dynastic bombshell of Edward's secret marriage to her daughter Elizabeth, a widow with two young sons. Edward's companions noted his state of blissful exhaustion in the days following the marriage, and anyone who doubts that Elizabeth's sexual virtuosity closed the deal simply does not know much about young men.

It is prissy as well as unhistorical to underplay traditional female strengths. Also, given the appalling rate of death in childbirth and infant mortality, a proven record of bearing healthy sons was certainly an asset we should not undervalue. Nor should we doubt the influence of mothers on their children. There is little doubt Cecily poisoned her younger sons' minds against Edward, but the outstanding example was Lady Margaret Beaufort, who was to be the most intimate and influential adviser to her only child Henry VII throughout his reign.

Marriages among people of property were regarded as the cement of family alliances, and love matches were extremely rare. Arranged marriages, such as Warwick's with Anne Beauchamp, which made him the heir to most of the large Beauchamp, Montague and Despenser estates, were active partnerships. Wives retained their property rights, and for wealthy widows there was a brisk sellers' market in which, barring royal interference, they could dictate the terms of new partnerships.

It has been a more demanding task to organize this colourful cast of characters into a coherent theme for the quarter century following Edward's accession than it was for an equal period preceding it. There was a grim inevitability in the steady slide from the start of Henry VI's feeble and erratic personal kingship to the chaos and war that ended it. By contrast, Edward had done much to restore stability before Warwick rebelled in 1469–71, and had done so again by the time he died in 1483.

Yet his story ends with arguably the most tragic and certainly one of the most disputed events in English history. The recent discovery of Richard III's bones has only underlined the durable fascination of a period that culminated in one king being buried with full honours in the magnificent chapel he built at Windsor, and his successor brother's naked body cast into an unmarked grave and historical obloquy twenty-eight months later.

There was nothing inevitable about the outcome, but it is difficult to dismiss the suspicion that the fate of the Yorkist dynasty was written from the moment Edward was conceived. In the end it is wonderfully ironic that the issue of legitimacy should have fatally undermined the House of York, because the only Plantagenet blood in the veins of the Tudors came from Cecily Neville and Margaret Beaufort, both descendants of the family John of Gaunt bred with his mistress Katherine Swynford while he was married to Constance of Castille.

EDWARD

WHEN WE REVIEW THE ACTIONS OF YOUNG EDWARD IV during his early reign we should consider the possibility that the appalling experience of Towton may have influenced him profoundly. He was at the forefront of a prolonged hand-to-hand battle, much of it spent grimly retreating in the face of superior numbers, his height, distinctive tabard and banners making him a magnet for war arrows, while hacking down determined warriors who burst through his bodyguard, seeking to claim the glory of killing the usurper king.

Historians are often faulted by combat veterans because 'they were not there' – that while hindsight may permit them to see the big picture better than those who were involved, they lack the personal experience to get the details right. This is undeniable; but the antiseptic nature even of most accounts written by combatants suggests the main obstacle is the almost universal reticence of the veterans themselves.

Such reticence, born of a once general belief that feelings are a private matter, is the overt manifestation of the mind's ability to 'seal off' traumatic events, which, for some, can have a disabling psychological or even physiological cost. Ancient Mesopotamian texts reveal that the symptoms of post-traumatic stress disorder (PTSD) following combat had been identified over 3,000 years ago. Herodotus wrote of an unwounded Greek hoplite who went blind after a comrade was killed next to him at the Battle of Marathon in 490 BC.

No amount of training or mock combat in tournaments could have prepared Edward for the reality of thousands of men snarling and screaming around him, or for the experience of trampling over dead and dying men, or being spattered with blood and brains, or the overpowering stench of bowels voided in terror and agony. Add the stunning effect of repeated heavy blows to helmet and harness and sheer physical exhaustion, and it would be strange indeed if it did not affect his thinking and behaviour for many years to come.

Some men thrive on combat, but – probably because of Towton – Edward was not one of them. He fought well, when it was necessary, but he lacked the thirst for war that distinguished Edward III, the paternal and maternal great-great-grandfather after whom he was named. No doubt royal sycophants evoked the memory of his very distant ancestor Edward I, known as 'Longshanks', to explain the young king's exceptional physical stature, but he notably lacked the implacable ferocity of the dread 'Hammer of the Scots'.

The canonical view is that Edward pursued a policy of reconciliation to the point of endangering his regime – but would a harder line have stamped out the Lancastrian embers sooner? There is abundant evidence that well-established regional lords commanded deep loyalty, often reinforced by ties of kinship, and that beheading the lords did not decapitate their following. Indeed, some families were so deeply entrenched as to be seemingly untouchable. The outstanding example was the Stanleys of Lancashire and Cheshire, who retained their titles, lands and even royal offices despite serial betrayals of successive kings.

· ∾ ·

This loyalty is commonly attributed to the network of patronage or 'good lordship', which some call 'bastard feudalism'. If that had been all there were to it, decapitation and legal dispossession (attainder) would have worked, since no practical benefit could derive from remaining loyal to a family no longer able to offer 'good lordship'. Kinship built up over generations of intermarriage with the local gentry was also a double-edged sword, because extended families were more often than not rent by envious rivalries and vendettas. Clearly something more profound was involved.

The phenomenon is better described by the term 'affinity', which, born of the faithful performance of reciprocal obligations, over time became more akin to a deeply ingrained custom that defined each individual's way of thinking about himself. We use the term 'land-lord' to describe mere possession of a property, without considering its etymology. Smallholders were no less lords to those who share-cropped their fields than were nobles to the gentry who prospered under their tutelage. It was a deeply habit-forming relationship.

Custom and customary right were once the soul of Common Law. Although Rudyard Kipling cast the poem at a time not long after the Conquest, 'A Norman Baron's Advice' describes what he believed to be the defining characteristic of the English:

> The Saxon is not like us Normans. His manners are not so polite.
> But he never means anything serious till he talks about justice
>   and right.
> When he stands like an ox in the furrow – with his sullen set
>   eyes on your own,
> And grumbles, 'This isn't fair dealing', my son, leave the Saxon
>   alone.

It was considered 'fair dealings' to execute a man for his transgressions, but not to deprive his family of its property rights. Attainder, also known as 'corruption of blood', was a legal way around this. It declared an individual a non-person, and so without rights of any kind for his heirs to inherit. However, punishing the innocent sat so ill with the medieval concept of kingship that attainder was rarely sustained to the point of permanent deprivation.

There was also an element of practical politics involved. Members of attainted families with no hope of a reversal had every reason to seek the overthrow of the regime responsible for their deprivation as soon as possible, before whoever had been granted their lands could establish himself as the customary lord and win over their affinity. The longer a family had been in possession the deeper the roots, and so Edward's attainders tended to 'stick' in the case of newer creations, and to be reversed for those with older titles.

• ℯℑ •

Contemporaries and historians have generally been critical of the supposedly over-indulgent policy of reconciliation Edward pursued with those lately his mortal enemies. It would not have seemed so to Thomas Courtenay, Earl of Devon, and James Butler, Earl of Wiltshire in England and of Ormond in Ireland, both executed and attainted after Towton. Also attainted were Henry Percy, Earl of Northumberland, John Talbot, Earl of Shrewsbury, and Lords Clifford, Welles and Dacre of the North, all of whom had fallen in battle.

Of those who lived, the titles and lands of the deposed king, his queen and their son were of course forfeit. Dukes Henry Beaufort of Somerset and Henry Holland of Exeter, and Lords Roos and Hungerford, who fled to Scotland with the royal party, were also attainted. So was Jasper Tudor, Earl of Pembroke, who remained at large in Wales after defeat at Mortimer's Cross. Though William, Viscount Beaumont, was not still in rebellion, his attainder was sustained because Lord Hastings, Edward's closest friend, coveted his lands.

Edward offered an amnesty to those who had the prestige and affinity to cause him serious trouble. All they had to do was submit, swear allegiance to him, and prove the sincerity of their conversion through service to his cause. A different policy governed the lower-level attainders after Towton, which were part of a general score settling demanded by Edward's followers and tended not to be reversed because they contributed to stability by resolving minor vendettas. The 'hearts and minds' strategy was mainly applied to magnates.

Somerset was to prove the most notable failure, but Ralph Percy, brother of the slain Earl of Northumberland, repeatedly abused the king's mercy. Percy's recidivism showed indifference to the fate of his young nephew Henry, heir to the earldom, who was held in the Fleet prison as a hostage. This could be because, with older brothers Henry and Thomas killed in battle and his only other brother George a priest, Ralph and his sons would become the heirs to the earldom if young Henry were executed.

The back story is that the royal castles of Bamburgh and Dunstanburgh, along with the Percy stronghold of Alnwick, all in Northumberland, initially resisted the Yorkist tide after Towton. Alnwick and Dunstanburgh capitulated to Warwick in the autumn of 1461. Ralph Percy, royal constable at Dunstanburgh, was pardoned and reappointed, only to declare for Lancaster again in November after a Lancastrian-Scots force led by the proscribed and attainted William Tailboys recaptured Alnwick.

Tailboys was a knighted thug who had contributed greatly to the climate of lawlessness that undermined Henry VI's regime – in 1449 he was the first man impeached by the Commons in nearly seventy years, for assaulting a peer inside the parliamentary precinct. His principal properties were in Lincolnshire, but he also held a large moorland estate in Northumberland between Harbottle on the upper Coquet River and Redesdale, home to some of the most notorious border bandits. For the Yorkists, he was a dead man walking.

Percy continued to hold out after Alnwick and Bamburgh capitulated again in July 1462. Dunstanburgh is built on a headland jutting into the North Sea and encloses the largest space of any medieval English castle, but port facilities were better further north at Bamburgh. There, on 25 October, Henry VI, Queen Marguerite and an entourage including the attainted Earl of Somerset, Earl of Pembroke, Lord Roos and Lord Hungerford, landed with an 800-man French force led by Pierre de Brézé.

Brézé was once the most powerful man at the court of Charles VII, who made him Grand Seneschal of Normandy in recognition of his leading role in the 1449–50 reconquest of the province. He had also led a damaging amphibious raid on Sandwich in 1457, and to the English he was the French bogeyman personified. Nonetheless, he had been devoted to Marguerite's mother Isabelle, and his loyalty carried over to her embattled daughter.

In late March 1462 Marguerite had travelled, alone, via Brittany, to meet Louis XI, and obtained a limited amount of support in exchange for the promise to cede Calais once she regained the throne. Louis released Brézé, whom he had dismissed and imprisoned after he became king, and provided ships and a modest war chest. Brézé was permitted to mount a partially successful invasion of the Channel Islands, the right to which Marguerite also ceded, and to raise troops for the expedition to Northumberland.

They sailed first to Leith, Edinburgh's port, to pick up Henry VI and the other exiles, before landing at Bamburgh. Even though Marguerite had already surrendered the border fortress of Berwick to the Percys' ancestral Scots enemy, the Percy affinity still turned out for her in force. The massacre at Towton had created a blood feud that outweighed historical animosities, and it was the strength and depth of the Percy affinity that led Edward to show such seemingly reckless magnanimity to Ralph Percy.

Edward had to remain near the levers of power in London, learning on the job and trying to create an aura of permanence and stability. He also understood that a war of sieges and skirmishes offered no prospect of gain commensurate with the risk of death or disgrace. Consequently he did not become involved in the pacification of the North and delegated the task to Warwick, whose own regional hegemony was most directly challenged.

In early December 1462 Warwick began sieges of the three

□ Percy Manors and
■ Heads of Lordship

**5. SIEGES & BATTLES
IN THE NORTH-EAST
1462–4**

0   5   10
miles

Tweed Berwick

Norham

Lennel

Holy Isle

Bamburgh

Milfield

Till

Belford

Wooler

Hedgeley Moor

Dunstanburgh

Beanley

Breamish

Alnwick

Aln

Warkworth

CHEVIOT HILLS

Amble

Harbottle *(Tailboys)*

Rothbury

Coquet

Redesdale (Tailboys)

Otterburn

Font

Ashington

Morpeth

Wansbeck

Bellingham

North Tyne

Bothal *(Ogle)*

Blyth

Wark *(Grey)*

Belsay

Cramlington

Hadrian's Wall

Heaton *(Grey)*

Tynemouth

Langley

Corbridge

Newcastle

Hexham

Bywell

Tyne

Prudhoe

Gateshead

© Hugh Bicheno

castles. Based at the Percys' Warkworth Palace he directed the siege of nearby Alnwick by his ailing 57-year-old uncle William, now Earl of Kent, and his thirty-five-year younger deputy, the reconciled Lancastrian Anthony Woodville, Lord Scales. John Tiptoft, Earl of Worcester, and local magnate Ralph Grey besieged Dunstanburgh. Grey's family had a long history of affiliation with the House of York, but he had failed to hold Alnwick for Edward in 1461.

The main effort was at Bamburgh under Warwick's brother John, Lord Montagu, and Lord Ogle. Percy had moved there to join the Lancastrian high command, and as the northernmost of the castles it would be the first to be relieved should the Scots march south from Berwick. No such timely support developed thanks to Warwick's diplomacy and squabbles among the Scots, and with supplies running short Bamburgh capitulated on 26 December.

To shore up Scots support, Henry VI and Marguerite, along with Brézé and 400 of his men, had embarked on 13 November intending to make their presence felt at the Scots court. With their customary bad luck their little fleet was assaulted by a storm soon after it left Bamburgh. The French men-at-arms were wrecked on Holy Isle and were put to the sword by some of Ogle's men, led by his bastard brother. Their leader Jean Malet, lord of Graville in Normandy, was a prisoner in London for many years.

The ship carrying the royal couple and Brézé foundered, taking with it part of their war chest of gold crowns provided by Louis XI. They made it to Berwick in a small boat, but were now unable to influence events in Edinburgh. Meanwhile Edward, who had at last felt compelled to march north at the head of a large army, was incapacitated by measles at Durham. Fortunately by that time his show of force had produced the desired effect, and the alarmed Scots court requested and was granted a truce.

Brézé and the Earl of Angus defied the truce, cobbled together an army at Berwick and marched south, but word of their relief effort did not reach the defenders of Bamburgh and Dunstanburgh in time to prevent their capitulation. Warwick was only too well aware that Brézé was coming, and consequently the terms of capitulation were outrageously generous. To the bitter chagrin of Ralph Grey who, like Ogle, had struggled against Percy hegemony in Northumberland for many years, Ralph Percy was not only restored as royal Constable of Dunstanburgh, but appointed Constable of Bamburgh as well.

The rest of the Lancastrian high command were given the option of safe conduct to Scotland, or a full pardon if they swore allegiance to Edward. Pembroke and Roos, given no guarantee their lands would be restored, chose the first option. Somerset, Percy and several Lancastrian knights travelled to Durham, paid homage to Edward and were 'taken into the king's grace'. Somerset and his followers immediately joined the siege of Alnwick, where the defenders rejected all blandishments.

Warwick's army contained several other lords who had fought for Lancaster. They included his unattainted (but on probation) brother-in-law Lord FitzHugh, who had commanded the Lancastrian division opposite him at Towton – with little conviction – after Northumberland was mortally wounded. Three others, Lords Lovell, Grey of Codnor and Willoughby – the last also heir to the still-attainted barony of Welles – had benefitted from the reversal of their post-Towton attainders conditional on service against their old comrades.

Consequently it is not even slightly remarkable that Warwick broke off the siege and took up a defensive position when Brézé and Angus arrived at Alnwick on 6 January 1463. Apart from the doubtful loyalty of some of his subordinates, his army had suffered considerable attrition from exposure and desertion. The relief force must have been in little better shape after a rapid march south across inhospitable terrain in the dead of winter, but even so Brézé wanted to seek battle. Angus, who was mortally ill, settled for collecting the Alnwick garrison and marching back to Berwick.

Despite the setback at Alnwick, Edward had reason to believe that the policy of reconciliation was working for him. His offer of an open hand as an alternative to the mailed fist is the way lasting peace is normally made. It was also a notably mature policy for such a young man to pursue. Perhaps more to the point, with regard to the pacification of the North he acted in full agreement with the Earl of Warwick, who would not have hesitated to behead his defeated opponents had he believed it the wiser course of action.

II

WARWICK

WARWICK BENEFITTED HUGELY FROM THE RELATIVE failure of reconciliation. It permitted him to win a geographic concentration and regional hegemony akin to those enjoyed by cadet branches of the Valois dynasty in France, a fragmentation that weakened them so significantly in the confrontation with the English Plantagenets. One of the greater ironies of this saga is that by crushing their resistance in 1461–4, Warwick won the independent power that later made him the Lancastrians' last hope for reversing the verdict of Towton.

He was a schemer, not a warrior. His victory at Northampton was won by the treachery of Lord Grey of Ruthyn, and a similar odour emanates from FitzHugh's performance at Towton. Along with Lord Greystoke, FitzHugh had been encouraged to become Trojan Horses within the Lancastrian ranks by seeming to rally to Henry VI in 1459. Warwick's talents were not best suited to the grinding war against adamant enemies in the North, although intelligence from Greystoke did help him to identify covert Lancastrians among the Yorkshire gentry and burgesses, who were forced to take oaths of allegiance.

Warwick was able to depend at first on his veteran warrior uncle William, newly created Earl of Kent, and, following his death in January 1463, on his brother John, whom Edward had created Lord

Montagu as one of his first acts on seizing the throne.* With his uncle and brother largely taking care of military business, Warwick was free to play the statesman, a role he had relished as the virtually independent Captain of Calais and Keeper of the Seas during the last years of the Lancastrian regime.

The northern rebellion of late 1461 was supposed to be followed by a rising in East Anglia led by John Vere, Earl of Oxford, commanding his own and the Beaumont affinities, taking advantage of the fact that the Norfolk affinity was leaderless following the death of the sickly duke in late 1461. The plan may have been to attack Edward from the rear after he had been drawn north, or perhaps to join his army and assassinate him. They were also expecting Somerset to land in East Anglia with troops recruited in France or provided by his admirer Charles, Count of Charolais and heir to the dukedom of Burgundy.

Edward learned of the plan and Oxford, his eldest son, Thomas Tuddenham and a dozen accomplices, all of whom had previously avoided attainder, were arrested and imprisoned. Tuddenham had been a key player in a thuggish gang that terrorized East Anglia during the Lancastrian regime. To deal with them Edward appointed John Tiptoft, Earl of Worcester – already Lord Treasurer and Constable of the Tower – as Constable of England, with the power to try cases of high treason without reference to Parliament.

Tiptoft stood out among the generally philistine English peers. William Caxton, who brought the first printing press to England in 1475, wrote of him 'I knew none like [him] among the lords of the temporality in science and moral virtue'. After a pilgrimage to Jerusalem in 1458 Tiptoft spent two years studying at the University of Padua and brought the texts of the 'new learning' back to England. Something else he brought back from Italy was total ruthlessness in defence of the state, and he had Oxford, his heir and their fellow conspirators executed in a cruelly protracted sequence.

*John had been captured at the Second Battle of St Albans; his ennoblement was a signal that there would be reprisal against captured Lancastrian nobles if he were executed.

Bereft of support elsewhere, the 1461–2 rebellion in the North swiftly collapsed, leaving only Percy holding out at Dunstanburgh. When, as we have seen, it flared up again later in 1462, both Warwick and Edward were drawn north – but with the Lancastrian leadership now concentrated in Bamburgh they no longer feared a hostile landing to their rear. Following the capitulations of Dunstanburgh, Bamburgh and Alnwick, Warwick delegated the Wardenship of the East March to his brother Montagu while he and the king returned to London.

They had to deal with a mountain of decrees and legislation required to revoke or revalidate all the acts of the Lancastrian regime, now legally declared illegitimate from its inception in 1399. The crown was also vastly in debt, and even interest on the sums lent by the Calais Staplers, crucial to the success of the Yorkist insurgency, had to be declared 'in respite' until the royal finances could be sorted out.

This was no easy task. Even the resumption of crown lands alienated by Henry VI was not straightforward, as it generated an avalanche of petitions for exception, which had to be handled with delicacy. Edward made no fewer than eighty-four exceptions, no doubt grimly aware that each favour created several enemies and an ingrate. At the same time he had to deal with pleas from Yorkists seeking redress for wrongs done them under Henry VI, and from Lancastrians seeking relief from abuses committed by Yorkist supporters after Towton. He desperately needed a prolonged period of domestic and international peace.

Of course his enemies knew this, and combined to strike again before the new regime could establish itself. In late May 1463 Ralph Percy raised the banner of Lancaster over Bamburgh and Dunstanburgh once more. At the same time embittered Ralph Grey turned his coat, seized Alnwick castle and welcomed a Lancastrian column led from Scotland by Lord Hungerford. Meanwhile Scots queen mother Mary of Guelders and young James III, accompanied by Marguerite and Henry VI, marched with a Scots army to besiege the Bishop of Durham's border fortress of Norham, which was held by Lord Ogle.

With Ogle bottled up, the combination of the Percy, Grey, Tailboys and related affinities now dominated Northumberland. Montagu managed to prevent them seizing Newcastle, while ships under his command intercepted a French fleet before it could land supplies at Bamburgh; but he could only hold the southern border along the Tyne. At the same time there were Lancastrian risings in other parts of England. It was a well-coordinated offensive and, unlike the previous effort, took Edward and Warwick by surprise.

Montagu's situation was made even more precarious by the fact that the archdiocese of York had been solidly Lancastrian. Carlisle was not a problem, as Bishop William Percy died in August 1462 and his replacement died a year later. Archbishop William Booth had been Marguerite's chancellor, but the greater danger came from his half-brother Laurence, Prince-Bishop of Durham. Laurence had succeeded William as the queen's chancellor and had been Lord Privy Seal from 1456 to 1460. He had military obligations throughout the Marches, and retained a significant armed force.

Edward neutralized the prince-bishop by assigning his temporalities to Warwick, who immediately travelled north to raise his own Yorkshire and Richmondshire affinities. The Scots army at Norham fled before his approach and he chased it into Scotland. Meanwhile his brother George, Bishop of Exeter and Lord Chancellor, led a high-level delegation to negotiate a truce with France. Warwick was made plenipotentiary to deal with Scotland, and George was given almost unlimited negotiating discretion, including the prospect of a marriage between Edward and a suitable French princess.

Unusually, Parliament voted Edward the specific sum of £37,000 [£23.5 million], rather more than the usual fifteenth and tenth.* Stung by the fact that he had not made war on Scotland with the

---

*The basic form of direct taxation in late medieval England, on the assessed value of movables: one-tenth in towns and one-fifteenth in the shires. Land taxes were furiously rejected until the late seventeenth century.

taxes raised for the purpose in 1462, the new grant came with the proviso that the money was to be used solely for the defence of the realm. For the second time in three years the Church Convocations voted him a tenth of ecclesiastical revenues, over and above the loans individual bishops had made since he seized power. The City of London, whose leading citizens had also been generous to the new king, voted him additional funds to feed his army, and other cities did likewise. It was a massive, if conditional vote of confidence.

So it was that Edward marched north at the head of the best equipped and provisioned army he had ever led. The suspicion must be that he had tricked his loyal subjects into giving him money for a war he had no intention of fighting. He and Warwick knew the Lancastrian threat was ephemeral without French and Scots support, thus the solution would be diplomatic. Instead, to their chagrin, they had to spend much of the money to stamp out brush fires all over England.

The political ace Edward thought to play was Henry Beaufort, Earl of Somerset, whom he made every effort to win as a supporter and friend. He restored his lands, granted him a cash settlement to help pay his debts, and gave him a handsome annuity. Somerset played along so convincingly that he was made a Companion of the Bedchamber and appointed head of a new King's Guard, some 200 men recruited from his own retainers. It was an extravagantly trusting gesture, intended as a propaganda coup to dishearten the Lancastrians.

Edward's subjects were not impressed. Outraged to see their king surrounded by men they believed might kill him, the citizens of Leicester rioted and Somerset barely escaped with his life. Ruefully accepting that his gambit had backfired, Edward pacified the rioters with a tun [252 gallons] of wine and thanked them for their concern. He sent Somerset to the nearest of the duke's properties at Chirk Castle in Denbigh, and ordered the King's Guard to march on ahead to Newcastle. Edward himself proceeded to pay his respects to his mother at the family seat at Fotheringhay, then went to the royal castle at Pontefract, and finally to York.

The citizens of Leicester may well have saved Edward's life, as Somerset always planned treachery. He did not stay long at Chirk, stealing away by night with the intention of joining his men at Newcastle. He was identified when he stopped for the night in Durham and an angry mob formed. He had to flee the inn in his night-clothes, leaving his armour behind. His retainers were primed to seize Newcastle when he arrived, but by now Montagu was fully alerted and those of Somerset's men who did not flee in time were executed.

Somerset himself managed to reach Bamburgh, where the royal family had fled after the debacle at Norham. Henry VI remained, but in August Marguerite and their son sailed to Flanders. They were destitute and rescued by Charles, Count of Charolais, who helped them and their small band of followers to reach her father's duchy of Bar. Somerset was re-attainted in December and his estates awarded to Richard, Duke of Gloucester, Edward's 10-year-old brother.

Thus the sum total of Edward's contribution to the pacification of the North was a failed propaganda coup that could have cost him his politically irreplaceable life, and which cast strong doubts on his judgement. Thereafter he became little more than a spectator to a show run by the Neville brothers. First they cut off the Lancastrians from their French and Scots life support, and then they methodically crushed them.

Edward summoned Parliament to assemble at York in early February 1464, intending it to coincide with a peace treaty with the Scots. Things did not go to plan. While Somerset was posing as the king's friend his agents had been busy organizing revolts all over the country, which flared up as soon as he dropped the pretence. Though the coup at Newcastle failed, while at Chirk Somerset had set in motion local uprisings serious enough for Edward to send the young Duke of Norfolk to suppress them, with the power to execute and pardon at will. That he did not empower Lord Stanley, the nominally Yorkist local magnate, is significant.

Our only source for this rebellion is a letter in February 1464 from the younger John Paston, who rode with the king's friend John Howard, the real commander in Norfolk's name. Paston wrote that they had 'great labour here in Wales', where 'the commons in Lancashire and Cheshire were up to the number of ten thousand or more… but now they be down again'. There was obviously more to it than that. Many of the rebels would have come from Marguerite's dower lands in the region, where Lancastrian affinity ran deep, but the presumption must be that Stanley played an important part both in the rebellion and its suppression.

There was also dangerous unrest in the Midlands. In January Edward moved from York to Coventry, where Warwick and other Yorkist lords, plus his two chief justices, joined him. Their presence had the desired effect of overawing the city and the surrounding area. He then ordered his chief justices to Gloucester, where a revolt had broken out, and joined them in early February to conduct assizes (properly 'commissions of oyer and terminer'). Then came word of the intimidation of a commission appointed to deal with unrest in Cambridgeshire, presumably by members of the Oxford and Beaumont affinities, and Edward had to ride with Tiptoft and other lords to lend his personal authority to the proceedings.

Parliament, already postponed once, assembled at York on 20 February but had to be prorogued until 5 May with the humiliating explanation that unrest in the kingdom made it impossible for the king to be present. In fact he rode from Cambridge to London to meet a delegation from King Enrique IV of Castille, which brought him an offer of marriage to the king's sister and heir presumptive. This was none other than the lady known to posterity as Isabella of Castille, but one of history's more intriguing 'might have beens' became moot when Edward politely declined the offer.

With Edward buzzing around like the proverbial bluebottle fly (actually, as we shall see, more like a bee around a nectar-laden flower), it was left to the Nevilles to rip the heart out of the Lancastrian insurgency. At some point, in the absence of Lord Ogle, the Bishop of Durham's men at Norham mutinied, and it became imperative to conclude a truce with the Scots before they snapped up the border fortress. In April Montagu assembled a force of about 5,000 men and marched north to escort a Scots delegation from the border to York.

The march took him through the heart of the Percy lordship of Beanley, and on 25 April, at a place called Hedgeley Moor, he found his way barred by a Lancastrian army of about equal numbers commanded by Somerset. The bulk of the army was made up of northerners, but Roos and Hungerford led a battalion of supporters from elsewhere in England, including some of Somerset's affinity.

The difference in morale and determination between men fighting on their own ground and the rest became apparent once battle was joined, when the left wing under Roos and Hungerford broke and fled as Montagu's men advanced after an initial exchange of arrows. Abandoned by the other lords, Ralph Percy made a last stand and was killed. His dying words were 'I have saved the bird in my bosom', and historians have puzzled over them ever since.

Having failed to prevent the Anglo–Scots peace negotiations, Somerset's last throw, this time accompanied by Henry VI himself, was to march south in the hope of rallying the men of the Percy lordships of Langley and Prudhoe on the Tyne. On the night of 14/15 May the small Lancastrian force camped outside Hexham, and the next morning was dispersed with ease by a considerably larger force from Newcastle under Montagu, accompanied by Lords Greystoke and Willoughby.

All the Lancastrian high command were captured. Somerset and four others were immediately beheaded at Hexham; Hungerford, Roos and three others at Newcastle on the 17th. Seven more (presumably Neville turncoats) were executed at Middleham on the 18th, and fourteen more at York on the 26th, after being tried and convicted by Tiptoft. The last to be captured was Tailboys, found hiding in a Redesdale coal mine with the remains of Louis XI's gold. He was beheaded at Newcastle.

Henry VI, who had remained at Bywell Castle on the north bank of the Tyne, got away and, accompanied initially by Richard Tunstall and Henry Bellingham, two dog-loyal knights, wandered from one Lancastrian household to another in West Yorkshire, Westmorland and Lancashire for the next fourteen months. He was betrayed in July 1466 by Richard Tempest of Waddington Hall, near Clitheroe in eastern Lancashire. After a humiliating ride through London, riding a nag with his feet tied to the stirrups, he was imprisoned in the Tower.

At York on 27 May 1464 a delighted Edward created a new earldom of Northumberland for Montagu, endowed with the Percy estates not previously awarded to Warwick and Clarence. After Edward signed a fifteen-year truce with the Scots on 1 June, the new earl set out to reduce the Northumbrian castles. The Norham garrison's mutiny ended when they were paid, and the garrisons at Alnwick and Dunstanburgh capitulated in return for pardons on 23 and 24 June.

There remained Bamburgh, where the turncoat Ralph Grey knew he had no hope of pardon. With him was Warwick's cousin Humphrey Neville, whose father Thomas, brother and guardian of the demented Earl of Westmorland, had died with Clifford at Dintingdale, a few hours before the Battle of Towton. Humphrey had twice broken his parole to Edward and led damaging raids as far south as Yorkshire, so he also had no expectation of mercy.

Because of their strategic location Edward had been loth to see the Northumbrian castles damaged. This time the gloves came off and Montagu blasted Bamburgh's walls with huge bombards shipped years earlier to Newcastle from London and Calais, but only now brought along the coast by barges and put to work. After they brought down the roof of the central keep on Grey's head, Humphrey called for parley.

Perhaps believing Grey was dying, he gave up the castle in exchange for a pardon for himself. In fact Grey survived and was taken to Doncaster, where he was put on trial before the fearsome

Tiptoft. In recognition of his family's services to the House of York he was not degraded from the Order of the Garter or attainted before he was beheaded on 10 July. All the men around whom further resistance to the Yorkist regime might have coalesced were now either dead or reconciled.

In order not to burden the narrative I have set out the honours, offices and lands accumulated by Warwick in **Appendix D**. From the Warwick and Salisbury inheritance alone he held lands that had once endowed four historic earldoms, with estates in Welsh Glamorgan and Brecknock, and in every English county except Cheshire, Derbyshire, Lancashire, Lincolnshire and Shropshire. He had more land and enjoyed a higher income from it than any nobleman since John of Gaunt, the prototype of the 'over-mighty subject'.

To this he added revenues from the many offices he accumulated as the indispensable man in winning and securing the throne. He had more disposable income than the king, whose estates were heavily encumbered and whose overheads were vastly greater. While this may have rankled, it remains incomprehensible that Edward refused him a dukedom. It was possibly the least expensive gesture he could have made to ensure Warwick's loyalty.

Perhaps he intended to do so eventually, maybe even as a reward for pacifying the North; however, well before Hexham Warwick had made it clear that he considered himself the king's chief minister and the power behind the throne. Nowhere was this more evident than in his dealings with France, a role that appealed irresistibly to his grandiosity.

LOUIS

I F A RULER'S SUCCESS OR FAILURE DEPENDS AS MUCH ON THE ineptitude of his opponents as on his own skill, then Louis XI of France, wonderfully nicknamed 'the Universal Spider', was one of the luckiest monarchs in history. His principal antagonists were the last independent Duke of Burgundy Charles, nicknamed '*le Téméraire*' (which translates as 'the Rash' as well as 'the Bold'), Duke Frañsez II of Brittany, described by a contemporary Breton chronicler as 'weak in body and even weaker in mind', and the insecure usurper Edward IV.

On the minus side, the curse of genealogy lay heavily on the Valois dynasty. The legalistic justification for the devastating Hundred Years War was the English kings' claim to the throne of France, based on a superior right of succession through the marriages of the first two Edwards to the eldest daughters of the House of Capet. The powerful Dukes of Bourbon and Counts of Bourbon-Vendôme also had a separate but junior line of descent from the Capetian King Louis IX.* The greater problem was that the extended Valois clan, 'the princes of the blood', made the English Plantagenets seem like happy families.

The Dukes of Valois-Alençon were a cadet line descended from Count Charles of Valois, whose eldest son became the first Valois

---

* Thus becoming a new royal dynasty in 1598, after both the Valois and Valois-Orléans lines became extinct.

king. The Dukes of Valois-Anjou and of Valois-Burgundy were descendants of the second Valois king, and the Dukes of Valois-Orléans and of Valois-Orléans-Angoulême from the third. Their bitter rivalries had permitted relatively small English armies to conquer northern France. Even after Jeanne d'Arc shamed some of them into turning the tide, many years of ego massaging were required before they could be united to expel the invaders.

They were soon back to squabbling amongst themselves; but now, instead of hindering Charles VII (Louis's father), their divisions helped him to reduce their importance by building on the foundations of absolutism. The king's new measures included the 1438 Pragmatic Sanction, by which he 'nationalized' the Papacy's right to appoint French clergy and the revenues deriving from it, and a standing army paid for by a land tax (*taille*) on non-nobles. The *taille* was awarded to the monarchy in perpetuity by the Estates General in 1439, thereby rendering themselves irrelevant: Louis XI summoned them only once in twenty-two years.

Charles VII's reduced need to accommodate his nobles did not pass unnoticed, and the steps he took to rationalize the administration of justice and tax collection were seen for what they were – the thin end of a wedge of encroachment on traditional aristocratic prerogatives. His reforms provoked the short-lived 1440 Praguerie rebellion nominally led by Louis, his 17-year-old heir apparent, involving the Dukes of Bourbon, Alençon and Brittany, and the Count of Vendôme. There was a formal reconciliation, but Charles never forgave his son.

In 1441–3 Louis distinguished himself in operations against the English and the Count of Armagnac, and in 1444 Charles sent him to fight the fearsome Swiss at the head of an army of *écorcheurs*, savage and fiercely meritocratic French irregulars. Louis emerged with credit from the campaign, but received no reward. At court, relations between him and Agnès Sorel, Charles's influential mistress, became so bad that in 1446 he was sent to govern the Dauphiné, the traditional principality of the heirs to the throne, and a nest

6. KINGDOM OF FRANCE 1461

Calais
Flanders
B St
Artois
E Picardy
Rethel
Normandy
Île de France
Paris
Alençon
SEE MAP 7
Brittany
Maine
Perche
Champagne
Bar
Anjou
V
D
Orléans
Nemours
Touraine
Blois
S

SMALL
COUNTIES
B   Boulogne
C   *Comminges*
D   Dunois
E   Eu
M   *Mirande*
S   Sancerre
St   Saint-Pol
V   Vendôme

Poitou
Berry
Burgundy
Nevers
Bourbon
Saintonge
Angoulême
La Marche
Limoges
Périgord
Turenne
Auvergne
Forez
Duchy of
Savoy

Guyenne
Albret
Rodez
Dauphiné
(semi-autonomous)
Gascony
Armagnac
Papal
State
Kingdom
of
Castille
Kingdom of Navarre
Béarn
M
Bigorre
C
Foix
Languedoc
Narbonne
Provence
Kingdom of Aragon
Rousillon &
Cerdagne
© Hugh Bicheno

—————— **International frontiers**
············· **Territories of Burgundy-Nevers and Brittany**

Royal demesne in bold italics. Comminges and Mirande were semi-autonomous.

The Duke of Valois-Orléan's lands included Valois, Blois and Dunois
The Dukes of Angoulême were a cadet branch of the House of Valois-Orléans
The Duke of Valois-Anjou's lands included Provence and Bar
The Count of Maine was the son of Valois-Anjou
The Duke of Valois-Alençon's lands included Perche
The Duke of Bourbon's lands included Auvergne, Forez and Vendôme
The Counts of Sancerre were a cadet branch of the House of Bourbon
The Count of Armagnac's lands included Rodez and La Marche
The Counts of Nemours were a cadet branch of the House of Armagnac
The Count of Foix's lands included Béarn, Bigorre and Narbonne
The Lord of Albret's lands included Limoges, Turenne and Périgord

7. BURGUNDIAN LANDS 1461

Legend:

- - - - Frontier with Holy Roman Empire
——— **Burgundian lands**
——— Internal borders
✝ *Toul* Prince-Bishoprics
Italics Other principalities

Friesland

Zuiderzee

Holland

✝ *Utrecht*

Guelders

Zutphen

Cleves

Guelders

Zeeland

Bruges

Antwerp

Duchy of Brabant

Neuss

Cologne

Calais

Ghent

Flanders

Brussels

Boulogne

St Omer

Ypres

✝ *Tournai*

Ligny

Namur

Liège

Duchy of Limburg

HOLY

Artois

St Pol

Hainault

Duchy of Luxembourg

Frankfurt

Mainz

Hesdin

Arras

✝ *Cambrai*

Liège

Trier

ROMAN

Picardy

Guise

Amiens

Eu (Nevers)

Brienne

Rethel (Nevers)

Champagne

Lorr.

Palatinate

Île de

Reims

Bar

✝ *Verdun*

✝ *Metz*

Lorr.

EMPIRE

Paris

Duchy of Bar

✝ *Nancy*

Strasbourg

Montlhéry

France

Troyes

Bar and Lorraine governed by House of Valois-Anjou

✝ *Toul*

Metz

Lower Alsace

Iles (Nevers)

Bar

Duchy of Lorraine

✝ *Luxeuil*

Upper Alsace

Breisgau

Auxerre

Basle

Zurich

Berry

Duchy of Burgundy

Dijon

Free County of Burgundy

County of Nevers

Berne

Grandson

Morat

Swiss Confederacy

0 25 50 75 100
miles

Bourbon

Charolais

Mâcon

Geneva

Duchy of Savoy

© *Hugh Bicheno*

of interlocking feudal and ecclesiastical jurisdictions calculated to break the spirit of any ruler.

Once again Louis rose to the challenge. He humbled the local lords, favoured the gentry and the bourgeoisie, and introduced reforms such as the first regular postal service in Europe. He also ignored frequent attempts to recall him and in 1451, in defiance of his father's orders, he made a dynastic marriage with the House of Savoy. Charles intended to enforce Louis's obedience by invading the Dauphiné the following year, but had to turn aside to deal with the English reconquest of Guyenne. When the delayed invasion went ahead in 1456, Louis fled to the court of his uncle Duke Philippe of Burgundy.

Despite Charles's threats, Philippe set Louis up with his own establishment at the castle of Genappe in his sub-duchy of Brabant, a prudent arm's length south of the provincial capital at Brussels. By Valois standards Philippe's heir Charles, Count of Charolais, was a loyal son: but he questioned Philippe's benevolence towards Louis. He argued that it would be better to surrender the dangerously capable Louis to his father. If he lived he would promote sedition, and if killed his twenty-three-year younger brother would become Dauphin. Philippe thought otherwise, and fondly believed he was creating a bond of gratitude.

Louis's policy over the next five years was straightforward: he opposed anything his father did, thus he backed the Yorkists against the Lancastrians in England's civil war. Philippe took the same view, but Charolais was fascinated by the struggle between Warwick and Somerset over Calais. He became enamoured of handsome Henry Beaufort, and when he had to abandon the struggle for Calais gave him 1,400 livres [£135,000] to get himself and his men back to England and continue the fight.

I use the word 'enamoured' advisedly. Charolais's intense admiration for Somerset led him to support Lancastrian resistance after Towton, seemingly in defiance of his father's pro-Yorkist policy.* He felt Somerset's execution deeply, and once he became duke he sheltered Somerset's brothers and was reluctant to ally with the Yorkist regime. While he was also influenced by his adored mother Isabella of Portugal, a granddaughter of John of Gaunt, father of the Lancastrian dynasty, his motives appear to have been more personal.

The link may be that he was repelled by his father's monumental promiscuity – at least twenty-four mistresses and eighteen recognized bastards. Although Charolais managed to overcome his revulsion and engender a daughter in 1457, in general he shunned female and sought out exclusively male company. In 1470 his illegitimate half-brother Baudouin fled to France and accused him of 'unnatural vices'; but while he was almost certainly homosexual, it is more likely he sublimated his urges in violent sports and warfare.

During his time at Genappe Louis was at all times respectful of his uncle Philippe and also won over his sceptical son through their mutual passion for the chase. He even managed to remain friendly with Jacquetta's brother Louis de Luxembourg, Count of Saint-Pol, who had been his comrade-in-arms in 1441, even though they backed different sides in the English civil war. During his time in exile Louis obtained an intimate knowledge of the strengths and weaknesses of men who would later oppose him, without permitting any of them to catch more than occasional glimpses of the workings of his own mind.

On the other side of France, Duke Frañsez of Brittany seems to have calculated (if, indeed, any coherent mental process was involved) that his interests were best served by stirring the English pot. After the Lancastrian defeat at Northampton he welcomed Marguerite's emissary the Earl of Wiltshire, gave him the money to recruit Breton and Irish mercenaries, and the ships to transport them to join Jasper Tudor, Earl of Pembroke, in Wales. Few survived the rout that followed their defeat by Edward at Mortimer's Cross. Frañsez continued to support Jasper, as well as the last Lancastrian

---

*There may be less to this than meets the eye. Charolais lacked the means to conduct an independent foreign policy and Philippe could have stopped him if he wished. He was probably using his son to hedge his bet.

holdout of Harlech Castle in Wales, for many years.

When Marguerite's army marched on London after defeating and killing Richard of York and Warwick's father at Wakefield, Philippe gave generous sanctuary to Richard's two youngest boys. He also sent a contingent of hand-gunners, who shared Warwick's defeat at the Second Battle of St Albans. Arguably more significant was the choice of one of Louis's retinue, Lord de la Barde, to represent Burgundy to the Yorkists, and that he led a contingent of Burgundians to fight for Edward at Towton under the Dauphin's banner.

Philippe's greater contribution was to keep Charles VII in check. Charles was in poor health – he died four months after Towton – and desperate to be reconciled with his heir. Louis refused to go to him even when he was dying, and after he died shocked Philippe by making only a perfunctory gesture of mourning during the elaborate ceremonies the duke organized. Louis went along with the charade, making it clear he did so only to please his uncle, but eventually could bear it no longer and slipped away to get on with the business of ruling.

He immediately adopted many of the policies he had opposed while his father lived, among them support of the Lancastrians. Having been at the heart of the informal alliance between Burgundy and the Yorkists, Louis fully appreciated the threat it could pose to France. Also, France's allies the Scots had obtained Berwick by helping Marguerite after Northampton – could he not obtain title to Calais now that she was truly desperate? Yet, having obtained her undertaking to cede the enclave if she recovered the throne, he did the bare minimum to keep the Lancastrian resistance alive.

This was because he did not wish the issue of who governed England to become a major bone of contention between France and Burgundy. He was coldly pragmatic and the sole purpose of his limited support for the Lancastrians was to keep England divided and weak for as long as possible, in order to diminish the value of an English alliance in Burgundian eyes. In this he was successful, leaving both Philippe and himself free to deal with more important bilateral matters and their own internal problems.

• ❧ •

The Burgundian lands were separated by the duchies of Bar and Lorraine and by the Prince-Bishopric of Liège. Bar was ruled by Duke René d'Anjou, Marguerite's father, and Lorraine – in succession to his mother – by René's eldest son Jean. About half of Bar and all of Lorraine lay within the boundaries of the historic Holy Roman Empire, such that René and Jean owed nominal homage to the Emperor for them.

Considerably more significant was the homage René owed to the King of France for part of Bar, and all of Anjou and Provence. He was also titular King of Naples, having been expelled by the King of Aragon in 1441, a can of worms best left unopened here. More germane to our story is the war fought between René and Philippe over Lorraine in 1431, in which René was captured. He was eventually released in 1436 after agreeing a ransom that ruined him, even though he was never able to pay the whole amount.

Power abhors a vacuum, but the Angevins and their descendants clung on to Bar and Lorraine until 1766 because they were recognized as the legitimate rulers by both the Empire and France. The price of powerlessness was that their territory was regarded as a thoroughfare, and Nancy as an occasional alternative location for the courts of the French kings.

The existential threat to the Dukes of Burgundy was not so much that every duchy, sub-duchy and county recognized his overlordship according to its own laws and customs, a feudal overhang common to all the proto-nations of Europe. Their particular problem came from the example set by the autonomous Rhine valley cities outside their borders. Burgundy depended heavily on revenues from the commercial and industrial cities in Flanders, where a desire for comparable autonomy was never far below the surface.

• ☙ •

Louis XI added two substantial territories to his kingdom in 1462–3, both by purchase. The first opportunity came about in early 1462 when the province of Catalonia overthrew the authority of King Juan II of Aragon, who had exhausted his credit in a war over Navarre. In May Juan signed treaties with Louis XI for the loan of 4,200 knights plus their retainers and led by the Count of Foix for an agreed price of 200,000 gold crowns [£25.4 million]. As surety Louis was to hold Roussillon and Cerdagne, Catalan counties north of the Pyrenees.

The Catalans, hard pressed by King Juan's French army, invited King Enrique IV of Castille to become their ruler. He denounced the cession of Rousillon and Cerdagne and threatened to conquer the kingdom of Aragon in its entirety. In an adroit move, Louis persuaded Enrique to accept his arbitration, then prevailed on Juan to cede disputed territory in Navarre to keep Castille out of the war. The war dragged on for another decade though permutations including the Catalans' election of René d'Anjou, who ruined himself again by trying to make good his claim; but by 1474 Rousillon and Cerdagne were permanently incorporated into France.

Louis's other purchase seemed at first to be more straightforward. In 1435 his father had ceded the rich towns of the Somme valley in Picardy to Duke Philippe as part of the price he paid to break up the Anglo–Burgundian alliance.* The terms were that the towns would revert to the French crown in return for 400,000 gold crowns [£51 million].

Louis completed the supposedly prohibitive payment and, with the help of high-placed agents at Philippe's court, recovered the towns by the end of 1463. The complications here were that the taxes vigorously collected across France to raise the money were

---

*From west to east, the cities were Abbeville, Saint-Riquier, Amiens, Corbie, Péronne and Saint-Quentin. Also, south of the valley, Roye and Montdidier, and north of the valley Doullens, Arleux and Mortagne.

deeply unpopular, and that Philippe's son Charolais violently opposed the deal and swore to reverse it.

Not only Burgundian feathers were ruffled. As before in the Dauphiné, Louis had been a whirlwind since becoming king, constantly touring and making no effort to cultivate his nobles. Indeed, he seemed at times to go out of his way to offend them, and spoke rather too freely about their personal shortcomings. He also enforced royal prerogatives at their expense, notably by revoking the patronage previously enjoyed by secular and ecclesiastical lords under the terms of the 1438 Pragmatic Sanction.

Louis certainly knew he was playing with fire. He had, after all, helped to derail his father's more modest attempts to assert royal authority in the 1440 Praguerie rebellion. Since then Charles VII had committed the *taille* to setting up the salaried *compagnies d'ordonnance*, drawn from the lesser nobility and gentry. This was the standing army with which Charles threw the English out of France in 1449–51 and Louis, confident of his own military skill, believed it would deter his nobles from resorting to arms.

It did not deter the Duke of Brittany, who inspired little enthusiasm among his subjects but could depend on their unqualified support in resisting any attempt by the French king to infringe on Breton autonomy. So, when Frañsez defied him in 1463 and Louis found he needed the support of the French nobility, he did not get it. The step too far was to make an enemy of Charolais at the same time, when Philippe was showing signs of senility and could no longer be depended on to keep his intemperate son under control.

The paradoxical result was that England moved to the front and centre of Louis's diplomacy. He had created a critical mass of enemies and the last thing he needed was for an English army with its dreaded longbowmen to descend on Normandy. Thus the embassy sent by Edward IV, led by Chancellor George Neville, was manna from heaven. Louis agreed a one-year truce with Neville in October 1463, deluged the embassy with expensive gifts, and showed himself warmly disposed to the idea of a matrimonial alliance.

Not least, he expressed extravagant admiration for Warwick and requested he should lead a subsequent delegation to a peace conference to end the state of war that still existed between the two kingdoms. In what he thought was a masterstroke, Louis asked Duke Philippe to host the conference. Philippe, who, unlike his son, was rather pleased with the immense addition to his treasury from the redemption of the Somme towns, was flattered and moved almost permanently to his palace at Hesdin, the designated venue.

Warwick could not come because the Lancastrians and Scots continued to cause trouble well into 1464, and everybody – except Marguerite and Bishop Kennedy in Scotland, who begged in vain for further support – believed Louis was responsible. This was no longer the case: the Lancastrian gambit had outlived its usefulness. His aim was to prevent an Anglo–Burgundian alliance, and what better way than by winning over the man said to be the power behind the English throne?

In March 1464 Louis sent Lord de la Barde, who had fought for Edward at Towton, with an offer of marriage to Bona of Savoy, Louis's 14-year-old sister-in-law. Edward coolly replied that he would give it serious consideration. Warwick, on the other hand, leapt for the fly and promised to go to Hesdin to agree the final terms of the treaty. As spring gave way to summer, letters arrived from Warwick excusing himself because negotiations with the Scots required his presence in York, and Louis became increasingly nervous.

Meanwhile Philippe was becoming restless, and Louis rode to Hesdin to soothe his uncle's increasingly clouded mind. Finally an embassy arrived, but it was led by Warwick's retainer Lord Wenlock and had only come to negotiate a one-year extension of the truce due to expire in October. Warwick would certainly come, Wenlock said, before then. By now Louis was genuinely desperate. His diplomacy was unravelling, reports from his spies indicated serious trouble brewing among his nobles, and now he had involved Duke Philippe in a fiasco. Louis left Hesdin on 9 July, never to see his uncle again.

'I never saw a lord so ardently desire anything as this King desires this peace with the English', reported Louis's confidante Alberico Maletta, the Milanese ambassador. 'I believe that if the earl of Warwick came he would obtain anything from the King to obtain this peace'. 'Anything' almost certainly included a French title and lands to go with it.

Then rumour swelled to certainty – Edward had secretly married Elizabeth Woodville, a beautiful English widow, and had announced it at a meeting of his Great Council after first permitting the oblivious Warwick to extol the virtues of Bona of Savoy. It was a brutal rejection of the French alliance, and Duke Philippe exploded with rage when he learned of it. Then Charolais announced he had arrested a spy sent by Louis – a nephew of the Croy brothers, Louis's agents at the Burgundian court and the blackest of Charolais's *bêtes noires*. The Universal Spider's web had been torn apart.

IV

ELIZABETH

L IKE MOST WOMEN OF HER TIME ELIZABETH WOODVILLE
has no voice in the historical record. Inevitably, most of what
we 'know' of her as a person is based on gossip, because that
is all there is to work with. There are records of a few acts of charity,
patronage and household management, but none that illuminate
her closest relationships. Her presumed influence must be inferred
from the better recorded actions of those around her, in particular
Edward IV, because had she not become his queen we would know
even less about her.

One incontrovertible fact is that, like her mother Jacquetta,
Elizabeth was astonishingly fertile. Between 1466 and 1480 she bore
Edward ten children, eight surviving infancy. Since Edward was an
inveterate womanizer, clearly something more than sex continued
to draw him back to Elizabeth's bed. Perhaps, like Shakespeare's
Cleopatra:

> Age cannot wither her, nor custom stale
> Her infinite variety. Other women cloy
> The appetites they feed, but she makes hungry
> Where most she satisfies…

Edward would not have been easily impressed. He would have
started early with servants and worked his way up the social scale as

he grew older. He was young, tall, handsome and rich, and would have had little difficulty seducing lonely widows and women married to men who thought to profit from the liaison. The floodgates would have opened after he became king. Royal courts could be hothouses, and adultery was easily incubated behind the stylized flirting of courtly love, accompanied by staggering amounts of wine and spirits.

Married women were the safest option, as any by-blows could not definitely be attributed to him, and Edward is reputed to have bedded the wives of many London merchants. His taste ran to mature, sexually experienced women, but no doubt a fair number of maidens were happy to be deflowered by him. He had at least two recognized bastards.* English kings never adopted the well-ordered continental custom of 'official' mistresses (*maîtresses en titre*), but the families of their lovers still had much to gain, and their cast-offs could expect to make good marriages to men likewise seeking royal favour.

So – Edward lived any young man's dream of concupiscence, and if foreign observers were still commenting on his sexual appetite when he was approaching 40, he must have been truly voracious in his late teens and early twenties. It may have contributed to his reluctance to subject himself to the hardships of campaigning, and might help to explain his sluggishness in all except the most challenging situations. These were not qualities that inspired respect. However indulgent society might otherwise be of youthful exuberance, as king he had an obligation to ensure the succession and to set an example.

Accordingly, Edward was under pressure to marry and settle down. Warwick's earnest efforts to saddle him with Bona of Savoy were irksome, and Edward's decision to marry someone 'unsuitable'

---

*Elizabeth Lucy née Wayte, a widow, gave him a daughter, also Elizabeth, in the early 1460s, and may have died giving birth to a son, Arthur, *c.*1476. Elizabeth married Thomas Lumley and their son Richard (born *c.*1478) became the 4th Baron Lumley. In 1511 Arthur married Elizabeth Grey, Baroness Lisle by right, and was made a viscount in 1523.

was undoubtedly a defiant gesture both to him and to convention. Although it was a snub to Warwick, it was also a humiliating slap in the face to his aunt, Edward's insufferably proud mother. Duchess Cecily liked to think of herself as 'queen by right' and had no doubt been looking forward to dominating a young foreign-born queen. Her chagrin at being replaced by a mature and self-assured Englishwoman was boundless.

It went deeper than that: Jacquetta and Richard Woodville filled an emotional void in Edward's life before he ever set eyes on Elizabeth, and his close relationship with them preceded his marriage to their daughter by several years. When his reign began he was, just, 20 years old, Richard was 56 and Jacquetta 46. Edward's nominal father – had he lived – would have been 50 and Cecily was also 46. To some degree, the older Woodvilles became surrogates for the loving parents he never had.

Edward first got to know them when he was with Warwick in Calais. In January 1460 Lord Rivers, Jacquetta and their eldest son Lord Scales were captured in a raid on Sandwich. Jacquetta seems to have insisted on being taken with them to Calais, where Warwick and Edward submitted Rivers and Scales to a public humiliation, sneering at Rivers for marrying above himself. Jacquetta's presence may have saved their lives, as she was not only dowager Duchess of Bedford, thus outranking both Edward and Warwick, but also the sister of Louis, ruler of the neighbouring county of Saint-Pol. She would have demanded honourable treatment of her husband and son before returning to England.

While he did not bond with Rivers at this time, Edward did win over two other Lancastrians captured during his sojourn in Calais. John Tuchet, Baron Audley, and Humphrey Stafford of Hooke (later Southwyck) formed part of the expedition sent under Henry Beaufort to take Calais back for Lancaster. Captured in a skirmish, they were treated so well by Edward that they changed sides and became his devoted followers.

Edward's next encounter with the Woodvilles was at Towton,

where Rivers and Scales led the division that outflanked the Yorkist right wing and nearly won the battle before the tide was turned by the late arrival of the Duke of Norfolk's men. It was therefore remarkable that only ten weeks later Edward should have visited Rivers's manor of Grafton in Northamptonshire on his way back to London. Before departing he wrote to Chancellor George Neville saying he pardoned Rivers 'all manner of offences and trespasses of him done against us'. A month later he also pardoned Scales, conditional on service against the Lancastrians in the North.

Even Somerset was required to prove his loyalty – why not Rivers? The answer is almost certainly Jacquetta. Her feisty performance at Calais no doubt made a positive impression, but it would have been her subsequent actions that turned Edward into an admirer. She was one of the two noblewomen, both ladies-in-waiting to the queen, who were sent by the mayor and aldermen of London to beg Marguerite not to assault the city after her victory at the Second Battle of St Albans on 17 February 1461.*

In fact Marguerite's army was in no condition to fight its way into the city. It would also have been madness to do so with Edward's army approaching from the west following his victory at Mortimer's Cross. Contemporaries did not see it that way. They believed Marguerite was at the head of a horde of ravening English and Scots borderers, intent on rape and pillage. Consequently, when Jacquetta returned to reassure them the alleged horde would not try to enter the city, she became a secular saint to Londoners.

Arriving a few days later, Edward would have believed she had made it possible for him to occupy the capital peacefully, with all the political, financial and military benefits that flowed from this. Although her husband and eldest son tried earnestly to kill him at Towton, he owed Jacquetta a considerable debt of gratitude and went to Grafton to pay his respects – to her. No doubt she told her doting husband, in no uncertain terms, how he should behave.

*At which Jacquetta's son-in-law John Grey, Elizabeth Woodville's first husband, had been the only prominent Lancastrian killed.

Rivers was soon regularly employed on royal commissions and in 1463 became the first ex-Lancastrian to become a member of the Privy Council. Even so, Elizabeth did not judge her parents close enough to the king to plead her cause in a well-documented event immediately preceding her marriage to Edward, which may be crucially illuminating. It involved a negotiation with William Hastings, Edward's closest friend.

Hastings was an inveterate lecher and Edward had learned much from him when he was a lusty teenager enjoying the older man's hospitality as ranger of the Duke of York's chase at Wyre in Shropshire. Given Hasting's reputation, when we find Elizabeth appealing to him in 1464 to use his influence on her behalf in a lawsuit involving the fourth son of Viscount Bourchier, the king's uncle, it is a safe assumption that he demanded something more than the goodwill of a highly desirable widow in return.

The suit came about because Elizabeth's mother-in-law, Baroness Ferrers of Groby in her own right, tried to cheat her of a settlement made on her by the baroness's first husband, who had died in 1457. The baroness was urged on by her second husband John Bourchier, nineteen years her junior, both of them emboldened by the death of Elizabeth's husband at the Second Battle of St Albans and the sudden prominence of John's father, now Earl of Essex. At stake were not only three manors allocated by the terms of a trust, but also the Ferrers lands, which should eventually go to Thomas, Elizabeth's eldest son and heir to the barony.

By the terms of a contract signed on 13 April 1464 Hastings acquired the right – for which he paid 500 marks [£106,000] – to marry a daughter of his family to Thomas, or if he died to his younger brother Richard. If both died Elizabeth was to repay 250 marks. Hastings was also to have an equal share of the income from any Ferrers lands secured (implicitly by his influence) for Thomas before his 12th birthday.

It was an almost priceless warning shot across the bow of John Bourchier from the heaviest gun at Edward's court. As to the settlement, half of something is, after all, a great deal better than all of nothing, and 500 marks was not chicken feed. If part of the price Hastings demanded to ensure her son's inheritance was for Elizabeth to bed him, it would explain her hostility towards him in the years to come. It would, of course, have been very greatly in the interest of neither to tell Edward about it.

Given that the contract became moot after Elizabeth married Edward, he cannot yet have been a prospect. He was probably first smitten seventeen days later during a visit to Grafton, when Elizabeth is alleged to have petitioned him for justice in her dispute with Lady Ferrers. As early as 1468 an Italian author stated the marriage took place the next day, but it is just too neat to have it take place on May Day, the spring festival of fertility. The marriage took place after Edward returned from signing the Scots truce, at one of two subsequent visits to Grafton in June and July.

Jacquetta probably pimped her daughter, as any aristocratic mother would have done. Edward was always on the quest for nubile widows, but he would have hesitated before seducing the daughter of a couple he respected. No doubt the usual game of love was played out, with Edward becoming increasingly ardent. Jacquetta was the only family member to witness the informal marriage that preceded the consummation, after which Elizabeth set the hook so well that Edward's travelling companions remarked on his blissful exhaustion.

In the context of his policy of reconciliation it was politically shrewd for Edward to marry the daughter of Lord Rivers, the most prominent of the genuinely reconciled Lancastrians. But there was also an overwhelming dynastic argument with reference to the looming power struggle with over-mighty Warwick. With his older sisters already married, in mid-1464 Edward could dispose of only three siblings as matrimonial assets: 18-year-old Margaret, 14-year-old George and 11-year-old Richard.

By marrying Elizabeth he acquired two stepsons and nine brothers- and sisters-in-law, all except one, Elizabeth's sister Jacquetta, unmarried. The significance of this becomes apparent when we contrast the wave of marriage alliances that ensued with those of the Nevilles when they were seeking to affirm their power a generation earlier. Edward married his new in-laws to every eligible bachelor in the peerage to strengthen his family ties, and the grooms in turn expected to benefit from becoming members of the extended royal family. It was a transaction well understood by all concerned.

Petit bourgeois preoccupation with class has never bothered the nobility when money and power are involved, and despite sniffy comments by some contemporary chroniclers and most historians, Elizabeth's lineage was acceptable to the old aristocracy. Led by the Earl of Arundel, whose title dated back to 1138 and who had married one of the Nevilles a generation earlier, they were only too willing to enter into matrimonial alliances with the Woodvilles.

Some have suggested that Warwick was outraged by the marriage between 19-year-old John Woodville and wealthy, 65-year-old Katherine née Neville, dowager Duchess of Norfolk, Duchess Cecily's sister and Warwick's aunt. Yet Warwick did not object to his sister Katherine marrying newly created Lord Hastings or another aunt, the dowager duchess of Buckingham, marrying Lord Mountjoy, an even more recent creation.

The canonical accounts have it that Edward, like a guilty schoolboy, was forced to admit his marriage at the meeting of the Great Council in mid-September when pressed by Warwick to make a decision about Bona of Savoy. This is unlikely. The assembled peers would have regarded any proposal from Louis XI with extreme suspicion, and Warwick's sales pitch would have been addressed to them. The more likely reason why Edward delayed the announcement of his secret marriage is because there had not previously been an occasion when he could inform his magnates collectively.*

If it was always Edward's intention to announce his marriage to Elizabeth, then it was malicious to have permitted Warwick to

---

*The reason given for summoning them to Reading Abbey was to agree a recoinage, not to discuss royal matrimony.

NEVILLE MARRIAGES

Joan married (1438) William FitzAlan, Earl of Arundel.

Cecily married (1434) Henry Beauchamp, heir to the earldom of Warwick.

Richard married (1434) Anne Beauchamp, eventual heir of Henry, Earl of Warwick.

Alice married (1448) Henry FitzHugh, heir to the eponymous barony.

John married (1457) Isabel Ingoldisthorpe, wealthy heiress.

Eleanor married (1457) Thomas Stanley, heir to the eponymous barony.

Katherine married (1458) William Bonville, Baron Harington, heir to the Bonville barony.

William married (1422) Joan, *suo jure* Baroness Fauconberg (congenital idiot).

Edward married (1424) Elizabeth Beauchamp, *suo jure* Baroness Bergavenny.

Thomas married (1454) Matilda, co-heiress of Ralph, Baron Cromwell.

Margaret married (1458) John Vere, Earl of Oxford.

WOODVILLE MARRIAGES

Elizabeth married (1455) John Grey of Groby, heir to the barony, and (1464) Edward IV

Thomas Grey married (1466) Anne, heiress to the dukedom of Exeter

Anthony married (1459) Elizabeth, Baroness Scales

Jacquetta married (1450) John, Baron Strange of Knockyn

John married (1466) Katherine Neville, dowager Duchess of Norfolk

Anne married (1467) William Bourchier, heir to the earldom of Essex

Mary married (1467) William Herbert, heir to the earldom of Pembroke

Margaret married (1465) Thomas FitzAlan, heir to the earldom of Arundel

Eleanor married (1465) Anthony Grey, heir to the earldom of Kent

Catherine married (1465) Henry Stafford, Duke of Buckingham argue the merits of the French alliance in the presence of his peers. Thus it was not so much the supposed unworthiness of Elizabeth, nor even differences of opinion on foreign policy that lit the fuse for Warwick's future treason: it was the gratuitously insulting manner in which Edward let the assembled nobility of England know that he no longer heeded Warwick's advice.

Only one or two already knew. Rivers, a royal councillor since 1463, certainly; also Hastings, and one would have liked to have been a fly on the wall when Edward told him. The king would not have informed the other members of his household, as such a juicy piece of gossip would have spread like wildfire. Accordingly, the sound of mental gears changing would have been almost audible in the Council chamber after Edward's announcement until someone, probably Hastings, broke silence to be the first to congratulate the king.

Escorted by Warwick and Edward's brother Clarence, on the 29th Elizabeth was introduced to the Great Council and saluted by all present as Queen of England. The royal couple stayed at Reading after the Council disbanded, then moved to the royal palaces of Windsor in November and Eltham in December. Edward ordered her paid £466 [nearly £30,000] to cover her Christmas expenses, and later endowed her with lands producing about £4,500 [£2.86 million] per annum. Christmas gifts included the palaces of Greenwich and Sheen.

Elizabeth was crowned at Westminster Abbey on 26 May 1465, the date delayed to accommodate a high-ranking delegation from Burgundy, among them her brother Jacques de Luxembourg, lord of Richebourg. Edward rode into London on the 23rd and knighted thirty-nine men in her honour, including Elizabeth's brothers Richard and John. The City put on a splendid display at London Bridge. There was music and singing and a tableau of men dressed as St Paul, St Elizabeth and Mary Cleophas, the Virgin Mary's half-sister, flanked by angels with wings of peacock feathers.

Elizabeth spent the night at the Tower and the next day rode in an open litter through the streets of London to Westminster Hall, escorted by the new knights. During her procession to the abbey the following day the dowager Duchess of Buckingham, whose husband had been killed at Northampton by Warwick's men, carried her train. At the ceremony of bridal washing back at Westminster Hall after the coronation, John Vere, who had been permitted to succeed as Earl of Oxford and hereditary chamberlain after Tiptoft executed his father and older brother in 1462, poured the water.

Warwick and Tiptoft were away on conveniently timed official business. While obviously the ex-Lancastrian guests would have been glad not to rub shoulders with men who had killed their kin, one suspects Warwick was also sent away lest he spoil the joyous occasion by glowering. Also pointedly absent, of her own volition, was Cecily Neville, dowager Duchess of York and the king's mother.

The family of Henry Bourchier, Earl of Essex, the king's uncle by marriage, dominated the new queen's household. Her chamberlain was John, Lord Berners, the earl's brother, the most senior of her ladies-in-waiting was her sister Anne, wife of the earl's heir William, Viscount Bourchier, and one of her carvers was Humphrey, Baron Cromwell, the earl's third surviving son. Another lady-in-waiting was her brother Anthony's wife Elizabeth, Baroness Scales – but even she had a Bourchier connection, as she was the widow of Henry, the earl's second son. The only male Woodville was her brother John, her Master of Horse.

After the ceremony Edward created his new father-in-law Earl Rivers, and recreated the earldom of Kent for Edmund Grey of Ruthyn, whose timely treachery had given him victory at Northampton. He also ennobled Walter Blount, who became Lord Mountjoy, and gave him £666 [£42,400], perhaps to soften the blow of losing the lucrative office of Lord Treasurer to Rivers two months earlier. Like Grey of Ruthyn before him, Blount had done well out of his time in office, and in 1467 he married the dowager Duchess of Buckingham.

So many wheels within wheels. One of the biggest barriers to modern understanding of the late Middle Ages is how far from straightforward everything was: even the art of the period is layered with allusions and arcane symbols. So also the statements and actions of princes: they were always seeking to achieve more than one thing at a time, and form was often as important as substance. Whatever the original spark of Edward and Elizabeth's relationship, the marriage itself was a complex act of dynastic calculation and theatre.

In sum, Elizabeth was a beautiful and sexually skilled woman who could be expected to produce a healthy heir. Choosing her over Bona of Savoy delivered a deserved snub to Louis XI and strengthened Edward's ties with Burgundy, while announcing his emancipation from his mother and Warwick. She brought with her sons and siblings to expand the matrimonial links of a royal dynasty with shallow roots. Finally, she symbolized Edward's desire to heal the wounds of fratricidal strife.

It was a heavy load for a pair of slender shoulders to carry.

V

HENCHMEN

THE PROPAGANDA SPIN PUT ON THE EVENTS OF THE next few years by Warwick and his partisans at home and abroad has weighed heavily on historiography. Supposedly entranced by Elizabeth and her mother, Edward is alleged to have showered preferment on his grasping and parvenu in-laws, to the exclusion of the great lords (for which read Warwick) whose ancient lineage made them the custodians of historic customs, and thus of the nation's best interests.

It should not be necessary to refute such evidently self-serving piffle. There is little evidence any of the Woodvilles were promoted above their level of competence, and even less that they exercised undue influence on the king. It was hardly likely Edward should have declared his independence by marrying Elizabeth, only to become overly dependent on her family. He favoured them when it served his purposes to do so – but that is all he did.

The key men of his regime were three who rode with him after Mortimer's Cross, whom he ennobled after Towton. They were William Herbert, 38 years old in 1461, the first full-blooded Welshman to be made an English peer; 30-year-old William Hastings; and 22-year-old Humphrey Stafford of Southwyck. Also part of the group though less prominent was 30-year-old Walter Devereux, Baron Ferrers of Chartley by marriage. An outlier, not ennobled until 1470, was 36-year-old John Howard, whose timely arrival at the head of his cousin the Duke of Norfolk's men decided the outcome at Towton.

• ℯↄ •

Although Hastings was Edward's closest friend and fellow voluptuary, Herbert was the man on whom he depended most – after the Nevilles – to affirm his regime in the face of adamant Lancastrian resistance. The struggle for the North gets more attention because of the presence of the usurped royal family, but the challenge was more intractable in Wales. Only the south-eastern part of Wales was ever truly reconciled to Yorkist rule.

It is generally believed that the 'deep' Welsh never truly accepted English rule until the Tudors seized the throne, but it was more complicated than that. Underlying the York-versus-Lancaster rivalry was a blood feud among Welshmen whose forefathers had fought for or against Owain Glyn Dŵr, the last Welsh Prince of Wales. Superimposed on both were local clan rivalries, with the parties choosing sides in the greater conflict for tactical reasons.

Things were simplified after Towton. Herbert, who provided the best of Edward's army at Mortimer's Cross, was immediately appointed Chief Justice for South Wales and steward of royal Carmarthen and Cardigan. He, his brother and his Vaughan half-brothers also took possession for the king of the local lands of the variously killed Earl of Wiltshire (Laugharne and Walwyn's Castle in Wales), Earl of Shrewsbury (Goodrich and Archenfield in Herefordshire) and James Luttrell in northern Somerset. They also took possession of the lands of still living Jasper Tudor, Earl of Pembroke, and John Skydmore of Herefordshire.

Walter Devereux was a not a member of Herbert's affinity, but they acted in concert. Herbert was married to his sister, but Devereux was a Herefordshire and Leicestershire landowner in his own right and, through his wife, acquired the title and lands of the barony of Ferrers of Chartley in Staffordshire and Lincolnshire. Consequently he was content to play second fiddle in Wales to his brother-in-law, although Edward built up Ferrers's holdings in Herefordshire by making him steward of Goodrich and Archenfield, and adding his manor of Richard's Castle to Devereux's own manor of Weobley.

In 1461 Herbert and Ferrers received nominally joint custody of the Stafford lands in south Wales during the Duke of Buckingham's minority, but Herbert was appointed Chief Steward of the main manors of Brecon, Hay, Huntington and Newport.* In 1463 Edward created the Marcher lordship of Crickhowell and Tretower in Brecknock for Herbert (delegated to the Vaughans) and in 1465 another lordship, the last ever created, of Raglan, Carleon and Usk in Monmouth. Both were areas long held for the House of York by the Herberts and Vaughans, now made feudal fiefs.

A glance at Map 8 will reveal that Edward's intention was to build a *cordon sanitaire* around Warwick's Marcher lordship of Glamorgan and the lands of the barony of Bergavenny appropriated by Warwick from his compliant uncle Edward Neville. Fully occupied as he was in the North and with playing the statesman, Warwick could not object when Herbert was entrusted with pacifying Wales and was showered – as he himself had been in the North – with the appropriate royal offices.

Warwick's break with the Lancastrian regime had come about when his wife Anne Beauchamp's inheritance in south-east Wales and the Marches was assailed by the claims of her half-sisters and their husbands, the now dead and attainted Duke of Somerset and Earls of Shrewsbury and Wiltshire. His local affinity was shallow because of this and neglect during the war, and the promotion of Herbert further devalued his 'good lordship'. If to this we add that Herbert had been for many years his steward and Sheriff of Glamorgan, and it is clear why Warwick came to hate him.

The Herbertification of Wales was not confined to the south-east. After their ennoblement, on 30 September 1461 he and Ferrers

*Newport became a venomous bone of contention with Warwick – presumably to do with port rights.

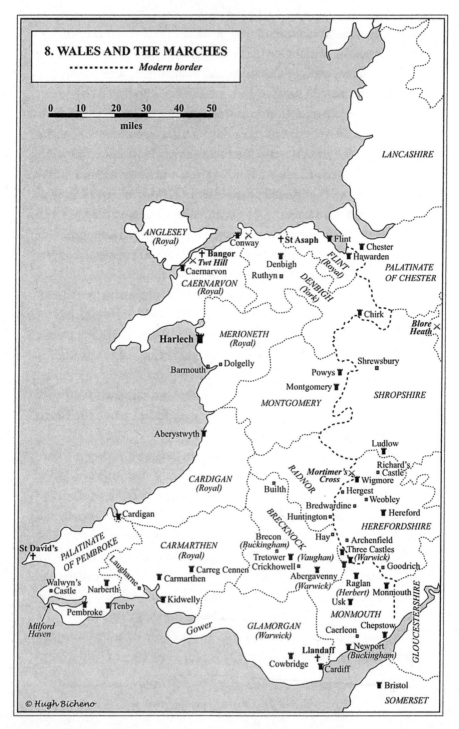

8. WALES AND THE MARCHES
------------ *Modern border*

0 10 20 30 40 50
miles

LANCASHIRE

ANGLESEY (Royal)
✕ Conway
† Bangor
✕ *Twt Hill*
Caernarvon
CAERNARVON (Royal)
† St Asaph
Flint
Chester
Hawarden
Denbigh
Ruthyn
FLINT (Royal)
DENBIGH (York)
PALATINATE OF CHESTER
Chirk
Blore Heath ✕
Harlech
MERIONETH (Royal)
Shrewsbury
Barmouth
Dolgelly
Powys
Montgomery
SHROPSHIRE
MONTGOMERY
Aberystwyth
Ludlow
Richard's Castle
RADNOR
Mortimer's Cross ✕
Wigmore
CARDIGAN (Royal)
Builth
Hergest
Weobley
Bredwardine
Hereford
Huntington
Cardigan
BRECKNOCK
Hay
HEREFORDSHIRE
St David's †
PALATINATE OF PEMBROKE
CARMARTHEN (Royal)
Brecon *(Buckingham)*
Archenfield
Three Castles *(Warwick)*
Tretower *(Vaughan)*
Crickhowell
Carreg Cennen
Abergavenny *(Warwick)*
Goodrich
Laugharne
Carmarthen
Raglan *(Herbert)* Monmouth
Walwyn's Castle
Narberth
Usk
Kidwelly
MONMOUTH
Pembroke
Tenby
Caerleon
Chepstow
Milford Haven
Gower
GLAMORGAN (Warwick)
Newport *(Buckingham)*
Llandaff †
GLOUCESTERSHIRE
Cowbridge
Cardiff
Bristol
SOMERSET

© *Hugh Bicheno*

secured the surrender of Tenby and Pembroke Castle from John Skydmore, Jasper Tudor's most trusted lieutenant, who was promised a pardon. Although Skydmore's attainder was revoked, by a separate bill he was pardoned only his life and goods – Ferrers kept his forfeited Herefordshire lands.

A bonus from the capture of Pembroke Castle was that 4-year-old Henry Tudor, Earl of Richmond, came into Herbert's custody. He placed him in the care of his wife at the great show castle he was completing at Raglan, and paid the king £1,000 [£636,000] for the boy's wardship and marriage. This was further grit in Warwick's eye, as the young earl's estates would have nicely complemented his own.

Herbert then rode north to recruit another army, with which on 16 October he defeated a force led by Jasper Tudor and the Duke of Exeter (who joined him after fleeing Towton) at Twt Hill near Caernarvon Castle. Jasper and Exeter fled to Ireland, whence Jasper continued the fight with support from Duke Frañsez. Exeter eventually reached Burgundy, where he remained until 1471, initially in a state of beggary but later in receipt of a pension from Charolais.

Three Welsh castles still held out for Lancaster. In the north, Edward declared the temporalities of the rebel bishops of Bangor and St Asaph forfeit, and without support from the surrounding area or hope of relief Denbigh Castle surrendered in January 1462.* In the south, Carreg Cennen capitulated in May. This left only Harlech in Merioneth, the most formidable of Edward I's castles and of enormous symbolic importance to the Welsh. It had capitulated to Glyn Dŵr in 1404 to become his headquarters for the remainder of the dying kick of Welsh independence.

Although now separated from the sea by a half a mile of sedimentary deposition, at the time Harlech had a functioning water-gate at the base of the cliff on which it stands, through which it was kept supplied by Jasper, first from Ireland and later from Brittany. Even if Edward had been prepared to ship his bombards to Merioneth, it

---

*The bishop and parishioners of St Asaph were so recalcitrant that in 1463 he was deprived of his see, which remained vacant until 1471.

is hard to see where they could have been sited. The county was also desperately poor and notoriously unruly, such that maintaining a siege was an expensive and risky proposition. Harlech's commander David ap Eynon, latterly joined by Richard Tunstall and Henry Bellingham, easily held out until late 1468.

In February 1462 Edward awarded Herbert the lands of Jasper Tudor's attainted earldom of Pembroke and custody of the Welsh estates of the Mowbray dukedom of Norfolk, including Chepstow and Gower. In 1468 he acquired them permanently, the first when he was made Earl Palatine of Pembroke, and the Mowbray manors in exchange for properties he held in East Anglia, a sensible act of territorial consolidation for both lords. Already a wealthy merchant in 1461, control of the south Wales ports made Herbert wealthier still.

By that time he had also replaced Tiptoft as chief justice and chamberlain for north Wales and had been given custody of the lands of Lord Grey of Powys, who had backed the wrong horse in 1463. Herbert was now either the dominant lord or the senior crown official of every county in Wales except Warwick's lordship of Glamorgan. In addition, in September 1466 Edward revived the extinct barony of Dunster for Herbert's 15-year-old namesake son prior to his marriage to Mary, the queen's youngest sister, and endowed him with lands confiscated from the late Earl of Wiltshire and James Luttrell in Somerset.

• ℰℑ •

The most cold-blooded injustice committed by Edward during the early years of his reign was the permanent dispossession of William, 2nd Viscount Beaumont. His father, the first viscount ever created in the English peerage, was a childhood friend of Henry VI, thanks to whom he built up large estates in Lincolnshire, Leicestershire, Norfolk and Suffolk. He also married the Duke of Norfolk's mother, Warwick's aunt Katherine, and enjoyed her dower of more than a third of Norfolk's patrimony. He was one of the lords killed at Northampton.

The sole reason for confiscating William's lands was to build up the Midlands lordships of William Hastings, who remains an enigmatic figure. The standard attack on the sacred person of a medieval monarch was through his favourites, the canonical 'evil councillors'. Hastings was certainly qualified for the role, yet with the notable exception of the queen and her family he was well regarded by everyone. This appears to be because he refused any title higher than baron and, content with Edward's generosity, did not abuse his influence to take more.

He had much to be content about. In addition to the Beaumont lands, some of which were entailed during her lifetime to the now widowed dowager Duchess of Norfolk, Edward awarded him the Midlands estates of the late and attainted Earl of Wiltshire and Baron Roos. Although Hasting's barony was a new creation, Edward also awarded him the lands recovered by the crown from the previous barony of Hastings, extinct in 1389.

Complemented by the stewardship of the local duchy of Lancaster and duchy of York lordships, Hastings became a prominent lord in Leicestershire, Rutland, Northamptonshire and Huntingdonshire, and even had a strong presence in Warwickshire. Additional estates in Norfolk, Suffolk, Cambridgeshire and Hertfordshire gave him an income appropriate for an earldom, which he was almost certainly offered but prudently declined.

Unlike Herbert, Hastings was not assigned a role that required him to tread on Warwick's toes, and they were potential allies against the Woodvilles. Perhaps because of this, in 1468 Warwick appointed Hastings steward of his own holdings in Leicestershire, Rutland and Northamptonshire. This should be highlighted, as it has a bearing on later events.

• ↄ •

One of the more persistent myths about the Woodville ascendancy is the supposedly scandalous nature of the marriage in 1465 between the elder of two dowager duchesses of Norfolk, 65-year-old Katherine née Neville, and the queen's 19-year-old brother John. This is based on a misunderstanding of women's property rights. What actually took place was that Katherine – who had another notorious liaison between her marriages to Norfolk and Beaumont – bought herself a young husband, and with him influence at court to offset Hastings' designs on the Beaumont estates she retained.

She was also a player in Edward's scheme to ensure the loyalty of East Anglia, which had not enjoyed the stability of a dominant lord for many years. When the 3rd duke, dissolute John Mowbray, died in 1461, his 17-year-old namesake heir became Edward's ward. Granted possession of his estates in 1463, he proved as ineffectual as his father. As a prince of the blood and hereditary earl marshal of England he should have provided a 'regime lock' on the region. In practice the dowers of previous duchesses consumed two-thirds of the revenues from his estates and he never played a role commensurate with his rank.

Also in 1463, Edward restored the dukedom of Suffolk to 19-year-old John de la Pole, whose father had been Henry VI's chief minister until murdered in 1450. In 1458 Richard of York had bound the teenager to his cause by marrying him to Elizabeth, his second daughter. Young Suffolk had at least one thing in common with his neighbour Norfolk: over half of his inheritance was held by his formidable mother Alice, granddaughter of Geoffrey Chaucer of *Canterbury Tales* fame. John himself proved to be a nonentity.

It was because the Mowbray and de la Pole affinities were temporarily leaderless that the third most important East Anglian lord, John Vere, Earl of Oxford, had dealt himself a hand in the Lancastrian conspiracy of 1461–2. His was one of the poorer earldoms and apparently genuine illness kept him side-lined during the battles of 1460–1, although his third son George fought for Lancaster at Towton. Urged on by Aubrey, his eldest, Vere rashly

boarded the sinking Lancastrian ship in 1462, and both paid with
their heads.

Vere's 20-year-old namesake second son thus became the 13th
earl and, as we saw on the occasion of Edward's marriage, the
king made every effort to win him over. But with regard to East
Anglia, one of the richest and most strategically vital regions of his
kingdom, there was no single lord Edward could back secure in the
knowledge that he could keep the peace. It is for this reason the
marriage between young John Woodville and the older of the two
dowager Duchesses of Norfolk deserves reconsideration – Edward
needed her on his team.

His chief agent in the region was John Howard, whom he had
knighted on the battlefield of Towton. Howard's mother was the
eldest daughter of the 1st Duke of Norfolk, and his paternal aunt
was married to John Vere, Earl of Oxford. His sister was married
to Warwick's dispossessed uncle Edward Neville, Baron Bergavenny.
During 1461 Edward took Howard into his household and
appointed him Constable of Norwich and Colchester castles, as
well as High Sheriff of Norfolk and Suffolk. He may have hoped
Howard could coordinate the fragmented Norfolk affinity and/or
keep an eye on the Oxford affinity.

Howard built up a moderate estate around his inherited manor
of Stoke-by-Nayland on the border of Suffolk and Essex, including
seven manors granted him by Edward and six bought from his
penurious Vere uncle after 1463. Like Howard and Hastings, he
was a wealthy trader who did not depend on land rents – he was
cash rich and relatively land poor. This may explain why he was not
ennobled until 1470, although another reason may have been not
to risk arousing resentment among the established but ineffectual
regional lords.

• ❧ •

In addition to the North and Wales, Edward had to contend with persistent Lancastrian unrest in the West Country. The dominant lords had been the Earl of Wiltshire in Somerset and the county from which he drew his title, the Courtenay Earls of Devon, and Baron William Bonville, who feuded throughout the 1440s and 1450s. Courtenay declared for Lancaster and Bonville for York in 1459, but the war proved a catastrophe for both. Bonville's son and grandson, who had recently become Lord Harington, were killed at Wakefield, and Bonville himself was beheaded after the Second Battle of St Albans. When Courtenay and Wiltshire were executed a few weeks later and attainted, the West Country was leaderless.

The man who became Edward's principal agent in the region was only three years older than the king. Humphrey Stafford inherited a modest estate around Hooke in Wiltshire from his father, killed during Cade's Rebellion in 1450. By the time he fought at Mortimer's Cross and Towton, however, he was the heir apparent of his namesake cousin, the largest landowner in Dorset with sizeable estates in Somerset as well. His cousin died on 7 July 1461 and twenty days later Humphrey was summoned to Parliament as Baron Stafford of Southwyck.

The West Country was not a blank slate. The large Bonville-Harington affinity needed to be treated with respect, and rewards had to be found for local Yorkist barons like the Earl of Essex's brother William Bourchier, Lord FitzWarin, and Lords Cobham and de la Zouche. It was also necessary to build up the holdings of John Dynham, a south Devon landowner who had helped Edward and Warwick to escape to Calais after Ludlow and taken part in the capture of Sandwich, to justify his recent ennoblement.

Warwick resolved the issue of the Bonville succession with the king's approval. Cecily Bonville was only eight months old when the deaths of her father, grandfather and great-grandfather made her Baroness of Bonville and Harington by right and the richest heiress in England after Warwick's own daughters. The child's mother was another Katherine Neville, Warwick's younger sister, and in early 1462 he arranged Katherine's remarriage – to none other than William Hastings. Warwick retained a veto over the child's marriage, which he exercised to prevent her betrothal to William Herbert's heir.

There remained the larger problem of what to do with the Courtenay affinity, one of the oldest and deepest rooted in all England, which had suffered grievously at Towton. This was the task Edward set Stafford of Southwyck, starting with his appointment to the traditional Courtenay stewardship of the royal duchy of Cornwall, also as keeper of the royal forests in Dorset, Wiltshire and Somerset, and Constable of Bristol and Taunton.

If the plan was to give time for Stafford to grow his affinity, it went out of the window when the Earl of Oxford's co-conspirators revealed that the Courtenays were involved in the 1462 conspiracy. In February Edward awarded Stafford their principal estates in Devon, and although Stafford moved into the Courtenay family seat at Tiverton Castle the transfer of ownership never 'took'. Legal challenges forced Edward to regrant the awards in 1464, 1467 and again in 1468.

Further evidence of Stafford's failure to get a grip on the West Country can be seen in additional awards throughout the 1460s. These included his appointment in 1465 as keeper of the dowager Duchess of York's castle and manor of Bridgwater and Petherton Forest in Somerset, the award of further Courtenay lands in 1467, and in 1468 the stewardship of the estates of the minor John, Baron de la Zouche, in Dorset, Somerset and Wiltshire.

Like the Woodvilles, Edward's henchmen owed everything to him and were supposed to be his 'regime locks' on the most problematic regions of his kingdom – other than the North, where the Nevilles all but reigned in his place. There was, however, another individual to whom he entrusted a more general responsibility, the man immortally damned by Shakespeare as 'false, fleeting, perjur'd Clarence'.

VI

CLARENCE

G EORGE, DUKE OF CLARENCE, WAS THE THIRD SON OF
Richard, Duke of York and Cecily née Neville to survive
infancy. He was born in Dublin in October 1449, when
his father had wisely absented himself from a court about to suffer
the consequences of the collapse of the English empire in France.
York was the king's lieutenant in Ireland, a senior office usually
awarded to princes of the blood but normally handled by a deputy.

Like his younger brother Richard, born two years later, George's
early life was dominated by their father's struggle to take over the
government of England. They were captured along with their
mother when York abandoned them at Ludlow, and later sent to the
Duke of Burgundy for safekeeping after their father and their older
brother Edmund were killed at Wakefield and the Lancastrians
marched on London.

George would have grown up with a deep-seated sense of inse-
curity, but apart from those two episodes we know next to nothing
about him before his oldest brother became king. Suddenly he was
elevated to the rank and status of heir presumptive to the throne, a
role for which, as a third son, he had no preparation whatever. Far
from celebrating his good fortune he appears to have been a more
than usually sullen adolescent, petulantly resentful of his older
brother and lacking any sense of loyalty or gratitude.

It is not difficult to deduce what tipped George into outright malignancy. At some point, probably not long after being replaced at court by Elizabeth Woodville, the enraged Duchess Cecily must have told him that Edward was not his father's son, and that he should properly sit in his place. The confirmation of what he probably already suspected would have had a dislocating effect even on a normal person: for Clarence it tied together all the inchoate strands of his emerging personality.

Two things made this catastrophic for the Yorkist regime. The first is that Elizabeth did not produce the expected male heir until November 1470. The second, closely related to the first, is that Edward needed Clarence to fill a void in his scheme of governance. Maps 9 and 10 seek to illustrate why this was the case. I am aware that they do not do justice to the complexity of English landholdings – they aspire only to show who was or had the potential to be a dominant lord in every shire.

There were only five noble houses with nationwide estates: the duchies of Lancaster, York, Norfolk and Buckingham, and the Warwick/Salisbury earldoms. No other came close – the independently governed ecclesiastical estates were a special case. Edward was duke both of York and Lancaster, and the young Duke of Buckingham was his ward. These holdings, combined with the crown estates, should have given him an overwhelming supremacy. In practice he had to delegate to subordinates of varying honesty, competence and loyalty, and the personal link essential to the maintenance of an affinity was tenuous.

The crown, Lancaster and York estates were all separately administered and as late as 1466 Edward had to call in returns from all his manors, honours, messuages, feudal rights and other forms of tenure just to establish where and what they were. Nor could he count on anything like the professional bureaucracy that might have knit the varied strands together. In fact the only unifying element was the law, and consequently the administration of justice was the touchstone of a monarch's reputation.

Royal progresses and assizes could only accomplish so much. For

9. PRINCIPAL ESTATES OF THE CROWN AND LEADING MAGNATES c.1455

A	Arundel (FitzAlan)	E	Essex (Bourchier)
B	Buckingham (Stafford)	G	Grey of Ruthyn
Bt	Beaumont	H	Hungerford
C	Clifford	K	King (inc. Lancaster)
Cr	Cromwell	M	Norfolk (Mowbray)
D	Devon (Courtenay)	N	Neville (Salisbury/Warwick)
Da	Dacre	n	Neville (Westmorland)
		P	Percy (Northumberland)
		Q	Queen's dower
		Qp	Queen/Prince of Wales
		R	Roos
		S	Somerset (Beaufort)
		St	Stanley
		T	Talbot (Shrewsbury/Lisle)
		V	Vere (Oxford)
		W	Wiltshire (Ormonde)
		Y	York (duchy)

The aim of this map is to illustrate the patchwork quilt nature of landholdings. Only named manors are shown in approximately the correct location. A third of all landholdings were ecclesiastical, but only the most important are marked with a cross.

© Hugh Bicheno

10. REDISTRIBUTION OF ESTATES
*c.*1468

A	Arundel
B	Buckingham
C	Clarence
Cr	Cromwell (Bourchier)
E	Essex (Bourchier)
G	Gloucester
H	Herbert
Ha	Hastings
Ho	Howard
K	Kent (Grey of Ruthyn)
L	Lancaster
M	Montagu (Neville)
N	Norfolk
n	Neville (Westmorland)
O	Ogle
P	Suffolk (de la Pole)
Q	Queen's dower
R	Crown estates
S	Stafford of Southwyck
St	Stanley
T	Talbot/Lisle
V	Vere (Oxford)
W	Warwick (Neville)
Y	York (duchy)

© Hugh Bicheno

the day-to-day running of his kingdom Edward needed dependable local lieutenants. It was easier to deal with the blank slates of
authority created by death, forfeiture and attainder in the North,
Wales and the West Country than in the rest of the country, where
Edward needed to fill the random gaps created across the patchwork quilt. Local Yorkists filled many posts, but his pressing need
was to unite under one authority the scattered, nationwide distribution of the remainder. The sum of the parts was adequate to endow
dukedoms, and the only candidates were his young brothers.

After his coronation Edward revived the duchy of Clarence for
12-year-old George. The first duke had been Lionel of Antwerp,
Edward III's second son, descent from whom in the matrilineal
line was the basis of the Yorkist claim to priority over the House
of Lancaster, which descended from John of Gaunt, the third
son. A few months later Clarence was the first candidate inducted
by Edward to the Order of the Garter. There were a number of
vacant stalls thanks to attrition in the battles of 1459–61, but even
Hastings, Herbert, Tiptoft (Worcester) and John Neville (Montagu)
were not inducted until the following year.

Edward also made Clarence Steward of England and Lieutenant
of Ireland, and endowed him with a larger estate than any previous king had given a brother. As he was too young to exercise the
offices or receive the income directly, all were handled by officials
appointed by Edward. But for outward show, Clarence was provided magnificently. One could hardly design a programme more
likely to bring out the worst in any teenager.

It proves nothing about how he felt towards her that Clarence
played a leading role in the ceremonies of Elizabeth's introduction
to the nobles assembled at Reading and at her coronation. He was
still a ward of the king, and when not performing ceremonial duties
lived with his brother Richard and sister Margaret at Elizabeth's
palace at Greenwich. The test came after his minority was termi-
nated early in July 1466, when he was still only 16, because Edward
needed him to balance Warwick in the Midlands.

Not for one moment after that date did Clarence show any indication of gratitude. He appears to have believed that everything he had was his by right, and by right he should have much more without doing anything to earn it. This element of unbounded entitlement so completely defined his life that it is fair to conclude he believed he was the legitimate king – and the only reason he can have been so fatally convinced of this is if his mother had told him so.

The most lucrative of the manors and boroughs assigned to Clarence were concentrated around Tutbury Castle in south Staffordshire, which was deeply associated with the House of Lancaster. The compact estate had previously been one of the jewels in the crown of Queen Marguerite's dower and produced about 30 per cent of the income from Clarence's own endowment. He moved there as soon as he was declared of age, a long way from his brother in London – but very close to Warwick's Midlands estates.

Clarence chose to regard Tutbury as an appanage, a form of tenure originating in France, where it was customary to assign a fief to the younger sons of a monarch. The system did not have a good record of discouraging rebellion and was the principal reason why so many French dukedoms became virtually autonomous. In England the results were no less inauspicious – suffice it to say that Edward III gave his sons Edmund of Langley and John of Gaunt the duchies of York and Lancaster as appanages.

There were several problems inherent in Clarence's belief, the first being that no part of his endowment was specifically given as an appanage. By regarding it as such, Clarence made apparent his belief that it came to him by right of his father, not his brother the king. Related to this, while Tutbury and the rest of the lands awarded to Clarence were an unprecedentedly generous endowment for a royal brother, they were inadequate if perceived as an appanage for the heir to the throne.

On 30 August 1464 Edward appeared to accept the logic of the last argument when he announced that he would grant Clarence the palatinate of Chester, traditionally part of the patrimony of the

Prince of Wales. This was no casual gift: a county palatine was an hereditary principality enjoying judicial autonomy from the rest of a kingdom. In England, apart from the duchies of Lancaster and Cornwall, only the bishoprics of Durham and the Isle of Ely and the abbacy of Hexham enjoyed similar status. Pembroke was the only formal palatinate in Wales, but the Marcher lordships were in most respects indistinguishable.

The timing of the grant also gives food for thought, coming as it did after Edward had married Elizabeth but before he made this public. When he did, the grant was left without effect and the Chester palatinate reverted to the endowment properly reserved for the future heir apparent. Perhaps there was an early pregnancy that did not prosper, another possible explanation for the timing of an announcement that marked a watershed in Edward's reign.

Less speculative is that the marriage deprived Clarence of the appanage he came to think he deserved, more than sufficient reason for him to resent Elizabeth. If Duchess Cecily, in her fury at losing her precedence at court to a woman she could not dominate, did indeed tell him at this time that Edward was the product of her adultery, it would explain a great deal of what ensued. It certainly explains the following:

> In 1468 he [Clarence] approved an ordinance that would have made his household the largest and most expensive known for any medieval nobleman. There were to be 399 staff, 188 in the riding household, and the annual cost was £4500 [£2.86 million]. This was considerably grander even than Edward IV's lavish endowment... The 1467 Act of Resumption reserved for Clarence a further 5500 marks [£1.16 million] a year and 1000 marks in reversions, three times the minimum qualification for a duke, but clearly insufficient to support Clarence's plans which, if implemented, must have left him short of money.*

*Extract from Michael Hicks, 'George, duke of Clarence (1449–1478)', *Oxford Dictionary of National Biography*, Oxford University Press, 2004.

• ᏋᎤ •

Clarence may have seen parallels between his own situation and that of Charles, Duke of Berry, who was 18 years old in 1465 when he did his best to depose and replace his twenty-three-year older brother Louis XI. When we left Louis he was contemplating the ruins of his diplomacy following Edward's marriage. Despite his own teenage rebellion against his father in the 1440, he did not anticipate that his brother and heir presumptive, notwithstanding his whining about Berry being an inadequate appanage, would reprise his disloyalty.

Most of Louis's domestic enemies were nobles he had offended, such as Duke Jean of Bourbon, Lord Charles of Albret, Count Antoine of Dammartin and Count Jean of Dunois, who were simply demanding respect. Incestuous Count Jean of Armagnac was eventually condemned and crushed by the Church. Finally Duke Jacques of Nemours and Jacquetta's brother Louis, Count of Saint-Pol, two relentless schemers, were long overdue an appointment with the headsman by the time Louis finally sent them to the block.

Louis did not think any of them posed a serious threat, but his greater error was to have believed that his deterrent, the *ordonnances*, were king's men, when their loyalty lay with the commanders who had led them to victory against the English. As he did with others who had served his father well, Louis dismissed the old commanders and they were understandably bitter. Fortunately for him Pierre de Brézé, one of the greatest of them and a man he had demoted as seneschal of Normandy and briefly imprisoned on coming to power, overcame his personal dislike of Louis and remained loyal to the crown.

To round things off, he was at daggers drawn with his bishops, outraged by their loss of patronage and revenues following his unilateral suspension of the Pragmatic Sanction. He cannot have underestimated how widespread resistance to his style of government had become, but he did not believe his opponents were capable of coordinated action, and expected to disarm or defeat them in detail. The most likely explanation for how he came to such a nearly fatal miscalculation of the danger he faced is that his enemies either 'turned' his informants or systematically fed them misleading information.

Even then, had he not simultaneously made it apparent to the Dukes of Burgundy and Brittany that he intended to assert his feudal rights over them, it was a storm he could probably have weathered without resort to arms. Working for him, in contrast to Edward IV, was that nobody doubted the sacred right of the senior branch of the House of Valois to occupy the throne – but that was precisely why the complicity of Louis's heir presumptive was vital to the rebel plan. Young Charles gave them a king they could control if Louis were taken off the board, and the only honourable way for him to be killed was by the judgement of God in battle.

Although Louis had won the fervent support of the new urban elites they were not militarily significant and the rebellion was as much directed at them as against the king. Indeed, the League of the Public Weal was socially reactionary – it was an attempt by the land-based aristocracy to assert their traditional political dominance over mere wealth creators. Nor was this conservatism limited to the socio-political sphere. The one major battle of the rebellion at Montlhéry, 17 miles south-south-west of Paris, was an affair of massed mounted charges, with archers and footsoldiers ridden down by heavily armoured lancers as though Crécy, Poitiers and Agincourt had never taken place.

What reasons did Berry have to lend himself to a rebellion that would ideally end with the death of his brother? Leaving aside the almost genetic predisposition to unrestrained sibling rivalry among the Valois, the most obvious explanation is the simplest. Between 1456 and the death of the father who had named him after himself, he was in effect Charles VII's only son, and grew up hearing the king vituperate against the defiantly absent Louis. Plus his doting mother, who died in 1463, was René d'Anjou's sister (thus Queen

Marguerite's aunt), and the Angevin interest was strong at court. When he became king, Louis dismissed anyone even suspected of loyalty to the House of Anjou.

René was one of the conspirators in 1465, but Louis was on his doorstep when the rebellion began and, as he thought, neutralized him by making René's brother Charles, Count of Maine, his deputy in the west. Maine was given command of the local *ordonnances* and assigned the task of containing Duke Frañsez of Brittany while Louis himself rode east to deal with the greater threat from his cousins of Burgundy and Bourbon/Auvergne. Instead Maine simply fell back in the face of Frañsez's slow advance, and deserted Louis at Montlhéry.

The signal for the rebellion to begin came when Berry slipped away from his royal minders to join Frañsez at Nantes. Simultaneously Louis learned that Count Jean of Dunois had shipped his valuables to Nantes and joined the Bretons. This was particularly bad news, as Jean was the renowned 'Bastard of Orléans' who had ridden with Jeanne d'Arc and played a key role in the expulsion of the English. Not even Brézé matched his stature among French fighting men, but fortunately for Louis he was crippled by gout and unable to fulfil the strategic objective of trapping Louis between the Breton and Burgundian armies.

Aided by Jean, Count of Nevers, who had deserted the Burgundian camp when his stepbrother Charolais became ascendant, and by his fanatically loyal followers from the Dauphiné, Louis forced Bourbon, Nemours and Armagnac to negotiate – but then had to make them generous concessions to free himself to march north to relieve Paris, besieged by Charolais. Thanks to Maine's treachery, the resulting battle of Montlhéry was a draw. What might otherwise have been the decisive stroke was delivered by Brézé, who was killed, against Saint-Pol's massed cavalry on the Burgundian right wing.

It was Charolais's first battle and he led a locally successful charge of his own against the right wing of Louis's army. In fact he was very nearly cut off and killed, suffering a wound in the throat, but thought he had won a great victory. Philippe de Commynes, who was in the thick of things with him, later commented:

> All this day my lord of Charolais remained very joyfully on the field, thinking the glory his. This has since cost him dearly because never afterwards did he heed the counsel of anyone except himself. Up to that time he had little use for war and liked nothing to do with it, but subsequently his attitude changed because he continued fighting until his death. By it his life was ended and his house destroyed.

The rebellion came to an end when Louis bought off Charolais with the return of the Somme towns. Berry was granted the duchy of Normandy as an appanage and Frañsez was given a formal undertaking to respect Breton autonomy. Bourbon was made governor of eastern France, other lords were granted pensions, and men Louis had dismissed were brought back into his service at the expense of those who had remained loyal. Thus Saint-Pol was made Constable of France, expensively married to Louis's sister-in-law, and granted the county of Eu, which Louis's ally Jean of Nevers had inherited from his mother.

It was a brutal check to Louis's ambition, but a Pyrrhic victory for the rebels. If they had killed him and put his brother on the throne they might have been able to turn back the clock. As it was, they left the Universal Spider free to devote his considerable *furbizia* to recovering lost ground. The first to fold was Berry, always the weakest link, who was overwhelmed by his new responsibilities and all but invited his brother to take Normandy back in early 1466.

To follow this thread further would diverge too far from our story. Where it impinges is that Louis was nearly fatally weakened in 1465–6 and knew his fate would have been sealed had the English come in on his brother's side. Accordingly, he persisted in his policy of preventing an effective Anglo–Burgundian alliance at all costs, while by insidious diplomacy he created alternative red rags for the Charolais bull to charge.

VII

EDWARD

A T THE HEART OF THE 'EVIL WOODVILLES' MYTH LIES the same historical misogyny that has demonized energetic Marguerite d'Anjou, one of the greatest heroines of English history. The implicit innuendo underlying the myth is that Elizabeth was a succubus who could get Edward to do whatever she wanted, which is ridiculous. Until she bore him a male heir she could not even obtain an independently administered endowment half as great as that granted, on her marriage day, to Marguerite – who, like Elizabeth, brought no dowry with her.

Unlike previous kings and their favourites, Edward did not grant the Woodvilles lands that elevated them far above their 'station'. But had he done so, in what way would it have distinguished them from the origins of any other noble house? The oh-so-grand Neville family fortunes were built on royal favour, and Warwick himself owed his eminence to a ruthlessly opportunistic exploitation of his wife's fortuitously grand inheritance.

Scrape away the mould of snobbery, and what remains are the practical ways in which the Woodvilles served Edward's dynastic, diplomatic and political purposes. It was he, not they, who arranged their marriages, and he who used Jacquetta's family connections to pursue an alliance with Burgundy against France. With one exception the Woodvilles played no part in the king's policy of building up other lords to contain Warwick's power and frustrate his unconcealed desire to be the power behind the throne.

That exception was Anthony Woodville, Lord Scales, whom the king helped to exchange some of his estates in Essex for the lordship of the Isle of Wight and constableship of Carisbrooke Castle in November 1466, and Porchester Castle a year later.* Commanding as they did the approaches to Southampton and Portsmouth, and Portsmouth harbour itself, the castles were an indication that Edward intended Scales to command the main squadron of the royal fleet.

In terms of royal offices the only notable beneficiary was Earl Rivers, the Lord Treasurer. In August 1467 Edward purchased the life term of Constable of England from Tiptoft and awarded it to Rivers, with reversion to Scales. Rivers's income from all offices was in the region of £1,330 [£846,000], which, added to the rents from Jacquetta's dower as Duchess of Bedford, was sufficient to sustain the dignity of his earldom. However and by contrast, William Herbert's income from lands alone was about £3,300 [£2.1 million].

Scales's younger brothers Edward and Richard did not receive any offices, and Lionel's career in the priesthood was not unduly accelerated until the last years of Edward's reign. Thomas Grey, the elder of Elizabeth's sons from her first marriage, was married to Anne Holland, previously betrothed to Warwick's nephew, who was the only child of Edward's sister the Duchess of Exeter. Richard, the younger royal stepson, received nothing.

Although the marriages affected Warwick by denying him the opportunity to marry his daughters to the heirs in question, the Woodvilles were not otherwise rewarded to the point of challenging the local dominance of any other lord. Whence, then, the oft-quoted words of Dominic Mancini (writing in 1483) that they were 'certainly detested by the nobles, because they, who were ignoble and newly made men, were advanced beyond those who far exceeded them in breeding and wisdom'?

---

*The Isle of Wight and Carisbrooke had been previously awarded to Geoffrey Gates, Warwick's marshal at Calais. Gates was to cause a great deal of grief for Edward in 1469–71.

Mancini was simply repeating, almost word for word, Warwick's manifesto of 1469; but that, in turn, also echoed Yorkist propaganda of ten years earlier. On both occasions the real target was the monarch. The Woodvilles were attacked as proxies for Edward himself, and the particular venom with which their alleged lack of breeding was denounced in 1469 owed more to Clarence and Duchess Cecily than it did to Warwick.

It should never be forgotten that Cecily was a Neville and a descendant of John of Gaunt through her Beaufort mother, and that even as a child she was known as 'proud Cis'. The few documented facts argue that she was implacably hostile to the Woodvilles. One is her boycott of Elizabeth's coronation, another her complicity in Clarence's rebellion. A third was her boycott of the reburial of her husband in 1476 because Elizabeth would be present, a less than subtle assertion of her belief that she was 'queen by right' and Elizabeth a usurper.

From her evidently malevolent behaviour towards Edward it is not much of a stretch to conclude that Cecily probably resented him from birth as the undeniable evidence of a far from 'classy' indiscretion that permanently diminished her in the esteem of her august husband. We tend to judge political figures by the success or failure of their policies, but like everybody else their principal lifelong endeavour is to come to terms with the legacy of their parentage and upbringing.

From that perspective, Edward's lifelong philandering may be seen as an obsessive fixation on an unattainable partner by someone emotionally crippled from childhood. Pursuing the thread, another manifestation of the same psychological deprivation would have been a subconscious attempt to build himself an alternative family – which incurred the potentially murderous hostility of his biological mother and half-brothers.

Another under-commented aspect of Edward's character was the romanticism displayed in his attempt to revive the Arthurian ethos of the Order of the Garter. Chivalry developed from the Church's effort to temper the brutality of societies defined by military might. The essential virtues were faith, hope and charity, from which came the cardinal virtues of justice, prudence, temperance and fortitude. Ironically, the English monarch who came closest to living according to these ideals was the hapless Henry VI.

Henry's usurper had every reason to tip the balance back towards the martial virtues. During the first half of Edward's reign membership of the Order of the Garter was preferentially a reward for courage and skill at arms. After Clarence, the next man inducted was the obscure William Chamberlaine, in his time a famous jouster, belatedly honoured in the last year of his life. John Astley, inducted the following year, had been the English champion at a tournament in Paris in 1438 and another at Smithfield in 1442.

Notable warriors such as the exiled Gaillard, lord of Duras in the Narbonnais, John, Lord Scrope of Bolton – to whom Edward gave Richard of York's garter – Robert Harcourt and James, the last of the fabled Scots Black Douglases. followed in 1463. They were joined by men who had achieved eminence by force of arms, including the great *condottiere* Francesco Sforza, Duke of Milan, and the Aragonese King Ferrante of Naples. By the time Anthony Woodville was inducted in 1466 he too had become the tourney champion of England.

Thanks to Sir Thomas Malory, whose *Le Morte d'Arthur* gave the myth its modern form in 1469–70, King Arthur and the Knights of the Round Table will forever inhabit the late medieval era. The myth of course was much older: 150 years before Malory, in *L'Inferno* V, Dante linked the doomed thirteenth-century passion of lovers Francesca da Polenta and her brother-in-law Paolo Malatesta to their reading about Lancelot and Guinevere.

Dare one suggest that Arthur's conception by trickery was particularly appealing to Edward, the cuckoo in the Yorkist nest? Tending to support the hypothesis, in 1474 he made Federico da Montefeltro, Duke of Urbino, a Garter knight. Federico was not only a usurper but also a cuckoo in the Montefeltro nest, and modelled his court on the Arthurian legend – to the point that his daughter-in-law Elisabetta Gonzaga was a leading figure of the Renaissance Camelot in Baldassare Castiglione's highly influential 1528 treatise *Il Cortegiano*.

The ladies of Edward's court entered fully into the Arthurian fantasy. The famously handsome Scales features in an anecdote that grants us a unique glimpse of the light-hearted atmosphere Elizabeth brought to the court. In April 1465, a month before her coronation, Scales was speaking with his sister when the ladies of the court mobbed him, tied a garter of gold and pearls with an enamelled 'flower of souvenance' around his thigh and gave him a roll of parchment tied with a thread of gold containing a task he must perform.

The required deed was revealed to be a challenge to a nobleman of 'four lineages and without reproach' for a two-day encounter, the first on horseback and the second on foot, to take place in London in October. The nobleman chosen was Anthony, known as the Grand Bastard of Burgundy, hardly an impeccable pedigree, who had already written to Scales saying he would like to break lances with him. In other words, this was a diplomatic initiative thinly disguised as a celebration of chivalry.

The challenge was sent to the Burgundian court and accepted in the presence of Duke Philippe, Count Charles and Jacquetta's brother Jacques de Luxembourg. Anthony could not meet the deadline because he had to serve in his father's war with Liège, and further delays robbed the tournament of much of its diplomatic significance. Intended to initiate the diplomatic process leading to an alliance between the two countries, when the joust at last took place in June 1468 it merely coincided with the climax of a long courtship.

Even though on several occasions Edward used taxes specifically voted for war in order to repair the royal finances, there can be no doubt that he was intent on creating and maintaining a credible threat of war with France. One motive was revenge for Louis having kept the Lancastrian resistance going for the first years of their respective reigns; but another was that no other enterprise would do more to heal the wounds of civil war and unite the English nobility and people under Edward's leadership.

Nobody could forget that Henry V's conquests would have been impossible without the Burgundian alliance, and that they were ultimately doomed after Philippe ended the alliance in 1435. Edward was also grateful for Philippe's support in 1459–61, and single-mindedly pursued a renewed alliance against France. Philippe's Valois sympathies and Charolais's infatuation with Somerset were an impediment, but the main obstacles were commercial.

• ∽ •

Especially for a period when the political actors were so entertaining, it is easy to forget how ephemeral they were. The dynastic conflicts in England engaged a decreasing number of the barons and, apart from those directly involved, the rest of the nation just wished it would all go away. The real, deep-seated changes took place in the economic and social spheres.

The driver of economic and social change in England was the wool trade. It constituted the principal wealth of the country and created a new upper middle class of merchants and financiers. The commercial relationship between the Calais-based Company of the Staple and the great, mainly Flemish textile manufacturing cities had been the cash cow that permitted the English to sustain the Hundred Years War, and in 1436 it was the rock on which Duke Philippe's attempt to conquer Calais broke. Its historic importance was so great that to this day the Lord Chancellor sits on the Woolsack in the House of Lords.

Like all monopolists the Staplers abused their privilege, paying suppliers as little as they could get away with, while charging buyers as much as possible. Consequently a cottage textile industry grew up in England to compete for raw wool with the Staplers, while greatly undercutting imported Flemish textiles on price. The Flemings could live with losing England as an outlet for their finished products, but were adamantly opposed to permitting competition from high-quality English textile exports in the western European market.

The Staplers were the principal suppliers of raw wool to the Flemish cities and their interests were inseparable. The crown also owed them enormous sums, and by the Act of Retainer of 1466 their monopoly was extended to the collection of all customs duties on their own wool, both to repay themselves and to cover the likewise burdensome arrears and future wages of the Calais garrison. Consequently the strategically vital but declining traditional wool trade absolutely required the preservation of the status quo, but freer bilateral trade would benefit a growing new class of merchants seeking to export English manufactures.

• ‿ •

Thanks to education and facilitation by Herbert, Howard and Hastings, Edward was the first English monarch to draw significant revenues from personal participation in trade. Exactly how much is hard to establish, but it was sufficient for him to assure Parliament in June 1467 that he intended to 'live of his own'. Of course 'his own' included revenues regularly 'volunteered' by the nominally tax-exempt Church, which owned a third of the land in England; but it indicated his desire to achieve financial independence.

The conflict of interest was manifest. Edward, trading on his own account, was also solely responsible for concluding commercial agreements with the nation's trading partners. It is impossible to say to what degree his diplomacy was conditioned by considerations of personal gain, but there is no reason to suspect he had any more ethical reservations in commerce than in his pursuit of women. Despite his Arthurian pretensions he was sleazy, and this was the main reason he commanded little respect from his peers at home and abroad.

The clearest example we have of his dubious trading is that Italian merchants continued to enjoy unilateral trading privileges in England. We know Edward made extensive use of Italian ships to carry his own trade goods, mainly wool, to the hugely profitable Italian market, without demanding reciprocity from the Italians for English merchants in general. The special deal the Italian merchants offered him was, in effect, a massive bribe to act against the interests of his own subjects.

This said, no hint of rent-seeking contaminated Edward's desire for a Burgundian alliance. It was a purely strategic choice and actually cost him a great deal. The decision was also plainly his to make, and Warwick's opposition to his sovereign's clearly expressed will in this matter went well beyond merely flirting with *lèse majesté*. Before turning to his motives for doing so and the pros and cons of the alternative he proposed, it is essential to bear in mind that it was an outright challenge to the king's prerogative.

VIII

WARWICK

T HE CASE FOR WARWICK'S DEFENCE IS THAT HE WAS denied the honour due to him and acted to prevent a clearly signposted attack on the sources of his power. That hypothesis can only be sustained if taken in isolation from Warwick's no less clearly signposted desire to dominate. Unarguably Edward could have taken back Warwick's offices and the lands he held by royal favour – but to assume he intended to provoke an inevitable rebellion by doing so is to brush aside the entire theory and practice of deterrence.

Edward desperately needed domestic peace, and depended on Warwick to ensure it in the most troublesome area of his kingdom. Once the North was pacified, the question was whether being the king's virtual viceroy for the region would satisfy Warwick's grandiosity. Edward's policy of containment indicates he was certain it would not. Close collaboration with Warwick had given him an unequalled opportunity to study the man, and it is most unlikely he misread him.

To unconstrained egos any limit placed on their freedom of action is intolerable, and aggressive individuals will indeed perceive deterrence as an imminent attack – because that is what they would do if the roles were reversed. Rational people are always at a disadvantage when dealing with such people, because compromise is impossible. Concessions are taken as no more than their due and as a sign of weakness, therefore requiring no quid pro quo. It is a psychopathic condition known as malignant narcissism – and the only cure for it is death.

Not coincidentally, Warwick was a pioneer of mass propaganda. The 'big lie' was first deployed against Henry VI, but that was just a rehearsal for the full force of the technique he was to unleash on Edward. One can forgive the contemporary commons for believing him because, in the words of Adolf Hitler, the master practitioner, 'it would never come into their heads to fabricate colossal untruths, and they would not believe that others could have the impudence to distort the truth so infamously'. Historians should not be so credulous.

Nobody understood better than Warwick how fragile Edward's authority was, or had more to lose if his erstwhile apprentice managed to unite the country behind him in a successful military campaign against France. Louis XI perceived this early, and shaped his diplomacy accordingly. Their common interest was cemented when Edward insultingly rejected Warwick's guidance. A less grandiose individual might have accepted it as a warning not to presume too much – but to Warwick it was an unforgivable affront.

Bitter at the loss of the titles and lands Louis had promised him for delivering a marriage alliance with France, and enraged to have lost face, Warwick immediately wrote to Louis and said he hoped soon to have news that would please him. An oral message would, as usual, have accompanied the letter, and afterwards Louis told the Milanese ambassador he believed Warwick intended to seize the throne, and that he would help him.

So yes, the marriage and the matter of the Burgundian versus the French alliance were indeed the issues that led to war between Warwick and Edward – but because they were a trial of wills. Warwick could only be the power behind a throne occupied by a weak king, and looking back at the compromise he brokered in 1459, which left captive Henry VI on the throne and denied it to Richard of York, we can see he was always guided by that calculation.

The benefits to Louis were immense. During the Public Weal revolt Warwick thwarted Edward's efforts to profit from it by secretly assuring Louis there was no danger of an English invasion of Normandy. The Universal Spider was wary at first, finding it hard to believe that Warwick and his brother the Lord Chancellor should be so naive as to leap into his web by committing treason. In the event he never had to use the leverage they gave him: he had only to encourage them to do what they were set on doing anyway.

When George was made Archbishop of York in 1465, Warwick turned the week-long celebration of his installation into a display of magnificence intended to outshine the festivities following Elizabeth's coronation four months earlier. There were over 6,000 guests, including six bishops, five abbots and their retinues. Apart from Richard, Duke of Gloucester, whom Edward had placed under Warwick's tutelage, and the king's easily influenced brother-in-law John de la Pole, Duke of Suffolk, the rest were members of the Neville affinity.

The earls were Warwick himself, his brother John of Northumberland, his future brother-in-law John Vere of Oxford and the newly restored John Talbot of Shrewsbury. Barons FitzHugh, Stanley, Lumley and Hastings – who was made comptroller of the event – were Warwick's brothers-in-law, while Scrope of Bolton, Greystoke and Ogle were retainers. Young Lovell, who was wealthier than many earls (he was also Baron Holland, Deincort, Bedal and Grey of Rotherfield), was also living at Middleham, and Willoughby was a kinsman through his wife, to whom he owed the title that remained to him after the attainder of his father, Lord Welles.

Most of them had benefitted from Warwick's good lordship. Northumberland, Lumley and Ogle owed their titles to him, and he had saved FitzHugh, Greystoke and Lovell's father from attainder after Towton. His role in the restoration of Shrewsbury to his attainted title, Oxford's immunity following his father's treason and Willoughby's later recognition as Baron Welles is less clear, as they were in keeping with Edward's policy of reconciliation. What matters is that they believed Warwick had persuaded Edward to show them grace.

Hastings's prominent presence is intriguing. Edward could not very well have forbidden him to attend the installation of his brother-in-law, but would have been displeased by his acceptance of a leading role in such a defiant celebration of Neville power. The most likely explanation is Hastings's guilty certainty that he could never be reconciled with the Woodvilles. The key to Hastings's behaviour in 1465, as it would be again in 1469 and 1483, was the conflict between his personal loyalty to Edward and his justified fear of Edward's queen.

George's elevation to the archbishopric of York was the last of the grand concessions Edward made to the Nevilles. This was partly because he had no more major offices or substantial forfeited estates to award, but also in the hope that they would be satisfied with their virtual hegemony in the North. Even so, he would have expected that his brother Clarence, whose estates included the ex-Percy lordship of Spofforth in Yorkshire and royal Richmond Castle, would act as his loyal representative. He could not have been more mistaken.

Elizabeth bore Edward three daughters, Elizabeth in February 1466, Mary in August 1467 and Cecily in March 1469, before producing Prince Edward, the required male heir, in November 1470.* Each pregnancy might have ended Clarence's status of heir presumptive, and with it his aspiration to the appanage he thought he deserved. In the absence of any prospect of further endowments from his brother, he was highly receptive to the alternative offered by Warwick, who had his sights set on Edward's brothers as husbands for his daughters Isabel and Anne.

The heir to Warwick's Salisbury patrimony in Yorkshire, the South-West and the Home Counties was his brother John, now Earl of Northumberland, who did not produce a male heir until

*Louis XI's first surviving son, the future Charles VIII, was born in June 1470.

1465. Through their mother Warwick's daughters were heirs to the rest, including the entirety of the Beauchamp/Despenser estates in the west Midlands, the Welsh Marches and Barnard Castle in County Durham. These were complementary to the lands Edward had given Clarence, and best of all would become his by right of marriage and not by royal favour.

Warwick was not a personally attractive man. He completely failed to win over Richard of Gloucester and Francis, Lord Lovell, two young men who grew up in his household at Middleham. Outside his family and the northern retainers he inherited from his father, his principal following was in Kent, which was economically symbiotic with his Calais stronghold and whose men had been well rewarded after turning out for him in 1460. In general his free-spending magnificence was much admired by the common people, but not by his peers.

His immensely high opinion of himself was not something he could conceal beyond superficial acquaintance and, in an age that believed the face was the mirror of the soul, he was strikingly ugly. The only likeness we have of him is an ill-visaged figurine on the funerary monument of Richard Beauchamp, his father-in-law. Since Warwick oversaw the construction of the tomb, presumably he thought it portrayed him to best advantage. At a purely personal level it is not surprising he believed Louis XI, almost as ugly as himself, a kindred spirit, and that he envied Edward and felt a reciprocal loathing for handsome Charles of Burgundy.

Apart from making the French king a gift of priceless intelligence, whatever else Warwick may have intended to do was put on hold while Louis was fully taken up with the Public Weal revolt and its aftermath. Louis retreated to the Loire valley for a year and put his reform programme on hold while he built up the standing army from seventeen to twenty companies of heavy cavalry and established an artillery factory and park so that he should never again be outgunned, as he had been at Montlhéry.

Louis had also been shocked by the presence of several hundred mercenary English longbowmen at Montlhéry. Although Count Charles wasted the advantage they might have given him, the prospect of a larger contingent taking part in a future war under competent leadership was something that must have given Louis sleepless nights. If he could not prevent an Anglo–Burgundian alliance, Edward must be kept distracted by other challenges, to make it impossible for him to embark on the expedition against France for which Parliament was only too willing to vote the necessary funds.

It took Edward an unconscionably long time to subtract the Nevilles from the diplomatic initiatives they invariably sabotaged. Chief among them was the opportunity that opened up when Charolais's second wife died in late September 1465. Louis promptly offered him the hand of his 4-year-old daughter Anne along with an enormous dowry, but the count did not wish to reaffirm the Valois link. Even though the exiled Lancastrians had served in his army and Somerset and Exeter were still pensioners at his court, in early 1466 Charolais put out diplomatic feelers for a marriage with Edward's sister Margaret.

The Nevilles argued that the suggestion had not been made in good faith, and Warwick got himself appointed to lead a delegation, which included Lords Hastings and Wenlock, to discuss Charolais's initiative but also to treat with Louis, supposedly to strengthen Edward's bargaining position. Warwick clashed with Charolais when they met at Boulogne on 15 April, but all was sweetness and light when he met Louis's representatives at Calais three days later.

Louis, suspicious that Warwick was playing some unfathomably deep game, took the precaution of sending a copy of his ambassadors' instructions to Charolais. His doubts were resolved when Warwick agreed a truce to last until March 1468, in which both sides undertook not to support each other's enemies, with a final peace settlement to be negotiated in October. With Warwick's complicity, and in return for merely disowning the spent Lancastrian resistance, Louis had sabotaged Edward's hopes for a Burgundian marriage.

In the light of future events it is highly significant that Hastings, supposedly Edward's eyes and ears, went along with this attempt to subvert his king's intentions. Like Warwick, he associated Edward's pro-Burgundian policy with Jacquetta, and this is merely the first clear evidence we have of what we may presume was his constant effort to diminish Woodville influence, for fear that it might grow strong enough to drive him from Edward's side.

In further discussions Warwick and Louis's ambassadors drew up a draft treaty by which Louis would pay 40,000 gold crowns [£5 million] a year during the truce and for as long as it might be extended. He also undertook to arrange a suitable husband for Margaret, to provide her dowry and to pay for a magnificent marriage ceremony. The candidates discussed included Galeazzo Maria Sforza, the new Duke of Milan, and Prince Philibert of Piedmont, heir to the duchy of Savoy and Louis's nephew by marriage.

The Nevilles were now in the awkward position of arguing that the notoriously slippery Louis was more trustworthy than Charolais. It did not help their cause that the deal Warwick brought back was transparently aimed at derailing Anglo–Burgundian understanding, and that he had plainly exceeded his instructions. Also, while he was away Edward had rebuked Chancellor George Neville for obstructing safe conducts for the Grand Bastard of Burgundy to come to England for his contest with Anthony Woodville. As it happened, the event was again postponed because the Burgundian was required to serve in the siege of Dinant.

If Count Charles had made a formal offer for Margaret's hand in 1466, the showdown between Edward and the Nevilles would have been brought forward by a year. He did not because Louis sent him a copy of the draft treaty. Having himself just spurned a far greater bribe, Charles's lip must have curled. Far from strengthening Edward's hand in his dealings with Burgundy, the Nevilles had deliberately undermined him by giving the impression he was only toying with Charles in order to increase the money he could obtain from Louis.

Edward let the Nevilles think he remained amenable to a French alliance because his own position was not strong. The reconciliation with the Lancastrians had not been popular among the Yorkist nobles, and the advancement of newly created peers, particularly the Welshman Herbert, had generated further resentment. Regional magnates such as his uncle the Earl of Essex, the Earl of Arundel and Lord Stanley did not feel they had sufficient influence.

By over-rewarding Warwick and subsequently finding himself obliged to build up his henchmen in order to contain him, Edward had dangerously narrowed the scope of his patronage. Every attainder he reversed also reduced the spoils available for distribution, and after endowing his brothers there was little left over for his other supporters. They did not become hostile, but rather were neutral between Edward and Warwick, although many would have let Warwick know they shared his disappointment with the king.

The result was that Edward had to move carefully, and while pursuing the tournament and the Burgundian marriage he did not reject the French alternative. Just prior to the long-heralded arrival of the Grand Bastard of Burgundy, he again commissioned Warwick to treat with Louis. In early June 1467 Warwick sailed up the River Seine with a 200-man retinue to meet the king himself in Rouen. Louis went to greet him at La Bouille, about 15 miles (24km) downstream from Rouen, and then let him go on by river while he followed by road. He had organized a royal reception for his guest and did not want the effect diluted by his own presence.

For eight days Warwick and his followers were showered with expensive gifts. During their daily meetings Louis suggested his guest could better control England with a Lancastrian restoration, but Warwick was adamant that he was still the power behind the throne. They drew up a draft treaty by which in return for a military alliance against Burgundy Louis would pay a yearly pension of 4,000 marks [£845,000]. The spoils of the conquered Netherlands would be shared, and Louis floated the idea that Warwick should become Prince of Holland and Zeeland. The king also repeated his offer to provide a fitting groom for Margaret entirely at his own expense, and free access to French markets for English goods.

The love fest broke up when news arrived that Duke Philippe was dying. Both judged that Warwick should hurry back to London and on 16 June he departed, accompanied by a high-level French delegation. On their way back they learned that on the 8th, the very day the Rouen conference had begun, Edward had ridden with Clarence, Herbert and other henchmen to Archbishop Neville's palace and required him to surrender the Great Seal. The following day Edward had signed a thirty-year truce with Duke Frañsez of Brittany, promising him military support if Louis attacked him.

Warwick could not have been more humiliated.

IX

KINGSHIP

THE DEATH OF DUKE PHILIPPE BROUGHT AN ABRUPT end to the tournament designed to strengthen Anglo-Burgundian ties, as the Grand Bastard had to return for his father's funeral. Charles's accession also ushered in a new, more urgent phase of French diplomacy, as it revived the hopes of the nobles dissatisfied by the outcome of the League of the Public Weal. So keen was Louis on keeping England out of the mix that the French delegation Warwick brought back with him even offered to submit Edward's territorial claims to papal arbitration.

Birds in a bush proffered by Louis were of no interest to Edward. Whether or not he genuinely aspired to recovering Normandy and/or Guyenne, in the short term it made eminently good dynastic sense to seek an alliance with Burgundy. With the exception of Marguerite's shabby court in Bar and Jasper Tudor in Brittany, the main Lancastrian exiles were now pensioners of Duke Charles. Burgundy was also England's most important trading partner and its territories surrounded Calais.

On 14 July, after being treated as unwanted guests, the French ambassadors went home. Warwick escorted them to the coast, assuring them he would reassert control of the realm, and then rode to his estates in the North. Unfortunately, no record survives of where he went and whom he met; but it is a safe bet they included his brother John and Lord Ogle in Northumberland, Lords FitzHugh, Scrope of Bolton and Greystoke in Yorkshire and Richmondshire, and Lord Stanley in Lancashire.

Warwick did not make direct contact with teenaged John Talbot, Earl of Shrewsbury, whose father he had killed at Northampton. Shrewsbury's involvement came through Clarence, who was the same age and held adjacent lands. Clarence had been seduced by the prospect of marriage with 16-year-old Isabel, Warwick's elder daughter, some time in 1466. The mission sent that year to follow up Charles's suggestion of a marriage alliance proposed an additional match between Clarence and Charles's only child, Marie of Burgundy. It was an unrealistic proposal, its purpose to justify Edward's rejection of Clarence's betrothal to Isabel.

Edward put himself in the wrong by continuing to block it – having married an English wife it was hypocritical to oppose Clarence marrying another. Isabel was the best prospect Clarence could hope for, and sympathy for him was not limited to his mother and sister. The Bourchiers saw no harm in it, and other senior Yorkists would have agreed. When they were eventually married it was with Archbishop Bourchier's blessing and with a papal dispensation (they were second cousins) obtained by Bourchier's representative in Rome.

If we broaden our focus beyond the growing tension between Edward and Warwick, we can see that Edward had been reasonably successful in repairing his deeply fractured kingdom. Political stability seemed to have been restored, the royal finances were improving and flagrant abuses of authority by the nobility were restrained. Public order and the impartial administration of justice remained very distant ideals, but if any proof were required that he had succeeded in returning the genie of anarchy to the bottle, it came after Warwick pulled the cork.

The main source of unrest was that the economy was still in the recession that began around 1440, exacerbated by the initial contraction of the money supply and exchange rate confusion following the debasement of the coinage in September 1464. It was actually a devaluation of about 25 per cent, agreed with rare unanimity by the heavily indebted members of the Great Council. As the country's greatest debtor, Edward had the most to gain from it, and he also charged a fee for the new coinage; but it did make English exports more competitive.

The same desire to act in concert with his nobles inhibited him from a more vigorous style of kingship. He could have made royal progresses to every corner of his realm in the manner of Louis XI, but he did not. This is commonly attributed to indolence, but a less facile explanation is that he needed to avoid any perception of seeking to undermine the authority of local magnates. Given that Louis was nearly overthrown for doing so, it is hard to fault Edward's judgement.

Edward's greatest weakness as a politician was that he lacked his opponents' insatiable will to dominate. With relatively little effort he had achieved all the wine, women and song a man could wish for, his life punctuated by leisure activities and peregrinations from one palace to another, with teams of people devoted to making his existence as pleasurable as possible. He was a self-confident, spoiled child of fortune, revelled in it and had no burning desire for more.

It follows that he resented the Neville fly in his brimming pot of ointment mainly because it would not stop buzzing. He did not anticipate how far Warwick was prepared to go, and one cannot fault his reasoning. Objectively, the earl had nothing to gain commensurate with what he stood to lose. The king's legitimacy might be questionable, but without him Warwick had none at all, and the only people who wanted to depose Edward hated Warwick even more.

Clarence supplied the missing ingredient, but again it is hard to see how Edward could have anticipated this. Clarence owed everything to his brother, he had no following among the nobles and any affinity he might have developed in his scattered domains since 1466 was wafer thin. There is every reason to suspect his mother's influence was crucial – and that was Edward's blind spot.

This said, we cannot acquit him and his courtiers of a failure to focus on the essentials. They only began to pay county sheriffs for political information in 1468, and they should have maintained the commissions of array. These were summons of all men between the ages of 16 and 60 for the defence of the realm, through royal orders sent to the sheriffs through local lords. Edward's predecessors regularly summoned the levies for inspection and basic training, a useful reminder of royal authority, but he let the custom decay. Consequently the permanent militias, responsive to the will of local authorities, assumed greater military significance.

Arguably a greater failure was to regard the Church as little more than a cash cow. If properly handled it would have been an invaluable source of intelligence as well as being the most important institutional foundation of the monarchy. Two of the three most senior non-ceremonial officers of state were traditionally clerics: the Lord Chancellor, who was the senior legal officer and also the king's senior adviser in matters spiritual – hence normally the Archbishop of Canterbury; and the Lord Keeper of the Privy Seal, the king's personal signet.

Thomas Bourchier, Archbishop of Canterbury, had been Lord Chancellor during Richard of York's Protectorship in 1455–6, but Edward did not reappoint him even after he dismissed George Neville. In part this may have been because the archbishop seems to have been an indecisive individual; but mainly it was because Edward wished to be his own chancellor, to which end he appointed the yes-man Robert Stillington, Bishop of Bath and Wells. Although he did petition the pope to make Thomas a cardinal, this was because George Neville was lobbying the pope to appoint him instead. When Thomas's nomination came through in September 1467, Edward maliciously forwarded the letter to his recently sacked ex-chancellor.

The Bourchiers were of royal blood and were a pillar of the Yorkist cause, but Edward appears to have taken them for granted. Although he did arrange the marriage of Viscount Bourchier, Earl Henry's heir, to Elizabeth's sister Anne, and packed the queen's household with Bourchiers, Edward did not bring the older Bourchiers back into government when he humiliated the Nevilles. The reason is uncomplicated – he wished to be surrounded by men unlikely to volunteer unwelcome advice. Consequently he did not pay enough attention to the nuts and bolts of the scaffolding on which he stood until it collapsed under him.

Warwick had not sought royal permission to withdraw to the North and Edward overplayed his hand by peremptorily summoning him to answer an accusation of treason made by a Lancastrian courier captured by Herbert. Warwick refused, and Edward had to back down. In January 1468 Warwick rejected another summons to a Council meeting in Coventry, saying he would not come while Rivers, Scales and Herbert were at the king's side, but Archbishop Neville persuaded him to attend. He was civil to Herbert and Stafford of Southwyck, but refused to have anything to do with the Woodvilles.

Edward resorted to appeasement. After Warwick rejected the first summons, he formally confirmed the earl's wardship and marriage of wealthy Francis, Lord Lovell. After Warwick ended his sulk and attended the Council meeting, Edward appointed him Constable and Steward of the nearby duchy of Lancaster castle and honour of Kenilworth, previously the jewel of Queen Marguerite's dower. Later in the year he also granted him a share of the profits from all the royal gold, silver and lead mines north of the river Trent.

Thus the carrot: it did not work because Warwick could not be won or even mollified by an accumulation of offices, wardships and modest territorial concessions. He had no desire for a subordinate role in the administration or the other mundane occupations of indirect power. Following further defiance, Edward reverted to the stick. After Warwick opposed an expedition to help Brittany against a French invasion in July 1468, the king appointed Scales to lead it – and made him Keeper of the Seas.

The office of Keeper of the Seas had been Warwick's since the late 1450s when Marguerite, in a vain attempt to win him over, had made him lord of Calais in all but name. In the peculiar circumstances then prevailing it had given him extraordinary power.

The trade conducted through the town was the crown's principal source of bullion, and it even had its own mint. The garrison was England's only standing army and Warwick was given full charge of the fleet. Warwick once said he would give up all his lands in England if he could keep Calais, and he could not now ignore a threat to the constellation of power built around it.

Insult was added to injury. Although the expedition arrived too late to help Duke Frañsez, it turned aside to help the locals retake Jersey from the heirs of Pierre de Brézé, who had seized it in 1461. The Channel Islands formed part of Warwick's wife's Beauchamp inheritance, so it was a further slap in the face when the king resumed them and made Scales Warden of Jersey.

Nothing Edward had to offer could compensate for this thrust at the heart of Warwick's power, but the king does not appear to have understood the gravity of what he had done. As late as February 1469 he granted Warwick three more Percy manors in Cumberland and two in Warwickshire. This sent entirely the wrong signal, as Warwick rightly concluded that Edward did not intend to attack his power further. He was mistaken, however, in believing that if he could get rid of the king's inner circle he would recover his dominance over him.

Fear will do in the absence of respect, but Edward inspired neither. This was a disappointment to his subjects, who had hoped for firm leadership once woeful Henry VI was deposed. Another factor in the growing disaffection among Edward's subjects was the reappearance of a virulent new strain of the plague in 1463–5 and again in 1467, which would have been seen as an indication of divine disapproval. But thence to rebellion and a return to the anarchy of 1459–61 was a very big step indeed, one nobody except Warwick and his affinity was prepared to take. Accordingly, he had to prepare the ground, and did so in a remarkably modern manner.

Latin-based languages use the same word for 'discord' and 'tares', the Biblical term for harmful weeds that grow in wheat fields. Warwick set his agents to sowing tares in the ever fertile ground of endemic discontent – much as left-wing 'grass roots organizers' do today. Sometimes this took the form of direct action. It is not difficult to identify the hidden hand of the Nevilles in a conspiracy among the London craft guilds to maim Flemish artisans resident in Southwark, discovered in September 1467. More blatantly, one of Clarence's retainers led a mob assault on one of Earl Rivers's manors in Kent in January 1468.

Meanwhile Warwick and his brother used their now assiduous attendance at Council meetings to steer government policy in unpopular directions. The most clear-cut example came when they prevailed on Edward to levy a huge fine backed by the seizure of Hanseatic League merchants and their goods, over what was actually an unrelated matter. This led to a guerrilla war at sea with the Hansards, who commanded a considerably larger fleet.

In this, the dog that did not bark in the night was the passivity of Warwick's Sandwich-Calais squadron, previously only too willing to maraud against Hanseatic shipping. The resulting losses were extremely damaging to the London merchants, to whom Edward was heavily indebted and on whom he depended to finance temporary shortfalls in his general revenues.

That Edward ignored so many indications of their ill will bears testimony to the personal plausibility of the Nevilles. He should have noticed that the 'great riots and oppressions done to our subjects' were increasing in counties where Warwick and Clarence were supposed to keep the peace. He did not join the dots even after he judged it necessary to travel with a large bodyguard to Coventry at the end of 1467. Again, he should have dealt with the situation in person; instead – and in keeping with his governing philosophy – he commissioned Warwick and Clarence to conduct assizes to deal with unrest in six Midlands counties.

To continue listing examples would merely labour the point that Edward sleepwalked into a world of trouble. Not all or even most of the ignored warning signals were engineered by the Nevilles. It was sufficient for them to sow their tares and let nature take its course, never openly espousing treason, such that their troublemaking blended into the normal background noise of grumbling dissatisfaction. Edward was also distracted by a revival of Lancastrian subversion, which could not have served Warwick's purpose better had he devised it himself.

In May 1468, two months before Margaret of York's long-delayed marriage to Charles, Chancellor Stillington informed Parliament that the king had concluded encircling alliances with Burgundy, Brittany, Castille and Aragon, and was now ready to lead an invasion of France. Despite previous disappointments, Parliament once again granted him an exceptional tax of three-sixteenths and tenths for the purpose. As before, there is no indication that Edward seriously contemplated jumping into the financial bottomless pit of a continental war.

Taxes voted by the Commons between 1461 and 1470 averaged about £10,000 [£6.36 million] per annum, with a further £7,000 per annum from the Church. Against this, regular annual charges against the royal purse – in peacetime – totalled about £50,000. To put this into perspective, the down payment on Margaret's dowry and the cost of her trousseau and related expenses was about £15,000. The peacetime military establishment demanded about the same amount annually until the Staplers assumed responsibility for the Calais garrison in 1466.

Edward was also still struggling to pay off the massive overhang of debts run up by Henry VI, and those incurred to overthrow him. Even quite modest military campaigns added significantly to the burden – in 1468 the relatively small expedition to Brittany under Scales cost about £18,000. Before condemning Edward's apparent embezzlement of funds voted for war, we should perhaps consider that the gulf between what people demand of their government and what they are prepared to pay was at least as great in the fifteenth century as it is today.

We have noted his neglect of the commissions of array, but one of the reasons for it highlights a military constraint on Edward's freedom of action. Service abroad had always been through paid indenture, and without the prospect of earning good money there was little incentive to put in the years of practice necessary to become a skilled longbowman. Many of those who did became mercenaries – Charles of Burgundy was a major employer – and as a result the military value of the unpaid levies declined. Even if it were possible to survey every subsequent battlefield of the Wars of the Roses as thoroughly and fruitfully as Towton has been, the number and concentration of arrowheads would be decreasingly informative.*

Although the levies still provided the billmen who made up the bulk of the armies, and the longbow still deterred mounted charges, the bow's slow eclipse increased the relative importance of the more expensive, fully harnessed (armoured) and more independent men-at-arms. In terms of the internal balance of military power, the dying out of the generation of southerners with experience of war in France shifted the preponderance of combat-tested men-at-arms to the North, where the years of war against the Scots and the Lancastrian die-hards had provided the Neville affinity with continuing on-the-job training.

Edward's promotion of Herbert to become the dominant lord of the Welsh Marches, the other area with a strong martial tradition, argues he was alert to the danger this posed. He could not himself maintain his father's affinity once the crown subsumed the duchy of York, and delegating to Herbert, Stafford of Southwyck and Hastings was his best option. The insuperable problem was that being a step removed from affinity maintenance meant he could no longer summon a large body of men-at-arms personally loyal to himself. This was to prove the decisive factor in the early stages of the storm that nearly washed away the Yorkist regime.

---

*Before investing in a metal detector, consider that differences in land use and soil chemistry make some sites considerably less promising than others. In many places the survival of battle artefacts would be miraculous.

X

TREASON

EDWARD BEGAN TO SUPPLY FUNDS TO THE COUNTY sheriffs to pay informers because there was no doubt that Louis would retaliate for the Anglo–Burgundian alliance. The harvest was not long in coming, contaminated by confirmation bias, a problem no intelligence service has ever resolved. If you demand details of a specific threat you will get it; and the more insistent you are, the more your informers will tailor their reporting to your demand. Also, by narrowing the focus of inquiry you shut out intelligence that might have led you to ask better questions.

To employ a phrase coined in a later age, Renaissance princes surrounded their intentions with a bodyguard of lies. The Universal Spider was a master of the craft, and his preferred outlet for disinformation appears to have been the Milanese ambassador. While dealing with more urgent threats nearer home, Louis confided in him that he was equipping Marguerite and the exiled Lancastrians with money, ships and troops. This was false, but after it leaked back to England it served the dual purpose of alarming Edward and encouraging unreconciled Lancastrians to give him something to be alarmed about.

The only hostile action that can be unequivocally attributed to Louis is the help he gave Jasper Tudor after he was compelled to leave Brittany following the Anglo–Breton treaty. The loss of support from Frañsez doomed Harlech Castle, the last Lancastrian toe-hold, and when Jasper sought alternative patronage from France, Louis made another of his small investments in the hope of creating disproportionate trouble for his enemies. In June–July 1468 Jasper sailed with fifty men in three small ships to the relief of Harlech, but finding it too closely invested he landed at Barmouth instead (Map 8).

The Principality was still so strongly Lancastrian and lawless that no rents had been paid to the monarchy since 1461, and with the peasantry flocking to his banner Jasper marched inland to strike at the Yorkist borough of Denbigh, which he sacked and burned. He retreated along the coast when a royal army under Lord Herbert's brother Richard approached, but was caught and crushed near Conway. Jasper escaped into Snowdonia, and thence back to France, but the royal army, 'pursued its course up the Conway valley, ravaging it with fire and sword. The entire Snowdon district experienced such unparalleled desolation that it had barely recovered more than a century later. Echoes of the slaughter survive in song and story'.*

The commissions of array for the Marches issued by Edward to the Herbert brothers in early July marked the abandonment of his hope that Lancastrian resistance in Wales would wither on the vine. While one would hesitate to attribute humanitarian concerns to any monarch of the period, Edward's patience with the unreconciled Welsh appears to have been based on an intelligent appreciation that, as several of his predecessors had discovered, scorched earth simply provided more fertile ground for future rebellions.

The Herberts' view was that the scorching had not been done thoroughly enough. Lord Herbert gathered an army in Pembroke and marched north through Cardigan, the passage of a large army alone sufficiently punitive for such a poor county. When he reached Harlech the defenders repulsed a first assault, but with no prospect of relief following Jasper's defeat they surrendered on 14 August.

*From Howell Evans's indispensable online *Wales and the Wars of the Roses*.

The garrison of about fifty men was sent to London to await the king's judgement. Only two, presumably turncoats, were executed.

Edward not only spared but also honoured David ap Eynon, the Captain of Harlech, and showed similar grace to Richard Tunstall and Henry Bellingham, who had fought against him in all the Northumbrian sieges and battles, and had also escorted Henry VI during part of his peregrinations. A general pardon followed on 1 December. Although Tunstall and Bellingham declared for Lancaster in 1470 and were subsequently attainted, they were pardoned again and Tunstall served Edward faithfully for the rest of his reign.

William Herbert was rewarded with the earldom of Pembroke and Edward confirmed his wardship and marriage of 11-year-old Henry Tudor, Earl of Richmond and Jasper's nephew. Herbert had married his namesake son to the queen's sister Mary, and also had the wardship and marriage of 19-year-old Henry Percy, heir to the attainted earldom of Northumberland, currently held by John Neville. It was clearly his intention to marry Percy and Tudor to his daughters, hoping thereby to supplant Neville supremacy in the North.

Louis must have been delighted with the return on his miniscule investment, but it is not possible to detect his or Warwick's hand in the other domestic troubles that distracted Edward. The first pebble of the landslide was the arrest of a Lancastrian courier named Cornelius, who was captured with incriminating documents. Handed over to the tender mercies of Tiptoft, under torture Cornelius implicated Thomas Malory, a number of prominent Londoners and John Hawkins, who in turn implicated London Alderman Thomas Cooke.

For Edward the timing could not have been worse. Hawkins was a servant of Lord Wenlock and claimed to have been acting with his approval. Wenlock was about to accompany Margaret on her journey to marry Duke Charles, and Cooke was one of the merchants who had stood surety for the payment of her dowry. After bidding farewell to Margaret, Edward returned to London for the trial of some of those accused by Cornelius and Hawkins. Clarence, Warwick, Northumberland and Rivers headed the commission, but the man really in charge was Chief Justice John Markham, renowned for his integrity.

Possibly convinced of Cooke's guilt but certainly anxious to lay hands on his wealth, Edward sent Lord Treasurer Rivers and household treasurer John Fogge to loot Cooke's London and country homes. After the jury acquitted all the prominent Londoners Edward was particularly incensed by the verdict in the case of Cooke, who at the direction of Markham and despite royal pressure was acquitted of treason but found guilty of 'misprision' – a failure to report treason to the authorities. The king subsequently fined him £8,000 [£5 million] and Elizabeth added a demand for 800 marks under the ancient right of 'Queen's Gold'.

Before his execution Hawkins confessed he had defamed Cooke, but by then Edward was in too deep. Despite the fact that the goods taken and money extorted from Cooke were promptly paid to one of Edward's creditors, and that he dismissed Markham a few months later, this sordid tale has been spun as the work of the evil Woodvilles. One can understand why contemporaries would be extremely careful to avoid pointing the finger directly at the king; but not historians for seizing on it as, in fact, the sole example any of them has been able to produce to prove what nasty, grasping parvenus the Woodvilles were.

As though unhinged by the flagrant injustice he had committed against Cooke, Edward embarked on a witch-hunt based on hearsay evidence from paid informers. The victims were Henry Courtenay and Thomas Hungerford, heirs respectively to the attainted earldom of Devon and the barony of Hungerford, both arrested in late September and imprisoned at Salisbury to await trial. In January 1469 a special commission consisting of the king's brother Richard of Gloucester, the Earl of Arundel and Lords Audley, Scales, Stafford of Southwyck and Stourton presided over a trial in which the accused in desperation opted for a verdict by a local jury.

With no one to play the role of Markham and in the presence of the king, the provincial jurors found the two men guilty of plotting the king's overthrow and murder. Although Courtenay had availed himself of a general pardon dated subsequent to his alleged offence, they were hanged, drawn and quartered. It is hard to escape the conclusion that they had the misfortune to be brought to trial when Edward, frustrated in London, wanted to make an example of someone, and did not much care who it was.

The effect was wholly negative. The scholarly John Warkworth, whose *Chronicle* is generally unbiased and can be taken as a record of what well-informed Englishmen then believed, wrote that the two men were the victims of the malice of Stafford of Southwyck, who had been made Earl of Devon in May. Perhaps so, but the award of their lands fits the pattern of Edward's attempt to build up Stafford as his regime lock on the West Country. The blame and dishonour for an outrageous perversion of justice lay entirely with the king.

John Vere, Earl of Oxford, was detained and consigned to the Tower shortly after the arrest of Courtenay and Hungerford. There was no doubt of his guilt, as he promptly turned king's evidence and betrayed Thomas Tresham, a former speaker of the Commons. Oxford also identified three other men as Lancastrian couriers, one a servant of the exiled Duke of Exeter and the other two servants of the Duke of Norfolk. The three were convicted and executed in haste, but Oxford was Warwick's brother-in-law and so was released in January 1469. In April Edward pardoned him but kept Tresham in prison.*

After a regime falls it is tempting to explain the event by reference to a catalogue of grievances. Unfortunately reason plays a limited role in politics; what matters is the spirit of the moment, which is elusive. Having lived through such a moment a couple of times, I

---

*Also Thomas Malory, who wrote *Le Morte d'Arthur* during his two-year imprisonment in the Tower.

can only describe it as a form of psychic electricity that galvanizes and disorders each component part of a society in its own way, such that people think and act in a manner they later have difficulty reconciling with their self-image as rational beings.

To pursue the analogy, there was undoubtedly an ominous build-up of electricity in 1468–9, and Edward's behaviour may have been as much a symptom as a cause. As king he could do no wrong, and the contradiction that arose when he committed a flagrant injustice could only be resolved if he were not in fact, the legitimate king; which, if believed, explained everything. The deadliest of the tares sowed by Warwick's agents was that Edward was not Richard of York's son, which had the great advantage of being highly believable.

None of this was regime-threatening so long as the regional magnates were on board, but by 1469 Edward's support among them was fragile. Of the dukes, Norfolk was ineffectual and also offended by the execution of his servants. Suffolk, even though Edward had recreated the earldom of Lincoln for his 5-year-old son in 1467, continued to avoid becoming closely identified with the regime. The king had neglected to cultivate the extensive affinity of his ward Buckingham, and only in 1470 – far too late – sought to revive it by recreating the earldom of Wiltshire for John Stafford, the youngest son of the duke killed at Northampton.

The senior Yorkist earls felt excluded and Arundel, who was Warwick's brother-in-law, may have been disgusted by his enforced participation in the judicial murder of Courtenay and Hungerford. The rest, apart from Tiptoft, Rivers and Edward's recently promoted henchmen Pembroke and Devon, were at best neutral, while Oxford and Shrewsbury had family wrongs to right. Most of the barons kept their heads down while those who owed their titles to Edward and Warwick lined up behind their patrons in roughly equal numbers.

The key figure in the equation was John Neville, Earl of Northumberland, with whom Edward believed he had a special understanding. Why this should have been the case cannot be established with certainty, but John probably distanced himself from his ambitious brothers in private conversation with the king. This was eminently believable because, sitting atop the unreconciled Percy affinity, a long way from London and next to Scotland, he stood to lose everything if there were a breakdown of the Yorkist order. Edward had also made him a Garter knight, and perhaps put too much faith in the ancient tradition of blood brotherhood.

When reports filtered back to London of a rebellion in Northumberland in April–May 1469, led by a man calling himself Robin of Redesdale (notorious bandit country) or Robin Mend-All, Edward had no reason to doubt John Neville's report that it was just another minor revolt, dispersed without bloodshed. The truth of the matter is revealed in a letter to Louis XI from his chamberlain, the Scots William, Lord Monypenny, who was in England to liaise with Warwick:

> In the county of Surfiorkshire [South Yorkshire] more than three hundred archers were in arms, and had made themselves a captain named Bobin, and sent to the Earl of Warwick to know if it was time to be busy, and to say that all their neighbours were ready. But my lord answered bidding them go home for it was not yet time to be stirring.

Redesdale had been awarded to the Neville retainer Lord Ogle following the attainder of Tailboys in 1461. Thus the alias 'Robin of Redesdale' strongly suggests that the most experienced military commander in the Neville camp was primed to act on Warwick's signal, a plan put at risk by the impatience of some of those on standby to join him in Yorkshire. It is most unlikely these preparations could have been made without John Neville's complicity.

Happily for the Neville conspiracy, in late May a genuine rebellion erupted in Holderness, in the East Riding. It started as a protest against an ancient corn tax levied by the monks of St Leonard's hospital in York, supposedly for the benefit of the indigent but notoriously spent on luxuries. It grew into a revolt against the corruption that flourished in the archdiocese of York under George Neville, and thence to a demand for the reinstatement of the Percy family. The main landlord in Holderness was the Duke of Buckingham, and nearby Hull was one of the Duke of Norfolk's boroughs – but they abutted on one of the largest forfeited Percy estates around the head of lordship at Leconfield, which had been awarded to John Neville.

The leader of the revolt, who adopted the name 'Robin of Holderness', was Robert Hildyard, lord of Arnald and heir to his namesake father, lord of Winestead, which was located next to the ex-Percy manor of Partington. The Hildyards had fought for Lancaster but avoided attainder and were the largest resident landlords in the 'beak' of the East Riding. Massively joined by the Percy affinity, Robert marched through Leconfield towards York. Edward Hall's and Polydore Vergil's accounts are virtually identical:

> [Hall] When the fame of this great commotion and assembly came to the ears of the citizens of York they were first greatly astonished: but leaving fear aside they were in great doubt and

11. EAST RIDING, YORKSHIRE

uncertain whether it were best for them to issue out of their walls and to give battle to the rebels, or to keep their city and repulse the violence of their enemy by manful defending of their walls and port [gate].

[Vergil] But [John Neville], lieutenant of that county for the king, delivered the city of that fear, who, taking a very fit way for avoiding further danger encountered with the commons as they came at the very gates of the town, where, after a long fight he took their captain Robert Hulderne and forthwith struck off his head, which when he had done he caused all his army to retire from the battle, very late in the night, and withdrew them into the town.

Robert Hildyard was still very much alive and seeking the king's pardon at York in late March 1470, so the report of his execution was Neville's attempt to put a brave face on what was, at best, a drawn battle. The truth was that he fell back into York and the rebels returned unmolested to their homes. Neville, an experienced commander at the head of family retainers, must have been deeply shocked to be fought to a standstill by men from lands that were nominally his, and this was to have repercussions two years later.

The episode – as reported to him – confirmed Edward in two related errors of appreciation. The first was that the threat to his regime in the North was simply a revival of the adamant Percy affinity, which had been the mainstay of Lancastrian resistance in 1461–4. The second was that he could depend on John Neville to suppress it.

XI

COUP D'ÉTAT

HISTORY IS NOT A COURT OF LAW. THE BEST ONE CAN do is apply the Sherlockian dictum that when you have eliminated the impossible, whatever remains must contain the truth. Thence to proving something beyond reasonable doubt is usually beyond the historian's grasp. In the preceding chapters we have reviewed a deep background broadly agreed by historians, give or take a nuance. This one deals with the series of explosive events born of that background.

As had been the case with the Public Weal conspiracy in France, the inescapable logic of the Warwick–Clarence rebellion in mid-1469 was that Edward must die in battle. Warwick and Richard of York had failed to rule through docile and compliant Henry VI in 1460–1. Merely capturing a king as vigorous as Edward could not bring about the changes the conspirators desired, while assassinating him risked unleashing a free-for-all they were unlikely to win. Only if armed with evidence of God's judgement could they seize and retain power

While Warwick was nearly as clever as he believed himself to be, he had the psychopath's signature inability to think through the likely consequences of the crimes he planned so carefully. Removing Edward and his henchmen from the board would certainly create a void of authority, but it was a delusion to believe the Yorkist magnates would be so anxious to avoid chaos that they would tamely accept it being filled by Warwick's puppet king. It was also a certainty the unreconciled Lancastrians would seek to exploit the divisions in their opponents' ranks, so the civil war Warwick needed to avoid at all costs would have been inevitable.

Accordingly, the story of the coup is that the best laid plans of mice and men 'gang aft agley'. At the operational level it was a story of the mistaken preconceptions the two leading protagonists drew from the battles of 1461. Edward believed Warwick was a blustering coward who would not dare draw sword against him, and Warwick believed Edward was stupidly brave and would charge to destruction rather than surrender.

The precise timing of the rebellion was opportunistic. Edward was due to accompany Warwick to the blessing of his rebuilt flagship *Trinity* and to review the fleet at Sandwich, and then to visit Calais, but cancelled the expedition on learning of the Robin of Holderness rebellion. The trigger was Edward's precautionary issuance of countrywide commissions of array. Warwick took the opportunity to mobilize his followers in the North and the Midlands under royal warrant, and decided to strike before the king could gather sufficient forces of his own.

One of the unexamined factors in what followed is the generally accepted view that Edward did not know his brother intended to defy him and marry Isabel Neville – which is absurd. Given the certainty the king would learn of it from his own agents in Rome, Cardinal Bourchier could not have obtained the papal dispensation for the match – which was granted long before, on 14 March 1469 – without Edward's tacit approval. It follows that the king was also informed when Bourchier authorized Archbishop Neville to perform the marriage ceremony in Calais.

The significance of this lies in the fact that the furtive toing and froing by the conspirators before the event was probably regarded with wry amusement by Edward, who set off from Windsor on a pilgrimage to the shrines at Bury St Edmunds and Walsingham on 13 June. There is even a hint of sly humour in his choice of itinerary.

The first stop for the royal party was at Archbishop Neville's palace of More in Hertfordshire, where they had to be expensively entertained and which required the archbishop to hurry back from blessing the *Trinity*.

Edward would also have known that his mother went to Sandwich with Clarence in mid-June to give the young couple her blessing – the movements of the duchess and duke and their retinues could hardly have been kept secret. From his point of view it was an act of tolerable defiance by his own family, which spared him the necessity of officially revoking his prohibition of the wedding. His own secret marriage had, after all, set a precedent. No doubt he intended to accept the fait accompli gracefully, perhaps taking the opportunity to embrace Warwick as a brother-in-law when he received the newly-weds at court.

He clearly had no inkling that the preparations for Clarence's marriage were functioning as effective cover for the well-kept secret of the rebellion that Warwick initiated before sailing to Calais. Reports of a major northern uprising led by Robin of Redesdale reached Edward at Bury St Edmunds on 18 June, along with the disquieting news that the rebels had issued a manifesto comparing the current state of England to that prevailing under Edward II, Richard II and Henry VI when they were deposed. As usual it denounced 'evil councillors', naming the Woodvilles, the Herberts, Stafford of Southwyck and Edward's friend Lord Audley.

This was a bombshell – Edward still did not doubt John Neville's good faith, but clearly he had failed to keep the peace in the North. Working on the false assumption that the rebels had somehow slipped past Neville to march south, and that they were a spontaneous, probably Lancastrian rabble, Edward decided to deal with them from his own resources. He ordered the royal artillery to set out along the Great North Road and the royal wardrobe to send Yorkist banners and 1,000 liveries to his castle-palace of Fotheringhay in Northamptonshire, while he continued his leisurely progress through East Anglia.

Edward had very recently prevailed on his mother to exchange Fotheringhay, once the administrative centre for the duchy of York in eastern England, for the castle-palace of Berkhamsted in Hertfordshire, with nearby Kings Langley palace added to sweeten the deal. The Hertfordshire palaces had been royal residences, set in large parks and much nearer London, but Fotheringhay was particularly dear to Cecily, four of whose children had been born there and where she had spent much of the 1450s with her younger children. She would have been furious that even in this she was being supplanted, as she saw it, by Elizabeth.

The uprising was very far from being a rabble. The nucleus was made up of tough borderers led south by the highly competent Lord Ogle. They were joined by Warwick's Richmondshire and Yorkshire retainers, quietly summoned by Lord Scrope of Bolton and by John Conyers, Warwick's steward at Middleham. A proportion of the Neville affinity under John Neville, probably based at Pontefract, and in Westmorland and Cumberland under Lord FitzHugh and Richard Salkeld, Warwick's Warden of Carlisle, remained to guard against a genuine uprising by the Percy affinity. John Conyers also stayed behind for the same reason, although his brother and namesake eldest son marched with Ogle.

Despite this, starting with Warkworth, Hall and Vergil, historians have agreed Robin of Redesdale was the elder John Conyers, or failing that his brother William. Apart from the highly suggestive *nom de guerre*, the principal reason for believing he was more certainly Lord Ogle is the skill and boldness with which the campaign was conducted. Neither John nor William Conyers had experience of independent command, and the only other candidate with the necessary qualities was Scrope of Bolton, who dropped out of the conspiracy once he realized its lethal intent towards his king and Garter brother.

Warwick's initial plan was to draw Edward north so that he and Clarence should not encounter any opposition when they landed in south-eastern England and made a triumphal entrance into

London, just as he and Edward had done in 1460. If all went as anticipated he would then march up the western spur of the Great North Road (Map 4) to trap Edward between his anvil and Ogle's hammer. Meanwhile his retainers in the east Midlands would create a blocking force to prevent Edward escaping to the Yorkist heartland in the Welsh Marches.

Edward was remarkably ill-informed throughout the campaign. He had neglected to cultivate alternative eyes and ears in the North, such that Clarence's treachery meant the only news he received about events north of the Trent was what the conspirators wanted him to believe. For their purposes he needed to know about the Robin of Redesdale revolt, but not that it was sufficiently serious to warrant his prompt return to London, there to await reinforcement by the Yorkist magnates.

However, his fateful decision to deal with the rebellion from his own resources also suggests that someone close to him was giving him very bad advice indeed, and the only viable suspect is William Hastings. Not only was he Warwick's brother-in-law, he was also (since late 1468) steward for the earl's estates in Northamptonshire, Leicestershire and Rutland, where he was a major landowner in his own right.* Edward had also entrusted Hastings with stewardship of the Yorkist affinity in the east Midlands, including Stamford, Grantham and, most recently, Fotheringhay. Their peregrination had taken them through or close to Hastings's own estates in Norfolk and Lincolnshire.

Even though Edward was belatedly joined by the Dukes of Norfolk and Suffolk, they would have come only with their retinues and most of the troops who marched with him to Newark were Hastings's men. This would explain why Edward sent the Woodvilles away on 9 July, when he belatedly obtained accurate information about the size of Robin of Redesdale's army and learned that it was

---

*The core of his lordship were the castles at Ashby-de-la-Zouche, Bagworth and Kirby, occupying a broad band of territory running north-west from Leicester and equidistant from Nottingham and Coventry.

12. EDGCOTE CAMPAIGN 1469

0   25   50   75
miles

© Hugh Bicheno

CHRONOLOGY OF THE 1469 EDGCOTE CAMPAIGN

End May	Edward learns of 'Robin of Holderness' rebellion, cancels plan to go with Warwick to Sandwich for the blessing of Warwick's rebuilt flagship *Trinity*, to review the fleet and travel to Calais.
Early June	Edward issues commissions of array to dukes, earls, barons and judges across the country.
9 June	Warwick is joined in Sandwich by Archbishop Neville.
12 June	The archbishop blesses the *Trinity*.
13 June	Edward, Gloucester, Hastings, Rivers, Scales *et al* depart Windsor on pilgrimage.
14 June	Edward visits Archbishop Neville at More Palace in Hertfordshire; Clarence at Canterbury.
15 June	Clarence and Duchess Cecily to Sandwich.
15–17 June	Edward at the shrine of St Edmund in Bury St Edmunds.
18 June	Edward first learns of Robin of Redesdale manifesto and uprising.
19 June	Edward at Norwich; Duchess Cecily to Canterbury.
20 June	Edward orders royal artillery sent from London up the Great North Road and royal wardrobe to supply 1,000 House of York liveries, banners, etc.
21 June	Edward at the shrine of Our Lady of Walsingham; Duchess Cecily in London.
22–24 June	Warwick at Canterbury, sends 'get busy' order to Yorkshire, travels to Sandwich.
24–28 June	Edward at Castle Rising, Bishop's Lynn and Crowland Abbey.
29 June	Edward at Fotheringhay, joined by Elizabeth; Warwick in London, announces he will join Edward after the forthcoming marriage of Clarence and his daughter Isabel.
1 July	Edward's party joined by Dukes of Norfolk and Suffolk.
4–6 July	Conspirators joined at Sandwich by Earl of Oxford, sail to Calais.

5–8 July	Edward marches up Great North Road through Stamford and Grantham to Newark.
9 July	Edward marches to Nottingham, sends Rivers, Scales and John Woodville away; summons Pembroke and Devon to join him in all haste, summons archers from Coventry.
11 July	Archbishop Neville marries Clarence and Isabel in Calais.
13 July	Conspirators to Sandwich, issue manifesto enlarging on Robin of Redesdale's.
16–19 July	Conspirators recruit at Canterbury.
20 July	Warwick's army enters London; Clarence and Isabel with Duchess Cecily.
26–27 July	Warwick and army march to Northampton.
26 July	BATTLE OF EDGCOTE
27 July	Warwick beheads Pembroke and brother Richard at Northampton.
28–29 July	Edward disperses his troops, departs Nottingham with Gloucester and Hastings, surrenders to Archbishop Neville at Olney.
10–12 August	Rivers and John Woodville captured near Monmouth, beheaded by Warwick at Coventry.
13 August	Thomas Herbert beheaded at Bristol.
17 August	Humphrey Stafford (the 'three-month earl') lynched in Bridgwater.

marching down the western spur of the Great North Road. Facing a far more serious challenge than he expected, the bad blood between the Woodvilles and Hastings made it impolitic to keep them by his side. No doubt Hastings also urged him to send them away, supposedly to make it easier to negotiate with the rebels.

The most likely explanation is that Hastings was privy to Warwick's plans, but only with regard to their common desire to depose the Woodvilles. Expecting the usual show of force followed by negotiation, he would have been as shocked as Edward by the size of the northern army and the purposeful speed with which it marched south. There is ample reason to suspect Hastings had crafted a situation where Edward would be powerless to protect his in-laws, but did not anticipate that the purpose of the revolt was to supplant the king as well.

Warwick must have assured Hastings that he would continue to enjoy his status at court in a Warwick-dominated administration. Now, when it became clear the threat from the North was far deadlier than he had anticipated, Hastings realized that Warwick intended the king's destruction. As he and Edward marched from Newark to Nottingham to stand across the rebel line of advance with what they now knew was an inadequate army, frantic summons were sent galloping to Herbert in south Wales and Stafford of Southwyck in the West Country.

Meanwhile the main thrust of Warwick's strategy went ahead. The first step was to cement his alliance with Clarence, who duly signed a prenuptial agreement to make Warwick his chief councillor and restore Archbishop Neville to the chancellorship when he became king. Clarence and Isabel were married on 11 July and on the 13th Warwick, Clarence and Archbishop Neville issued a manifesto echoing Robin of Redesdale's word for word, and expanding on it. Published under the seals of the two richest laymen and the richest prelate in the kingdom, the insolent audacity of the text was breathtaking:

> First, when the said Kings estranged the great lords of their blood from their private Council and not advised by them, and taking about them others not of their blood and inclining only to their counsel, rule and advice, the which persons take no consideration to the weal [welfare] of the said princes, nor to the commonweal of this land, but only to their singular lucre and enriching of themselves and their blood, as well in their great possessions as in goods; by which the said princes were so

impoverished that they had not sufficient of livelihood nor of goods, whereby they might keep and maintain their honourable estate and ordinary charges within this realm.

The proclamation went on to allege that Edward's alienation of crown lands – of which Warwick and Clarence had been major beneficiaries – had prevented him from living within his means, as he had promised, and so led to burdensome taxation, the misappropriation of money voted for war with France, and of church contributions intended for a crusade.

The 'evil councillors' were enumerated, to reassure Hastings and others that they were not threatened. They were Earl Rivers, his wife Jacquetta and their sons, the Earls of Pembroke and Devon, Lord Audley and John Fogge. Audley's inclusion probably stemmed from a desire to distribute his lands among Warwick's Midlands affinity. Fogge was Edward's household treasurer and had participated in the despoiling of Thomas Cooke, but he was also an unpopular landlord in Kent, the next stop for the conspirators.

The manifesto announced they would be at Canterbury on 16 July and summoned all 'true subjects' to be there in arms. As Warden of the Cinque Ports Warwick had prepared the ground in Lydd, Rye, Hythe and Dover, which sent contingents to meet him at Sandwich when he arrived with part of the Calais garrison on 13 July. The conspirators were already at the head of a large, well-armed force when they arrived at Canterbury, where the mayor paraded the militia to greet and join them. Their numbers swelled rapidly as the commons of Kent, led by their captains, flocked to join what promised to be a profitable party.

One of the stronger indications of Warwick's hope to kill Edward in battle is that he was careful to keep his new son-in-law uncontaminated. Clarence remained with his mother in London, and his retainers in Yorkshire did not join Ogle's army. It was still Warwick's intention to trap Edward in the Midlands, but the king's move to Nottingham and the speed with which Herbert and Stafford responded to his summons required a change of plan. Ogle left the western spur at Rotherham, marched south to Chesterfield and then rapidly across country to Coventry, bypassing Edward at Nottingham.

The next stage was crucial. When Ogle left Coventry he marched towards Northampton to rendezvous with Warwick, who was marching up the St Albans–Bedford branch of the western spur. Warwick's advance was slowed by the guns required to give battle to Edward, who was well equipped with them, so he sent his fore-riders on ahead to Northampton under Geoffrey Gates, his marshal at Calais. Among them were Thomas Parr, youngest son of William Parr, lord of Kendal in Westmorland (who was riding with Ogle), and John Clapham, one of Warwick's Midlands esquires of the body.

Ogle's march took him across the path Herbert and Stafford would have to follow if they were to join Edward at Nottingham, and their respective outriders soon came into contact. The stage was set for one of the most fiercely fought battles of the Wars of the Roses after Towton, which it uncannily resembled in terms of battlefield evolution. It may well have been even bloodier as a pro-portion of the men engaged, and its impact on English history may have been greater.

SHOWDOWN

NEITHER EDWARD NOR WARWICK WANTED THEIR subordinates to fight. Edward desperately needed re-inforcements, and Warwick's revised plan was for a united army to stand on ground of his choosing between the king and London, forcing him to attack. The plan was the same as it had been when he was defeated at the Second Battle of St Albans in 1461 – it was typical of the man that he did not doubt its essential soundness. Instead, their subordinates sought each other out for reasons of their own – and what those reasons were defined the battle that ensued.

Ogle's decision to seek a battle was probably the result of learning Herbert and Stafford had divided their forces, with Herbert at Banbury and Stafford several miles away on the Fosse Way. This was the Roman road running from Exeter through Cirencester, where they had initially joined forces, which would take them most directly to Edward (Map 3). Ogle, immensely experienced in the fast-moving northern Marcher tradition, would have jumped at the opportunity to attack before they could join up again.

So, the key question is why the two royal contingents became separated. The generally accepted version, based on Edward Hall's account, is that Herbert and Stafford, responding to the urgent summons to join him as soon as possible by the king, inexplicably turned aside to seek battle with Ogle. They then fell out with one another when battle was imminent, allegedly over lodging at Banbury and/or a wench. As a result, Herbert fought the battle without archers, who were under Stafford's command.

To take the last point first, it is absurd to believe that Herbert, who won Mortimer's Cross for Edward with an arrow storm, would have marched without a full contingent of Welsh longbowmen, or that he might have transferred them to Stafford. It is far more likely that, surrounded by the flower of Welsh chivalry, Herbert saw it as a unique opportunity to save the regime singlehandedly and to smash the northern Neville affinity, paving the way for the restoration of Henry Percy, his ward and soon-to-be son-in-law.

Another – improbable but not inconceivable – explanation is that Stafford was a traitor, in keeping with Warwick's modus operandi of cultivating Trojan Horses within enemy ranks. This was the view of the mob in Yorkist Bridgwater that lynched Stafford when he returned there after the debacle, according to Hall on Edward's orders. The unanswerable objection to this theory is that Herbert rushed into battle knowing full well that Stafford was out of supporting range.

No – Herbert side-lined Stafford so that he should not share the glory, and both sides sought battle for the oldest of all reasons: from time to time men are overcome by an impulse to do reckless things simply because they are men. Herbert and Ogle were alpha males in their respective warrior cultures, in command of men trained for combat from childhood and accustomed to victory in battle. The intoxicating prospect of putting their skills to the test against a worthy opponent was irresistible.

The decisive pre-battle event was a major skirmish on the 24th, which came about after Herbert's fore-riders reported sighting enemy stragglers somewhere between Daventry and Northampton. He sent a large mounted force to attack them, which found that the alleged stragglers were the rearguard of a considerable army. Now aware of each other's presence, Ogle returned to Daventry and Herbert left the Fosse Way and marched towards Banbury, a distance of 12–15 miles. This is when he parted company with Stafford, after a violent disagreement over disregarding Edward's orders.

The 25th would have seen the two armies closing on each other behind screens of mounted scouts, and in one encounter Henry Neville, eldest son of demented Lord Latimer, was captured and beheaded. This announced there would be no prisoners taken in the impending battle. Ogle marched south from Daventry and diverged from the main Banbury road to camp for the night on Byfield Plain, next to a ford over the River Cherwell (today's Trafford Bridge), which at this point is only 20 feet wide and 2 feet deep.

That night Herbert rested his army at Banbury and the next morning marched through Upper Wardington to Edgcote Hill, knowing Ogle had crossed the Cherwell and formed up on a hill about a mile away between two rivulets and overlooking the plain of Danes Moor, an area of fields divided by another rivulet and belonging, according to *Hearne's Fragment*, to Richard Clarell, 'a gentleman of Edgcote', one of many villages depopulated by the Black Death.

By this time both commanders knew whom they were facing and in what strength, so if they sought battle it was because they were of roughly equal numbers – perhaps 6–7,000 each. If the planned high speed railway project (HS2) goes ahead it will create an unrepeatable occasion for archaeologists to obtain funding to excavate the Edgcote battlefield before it is destroyed. Should that come to pass we will have some definitive answers. Until then the following is an interpretation based on the terrain and the personalities involved.*

Supposedly Ogle induced Herbert to leave his strong position by harassing him with archery, to which he could not make reply because of Stafford's absence. This is a variant on Hall's account of the opening phase at Towton and is no less nonsensical. The killing range for heavy war arrows was not much greater than 50 yards, and archers did not waste their arrows in the long-range parabolic shooting beloved of film-makers. Herbert paused only long enough to dress his lines and then attacked. If anyone was short of archers it was Ogle, as the Welshmen came to hand strokes without any serious check to their momentum.

Ogle's men would have made a short charge down the hill to meet them and so, if my reconstruction is correct, the first brutal encounter would have taken place more or less exactly on the line planned for the HS2 railway. The northmen gave way and were driven back over the hill where they had first formed up, suffering terrible losses. Ogle himself was mortally wounded and with him fell the only son of Lord Greystoke and both John Conyers's namesake son and his brother William. The fall of so many senior officers was a sign their army was disintegrating, a view that supports an anecdote in Hall's account:

---

*N.B. The depth of the rectangles in this and other battle maps is dictated by labelling and bears no relation to the likely deployment, which would have been perhaps 5–6 ranks deep and far less ordered in attack.

The Earl of Pembroke behaved himself like a hardy knight and expert captain, but his brother Sir Richard Herbert so valiantly acquitted himself that with his poleaxe in hand (as his enemies did afterwards report) he was by fine force passed through the battle of his adversaries and without any mortal wound returned. If every one of his followers and companions in arms had done but half the acts which he that day by his noble prowess achieved, the Northmen had obtained neither valour nor victory.

But then it was Towton all over again – an army on the point of annihilation was saved by the last minute arrival of reinforcements who appeared to the enemy rear, and the sudden dislocation of expectations turned the exultant Welshmen into a fleeing mob:

> When the Welshmen were at the very point to have obtained the victory (the Northmen being in manner discomforted) John Clapham Esquire, servant of the Earl of Warwick, mounted up the side of the east hill accompanied only with 500 men gathered of all the rascals of the town of Northampton and other villages about, having borne before them the standard of the earl with the white bear, crying 'a Warwick, a Warwick'. The Welshmen thinking that the Earl of Warwick had come on them with all his puissance, so that as men amazed fled: the Northmen then pursued and slew without mercy for the cruelty they had shown Lord Latimer's son. So that of the Welshmen there was slain about 5,000 besides them that were fled and taken.

Some of Herbert's men crossed the Cherwell and were hunted down as they fled. The road running between Chipping Warden and Job's Hill is still known as the Welsh Road, and there are indications there may be mass graves in the nearby churchyard. Welsh sources confirm that Herbert's affinity, the cream of the south Wales aristocracy, was slaughtered, but not before doing terrible damage to the northern Neville affinity.

· ❧ ·

Ironically, in defeat Herbert still achieved one of his objectives. The reduction in Neville military power permitted and to some extent demanded the restoration of Henry Percy as Earl of Northumberland, and he kept his word and did eventually marry one of Herbert's daughters. Neither William nor Richard Herbert lived to see it. The earl and his brother were captured and brought before Warwick at Northampton. Despite William's pleas that his brother be spared, both were beheaded without even the pretence of a trial.

Warwick also sent Clapham and others including Edward Grey, Queen Elizabeth's brother-in-law from her first marriage, to seize Earl Rivers at his manor of Grafton, 10 miles south of Northampton. On 12 August both he and his son John, the dowager Duchess of Norfolk's young husband, were summarily executed at Gosford Green outside Coventry. Even nobles who had resented the rise of the Herberts and the Woodvilles, and would have celebrated their fall from power, were appalled by these cold-blooded murders.

Warwick may have forced Edward to witness the death of his father-in-law, for by this time the king was his captive at Coventry. On learning of the disaster at Edgcote Edward had set off from Nottingham towards London, ordering his army to disperse. Suffolk and Norfolk returned to their counties. The king travelled only in the company of his brother Richard and Hastings, and at the village of Olney, 10 miles south-east of Northampton, he surrendered to Archbishop Neville, who arrived in full harness.

The surrender was probably negotiated by Hastings, by now horribly aware his friend might be killed should he fall into the hands of Warwick's servants. By accepting Edward's surrender George Neville became the guarantor of his life, which suggests he also feared his brother would commit the ultimate act of *lèse majesté*, which Cardinal Archbishop Bourchier would condemn in the strongest terms, and which risked turning every man's hand against them.

Sadly there is no record of what passed between Warwick and Edward at Coventry, whence the king was transferred to Warwick Castle. While there, a repellent individual called Thomas Wake, a Northampton man whose son had been killed at Edgcote and who was among those who seized Rivers, produced alleged proof that Jacquetta had employed witchcraft to bring about the marriage of her daughter and the king, and the destruction of Warwick. The 'proof' of the latter was a leaden figure like a man-at-arms, broken in the middle and wired together.

Jacquetta appealed to the mayor and aldermen of London, who demanded to examine the case against her. In due course Wake and a parish clerk who had testified to the existence of two other images, of the king and Elizabeth, were questioned and the clerk recanted his testimony. They were not punished for their perjury, but in January 1470 Jacquetta obtained a formal and published vindication by the Great Council, which both Warwick and Clarence signed.

Before travelling to London Warwick transferred Edward to the custody of John Conyers at Middleham, where he could be kept isolated. Warwick may have hoped for a popular apotheosis when he rode into London, similar to the last occasion he had rebelled against a king in 1460, but if so he was disappointed. He also found that the king's senior officials accepted his orders so long as they bore the king's signet, and gave him no excuse to dismiss them.

Accordingly, he could promote only one of his followers to high office. This was John Langstrother, acting Prior of St John's Hospital, a lucrative post Edward had wished to award to the younger Richard Woodville. Warwick made Langstrother Lord Treasurer to replace Rivers, while taking Herbert's Welsh offices for himself and, tellingly, making Hastings chamberlain of north Wales. To punish Archbishop Neville for having guaranteed Edward's life he chose not to appoint him Lord Chancellor, as previously agreed.

One can deduce that the Bourchiers and other leading magnates told Warwick that he had gone far enough, and that they would come out against him if he harmed the king. He must, perforce, govern with the king's consent. Baffled to find that victory had won him so little, on 8 August Warwick obtained Edward's signet on a summons for a Parliament to meet at York on 22 September. The stated agenda was to 'arrange the government of the realm', but the realm rapidly demonstrated that there was no time for such formalities.

First, there were riots in London that threatened to overwhelm authorities uncertain whether the disturbances were prompted by Warwick. They were only subdued when a large embassy of Burgundian knights, in town to arrange the reciprocal appointments of Duke Charles and Edward to their respective orders of chivalry (the Golden Fleece and the Garter), made it clear they would act if the authorities did not. Charles also sent a letter to the mayor and aldermen promising help and protection if they were faithful to Edward and to the Burgundian alliance, and dire retribution if they were not.

The London riots were only one of many breakdowns of law and order. Thanks to the *Paston Letters* we are best acquainted with the Duke of Norfolk's assault on Caister Castle. Having failed to win it by legal means, on 21 August Norfolk besieged the castle with a large force and artillery, and repeatedly rejected demands from the Council in London to submit to arbitration by Archbishop Neville. He also treated personal pleas from Clarence with contempt. 'He would not spare to do as he is purposed for no duke in England', he replied.

The defenders capitulated on 27 September and Norfolk held the castle until his death in 1476, when at last the Pastons secured possession of a property whose title they had obtained in the first place by prevailing on a dying old man to will it to them, or possibly forging the will. It is a fascinating story of stubbornly maintained legalistic skulduggery by commoners in the face of apoplectic outrage by two generations of one of the most eminent noble families in the land, something unimaginable in any other European kingdom.

As it affects our main narrative the siege of Caister simply serves to highlight that while Warwick had won a measure of control over the apparatus of government, he had failed to achieve authority. Warwick found himself at a loss, probably for the first time in his life, and then things got humiliatingly worse. He had to admit failure and cancel the Parliament because the next major challenge underlined the degree to which the coup had also eroded his own power, in his ancestral heartlands.

It will be recalled that Humphrey Neville, a nephew of the demented Earl of Westmorland, managed to negotiate a pardon when he surrendered Bamburgh Castle in 1464. Although his branch of the Neville clan was senior, they had lost much of their birth right when the 1st Earl of Westmorland willed it to the children of his second marriage to Joan Beaufort, who included Warwick's father and Cecily, the king's mother. As a result the Nevilles of Brancepeth and Raby hated their cousins of Middleham with an abiding passion.

Consequently, when Humphrey and his brother Charles raised the standard of Lancaster in Northumberland in August 1469 it was above all a threat to Warwick's northern hegemony. Despite this, the earl found he could not raise sufficient troops from his own resources to suppress the rebellion. This was a startling development and strongly suggests that, following the bloodbath at Edgcote, Warwick's most dependable retainers were no longer willing to go to war at his command. Even his brother John, Earl of Northumberland, held back.

Defied on every side, Warwick had to yield to pressure from his peers to release Edward, who regained freedom of action in calculated stages. On 10 September he was allowed to make a public appearance in York, where his call for men to join Warwick against the rebellion met with an immediate response. Warwick marched north and quickly dispersed the uprising, capturing Humphrey and Charles. In his absence Edward moved to Pontefract and summoned brother Richard, his uncle the Earl of Essex and the Earls of Arundel, Suffolk and, most tellingly, of Northumberland, plus Lords Hastings and Mountjoy.

When Warwick returned to York with his captives, who were beheaded in Edward's presence on 27 September, he found the king acclaimed by the populace and flanked by some of the highest in the land. There can be no doubt Edward was coldly determined to be avenged, but a combination of prudence and the unanimous urging of his loyal lords to avoid a civil war led him to do no more than announce he was returning to London, and that Warwick should remain in York to complete the pacification of the North.

Warwick tried to salvage something from the wreck by sending Archbishop Neville to join the king's party as it entered London, but when he and the Earl of Oxford approached, according to John Paston 'the king sent them a messenger that they should come [when] he sent for them'.

XIII

BITER BIT

THE BALANCE OF POWER HAD TIPPED BACK TO EDWARD, but not enough to permit him to punish the crimes committed against him. He promptly set about shifting it further in his favour, but he had to move carefully. Expecting more immediate retribution, Clarence joined Warwick in the North and they ostentatiously rode around the region with a small army of their respective retainers. Any military move against them would have precipitated the civil war that even the most loyal Yorkist magnates were anxious to avoid.

Since Warwick had done so little to change government personnel it was uncontentious to reverse the few appointments he had made. Langstrother was dismissed as Lord Treasurer but confirmed as Prior of St John's. William Grey, the immensely wealthy Bishop of Ely, was appointed in his place. With the Herbert affinity almost annihilated, Edward appointed 17-year-old Richard, Duke of Gloucester, with the guidance of Lord Ferrers, as the temporary custodian of the Welsh offices that Warwick had awarded himself and Hastings.

This was the only sign Edward ever gave that he disapproved of Hastings's conduct. Hindsight permits us to be tolerably sure his role during the early stages of the Edgcote campaign was disloyal, but the irresponsible behaviour of Herbert and suspected treachery of Stafford had been much worse. With his scheme for regional control of the West Country and Wales in ruins, Edward could not afford to alienate his remaining henchmen.

He did signal a major policy reversal with regard to the North by releasing Henry Percy, whom Warwick and Clarence had placed in the Tower, and accepting his oath of fealty on 27 October. The presence of Cardinal Bourchier, two bishops, two dukes and five barons underlined the importance of the ceremony. The Earls of Arundel and Kent, Lord Treasurer Bishop Grey, and Lord Ferrers in representation of the late Lord Herbert, whose ward Henry had been, posted surety of £8,000.

The writing was on the wall for Percy's restoration to the earldom of Northumberland in place of John Neville, whose loyalty Edward still seems not to have doubted. John had to go because he had failed to win over the Percy affinity, and who knew how long the Scots court, egged on by Louis XI, would resist the traditional temptation to take advantage of English weakness? Restoring Percy had become a geopolitical imperative, and all that could be done was to soften the blow for John Neville.

Edward strained the limits of appeasement to keep John from making common cause with his brothers. On 6 November he announced his intention to recreate the dukedom of Bedford, previously reserved for members of the royal family, for John's 4-year-old son George, effective on 5 January 1470. He also announced the betrothal of young George to his eldest daughter, 3-year-old Elizabeth. Edward ruled that the Yorkist claim to the throne through the female line would continue, and this was duly certified by the Great Council. If no male heir was born and the two children outlived Edward, a Neville would become king. George would also inherit the pick of Warwick's northern lands, which were entailed in the male line.*

Percy was restored to his family estates as the months advanced, at the expense of the Nevilles and Clarence. Edward compensated

*The large lordships of Penrith (Cumberland), Sheriff Hutton (Yorkshire) and Middleham (Richmondshire).

only John, awarding him many of the lands, offices and wardships previously enjoyed by Stafford of Southwyck. As well as making him an honorary member of the royal family, he was clearly being invited to become the regime lock on the West Country. Eventually, when Percy was restored as Earl of Northumberland, Edward created the new marquessate of Montagu for John, which gave him a higher rank than Warwick. It is hard to see what more the king could have done.

This has not stopped historians citing the alleged poverty of John's new endowment as the reason for his later disaffection, without considering how little income he had derived from the surly Percy estates. Edward failed to keep his loyalty because he never had it. John was guilty, at best, of 'misprision' in the Robin of Redesdale conspiracy, and of conflating it with the Robin of Holderness revolt. His misrepresentations persuaded Edward not to follow up on the nationwide commissions of array he had issued, and to embark on a pilgrimage with only a ceremonial retinue. There is more than sufficient reason to believe John Neville, not the unfortunate Stafford of Southwyck, had been Warwick's Trojan Horse all along.

Edward summoned Warwick and Clarence to attend the Great Council that convened on 18 November. They eventually came, no doubt persuaded to do so by Edward issuing commissions of array on 29 October to everyone except those who had lately rebelled against him. It was an imposing display of the king's latent power, attended by the Dukes of Gloucester, Norfolk and Suffolk, the Earls of Arundel, Kent, Essex and Northumberland, and Barons Dacre, Dynham, Ferrers of Chartley, Hastings and Mountjoy. Cardinal Bourchier and five bishops also attended. Polydore Vergil's account rings true:

> Both the authority and the entreaty of the nobility so moved the mind of the king and earl, that, upon mutual promise of assurance made, the earl himself and the Duke of Clarence came to London, guarded with a slender crew of soldiers in respect of so

great danger, and had at Westminster long talk with the king concerning composition [settlement].

The Council persuaded Edward to issue a general pardon for all offences committed before Christmas, an insolent demand by Warwick and Clarence that allowed a further month of impunity for crimes yet to be committed. Against this they were compelled to assent to a series of measures transparently aimed at them. The stinging vindication of Jacquetta was one, and they could hardly oppose either the promotion of young George, the sole legitimate male heir any of the Nevilles had produced, or the appointment of Richard of Gloucester to Herbert's Welsh offices and as Constable of England in replacement of murdered Earl Rivers.

Although Anthony, Lord Scales, did not attend the Council, he reappeared at court using his father's title, and there were other indications Edward regarded the 'composition' as no more than a truce, among them measures to repair the Herbert affinity. Herbert's widow, resident at her brother Lord Ferrers's manor at Weobley in Herefordshire, was granted the wardship of her 14-year-old son, now Earl of Pembroke and also married to Mary Woodville. The idea was that in due course he would fill his father's shoes, but he proved a disappointment and never assumed the offices held for him by Gloucester.

Further writing on the wall was the partial rehabilitation of Humphrey Dacre, heir to the attainted Dacre barony whose lordship around Norham Castle in Cumberland was exercised by Warwick. Although Dacre was not yet restored, the intention was plain and in conjunction with the return of the large lordship of Cockermouth to Henry Percy it would undermine the hegemony in the West March enjoyed by Warwick since 1461. Also, when Warwick's demented uncle Lord Latimer died on 30 December, Cardinal Bourchier was awarded the wardship of Latimer's baby grandson and heir, and Warwick lost the custodianship of the large estate around Corby in Northamptonshire he had exercised since 1447.

Clarence's situation was even more precarious. He held all his lands at the king's pleasure, what he had regarded as his appanage was shrinking, and his status as heir presumptive was officially revoked in favour of Princess Elizabeth. It is not remarkable, therefore, that he initiated the next roll of the dice – the only surprise is that Warwick went along with a scheme not under his complete control. This may be evidence of a fracture in his carapace of self-regard, brought about by the abject failure of his *coup d'état*.

The Council was dissolved in early February and Edward immediately initiated a sequence of events that was to end with Warwick and Clarence fleeing the country. The contemporary *Chronicle of the Rebellion in Lincolnshire* has so much corroboration from other sources that it was not until 1988 that any modern historian took a close look at the timing. This argues persuasively that Edward set a trap for his enemies and fabricated evidence, and that the *Chronicle* is a masterly work of propaganda. The chronology opposite Map 14 is based on the *Chronicle*, with the points of factual manipulation in italics.*

This being the case, the idea of Edward as merely a gonad-led playboy crumbles. There were no 'evil councillors' – Edward alone was the architect and protagonist of his cause. He showed intelligent resolution in working his way free of Warwick's control, and in the months that followed acted moderately at the urgent behest of the Council; but from the start he hoped to provoke his enemies into breaking the peace and, once freed of the Council's restraint, did so.

· ❧ ·

*See P. Holland, 'The Lincolnshire rebellion of March 1470', *English Historical Review* (October 1988). In 1903 Charles Oman had come to the same conclusion, but on the basis of intrinsically fallacious 'after which therefore because of which' reasoning.

The fuse for the next round of violence was lit by Lord Welles, a supposedly reconciled Lancastrian and Lincolnshire magnate who had served (as Lord Willoughby, his secondary title) under Warwick in 1462–4, and owed him a debt of gratitude for the reversal of the Welles attainder. While Welles was of his affinity, Warwick had no local landed presence, whereas the king had given Clarence the extensive Lincolnshire lands of the attainted and executed Lord Roos and the infamous Tailboys.

Edward summoned Lord Welles and his brother-in-law Thomas Dymock to London to answer for the destruction of the main Lincolnshire manor house of Thomas Burgh, the king's Master of Horse. Burgh had risen to local prominence thanks to Edward's patronage, and the Welles affinity would not have dared attack him had they not believed the king too weakened by Edgcote and his captivity to retaliate. If, as seems likely, the assault took place in November or December 1469, it was covered by Edward's general pardon.

It is believable that Welles's defiance of Edward's authority should have prompted Clarence to invite him to join some future uprising; however, the chronology too neatly assigns this to early February, before Edward issued an order for his local retainers to meet him at Grantham on 12 March. The *Chronicle* had to make this assertion, because otherwise it was Edward's order that tipped the first domino. When he subsequently summoned Welles and Dymock they may have believed they were sheltered by the general pardon, and only fled to sanctuary at Westminster Abbey when they learned that the king did not share their view.

Clarence apparently did stir the pot by warning Welles's eldest son Robert that the king intended to lead a punitive expedition into Lincolnshire – but this was also the only interpretation that could be placed on Edward's military preparations. The pardon for the assault on Burgh's manor he issued on 3 March was belied by his order on the same day to start the royal artillery rolling up the Great North Road. There followed an episode that awoke Edward

14. LOSECOTE CAMPAIGN 1470

CHRONOLOGY OF THE 1470 LOSECOTE CAMPAIGN

2 February	Clarence invites Richard, Lord Welles, to join a 'great uprising'. *Some time before this* a mob incited by Welles, his son Robert and his brothers-in-law Thomas Dymock and Thomas de la Lande sack the manor house of Thomas Burgh at Gainsborough, Lincolnshire.
9 February	Edward orders Yorkist retainers to meet him at Grantham on 12 March.
22 February	Edward summons Lord Welles and Dymock, who seek sanctuary in Westminster Abbey.
3 March	Clarence warns Robert Welles the king is coming in force to punish Lincolnshire. Edward issues a general pardon for the sack of Burgh's manor, but also mobilizes the royal artillery.
4 March	Robert Welles summons the Lincolnshire commons to assemble at Ranby on 6 March. Clarence at Duchess Cecily's London palace – *they delay Edward's departure for two days.*
6 March	Edward, Clarence, the Earl of Arundel, Henry Percy, Hastings and other lords travel to Ware.
7 March	Edward to Waltham Abbey. *Clarence returns to London with commissions of array for himself and Warwick,* meets Welles, Dymock and John Langstrother, Prior of St John's Hospital.
8 March	Edward to Royston, learns of the rebellion and sends for Welles and Dymock. Receives first letter from Warwick and Clarence, who are together at Warwick.
9 March	Edward to Huntingdon, interrogates Welles and Dymock who confess *but do not implicate Clarence and Warwick.* Welles ordered on pain of death to instruct his son to stand down.
10 March	Warwick and Clarence send second letter. *Robert Welles marching to meet them at Leicester.*
11 March	Edward at Fotheringhay. Warwick and Clarence to Coventry, joined by William Parr. On receipt of his father's letter, Robert Welles turns south down the Great North Road towards Stamford.

12 March	Edward arrives at Stamford at midday, writes to Warwick and Clarence thanking them for their promised support, learns the rebels are arrayed for battle 5 miles to the north. BATTLE OF LOSECOTE FIELD – Lord Welles and Dymock beheaded.
13 March	Warwick and Clarence still at Coventry. *Captured letters confirm their treachery. Edward summons them to his presence, appoints Worcester Constable of England.*
14 March	Edward at Grantham. *Robert Welles's confession.* Warwick and Clarence write that they will join him at Retford. Scrope of Bolton and John Conyers disband troops assembled in Richmond.
16–17 March	Edward at Newark. Warwick and Clarence at Burton-on-Trent, Derby and Chesterfield.
17–19 March	Edward at Doncaster, executes Robert Welles and de la Lande. Warwick and Clarence march to Sheffield, hoping to rendezvous with Conyers.
20 March	Edward to Rotherham. Warwick and Clarence to Manchester, Lord Stanley stays away. Viscount Lisle killed in private battle with Lord Berkeley at Nibley Green.
21 March	Edward to Pontefract, Richard of Gloucester approaching Manchester from the west. Warwick and Clarence march south and collect Warwick's family. William Parr defects.
22–28 March	Edward at York. Scrope, Conyers, Parr and Robert Hildyard make submission and are pardoned. Henry Percy restored as Earl of Northumberland. Warwick and Clarence at Bristol with 5,000 men, they disband them and abandon their artillery.
29 March	Edward at Nottingham, marches south through Coventry and Warwick.
3–10 April	Warwick and Clarence at Exeter, then set sail from Dartmouth.
11–14 April	Edward at Wells and Exeter. Warwick's raid on Southampton defeated.

to the possibility of using the disturbance to smoke out his brother and Warwick.

The *Chronicle* would have it that Clarence invited Edward to meet him at Baynard's Castle, their mother's London palace, in order to delay his departure, giving time for Robert Welles to summon the Lincolnshire commons. Yet why would Edward have set out on the heels of his artillery? The guns needed several days' head start, and his aim was to be in Lincolnshire by 12 March, which indeed he was. Clarence's amiability and professed willingness to join him in the expedition was transparently a ruse – how best to take advantage of it?

Clarence set out with the royal party, but after the first stop at Ware he returned to London with commissions of array issued for himself and Warwick. Since Edward had returned from captivity they had been pointedly excluded from all judicial and military commissions, and he did not need their support to overawe Lincolnshire – indeed, he only learned of the uprising the following day; so what was this all about? Bearing in mind the manner in which Warwick had exploited commissions of array to prepare the 1469 *coup d'état*, much the most likely explanation is that Edward was enticing his enemies to try again.

The great unknown of the ensuing campaign is why Warwick let himself be carried away by Clarence's opportunism. Robert Welles certainly appealed to them for help, and he and many of his followers sported Clarence's livery. How many of Clarence's Lincolnshire affinity joined the rebellion is unknown – only two were later accused of participation, but this probably reflected Edward's desire to underplay his brother's role to Warwick's detriment. A mere eight days separate Welles's call for the commons to rally at Ranby and the Battle of Losecote, so the livery coats constitute prima facie evidence of Clarence's prior complicity.

Even the *Chronicle* does not claim that Lord Welles and Dymock, when summoned by Edward to Huntingdon, implicated Warwick and Clarence in their confession to having plotted treason. The uprising seems to have been a rash initiative by Robert Welles, seeking to precipitate the more general rebellion that Clarence's messages had led him to believe was in preparation. If there were any such preparation it was in its early stages and, even with commissions of array for the Midlands counties, Warwick and Clarence were finding it difficult to recruit an army. They were still at Coventry when the battle took place.

The *Chronicle* says Robert Welles was leading his men to a rendezvous with Warwick and Clarence at Leicester when he received the letter from Lord Welles begging him to desist, at which point he marched south to rescue his father. When the armies came face to face just north of Stamford, with a ruthlessness he had not previously displayed Edward had Lord Welles and Dymock beheaded in full view of both sides. Robert, to whom his father had earlier passed the subsidiary Willoughby title, thus also became – very briefly – Lord Welles.*

The battle barely deserves the name, as Welles's men broke under artillery fire and fled, those wearing Clarence's livery shedding it as they ran – hence 'Losecote'. Edward had his brother dead to rights, but needed to implicate Warwick. This he did with the impossibly convenient battlefield capture of a box of incriminating letters, never published, and an alleged confession by Robert Welles: '[without] the said Duke and Earl's provoking we at this time would nere durst have made any commotion or stirring; but upon their comfort we did that we did'.

It was time to slam shut the jaws of the trap Edward had set when he issued the commissions of array to Clarence. He did this *before* Robert Welles was captured, but allegedly after the box of incriminating letters was discovered. In the morning of the day after the battle he sent letters sealed with his signet to the sheriffs of twenty-six counties ordering them to proclaim the victory and to announce that:

*Both titles passed to Richard, Lord Hastings's younger brother, through his marriage to Welles's sister Joan.

None of his subjects presume… to rise, nor make any assembly or gathering by reason of [commissions of array previously issued nor by the] commandment [of] any person or persons of whatever estate he be, unless it be by the King's commission newly issued after this 13th day of March.

It would not have taken long for Warwick and Clarence to have sight of this letter and to appreciate the snare Edward had set for them. Their efforts to recruit were being disowned and portrayed in a sinister light, yet the day before the battle Edward had written thanking them for their support and urging them to make haste to meet him. Had they done so, he would have defeated and slaughtered them along with their retainers.

Even if historians for years to come have bought the king's version, Warwick and Clarence knew he had trapped them. Worse, he had shown a previously unsuspected capacity for fair-faced deceit and malevolent *furbizia*. Six months later they complained that they had been the victims of 'false means and dissimulations', and indeed they had. Edward had paid them back with their own coin, and now they had to salvage what they could from the wreck.

XIV

NOISES OFF

R EADERS MAY BE WONDERING WHY LOUIS XI AND DUKE Charles abstained from involvement during the turmoil in England in 1469–70. The explanation is that they were fully occupied with matters that concerned them more, a reminder of how relatively unimportant England had become since losing its empire in France. Charles's attention was almost fully absorbed by his efforts to assert and expand his areas of authority, and Louis was still working to recover the authority he had lost by the Public Weal rebellion.*

As soon as Duke Philippe died on 15 June 1457, Louis began receiving reports of a revival of the alliance among Brittany, Burgundy, Alençon, Armagnac, Nemours and Savoy to replace him with his brother Charles. He was forced to negotiate short and humiliating truces with Burgundy and Brittany, later extended to 15 July 1468. In April he convoked the only assembly of the Estates General during his reign and listened to their grievances with every appearance of sympathy, and a ready wit that won over many.

He took only a little time out of his busy schedule to stir the English pot with Jasper Tudor's tiny expedition to Wales, mainly because Warwick was doing such a good job unprompted. He also vigorously libelled Edward's sister Margaret, but could not stop

---

*Readers will find it useful to bookmark Maps 6 and 7 for ease of reference while reading this chapter.

Duke Charles marrying her on 3 July, 'against his heart and nature' as Philippe Commynes put it. In the midst of the extravagant celebrations of the event Charles agreed to extend the truce for himself and his allies from 15 July to 1 August.

Duke Frañsez, who was sheltering Louis's brother, omitted to ratify the agreement and on 15 July Louis sent three armies into Brittany. Edward's expedition, led by Scales, failed to provide timely support, and on 10 September Frañsez was forced to sign the Treaty of Ancenis, by which he renounced all his alliances. Duke Charles was so enraged that Brittany Herald, the bearer of the bad news, feared for his life. Louis had created a situation where it was imperative to persuade the duke that, contrary to the evidence, he had not been duped.

There was no hope of renewing the truce whose spirit Louis had violated, and mercenaries flocked from all over Europe to join Charles's army in Picardy. Louis could see nothing he might gain that outweighed the likelihood of a revival of the Public Weal alliance should he suffer a military check, and was determined to avoid war. Confident he could charm the duke if they met face to face, he committed a potentially fatal error.

When Duke Philippe died the citizens of Liège, smarting from the loss of municipal privileges following a 1465 revolt against the installation of Louis de Bourbon as prince-bishop, and undeterred by the brutal suppression of the Dinant revolt the following year, rebelled again. They were crushed in battle and surrendered in November 1467, after which Charles made them degrade the city walls and declared Liège a Burgundian protectorate under his deputy Guy de Humbercourt.

Louis had encouraged the revolts with false promises of military support, but the Liègeois were slow learners. Incited by French agents, they rebelled again on 9 October 1468, capturing Humbercourt and the prince-bishop, whose palace was occupied by the rebel leader. On the same day Louis left behind the army that had lately overawed Brittany and rode to Charles's headquarters at

Péronne, 50 miles east of Amiens, with only a small retinue. If he had prior knowledge that the Liège revolt was imminent, it was a breathtakingly rash bluff.

We know a great deal about the sequel thanks to Philippe Commynes, who was closely involved in the proceedings. There is no reason to doubt that, as he boasted in his memoirs, he played a key role in the encounter between the king and the duke at Péronne. After he defected to Louis four years later the king's deed of gift to him specified that 'our councillor and chamberlain, without fear of the danger that could come to him, informed us of all he could for our welfare and so employed himself that by his means and aid we escaped'.

The meeting between Louis and Charles was arranged by Jacquetta's brother Louis, Count of Saint-Pol. While one would normally assume that anything involving Saint-Pol was steeped in treachery, Louis himself insisted on meeting Charles protected only by a safe conduct. His confidence was severely shaken on the day he arrived when four of his most bitter enemies, including his Savoyard brother-in-law Philippe of Bresse, rode past the splendid palace allotted to him. The mutual hatred of Louis and Bresse, born of reciprocal acts of treachery, was boundless, and the king immediately requested a move to the dilapidated castle of Péronne.

While assuring Louis that Bresse was merely on his way elsewhere, after negotiations on 9 October proved unsatisfactory Charles brought Bresse to their meeting the next day and insisted on presenting him to the king. This was considerably more than a nod as good as a wink, introducing an element of menace even before news of the Liège revolt arrived. Initial reports falsely asserted that Humbercourt and the prince-bishop had been murdered along with their retinues, and identified two royal emissaries among the rebels.

Although he soon learned that Humbercourt had been released and that the prince-bishop was being well treated, Charles was (allegedly) consumed with rage and ringed Péronne Castle with his English archers. Louis quickly professed himself shocked by the revolt and offered to accompany Charles to chastise the rebel city. If Commynes is to be believed Charles would have none of it and was only with difficulty dissuaded from violating his safe conduct by his half-brother Anthony and other knights of the Golden Fleece.

Louis was both appalled and relieved to learn of this – from Commynes. Now then: whose interest was Commynes serving? In all probability Charles never had any intention of harming Louis, but wanted him to believe he might. After all, Commynes's message was that Louis should agree to everything Charles demanded, on pain of death. There is ample reason to suspect that he was serving the interest of his master in falsely persuading Louis that his life was in danger.

On 14 October Louis presented Charles with a peace treaty by which the king promised to abide by the 1435 Treaty of Arras and the 1465 Treaty of Conflans. Charles would not be required to renounce his alliance with England, but each undertook to aid and defend the other against aggression by third parties. Full territorial restitution was to be made to Philippe of Bresse and reparations paid for the harm done to him. Louis surrendered his claim to Bruges, Ghent and Ypres in Flanders, and accepted that if he broke any of the treaties, all feudal obligations Charles owed for his French possessions would be permanently cancelled.

Louis also accepted an addendum Charles had perhaps put forward more as a negotiating tactic than a serious proposal. This was that Berry was to be granted the appanage of Champagne, the strategically vital province bordering on the principalities lying between the northern and southern concentrations of the Burgundian empire. To reassure Charles further, Louis ordered his army to disperse and repeated his offer to join him in the suppression of the Liège rebellion.

They signed the treaty under the reliquary cross worn by the Emperor Charlemagne, held aloft by Cardinal Jean Balue, Louis's chief negotiator and, although unknown to him at this time, a traitor. Charles, for the first time, grudgingly knelt before Louis in homage for his French dukedom, stating he did so on condition that the king kept his promises. They then put their hands on Charlemagne's cross and solemnly swore to uphold the terms of the treaty.

Louis could not wriggle out of his commitment to ride with Charles against Liège, and they set out the next day. Humbercourt and the prince-bishop soon joined them, the latter released by the rebels to negotiate a capitulation, having given his word to return. Charles forbade him to honour his commitment. He also tested Louis, saying he was free to go if he wished, but the king continued to ride alongside him, separated from his own councillors and bodyguard.

On 28 October, when they were lodged in the Liège suburbs, 600 rebels wearing Burgundian livery made a night raid that came close to killing or capturing both. The raiders were all killed and defenceless Liège fell to an unnecessarily massive assault on the 30th. Most of the citizens had fled, and those who had not, thinking to indicate their loyalty, suffered the same treatment as those who made a last desperate stand in the cathedral. Hundreds were put to the sword, hundreds more tied together and hurled into the river Meuse, and the city was torched.

By associating Louis with this barbarity Charles ensured he would not find it easy to stir trouble in the Burgundian back yard in the future. He was still reluctant to let him go, but the king pointed out that the peace treaty would not be valid until registered by the Paris Parlement, which required his presence. Before departing, Louis casually asked Charles what he should do if Berry was not satisfied with his new appanage. 'If he does not want it and you can satisfy him some other way, I leave it to you two', Charles replied, confirming that it had never been high on his list of priorities, probably because he knew how undependable Berry was.

When Louis returned to French territory he was startled to find his subjects celebrating the news of the treaty with unreserved joy. They were weary of wars and, like the prime ministers of France and

Britain after selling out Czechoslovakia at Munich in 1938, Louis found himself cheered for what he knew to have been a humiliating act of appeasement. This, as much as the terms of the treaty, explains why he was so quiescent during 1469, and refrained from meddling in the affairs of England.

He was also fully taken up with the protracted wooing of his brother. There was no question in France of the throne descending through the female line – that had been ruled out forever when the English Angevin claim was rejected and the Valois dynasty installed in 1328, kicking off the Hundred Years War. In eighteen years of marriage Queen Charlotte had born him only two surviving daughters; three sons had been stillborn or died in infancy. It seemed likely that Berry would succeed Louis, and reconciliation was a dynastic imperative.

It took Louis a year to overcome his brother's fear that he had committed an unforgivable act by his dalliance with Charles. Early in 1469 Louis offered him the far richer – but safely separate from Burgundy – province of Guyenne in exchange for Champagne. In the midst of the negotiations a treasonous letter written by Cardinal Balue came into Louis's possession, in which the cardinal urged Duke Charles to resist the proposed exchange by force of arms. Although the pope refused to revoke their clerical immunity, Balue and his confederate the Bishop of Verdun were imprisoned for the next eleven years.

In April Berry accepted the exchange, but still refused to meet. Louis's next gambit was to create the chivalric Order of Saint-Michel and to appoint the new Duke of Guyenne as its first member. The order was exclusive, such that members could not also accept the Burgundian Golden Fleece or the English Garter. On 7 September the brothers finally met on a bridge of boats across a river, with a fence in the middle. Overcome with emotion, the younger man got around the fence and threw himself at the king's feet. For a week they were inseparable and Louis had little cause for serious concern for the remaining three years of his brother's life.

Meanwhile, with his back now covered, Duke Charles presided over a conference at Ghent to arbitrate a long and violent dispute, which Charles had stoked, between Duke Arnold of Egmond and his son Adolf over the duchy of Guelders and county of Zutphen. In January Adolf kidnapped his father and a civil war ensued that drew in the Duke of Cleves and the Archbishop of Cologne. By appointing himself arbitrator Charles took a large step towards the occupation that followed in 1473. Friesland, flanked by the lands of Charles's bastard half-brother David, Prince-Bishop of Utrecht, was next on the list.

In the south, Charles acquired Upper Alsace by mortgage from Archduke Sigismund of Austria. The province was a rat's nest of sub-mortgages that created only liabilities for its nominal ruler, but Charles was not deterred. Like his father, he dreamed of re-creating Lotharingia, the central kingdom of the three into which the vast Carolingian empire was divided in 840. It ran from the Low Countries along a broad band of territory west of the Rhine, through western Switzerland and Savoy to Provence.

The difference between father and son was that Philippe's aspiration was long term and dynastic, while Charles, having overcome his repugnance long enough to engender a daughter in 1457, made no further effort to produce a male heir and thought only in terms of personal glory. Fatefully, this was to include subduing the formidable Swiss, now stronger than ever.

Sociological studies of the posturing hypermasculinity known as *machismo* concur in the paradoxical role of mothers in perpetuating it as a form of revenge on philandering fathers. They teach their sons that all women – apart from the sainted mother – are bitches on heat and all men treacherous dogs. Throw in the high testosterone levels commonly found in homosexual men, add almost unlimited wealth and power, and you get Charles 'the Bold'.

The dominant figure in Charles's life was his mother, Isabella of Portugal, who was obsessed by the fact that her grandmother had been John of Gaunt's eldest child. Charles was a mother's boy to such an extent that he used to speak of 'we Portuguese', and after the death his first wife in 1454 Isabella pressed him to strengthen his claim to the English throne by marrying one of Richard of York's daughters. In 1457 she became completely estranged from Philippe after he insisted Charles marry Isabelle of Bourbon instead.

When Charles became a widower again in 1465 he was free to indulge his mother's obsession. What Edward believed was a matrimonial alliance against France was seen in a completely different light by Charles and his mother, who handled the marriage negotiations. It was she who imposed conditions of such unilateral advantage to Burgundy that it undermined Edward's standing with his own people, and this may have been her intention. In her eyes the (junior) Lancastrians and Yorkists had lesser claims to the throne, and in a perfect world they would destroy each other to make way for her son.

Was this an unrealistic ambition? Perhaps – but no more than many other calculations in an age politically defined by genealogy. The clinching argument in favour of this interpretation is that on 11 November 1471, five weeks before his mother died, Charles ordered a notarized document drawn up in which he set out his right to the English throne as the sole remaining legitimate Lancastrian claimant, and promised to pursue it. One need look no further for an explanation of his ambivalent behaviour towards Edward.

Thus there were no 'noises off' when England fell into turmoil because the two most powerful princes of Christendom, who might have sought to turn the situation to their advantage, had backed away from confrontation and each had pressing reasons to do nothing to provoke the other. The eternal problem with peripheral disputes, however, is that the parties in conflict will draw you in, no matter how unwilling you are to get involved.

XV

OUT OF THE ASHES

PERHAPS UNEASY ABOUT CLARENCE'S ATTEMPT TO bounce him into exploiting the Lincolnshire rebellion, Warwick only tried to mobilize his wider affinity after Losecote, when Edward sprung the trap he had set for them. Warwick and Clarence protested their innocence and said they would meet him at Retford on the Great North Road, but instead set out for Rotherham via Burton upon Trent, Derby and Chesterfield, gathering retainers as they went.

With Richard of Gloucester and the Yorkist Marchers on his doorstep, John Talbot, Earl of Shrewsbury, declined to join them. Their hopes were now pinned on John Conyers and Lord Scrope of Bolton bringing reinforcements down the Western Spur from Richmondshire. When Edward advanced from Newark to Rotherham, Warwick and Clarence stopped at Sheffield. Learning that Conyers and Scrope were not coming, in a last throw of the dice they marched to Manchester in the vain hope that Lord Stanley would come off the fence.

When they turned south their followers began to desert them, notably William Parr of Kendal, a key figure in Warwick's north-western affinity who had fought for him at Edgcote and who had carried messages to and from the king after Losecote. Although Warwick and Clarence still had 5,000 troops when they arrived at Bristol, these were men from the region who only stayed with them because they were returning home. Few accompanied them on the last stage of their flight, and the fact that they abandoned their artillery at Bristol suggests a general disbandment.

Meanwhile John Neville put on a show of loyalty by raising troops in the king's name from his own inherited estates in north Yorkshire and joined Edward at Doncaster. Soon afterwards Robert Hildyard joined Parr, Scrope and Conyers in seeking the king's pardon, and Edward learned that John had deceived him about the 'Robin of Holderness' revolt. This may have been why he chose this moment to announce the restoration of Henry Percy, who had accompanied him throughout the campaign, as Earl of Northumberland. Despite this Edward continued to trust John, and we must assume he believed the elevation of young George Neville to the dukedom of Bedford and his betrothal to the eldest royal daughter would keep his father loyal.

In March, in a matter unrelated to what was going on elsewhere, Thomas Talbot, Viscount Lisle, decided it was an opportune moment to bring to a head a longstanding family feud with William, Lord Berkeley, and he formally challenged him to battle. Berkeley unsportingly arrived at Nibley Green with a larger army and one of his archers killed Lisle with an arrow to the throat. Thus the male line of the Gloucestershire Talbots was extinguished in folly just when Thomas's Shrewsbury cousin was opting for discretion over valour.*

About a week later Warwick and Clarence rode past Nibley Green on their way to Exeter, where another local fracas awaited them. Clarence had a strong presence in Devon and may have encouraged this uprising in the same way he had in Lincolnshire. Although the senior Courtenay line was Lancastrian, following the judicial murder of Henry Courtenay its leader was his brother John, an exile at Marguerite's threadbare court. The rival Courtenays of Powderham Castle, 7 miles south-east of Exeter, were intermarried with the Lancastrian Hungerfords and Luttrells, whose lands had

---

*The Lisle–Berkeley feud is more fully explained in *Battle Royal*, Appendix D. It was not resolved until 1609.

been seized without regard to the rights of, among others, James Luttrell's widow Elizabeth Courtenay.

Elizabeth later stood as godmother to Clarence's only child, and the Powderham Courtenays were probably members of Clarence's affinity in the hope of recovering family lands awarded first to Stafford of Southwyck and subsequently to the new Marquess Montagu. On 16 March Edward ordered Lords Dynham and FitzWarin, his chief representatives in the West Country following the lynching of Stafford, to arrest them and Hugh Courtenay of Bocconoc in Cornwall for a rebellion that must have started some time earlier, in the expectation that Edward would be overthrown and replaced by Clarence.

Things did not go well for Dynham and FitzWarin, and by 22 March they were besieged in Exeter Castle. Also in the castle was Isabel, Clarence's very pregnant wife, whom he had sent there from Tutbury before the Losecote campaign, which argues he prepared an escape route in advance. The siege was lifted when he and Warwick arrived, and Isabel was permitted to join them as they travelled to Clarence's borough of Dartmouth, where a fleet was assembled. The rebel Courtenays went with them.

While to this point Warwick had been scrambling to make something of the dire situation in which his new son-in-law had landed him, from the moment they sailed he was in total command and Clarence became increasingly irrelevant. The ships and crews were Warwick's and they sailed to Southampton intending to cut out *Trinity*, his flagship, now under the command of Anthony Woodville, Earl Rivers. Forewarned, Woodville's men not only killed or captured the raiding party, but took two of Warwick's ships as well.

The remainder sailed to Calais, where Warwick hoped to repeat the strategy he had followed in 1459 of using it as a springboard for invasion. Lord Wenlock, his deputy, and most of the garrison were his men; against which the commander of the garrison was Galliard, lord of Duras, who was fiercely loyal to Edward, while the garrison's Stapler paymasters were strong supporters of the Burgundian alliance. Consequently Warwick found the chain across the entrance to the port raised against him, and warning shots fired. Poor little Isabel endured the stillbirth of her baby on a ship tossing at anchor in the Calais roads.

Back in England Edward reached Exeter four days after Warwick had sailed. On learning of the Southampton raid he marched there and unleashed Tiptoft on what was by now a large collection of prisoners. John Clapham, whose arrival at Edgcote had doomed Herbert, was fortunate only to be beheaded. Geoffrey Gate, Warwick's Marshal of Calais, captor of Earl Rivers and leader of the Southampton raid, was inexplicably pardoned. Humbler rebels suffered the novel barbarity of being dismembered and having their torsos impaled upside down with their severed heads on their buttocks.

Edward's party now included two dukes, four earls, ten barons and about 10,000 men. With the Earls of Essex and Kent securing London and the Home Counties, Northumberland and Montagu having left to settle the North, Rivers organizing the fleet and three more nobles sent to arrest Archbishop Neville at his Hertfordshire palace, aristocratic solidarity was overwhelming. It was also opportunistic and ephemeral, as Henry VI had discovered after they all joined his triumphal Ludford Bridge campaign in 1459.

To return to the herding cats analogy, noble houses that do not put their own interests first, last and everywhere in between seldom last long. Loyalty, like respect for the law and paying taxes, is for the little people. While a monarch could not govern without the greater magnates, they needed him only to the extent that he could maintain the status quo at no expense to them. This is why Losecote proved to be such a hollow victory – it had been won very largely by Edward's cunning and by employing his own resources. Most of the glittering array of nobles that jumped on the bandwagon could be depended on only to jump off again at the first sign of trouble.

Warwick knew he had severely weakened Edward's regime and that he must strike again before the damage could be repaired.

He could probably count on his Trojan Horse brother, while Shrewsbury and Stanley would no doubt jump on his own bandwagon if he could get it rolling again. But Edgcote had diminished his northern affinity both in number and in their willingness to turn out for him again, especially after the restoration of Henry Percy, and the Losecote campaign had ended with a number of his Midlands retainers executed and the rest feeling abandoned.

With Calais closed to him Warwick's remaining bargaining chip was his fleet, soon joined by a squadron led by his illegitimate first cousin Thomas Neville, better known as the Bastard of Fauconberg, who had escaped from the Sandwich fleet, newly put under the command of John Howard. Warwick knew how fiercely Louis XI must resent his humiliation at Péronne, and used the fleet to put the shaky Franco–Burgundian détente under intolerable pressure.

Not long after Thomas joined him Warwick's warships raided along the coast of Flanders, Zeeland and Holland, capturing sixty to one hundred small vessels. Collecting the transports off Calais, they then sailed along the coast of Normandy but were intercepted by John Howard. Most of the recently pirated Burgundian prizes were lost, probably sacrificed to cover the retreat of the remainder. On 1 May they arrived at Honfleur, on the Seine estuary, where Warwick demanded sanctuary, and sent Louis a letter saying they must meet to discuss the restoration of the House of Lancaster, as the king had first suggested in 1467.

Back in England, Edward declared Warwick's lands forfeit but redistributed little of it apart from returning Barnard Castle to the Bishop of Durham, keeping for the crown most of the income from the remainder. He also made Henry Percy, whose restoration as Earl of Northumberland was still subject to confirmation by Parliament, Warden of the East March, leaving Richard Salkeld of Carlisle, Warwick's deputy, in charge of the West March. Showing that indifference to cause and effect characteristic of those who have conspired and failed, the Neville affinity in general and Montagu in particular felt aggrieved.

Elsewhere, apart from appointing Arundel Warden of the Cinque Ports, Edward did not bring the great magnates into his government and tried to rebuild his network of personally loyal key men. He brought Tiptoft back as Lord Treasurer and also appointed him Lieutenant of Ireland to replace Clarence – but, like the Woodvilles, Tiptoft had no significant affinity. Of Edward's remaining henchmen Hastings and Ferrers were only medium-size lords while John Howard, recently created a baron but not yet confirmed by summons to Parliament, was not even that. The king's brother Richard of Gloucester and John Stafford, created Earl of Wiltshire only in January, had not had time to develop their own affinities.

The gaping holes in the scheme were Wales and the West Country. Edward had bet so heavily on Herbert and Stafford of Southwyck that he was left scrambling for alternatives. Gloucester and Ferrers appear to have done a good job of containment with regard to Wales, but the shattered Herbert affinity would require many years to recover, if it ever did. In the West Country, even if Montagu had loyally accepted his new role the Courtenay affinity was no more likely to accept his lordship than it had Stafford's. Yet, for obvious reasons, Edward's main concern was whether his gamble on Percy had neutralized the threat from the North.

All of this is more apparent in hindsight than it was at the time. Whatever Warwick's failings as a tactician he was a masterly strategist. Bearing in mind that he had no following in the West Country and that his south Wales affinity had been deprived of his good lordship for most of the preceding decade, he still formulated a plan to strike not where he was strongest, but where Edward was weakest. He probably got a crash course in West Country politics from the Courtenays who joined him in exile, while for Wales he was soon to be joined by the indefatigable Jasper Tudor and other Welshmen driven into exile by Herbert.

The question was whether Louis XI could be persuaded first to bring about an alliance with the exiled Lancastrians, and secondly to provide Warwick with a large enough army to get the band-wagon rolling in England. Warwick succeeded because Louis's heart remained that of the innovative rebel he had been as a young man. His formative hero had been the *condottiere* Francesco Sforza, who won the duchy of Milan in 1450 and thoroughly reformed an administration that had become predatory under the extinct Visconti dynasty.

Louis saw Warwick as another Sforza and his English opponents akin to the reactionary nobles he himself had outmanoeuvred in the Dauphiné. He was wrong on both counts, but he was not the first nor would he be the last French ruler to underestimate the degree to which England diverged from the continental norm. Louis per-suaded himself there was a groundswell in favour of regime change in England, and that Warwick could make it happen.

Accordingly, on receipt of Warwick's letter Louis summoned Marguerite d'Anjou to join him at court, currently at Amboise in the Loire valley, while seeking to show favour to Warwick without provoking Charles of Burgundy, who was outraged by Warwick's piracy and demanded Louis treat him as their common enemy, as required by the Treaty of Péronne.

Initially Louis requested that Warwick take his ships to Barfleur on the Cotentin peninsula or to the Channel Islands, where he could be resupplied and reinforced away from the eyes of Saint-Pol, acting Governor of Normandy, who hated Warwick for his shabby treatment of his sister Jacquetta and was keeping Charles fully informed about Louis's machinations. Warwick refused, holding out for an interview.

In the face of Charles's fulminations and threats Louis came to the conclusion that, given the opportunity of at least destabilizing England for many years, the time was ripe for war with Burgundy. We are seriously hampered in our understanding of what fol-lowed because our best sources are reports citing Louis himself by the Milanese ambassador, which may have been disinformation and which in key places contradict a subtle piece of Warwickian propaganda called *The Manner and Guiding of the Earl of Warwick at Angers in July and August 1470.*

As with the *Chronicle of the Rebellion in Lincolnshire*, one must read between the lines of *The Manner and Guiding.* Selling Warwick's alliance with the House of Lancaster to the English people was a difficult task, to put it mildly, and the military alliance with France was not even mentioned. The restoration of Henry VI would bring with it the reversal of an enormous number of property transfers, which would hit Warwick's and Clarence's affinities particularly hard. They had to be reassured that Warwick would be the real power in the land and would take care of their interests. For this and other reasons *The Manner and Guiding* had to portray Warwick, not Louis, as the principal protagonist in the negotiations.

In battlefield analysis the sole unimpeachable witness is the terrain. So also in political analysis the only dependable contours are who had the power, and what they sought to gain. Louis XI had all the power in the negotiations between Warwick and Marguerite, and while he was flatteringly polite to the pieces on his chessboard they moved because he willed it. What followed was a French invasion of England with Warwick as its figurehead, and with Lancaster providing its political justification and supplementing his popular appeal. There was not the smallest chance they would co-exist peacefully once they seized power.

The alleged details of how these irreconcilable enemies were brought to sink their differences long enough to seize power are unimportant. Louis may have hoped Warwick would prevail in the ensuing power struggle to become a firm French ally against Burgundy, but he was too shrewd to count on it. What he wished to avoid was the immediate threat of an English invasion of Normandy in support of Burgundy, led by the dangerously competent Edward. If the English king could be permanently removed from the board, so much the better; but simply tying him down and exhausting his resources would be gain enough.

The agreement between Warwick and Marguerite was confirmed

on 25 July at Angers, the capital of Anjou. There was no formal treaty, but the immediate betrothal of 14-year-old Anne, Warwick's younger daughter, and 17-year-old Edward of Westminster, Marguerite's son, was supposed to guarantee an agreed course of action. Warwick was to go ahead with Jasper Tudor, the Courtenays and his brother-in-law the Earl of Oxford, who had lately joined them. He would defeat Edward, restore captive Henry VI to the throne and govern as his lieutenant until Marguerite and Edward joined him. What was to happen then remained to be seen.

Warwick believed his status would not change, but it is as near an absolute certainty as any historical 'what if' can be that fiery Marguerite intended to kill him once his usefulness was over. Ten years of metaphorically – if not literally – sticking pins in his effigy could not be abolished by a marriage forced on her by her manipulative cousin Louis. She had fought like a wolverine to defend her son's right, and the forlorn expedition to Northumberland Louis had embarked her on in 1462 must have been acid-etched in her memory. Neither she nor the Lancastrian exiles whose kin Warwick had slaughtered would tamely submit to putting their prince under his tutelage.

XVI

BLOODLESS VICTORY

PRIMED BY LOUIS DE LUXEMBOURG, DUKE CHARLES bombarded Edward with warnings that an invasion was imminent, but could offer no useful intelligence about where Warwick planned to land and in what strength. Edward had to assume it would be at places where disaffection ran deep and so had the south-east coast covered by Arundel and Howard, while Ferrers and the Yorkist Marchers could be expected to defeat any landing in Wales. That left the North, and at the end of July word came of another Middleham-based insurrection led by Lord FitzHugh.

Henry Percy reported he could not persuade the family affinity to turn out in defence of the Yorkist regime and with fatal naivety the king issued a commission of array to Montagu, who just happened to be in the North, but heard no more from him. We may fairly question whether the alleged insurrection was ever more than a ruse to permit Montagu to summon the levies with royal authority. The northern Neville affinity in fact played no significant part in the events that followed.

Edward decided he must go north himself. Before departing he ordered guns brought from Bristol and extra munitions, bows and arrows to reinforce the Tower, where he installed pregnant Queen Elizabeth and their daughters. By 5 August he was in Leicester and he reached York on the 14th. From there he marched directly towards Middleham but at Ripon, 24 miles north-west of York, word came

that the alleged insurrection had collapsed and FitzHugh had fled
to Scotland. Edward returned to York and on 10 September issued
a general pardon.

Inexplicably he stayed there, even after writing a warning to
Arundel and Howard that a landing in Kent was imminent. That
was not where it arrived. To explain how Warwick achieved strategic
surprise a background weather report is in order. The prevailing
winds in the English Channel are westerlies at 15 knots, but strong
easterlies can blow for days if a high-pressure system settles over
England. The tail end of Atlantic hurricanes sweep in from June to
November, with the historic peak of activity around 10 September.
Contemporary ships were square-rigged hulks and carracks, slow
and unhandy at the best of times and with poor performance into
the wind. Under normal conditions a fleet sailing from Normandy
would sail with the prevailing wind to south-eastern England.

Most accounts state that a Burgundian fleet 'blockaded' the
Normandy ports, but that would have been impossible without the
ship and signalling technology of a much later age. They would have
been cruising well out into the Bay of the Seine, and when the prevailing wind was blowing could swoop on ships tacking laboriously

15. THE CHANNEL 1470

out of Harfleur or Honfleur. When Warwick secretly moved his base of operations to Valognes, his followers left their own ships as decoys in Honfleur and transferred overland to Barfleur and Saint-Vaast-La-Hougue on the Cotentin peninsula. There, sixty French ships and about 5,000 soldiers, mercenaries hired by Louis, awaited them. The Burgundians were left guarding the wrong ports.

Strong easterlies were blowing in late August/early September, making exit from the Cotentin ports difficult, and the departure of the invasion fleet may also have been delayed because the French admiral had orders to avoid combat. But another explanation is that Warwick's strategic deception plan required a wind shift. If the fleet's departure were observed, with westerlies blowing his enemies would expect him to sail to the south-east and deploy accordingly to intercept him. Counting on that, he intended go in the opposite direction.

It was a fortunate bonus when the tail end of a hurricane dispersed both the Burgundian fleet and the high-pressure system over England, restoring the prevailing wind. On 9 September the invasion fleet sailed into the Channel then spent four days tacking *into* the wind to make landings at Dartmouth and Plymouth, near the centres of rebel Courtenay power. Unlike Duke Charles, who unjustly sacked his admiral, Warwick understood ships and the sea.*

Edward learned of the landing in mid-September and set out for London. At Doncaster he stopped to give Montagu time to catch up, but when the new marquess was 5 miles away loyalist deserters brought warning of his hostile intent. Edward was comprehensively wrong-footed, and not just by Warwick's Trojan Horse. He had not expected Louis to tear up the Treaty of Péronne by attacking him with a major expedition. Nor had he anticipated that the long bereft affinities of the attainted West Country earls would flock to Warwick's banner.

He could have turned and fought Montagu, but chose not to risk

---

*On Louis's orders the French admiral promptly sailed away.

the attrition of his closest followers. He could also have issued commissions of array to the southern lords, but his summons to local
people at Nottingham had such a poor response that he chose not
to put anyone else in a similar situation. He disbanded his army
and fled to Bishop's Lynn accompanied by Gloucester, Worcester,
Rivers, Hastings, Lord Saye and their retinues. On the way, in an
echo of Kings John's mishap in 1216, the royal party was nearly
wiped out by the notoriously fast-rising tide in the Wash.

Tiptoft chose to remain behind but on 2 October the rest set sail
for the Netherlands. The little fleet scattered after encountering hostile Hanseatic ships the next day. The Hansards pursued Edward's
group while Gloucester and Rivers sailed south to Walcheren island.
Edward's ships ran themselves aground next to Texel island. With
the Hansards waiting for the tide to turn, the islanders helped
Edward and his party ashore (see Map 16, page 171).

Five days later Lodewijk van Brugge, fellow knight of the Golden
Fleece and lord of Gruuthuse, welcomed them to his mansion at
Alkmaar. Gruuthuse had been in London on several occasions
and regarded the king as a friend. He gave the refugees clothes
and money, and on 10 October sent letters from Edward to Duke
Charles and to Edward's sister Duchess Margaret. On 11 October
he rode with them to his palace in The Hague, where they were
reunited with Gloucester and Rivers. We shall return to them in the
following chapter.

Back in England the Yorkist regime was effortlessly supplanted,
even though the only nobles to sail with Warwick had been Clarence,
Oxford and Jasper Tudor, the attainted Earl of Pembroke. Jasper
peeled off to rally his own people in Pembroke and the principality,
but Clarence and Oxford stayed with Warwick. They were met at
Bristol but accompanied no further by Shrewsbury and Stanley.
The rest of the nobility stood down: the only, – failed – attempt to
organize resistance was at Salisbury by Thomas St Leger, lover of
Edward's older sister Anne, Duchess of Exeter.

Although Warwick was determined to prevent the outrages that commonly accompany a mercenary army and hanged offenders, his own people stained his cause. The commons of Kent erupted when they learned of his landing and marched on London, where they looted the premises of Dutch merchants and indulged in drunken debauchery. The authorities placed guns to cover the bridge and the gates, and volunteers swelled the ranks of the militia; but then recently pardoned Geoffrey Gates released imprisoned Lancastrians and hundreds of criminals from the city's jails, and blood ran in the streets.

Elizabeth and her daughters moved to sanctuary at Westminster Abbey before the Tower surrendered to Gates on 3 October.* On the 5th Archbishop Neville arrived to install a new garrison and found King Henry living in monkish squalor. Two days later, after making a triumphal entrance into London, Warwick led Henry in procession to the Bishop of London's palace. On the 13th he held the king's train in another procession to St Paul's, where he was crowned to mark the 'Readeption' of his reign before moving to the palace of Westminster.

The arcane term 'Readeption', meaning 'recovery', was proposed by Dr John Fortescue, Marguerite's closest advisor, who along with Dr John Morton had accompanied Warwick since Angers. Along with Dr Ralph Mackerell they became the king's councillors. All three had been repeatedly pardoned by Edward, Mackerell as recently as November 1469, but they were convinced of the legitimacy of the House of Lancaster to the depths of their learned souls.

Henry was still capable of independent action and imposed a tone of forgiveness on the new regime. An early edict was that sanctuary should not be violated, protecting not only Elizabeth but also Edward's chief office holders, the Bishops of Ely, Bath and Rochester, who had taken refuge in St Martin's Le Grand, near St Paul's. It was probably also at Henry's insistence that the Duke of Norfolk, the Bourchiers (the Archbishop of Canterbury, the Earl of

---

*Among others, Gates released Thomas Malory, who died the following March, aged about 55. *Le Morte d'Arthur* was published by Caxton in 1485.

Essex and Lord Cromwell), the Earl of Wiltshire, Lord Mountjoy and even Richard Woodville were released from arrest, pardoned, and their rights regranted.

Richard Tunstall, the king's faithful companion after Hexham and who had helped to hold Harlech for him for so long, was rewarded with the influential and profitable offices of Royal Chamberlain and Master of the Mints in England and Calais. Another sly flicker of independence may have been the special favour shown to the Earl of Oxford, who had contributed little to the campaign but was the only non-renegade in the triumvirate that liberated the king. Oxford carried the sword of state before him at the coronation and was made steward of the royal household.

It was Warwick, however, who also made Oxford Constable of England, so that he should have the pleasure of presiding over the trial and execution of John Tiptoft, Earl of Worcester, who had done the same to Oxford's father and older brother.* Although it was a popular act of public vengeance, there may have been another reason to make an example of Tiptoft. His death released the estates he had held from his late wife and Warwick's sister Cecily, dowager Duchess of Warwick, while by matrilineal succession Montagu's young son George, Duke of Bedford, was heir to half of Tiptoft's own family estate.

On 15 October Warwick summoned Parliament, with none excluded save the lords who had accompanied Edward into exile and the Stafford Earl of Wiltshire. Intriguingly, it was by this summons that John Howard was officially recognized as Baron Howard. This was supposed to reassure loyal servants of the deposed regime that, despite the execution of Tiptoft, they need not fear for their lives. It did not reassure those in sanctuary, who remained there.

The new regime was faced with the impossible task of restoring forfeited Lancastrian estates without creating a pool of discontent among those dispossessed. Fortescue, Morton and Mackerell

---

*Unusual to the last, Tiptoft instructed the executioner to behead him with three strokes to honour the Trinity.

performed prodigies of legal adjustment, and Fortescue had set out a plan of action for government to be conducted through a permanent Council that must approve all the king's decrees. The details need not concern us because the regime never had time to evolve.

There were two reasons for this. The first was that Edward would certainly be back, and nobody could put any faith in a settlement until one or other of the parties was dead and buried. The other was that Marguerite stubbornly refused to cross the Channel with her son and his new wife. At first the excuse was that papal dispensation for the marriage was delayed, which is deeply unconvincing. The degree of consanguinity between Anne and Edward was very tenuous indeed, and dispensation may not even have been necessary. Furthermore, although Louis could have obtained it in a heartbeat, it was not forthcoming until December 1470.

Did Marguerite insist on it to delay their departure, or was it yet another strand to the Universal Spider's web? Probably both: even after the marriage was formalized Marguerite and Prince Edward did not cross the Channel for another four months, and it stretches credulity to believe Louis could not have forced them to travel sooner. He can have been in no doubt about Marguerite's cold loathing for Warwick, and her unwillingness to lend him legitimacy coincided with his desire to give Warwick as much time as possible to secure his hold on power. Failing that Louis's aim, as always, was to keep England in turmoil.

In late October Jasper Tudor, the restored Earl of Pembroke, arrived in London with his 14-year-old nephew Henry, Earl of Richmond, whom he had taken from William Herbert's widow. Clarence held extensive property pertaining to the Richmond earldom and Jasper's request that his nephew should have it back could not be granted. Although Clarence's possession was only confirmed for his lifetime, when Jasper returned to Wales with his nephew in mid-November he was justifiably resentful. So was Henry Stafford, uncle to his namesake the young Duke of Buckingham and second husband of Margaret Beaufort, Henry Tudor's mother.

Clarence did lose all his duchy of Lancaster estates, notably Tutbury, which reverted to Marguerite. He was awarded the duchy of York, but it was encumbered by his mother's dower and Warwick was in no hurry to surrender the revenue of any part of what had been Edward's royal domain. As for compensation elsewhere, none was available because previously attainted estates were returned to Lancastrians – thus the exiles William, Viscount Beaumont, and Edmund, Baron Roos, recovered lands Edward had awarded to his henchman Hastings.

Although the threat to his Richmond estates was averted, Clarence would lose more if John Butler, Earl of Ormond in Ireland, were restored to the English title and lands of his father's earldom of Wiltshire.* Whichever way he looked, the man who had sniffed at his brother's generous endowment could see only a future in which, at best, he would be hard pressed to sustain the income required of a duke. More ominously, his permanent removal from the scene would obviously resolve quite a large number of problems for his father-in-law.

A Spanish aphorism about government and opposition translates as 'it is another matter with guitar in hand'. Like many another charismatic narcissist swept to power on a carefully orchestrated wave of popular euphoria, Warwick had not thought through what tune he would play once he was standing in the spotlight, with the audience eagerly awaiting the magical performance he had led them to expect. He had promised peace and an end to burdensome taxation and constraints on trade. He could deliver none of these, and his secret military undertaking with Louis obliged him to strum increasingly unpopular chords.

There is no record of Warwick sending back the French mercenaries who marched with him to London, and he almost certainly kept them to act as his regime guard. They must also have been intended to form the bulk of the 8,000-man army he had agreed

*It did not happen because Ormond wished nothing to do with a regime dominated by Warwick.

to lead against Burgundy, as there was no other way he could have made good on the promise. Warwick could only make war if France paid for it, and this we know Louis did not do – directly. But what if the mercenaries were his subsidy? If so, they would continue to prop up Warwick only as long as he kept faith with their paymaster.

One could continue indefinitely reviewing the number and vigour of the worms that erupted from the can Warwick opened by seizing power as he did. One that deserves mention was the murder of Warwick's friend and retainer Robert Harcourt, a Garter knight who had been among those attending the wedding of Clarence and Isabel. In 1448, in a brawl with the Staffords of Grafton, he had killed Richard Stafford. In November 1470 Stafford's bastard half-brother took his revenge by ambushing Harcourt in London, and Warwick could do nothing because the head of the Staffords of Grafton was also his retainer and a local MP.

Chaos reigned. Henry VI was as unconvincing as ever and the monarchy's authority was at an all-time low, while Marguerite and her son, the real strength of the House of Lancaster, were waiting in the wings for Warwick to stumble. This he was guaranteed to do, because he had been put in power by Louis XI to deliver an active military alliance against Burgundy, which ran counter to the deeply ingrained prejudices of the English people.

Power in England was a three-legged stool resting on the aristocracy, the Church and the merchant class. The monarchy was supposed to be the seat that held it all together, but had ceased to do so because of what was basically gang warfare among the Houses of Lancaster, York and Neville. Nations can endure most things but not prolonged uncertainty, and there was a general desire for the turmoil to end, one way or another.

XVII

THE ARRIVAL

HAVING INVESTED SO HEAVILY IN THE ALLIANCE WITH Burgundy, and after being overthrown by their common enemy, Edward had the reasonable expectation of rapid and immediate support from Duke Charles. It was not forthcoming. Not only the duke but also his wife Margaret, Edward's sister, proved reluctant to meet him, and for several months Gruuthuse alone stood between him and abject penury. Edward's anguish was made worse when he learned that Elizabeth had given birth to the long-awaited male heir in Westminster Abbey on 2 November.

Not far from the forefront of Charles's megalomaniac mind would have been the thought that it was 'one down and one to go' until he could add England to his heterogeneous empire. Duchess Margaret's motives were more rational – like their malignant mother, she yearned to see her whole-blood brother Clarence replace the cuckoo Edward on the throne. If that was no longer possible, her main concern was to save Clarence from the consequences of his treachery.

A third strand was the Lancastrian exiles, Charles's pensioners. The most prominent were the younger brothers of Charles's lost love Henry Beaufort. Edmund, Duke of Somerset, and John, Marquess of Dorset, served with Charles against Louis XI and had his ear. A third pensioner was Edward's erratic brother-in-law Henry Holland, the dispossessed and cuckolded Duke of Exeter, who appears to have been kept at arm's length.

The Beauforts had remained in contact with Marguerite's humble court in Bar and with Jasper Tudor in Brittany and France during the long years of exile. How closely and to what purpose we can only guess, but the traffic of messengers among the exiles and with Lancastrian sympathisers in England multiplied after the two great usurpers came to blows.

In early October 1471, at about the time the Yorkists were reunited at The Hague, Charles sent Commynes on a mission to Calais. The message he bore was that Charles regarded the Anglo-Burgundian treaty as between the kingdom of England and the

16. EDWARD'S ITINERARY 1470-1

© Hugh Bicheno

duchy of Burgundy, and that he would accept whomever the English wanted as their king. This was also the view of the Company of the Staple, appalled at the prospect of a war with Burgundy.

Commynes found the garrison, which had already raided neighbouring Burgundian territory, wearing Warwick's livery. Duras, appointed governor by Edward, must by now have gone to join him at The Hague because Commynes dealt with Lord Wenlock. Wenlock gave evasive replies and Commynes reported that he had requested several hundred additional Warwick retainers to reinforce the garrison, and was openly preparing for war.

Charles ordered a crash programme of coastal fortifications – a new gatehouse built at Veere on Walcheren island was called 'de Warwijkse poort', making it clear what threat they were built to counter. Even so, Charles permitted reality to intrude on his dynastic delusion only after Louis XI declared war on 3 December. The king denounced the Treaty of Péronne, declared all Charles's French lands forfeit to the crown and mobilized the *ordonnances* against Picardy.

Louis should not have moved until his pieces were in place. It appears to have been a bad-tempered response to Charles's increasingly strident protests about the king's evident breach of the Treaty of Péronne by sponsoring Warwick, and it gave Charles time to assemble an army of mercenaries in Picardy. Louis's initiative was also diplomatically rash, as it put him in the wrong and also placed intolerable pressure on Warwick to deliver on his promise of armed support before he was in a position to do so.

In mid-December Charles requested his allies of the Hanseatic League to cease trading with France and England, to clear the way for his own fleet to attack any ship sailing to and from England. The aim was to prevent Warwick reinforcing Calais in order to attack the duke's army in Picardy from behind, but it also gave Marguerite another excuse to ignore Warwick's pleas to join him.

On 26 December Edward's party moved to Gruuthuse's castle at Oostcamp, near Bruges, and on 31 December he was summoned to meet Charles's mother Isabella, possibly accompanied by his sister Margaret, at Aire-sur-la-Lys in Artois, 35 miles south-east of Calais. Isabella informed Edward that her son, who was 25 miles south-west of Aire at Hesdin, directing his army in Picardy, had granted him a monthly pension of 500 écus [£53,000]. Charles himself came to Aire between 2 and 4 January, but what they discussed is unrecorded.

On 6 January St Quentin, one of the main Somme valley towns in dispute, declared for France. On 7 January Edward was at Saint-Pol with Louis de Luxembourg, his uncle by marriage and Constable of France. They were joined by Charles until the 9th, and although their talks are also unrecorded it probably involved an intricate negotiation whereby Luxembourg would not find himself obliged to come off the fence. Edward came away with the impression that Louis XI was disappointed with Warwick, and was not wedded to the new English regime.

Edward also wrote to Duke Frañsez asking for support. Whether related to this request or not, in January the Breton fleet under Frañsez's illegitimate brother intercepted a convoy carrying a French commercial delegation, returning from an attempt to win the support of the English merchants for the Anglo–French treaty. Louis XI was later obliged to pay 30,000 livres [over £7 million] to compensate Jean de Beaune, the cloth merchant who financed the expedition, for the loss of the cargo and the death of his son at the hands of the Bretons.

While Edward was at Saint-Pol, Duchess Margaret summoned her younger brother Richard to Lille, and twelve days later loaned him 6,000 gold florins [£11.4 million], advanced by five Dutch cities on her surety, with Charles's tacit approval, to be repaid in 1472 and 1474. Charles arranged it this way to disclaim responsibility to his Lancastrian pensioners, who had begged him to do nothing that might assist Edward to return to England.

Margaret's munificence was timely. On 19 January, after the two brothers returned to Bruges, Rivers had difficulty hiring ships at

Damme, a port downriver from Bruges, for lack of funds. Charles's pension took the form of credit and could not be spent without official approval. Not so Margaret's loan, but Edward and Richard kept secret the amount of cash at their disposal, both at her request and for fear of theft or piracy.

The exiles were joined by a stream of knights and esquires from England and two ships' captains who served at their own expense throughout the ensuing campaign. Edward also received at least £500 [£320,000] sent secretly by several of the Calais Staplers after Warwick signed a ten-year truce and mercantile alliance with France on 16 February. Warwick, Archbishop Neville, Clarence, Langstrother and the Earl of Kent signed for England.

In mid-February Charles did two things that showed his hand. He sent his Lancastrian pensioners to England, and he cut off Edward's pension, a signal that he wanted him, too, gone. Charles did not believe Edward would succeed, but at the very least he would distract Warwick from joining Louis, while the optimum result from his point of view would be if Edward, his brothers, Warwick, Henry VI and his son were all killed in a three-way civil war.

On 19 February Edward walked through cheering crowds from Bruges to Damme, thence by boat to Flushing on Walcheren island, where his invasion fleet was assembling. By 2 March Edward, Gloucester, Rivers, Hastings and Duras with about 2,000 troops, mainly English men-at-arms but including 500 hired Flemish hand-gunners, were embarked on thirty-six transports with an escort of Hanseatic warships. Edward had promised the Hansards great rewards once he recovered the throne, but the warships were hired by Charles. Their orders were to escort Edward to England and to remain at his disposal for fifteen days after he landed.

The flagship was the *Anthony*, property of the lord of Veere, Gruuthuse's father-in-law. Later Veere was to receive English trading privileges, and the captain an annuity of £20 [£12,720], but the most revealing reward was a munificent grant to the *Anthony*'s 'lodesman' (navigator), whose skills included identifying sediment brought up by soundings with a tallow-coated lead weight, essential for inshore navigation. He was Robert Michelson and his home port was Hull, fairly conclusive evidence that Edward always intended to land in the Humber estuary.

Our principal source for the following campaign, *The History of the Arrival of Edward IV in England and the Final Recovery of His Kingdoms from Henry VI*, was written immediately after the campaign by one of Edward's servants. As with Edward's propaganda about the Lincolnshire rebellion and Warwick's *The Manner and Guiding*, the *Arrival* adheres so closely to independently verifiable facts that the omissions acquire heightened significance.

The key omitted fact is that Edward had been in in correspondence with Henry Percy, Earl of Northumberland, since arriving at The Hague, and his invasion strategy was based on the earl's assurance that the Percy affinity hated Warwick more than they hated him. Edward planned to take a leaf out of Warwick's book and land where he was least expected.

After nine days of prevailing westerlies, the wind turned and Edward's fleet set out from Flushing on 11 March and made a fast passage to arrive at Cromer, on the north-east Norfolk coast, the next day. Here, the *Arrival* says, the landing party found there was no local support because the Dukes of Norfolk and Suffolk, the Bourchiers, the Earl of Wiltshire, Lord Mountjoy and Henry Stafford had been placed in the Tower and others forced to post surety. However, Edward would have known this before he sailed.

Also allegedly, Cardinal Bourchier had smuggled out a letter warning Edward that Oxford, based at Castle Hedingham in Suffolk, and Beaumont, from his east Midlands estates, controlled East Anglia. Again, Edward would have known this. The landing at Cromer was really a feint designed to draw Oxford and Beaumont to Norfolk, which it did. Edward lied about it because, like all good generals, he did not want to reveal the tricks of his trade.

On the run from Cromer to the Humber the fleet ran into a violent storm that sank one of the horse transports and scattered

**17. BARNET CAMPAIGN
1471**

York
Tadcaster   Beverley
Wakefield-Sandal   Pontefract   Hull
Doncaster   SEE MAP 11   Ravenspur

Montagu

Lincoln

Newark
Nottingham

Leicester   *Beaumont*   Bishop's
                                        Lynn   Cromer

                                                    Norwich

Coventry
Warwick   Daventry   *Oxford*
           Northampton   Bury St Edmunds

           Banbury
Burford   Dunstable   Hedingham
                     St Albans
Clarence   *Exeter*
           ✕ Barnet

Wells   London

0   25   50   75   100
miles

© Hugh Bicheno

CHRONOLOGY OF THE 1471
BARNET CAMPAIGN

14–15 March Edward lands at Ravenspur, Rivers at Paull. Local resistance under 'Martin de la Mare' melts away. Hull hostile, grudging acceptance by Percy affinity.

16–17 March Edward marches through Beverley to York.

18 March Edward enters York with retinue, persuades authorities to admit his army.

19 March Departs York, overnight at Tadcaster. Exeter, Oxford and Beaumont at Bishop's Lynn.

20 March Marches to his manor of Wakefield and Sandal Castle. Recruitment disappointing. Montagu afraid to emerge from Pontefract Castle.

23 March Edward at Doncaster. First significant addition to his army led by William Sutton. Montagu leaves Pontefract, marches south behind and parallel to Edward.

25–26 March Edward at Nottingham, joined by William Parr and James Harrington with 600 men. Marches towards Newark where Exeter, Oxford and Beaumont have arrived from East Anglia. They retreat north to join forces with Montagu.

28 March Edward at Leicester, joined by William Stanley with 300 men and William Noreys leading Hastings's affinity of about 3,000.

29 March Edward arrives at Coventry, where Warwick refuses to emerge.

1–2 April Edward marches through Warwickshire.

3 April Edward meets Clarence at Banbury, they reconcile and march together to Coventry.

4 April Rearguard at Leicester faces down Montagu, Exeter, Oxford and Beaumont. Howard announces for Edward in Suffolk. Louis XI and Duke Charles sign truce.

5–7 April Edward departs for London, from Daventry sends letters to London, as does Warwick from Coventry.

8 April	Palm Sunday. Archbishop Neville parades Henry VI through London. Somerset, Dorset and Devon depart for the West Country.
9 April	City authorities announce they will admit Edward's army.
10 April	Edward at St Albans receives letter from Archbishop Neville begging for grace.
11 April	Yorkists seize the Tower, release imprisoned lords. Elizabeth, her children and the Bishops of Ely, Bath and Rochester emerge from sanctuary.
12 April	Edward enters London, imprisons Lancastrian lords.
13 April	Good Friday. Warwick at St Albans.
14 April	Edward puts Elizabeth, their children and his mother in the Tower before setting out to intercept Warwick.
15 April	Easter Sunday. BATTLE OF BARNET.

the rest. Rivers eventually landed at Paull, a village near Hull, and Gloucester 8 miles further east; but Edward landed where he always intended, at Ravenspur, a village on the northern tip of the Humber estuary now lost to erosion. Why Ravenspur? Because there, in 1399, the future Henry IV landed from exile and announced he had come to reclaim his duchy of Lancaster, illegally taken from him by Richard II.

So also Edward, who proclaimed he had come to recover his duchy of York, professed loyalty to Henry VI and the Prince of Wales, and said that Warwick had forced him to claim the throne. One has to admire the breath-taking chutzpah. Edward also had two more convincing arguments – a war chest bulging with gold coins and a letter from Henry Percy to his affinity instructing them to let Edward pass. A combination of the two saw him through the challenge of several thousand local levies led by one Martin de la Mare.

Rivers reported that Hull was not well disposed and Edward marched to Beverley, and then through the Percy receivership of Leconfield to York. The civic authorities let him in with a few attendants and he rode into the city sporting the Prince of Wales's ostrich feather badge and crying out 'Long live King Henry'. After that gold coins worked their usual magic and the army marched in the next day.

Montagu, at Pontefract Castle, was wrong-footed. His experience with 'Robin of Holderness' in 1469 had given him a healthy respect for the fighting power of the Percy affinity, which he believed had rallied to Edward, and he needed strong reinforcement from the Neville affinity. He waited in vain because Scrope of Bolton never wished to fight against Edward, FitzHugh's feisty Neville wife could not, this time, goad him into action, and John Conyers had suffered irreparable personal loss at Edgcote.

Edward departed York on 19 March and marched down the Great North Road (Map 4) to begin a campaign that bears comparison with the greatest in history. For the first two weeks he had little more support than the men he brought with him and found no popular enthusiasm for his cause. The *Arrival* frankly admits that 'right few or almost none' welcomed him, and recruitment was disappointing even in ancestral Yorkist manors.

The first commented addition to his army was at Doncaster on the 23rd, where he was joined by 160 men-at-arms led by William, son of the 71-year-old West Midlands magnate John Sutton, Baron Dudley, who had fought and nearly died for Lancaster at Blore Heath in 1459.* Bypassed, Montagu emerged from Pontefract and shadowed Edward's army from a position well to the east of his line of march.

Meanwhile Exeter, Oxford and Beaumont marched out of East Anglia to confront Edward at Newark, only to find that he had left the Great North Road to gain the Western Spur at Nottingham, where 600 Lancashire men under William Parr, lord of Kendal, and James Harrington joined him. Edward then made a feint towards

---

*William Sutton's subsequent career in the Church was meteoric. Immediately made canon and then dean of the Chapel Royal at Windsor, Edward made him Bishop of Durham in 1476.

Newark and his enemies retreated to join forces with Montagu, putting themselves several days' march behind.

On 28 March Edward arrived at Leicester where he was joined by 300 men led by William Stanley, a signal that his weathervane brother Lord Stanley had deserted Warwick. The game-changer was the arrival of Hastings's east Midlands affinity, some 3,000 men led by William Noreys. Noreys had fought against Edward at Towton but was reconciled and made Sheriff of Buckinghamshire and Oxfordshire, and he also brought men of his own.

Numbers tell less than half the story, however. Even though Edward cannot have had more than 7,000 men by now, he had recovered his aura as a winner blessed by Lady Luck, and as an inspiring and dynamic military commander. Recruitment would have picked up markedly after Leicester and on 29 March Edward arrived at Coventry, where Warwick had shut himself up with 6–7,000 men,

Edward challenged him to personal combat but Warwick refused to emerge. He was waiting for Montagu and the others to close up behind Edward, but they were confronted by a strong rearguard left by Edward at Leicester, probably Hastings's men. It follows that Edward must have been posturing outside Coventry with considerably less men than Warwick had inside. It was a measure of Edward's reputation that Warwick preferred to be seen to play the coward than to risk a sortie.

The first three weeks of the campaign had seen a contrast between Edward's aggressive, direct English way of war and the continental style favoured by Warwick – of manoeuvre and of never risking battle unless the odds were stacked in your favour. The great heavyweight champion Jack Dempsey once defined the difference perfectly: 'All the time he's boxing, he's thinking, and all the time he was thinking, I was hitting him'.

XVIII

EPIC OF ARMS

W**HEN EDWARD LEFT COVENTRY AND MARCHED** through Warwickshire on 2 April, it was a non-destructive *chevauchée* to show that the earl could not protect the heart of his Midlands power, whose military-age men were closed up with him in Coventry. But it was also a move dictated by the approach of Clarence from the West Country with about 4,000 men. He had sent messages to his father-in-law urging him to avoid combat until he arrived.

In fact Clarence had been intending to turn his coat again ever since Margaret lent Edward and Richard the money to return to England. She and their mother had been urging him to take stock of his precarious situation since Louis XI brokered the alliance between Warwick and Marguerite at Angers. He did, but needed their assurance that Edward would not punish his treachery and would permit him to claim his wife's Neville inheritance. No doubt Margaret required a solemn undertaking from Edward as the precondition for the loan.

It cannot be coincidence that Edward met him at Banbury, 6 miles from Edgcote, where Clarence's treachery had cost him Herbert and his Welsh supporters. That he took his army with him indicates how little faith he put in Margaret's assurances that her favourite brother would, for once, keep his word. There was no chance Clarence would face Edward in battle and he duly grovelled.

Edward embraced him, but kept him by his side for the rest of the campaign and dispersed his men among the rest of the army.

We should spare a thought for Clarence's followers. His retainers would be resigned to sharing their lord's fortunes, but for the levies, recruited under commissions of array issued by Warwick in the name of Henry VI, profound relief after the royal brothers embraced at Banbury would have been followed by bewilderment. Many would have considered their terms of service fulfilled and returned to their homes in Somerset, Wiltshire and Gloucestershire.

Clarence brought more than dubiously dependable men with him. He had been Warwick's liaison with John Talbot, Earl of Shrewsbury, and was able to assure Edward that Talbot had no intention of getting involved in the latest round of fighting. William of Worcester wrote that Shrewsbury was 'more devoted to literature and the muses than to politics and arms', and he may not have been physically robust – he was only 24 years old when he died in 1473.

On 4 April the reunited brothers were back before the walls of Coventry, where Clarence attempted to persuade Warwick to surrender. The Kingmaker's rage can readily be imagined. Clarence's defection also meant that Warwick's allied lords chose not to fight Edward's rearguard at Leicester. Meanwhile Lord Howard declared for Edward in Suffolk. Oxford and Beaumont had drawn away all those ready to fight for Lancaster and, like Hastings's affinity in the east Midlands, the East Anglian Yorkists were now free to show their colours.

News that Louis XI and Duke Charles had agreed a truce on 4 April would have taken time to percolate, and it must have been a bitter blow to Warwick. He had spent much of his political capital to deliver the Anglo–French treaty and to prepare for a war that might see him become lord of Holland and Zeeland, all now for nothing. We may fairly doubt Louis ever intended to deliver on his promise, but now whatever chance there had been was gone.*

---

*Louis must also have recalled the mercenaries he had lent Warwick at this time, in accordance with the terms of the truce.

Edward IV and Queen Elizabeth, from life, as portrayed in the Royal Window at Canterbury Cathedral.

A portrait of Edward IV, painted *c.* 1471.

A copy of the earliest known portrait of Elizabeth Woodville
at Queens' College, Cambridge.

The only known image of Richard 'the Kingmaker' Neville,
on the Richard Beauchamp funerary monument at the
Collegiate Church of St Mary Warwick.

King Louis XI of France
– 'the Universal Spider'.

Duke Charles 'the Bold'
of Burgundy.

RICARDVS · III · ANG · REX ·

Richard III: the portrait that launched the cult.

The earliest known portrait of Richard III.

A painted terracotta bust of Henry VII by Pietro Torrigiano, *c.* 1509.

Edward recalled Hastings's men and on 5 April set out for London. The fastest route was along Watling Street, but he detoured through Daventry and Northampton, perhaps to punish them for supporting the 1469 rebellion. From Daventry on 7 April he sent a letter to the mayor and aldermen of London demanding they welcome him as their king. The same day Warwick also wrote to the authorities and to his brother Archbishop Neville, ordering them to hold the city long enough for him to close up behind Edward.

A few days earlier Mayor Stockton had developed a diplomatic illness and left Alderman Thomas Cooke in charge. There was probably no more fanatical Lancastrian in all England. Cooke had been cruelly victimized by Edward and Elizabeth, and his hopes for reparation rested entirely with Warwick's regime. However, he was no fool, and once Edward's and Warwick's letters arrived he loaded his worldly goods and sailed to France.

On 8 April, Palm Sunday, Archbishop Neville summoned all Lancastrian men-at-arms to assemble at St Paul's in harness but only 600–700 responded. He rode holding Henry VI's hand from St Paul's through London, but it was a dismal parade. The king himself was shabbily dressed and only one secular lord, 70-year-old Ralph Boteler, Baron Sudeley, led the way, holding the king's sword. As the *Great Chronicle of London* elegantly put it, the spectacle 'pleased the citizens as a fire painted on the wall warmed the old woman'.

Notably not taking part in the parade were the Beaufort brothers. The restored Duke of Somerset, his brother the Marquess of Dorset and John Courtenay, Earl of Devon, departed together for the West Country on 8 April to meet Marguerite, who was expected to cross the Channel soon. They were armed with the king's appointment of Prince Edward, his son, as Lieutenant of England in replacement of Warwick.

On 9 April the city fathers sent Edward a reply saying they would welcome him, and on the 10th Archbishop Neville sent him a letter begging for grace. On the 11th Yorkist supporters peacefully took over the Tower, freeing the Duke of Suffolk, the Bourchiers, the Earl of Wiltshire, Baron Mountjoy and Henry Stafford. Elizabeth and her children remained at Westminster Abbey, but the Bishops of Ely, Bath and Rochester, Edward's office holders, emerged blinking from sanctuary at St Martin's Le Grand.

On 12 April Edward marched his army into the city, according to the *Great Chronicle* led by 'black and smoky sort of Flemish gunners'. He was greeted by Stockton and all those dignitaries who had not committed themselves too publicly to the Readeption. Sudeley, Archbishop Neville and the Lancastrian Bishops of Lichfield/Coventry and Lincoln/Dorchester were sent to occupy the cells in the Tower so recently vacated by the Yorkist lords, but there was no purge of Lancastrian supporters. Even the mob prudently did not celebrate the occasion in the traditional manner.

Edward first gave thanks at St Paul's, and then went to the Bishop of London's palace to take possession of Henry VI. In a letter to her mother-in-law, Duchess Margaret said they shook hands and Henry greeted Edward with the words 'My cousin of York, you are very welcome. I know that in your hands my life will not be in danger'. It was a poignant remark, which also suggests he felt no such security with Warwick. He also went back to the Tower, perhaps to the old quarters from which he had been unwillingly plucked nineteen months earlier.

Finally Edward was free to be reunited with his family at the Abbey, and to hold his 5-month-old namesake son for the first time. There was little time to do more before he sent them, too, to the Tower – along with his mother. Whether Duchess Cecily was sent there for safekeeping or to make sure she did not try to deal herself a hand in the fluid situation we cannot know. Edward's meeting with his mother, no doubt accompanied by his brother Clarence, and her reaction to being forced to associate with Elizabeth are unfortunately not recorded, but no doubt all involved exercised a great deal of tight-lipped self-restraint.

Edward could spend no time on niceties because on Good Friday

Warwick arrived at St Albans with a large artillery train and an army that outnumbered his own. Edward was joined by contingents from the south-east led by Lord Saye and Humphrey Bourchier, Thomas FitzAlan and Anthony Grey, the heirs of Lord Berners and the Earls of Arundel and Kent. Lord Howard may also have arrived with men from Suffolk and Essex. The Duke of Norfolk, who had escaped from the Tower earlier, was still gathering his affinity.

Even allowing for wastage to ale and bawdy houses, and others who thought entering London was 'job done' and went home, the *Arrival* was propaganda and certainly understated Edward's numbers (9,000) while overstating Warwick's (20,000). More believable estimates emerge if we increase and decrease them proportionally, to give us 12,000 (the figure given in Duchess Margaret's previously cited letter) versus 15,000.

One can only guess where the others fought, but riding with Edward were Clarence, Duras and the Woodville brothers Anthony, Earl Rivers, and Edward, whom Anthony permitted to use his subsidiary title of Lord Scales. Richard of Gloucester led the vanguard with Lord Ferrers and William Blount, Lord Mountjoy's heir, and Hastings the rearguard with Henry Tudor's stepfather Henry Stafford, and another Humphrey Bourchier, Lord Cromwell.* Miserable Henry VI was with the baggage train – for what reason is hard to fathom.

Edward could expect Warwick to set up behind his artillery and wait to be attacked – it was what he had done at the Second Battle of St Albans, and what he had intended to do during the Edgcote campaign. The king might have contemplated marching around him, but by the time the foreriders of the two armies made contact his room for manoeuvre was severely limited. According to a very useful contemporary account by the well-connected Gerhard von Wesel, one of the Cologne Hansards' London representatives (my italics):

---

*Lord Cromwell was the son and Lord Berners the brother of Henry Bourchier, Earl of Essex.

18. BATTLE OF BARNET
15 April 1471

WOODS

Hatfield Road

St Albans Road

Deadman's Bottom

Warwick

Chantry

Oxford   Montagu   Exeter

Richard

Monken Mead Brook

Edward

Hastings

Monument

Beech Hill

Ancient hedge

Warwick

Traditional

Oxford   Montagu

Exeter

Modern A 1061

Hadley Green

Hadley church

Hadley Common

Richard

Edward

Hastings

N

Contours @ 15 feet intervals

Barnet church

London

© Hugh Bicheno

0   1/4   1/2

mile

On Easter Eve around seven o'clock in the evening, as King Edward marched away from here and came into the vicinity of Hornsey Park, six miles from London, Warwick's vanguard encountered him and they had a skirmish thereabouts and they chased each other in the dark as far as a village called Barnet, ten miles from London. Warwick and his lords and companions who had been in Coventry pitched their battle *a mile beyond the said village, just beside the highway to St Albans* on a broad green plot, and King Edward's people, not really knowing in the night where the opposing parties were, also in the night rode onto the same plot and set up their camp on the other side of the afore-said highway, *just opposite Warwick, in a hollow and marsh.*

Even without the support of Wesel's report, topography argues that the northern site in Map 18, across the St Albans and Hatfield (Great North) Roads, was the logical place for Warwick to deploy. The traditional location further south was unconvincing even before archaeologists failed to find any battle debris at the site. The clinching argument is that Warwick's guns fired over the heads of Edward's troops through the night. They were, therefore, either in the featureless hollow south-east of Hadley, or else marched along the Beech Hill road before descending into the Monken Mead valley and forming up on the far side of the brook, as described by Wesel. There is no question which was the more likely.

Thanks to the earlier success of his fore-riders Edward knew where the enemy was deployed, while Warwick did not. He held nothing in reserve and in thick mist at dawn on Easter Sunday he launched his entire force in an oblique attack. The tactic, later made famous by Frederick the Great, involves crumpling the opposing line pro-gressively from one flank. Ironically Edward learned the technique at Northampton, his first battle, where Warwick's uncle the veteran William Neville, Lord Fauconberg, employed it.

An oblique attack provides a unifying explanation for the known features of the battle. Warwick's guns were ineffective, which they would not have been had Edward made a frontal assault. Gloucester, on Edward's right, overlapped and drove in Warwick's left, under Exeter, and the main battle under Montagu could only wheel to face the oblique attack and to maintain contact with the retreating men. Warwick would have led the reserve to reinforce his left, which stabilized the fighting line roughly along the Hatfield (Great North) Road. The effect was to turn the line of battle through 45 degrees.

On Warwick's right Oxford and Beaumont did more than simply conform to Montagu's redeployment. They charged through their gun line to attack Hastings's approaching battle, which they out-flanked and drove back. It was probably here that Lord Cromwell was killed and Henry Stafford mortally wounded. If Oxford and Beaumont had managed to keep their men in hand they might have rolled up the outnumbered Yorkists, but they could not. The mist prevented the men from seeing that their success was not matched further north and they pursued Hastings's fleeing men as far as Barnet, where they found the Yorkist baggage train and fell to looting. They also found Henry VI, who was led away along the St Albans Road.

As so often in the Wars of the Roses, the outcome of the brutal struggle along the Great North Road was decided by a sudden col-lapse of morale. Oxford and Beaumont managed to rally about 800 men and marched back from Barnet. Prevented by the mist from seeing how far the battle lines had wheeled, they attacked what they believed was the rear of the Yorkist line. Unfortunately it was the flank of Montagu's battle, which had been holding its own against Edward's. The confusion was compounded by the similarity between the star with streams (rays) livery worn by Oxford's men and Edward's sun with streams.

Cries of 'treason' rippled through Warwick's army and it abruptly dissolved in flight. Local historian Brian Warren has identified the place where a chantry for the dead was built after the battle, which in our reconstruction would correspond to the place where Montagu and such of his men who did not flee made a last stand and were killed. Warwick, at the northern end of the line, rode away but was caught in the woods, killed and stripped of his armour. Severely wounded Exeter was also stripped and lay naked on the battlefield all day until his servants found him and bore him to sanctuary at Westminster Abbey.

Oxford, Beaumont and Oxford's brothers George and Richard Vere fled north, but the group escorting Henry VI abandoned him and he was recaptured and taken back to the Tower. Ten thousand arrows were said to have littered the field and about 3,000 men lay dead. A 3:1 ratio gives us a figure of 9,000 wounded for a staggering overall casualty rate. Wesel again:

> Those who went out with good horses and sound bodies brought home sorry nags and bandaged faces without noses etc. and wounded bodies, God have mercy on the miserable spectacle, but all men say that there was never in a hundred years a fiercer battle in England than this last Easter day as is aforewritten, may God henceforth grant us His eternal peace.

As well as Lord Cromwell and Henry Stafford, among the Yorkists Lord Berners's heir (the other Humphrey Bourchier), Lord Saye and William Blount were killed, while Richard of Gloucester and Earl Rivers were wounded, Rivers severely. Once again Edward, who would have been in the thick of the fighting, was unhurt. After a rest at Barnet he marched back to London, arriving in the evening at St Paul's, where the Archbishop of Canterbury and all the bishops not imprisoned in the Tower greeted him and a 'Te Deum' was sung.

The bodies of Warwick and Montagu were brought to St Paul's and exposed to public view for two days. Instead of quartering them and exposing their remains to further viewing around the kingdom, Edward permitted their burial alongside their parents at Bisham Abbey, the ancestral seat of the Earls of Salisbury in Berkshire. The once great Marcher and Midlands affinities of the Beauchamp,

Despenser and Montague earldoms would have no shrine to their lost leader.

Edward may have felt some regret it had come to this. Warwick had once been his admired mentor, and he had regarded Montagu as a friend. His greater regret, however, was for the sheer wastefulness of it all. The fruits of ten years of conciliation and moderate rule lay trampled into the blood-soaked earth north of Barnet. That the common people had favoured Warwick was something even the *Arrival* admitted and that, too, caused the iron to enter into his soul. He was a harder man and a more cynical monarch after Barnet.

With his battered army dispersed, and even as the corpses of Warwick and Montagu were on display at St Paul's, Edward learned that Queen Marguerite and her son Prince Edward had arrived from France at Weymouth in Dorset. It was no coincidence that they should have disembarked in the midst of the final showdown between Edward and Warwick – Marguerite and her supporters had been awaiting just such an opportunity.

XIX

CRUSH THE SEED

ONCE IT IS ACCEPTED THAT THE EVENTS OF 1470–1 were a three-way struggle, the pieces of the jigsaw come together, as they never did in Warwick's mind. On 17 December he obtained £2,000 from the exchequer to cross the Channel 'with an army of ships and men' to bring Marguerite and her son to England, but she would not move from Rouen. Again, in late February 1471, he travelled to Dover to receive them, having sent John Fortescue and Lord Treasurer Langstrother ahead to reassure her, but she still refused to move.

At some point he also sent Lord Wenlock from Calais, presumably with warships, but when Marguerite and Prince Edward eventually left Rouen they went to Harfleur, opposite Honfleur in the Seine estuary. The Cotentin ports or Dieppe would have been the appropriate choices if her intention were to sail with the prevailing wind to the south-east of England, where Warwick expected them to land. Harfleur was, however, an ideal place from which to sail to the West Country with an easterly wind. We know Edward sailed with just such a wind from Flushing on 11 March, which poses the pregnant question why Marguerite did not.

There was, of course, a credible threat of interception at sea by the Burgundians or Bretons, and Marguerite presumably convinced Langstrother and Wenlock that this was the reason for her unwillingness to risk the crossing. But with adequate escorts on offer, as excuses go it was almost as thin as the unnecessary, and needlessly delayed papal dispensation for her son's marriage that served to explain the first three months of procrastination.

The final pieces dropped into place in late March and early April, after Warwick had left London to confront Edward. Henry VI disempowered him by declaring his son Lieutenant of England, and in response to Warwick's urgent request that London should be held as the anvil on which he would crush Edward, the Beaufort brothers and the Earl of Devon marched their retainers out of the city to meet Marguerite at Weymouth, next to the Purbeck peninsula, the ancestral domain of the Beauforts.

Once the royal party did set out across the Channel, the ship carrying Anne, Countess of Warwick, sailed separately to Portsmouth, 75 miles east of Weymouth. This was either because her ship's captain had instructions to separate her from her daughter, now Princess of Wales, or because the countess belatedly realized that the Lancastrians intended to stab her husband in the back. After she learned that Warwick was dead she made no effort to join Marguerite and sought sanctuary in nearby Beaulieu Abbey.

We have already reviewed the motives of Louis XI and Charles of Burgundy. Louis had no further use for Warwick once it became apparent he could not deliver the promised military support. Charles's simultaneous release of his Lancastrian pensioners and pressure on Edward to sail as soon as possible was flagrant pot-stirring. One can interpret their truce on 4 April as recognition that Louis's gamble had failed, and that they should await the outcome of events in England as spectators at a sideshow that now affected them very little.

In sum, there is no indication that Marguerite ever intended to make common cause with Warwick. The Beauforts and Devon could never be reconciled with the man who had killed their fathers and had been the mainstay of the regime that killed their brothers. Their plan was to recruit a new army under the banner of Prince Edward, which would then join up with Jasper Tudor's Welshmen and the Lancastrians of Cheshire and Lancashire before marching on London to put the prince on the throne, which his father would willingly abdicate.

Marguerite was supposed to have crossed earlier, before Barnet, but adverse winds kept her in port a crucial week too long. News of Warwick's defeat and death on the day of her arrival was certainly unwelcome. She had been counting on him to eliminate Edward, and then find himself challenged by her son at the head of an army of unsullied Lancastrians. However her supporters were undismayed – indeed delighted that one of their blood enemies was dead and the other's armed strength severely depleted.

Flanked by Somerset, Dorset and Devon, Prince Edward and his mother led a growing army to Exeter, where it was joined by Devon's affinity and by Hugh Courtenay of Bocconoc. The Courtenays of Powderham who, like Hugh, had crossed the Channel with Warwick, did not respond and later joined Edward's army. They had not forgotten their bitter feud with the senior branch of the family in 1459–61. Their Hungerford and Luttrell relatives did, however, join the Lancastrian army when it marched through Somerset.

They stayed too long at Exeter. They were there from 19 to 27

April, which compounded the royal party's delay in crossing the Channel and gave Edward too much time to prepare. He sent out urgent summons for a new army to assemble at Windsor, where he arrived on the 19th. Windsor was on the highway from Dorset to London but on the 24th, deciding that reports of a Lancastrian advance through Salisbury were probably a feint, he set out to prevent it joining forces with Jasper Tudor.

Edward marched with the hard core of the Barnet army and a large contingent brought by the Duke of Norfolk. Apart from his brothers and Hastings, the only other peer was John Brooke, Lord Cobham, following in his father's footsteps as the most doggedly loyal Yorkist baron. Other companies from all over England joined during the march. After Tewkesbury Edward honoured nine company commanders by making them knights banneret. They came from Suffolk, Norfolk, Cambridgeshire, Northamptonshire, Bedfordshire, Warwickshire, Staffordshire, Dorset and Devon (Powderham).

He covered only 36 miles in the first four days and spent 27–28 April at Abingdon, south of Oxford, gathering strength and waiting for his scouts to confirm that the enemy was indeed marching north, but ready to double back if necessary. Once sure, he covered the next 33 miles in a day, arriving at Cirencester on the 29th. Map 20 shows the strategic significance of the town, at the intersection of the main highway from south Wales, of Akeman Street to St Albans, and the Fosse Way between the West Country and the Midlands.

Meanwhile the Lancastrians arrived at Wells on the 28th, where, according to Edward's once and future Lord Chancellor Bishop Stillington, they sacked his palace and emptied the jails. He was not believed and later fined for not having ensured the secure custody of Lancastrian prisoners. The Lancastrians then returned to the Fosse Way to arrive at Bath on 30 April, where they learned that Edward was 31 miles away, across their line of march. A game of cat and mouse ensued, in which the Lancastrians initially had the better part.

First, they led Edward to believe they intended to continue along the Fosse Way, causing him to advance 12 miles to Malmesbury on 1 May. Instead they marched west to Bristol, where they reprovisioned, equipped their troops from the royal armoury, including field artillery, and were joined by the city militia led by City Recorder Nicholas Hervey. The next day they made a feint towards Sodbury, and Edward marched 14 miles overnight to arrive at the village in the morning of 2 May. He stayed there, without news of the enemy, until early the next day.

He had been sold a dummy, as the Lancastrians marched instead to Berkeley, 13 miles north of Sodbury. They had stolen a march and if they could have crossed the Severn by the causeway at Gloucester it might have changed the complexion of the campaign. Their hopes were dashed when they arrived at ten in the morning of 3 May, having marched the 37 miles from Bristol with only a brief pause at Berkeley.

The *Arrival* admits 'many of the inhabitants of [Gloucester] were greatly disposed towards them', but a loyal Yorkist forewarned by Edward held the town, and the Lancastrians found the gates barred and the wall guns manned against them: 'Of this demeaning they took right great displeasure, and made great menaces, and pretended as though they would have assaulted the town... but, as those that kept the town and [those] that so pretended knew well, the king with a mighty puissance was near to them.'

The footsore army could not stay and marched on towards the next Severn crossing at Lower Lode, a ferry crossing 10 miles away outside Tewkesbury. There was no question of trying to ferry the army across with Edward so close behind, and they rested for the night about half a mile from Tewkesbury, around some old earthworks today known as Queen Margaret's Camp. The queen herself is believed to have spent the night in nearby Gupshill Manor.

Edward's army was no less exhausted. On 3 May he drove it over the 31 miles from Sodbury to Cheltenham in twelve hours, arriving at 5 p.m. The town was 6 miles from Tewkesbury, but his scouts confirmed that the Lancastrians intended to make a stand:

> Upon the morrow following, Saturday the 4th day of May, [Edward] apparelled himself, and all his host set in good array; ordained three wards; displayed his banners; did blow up the trumpets; committed his cause and quarrel to Almighty God... and advanced directly upon his enemies; approaching to their field, which was strongly [placed] in a marvellously strong ground, full difficult to be assailed.

Assuming that neither the contours nor the courses of the river Swilgate and the Coln Brook have changed radically over the intervening centuries, the 'marvellously strong ground' lay across half a mile of undulating ground between the two streams, facing the Cheltenham road. From east to west the three battles were commanded by Devon, Wenlock and Somerset. A hill, now crowned by a cemetery, within the boundary of what was a cultivated area known as The Gastons, gave a commanding view of the area where the Yorkists deployed. The Lancastrian reserve, under Prince Edward, would have been stationed on its slopes.

The traditional deployment has Edward commanding the main battle, flanked on the left by Richard of Gloucester and on the right by Hastings. This cannot be correct. Norfolk was a royal duke, the hereditary Earl Marshal of England, and he had brought the largest contingent to join Edward's army. He was certainly in command of the main battle, while the king would no less certainly have commanded a reserve of hand-picked knights behind him. Edward also sent 200 'lances' to a wooded hill on his left flank.

A 'lance' was a unit of military accounting and usually meant a mounted man-at-arms *and his personal retinue*, so this was a force three or more times greater than 200. It was not a reconnaissance in force but a major tactical deployment with which Edward always intended to outflank the Lancastrian army. The absence of tactical details in the *Arrival* was quite deliberate – as before, with regard to the landing at Ravenspur, Edward did not want to advertise his skill.

It was a relatively small battle, with no more than 7–8,000 men on either side. The Lancastrian position was strong, with its flanks covered by the river Swilgate and Coln Brook, and could be attacked only over broken ground that would make it difficult to maintain formation, against an enemy partially concealed by vegetation. Unaware of the threat from the wooded hill, the *Arrival* describes how Somerset sought to use the terrain to deliver a flank attack of his own:

> In the front of their field were so evil lanes, and deep dykes, so many hedges, trees and bushes, that it was right hard to approach them near, and come to hands: but Edmund, called Duke of Somerset, having that day the vaward, whether it were for that he and his fellowship were sore annoyed in the place where they were, as well with guns-shot as with shot of arrows... or else of great heart and courage, knightly and manly advanced himself with his fellowship, somewhat aside-hand the king's vaward, and, by certain paths and ways before surveyed, and to the king's party unknown, he departed out of the field, passed a lane, and came into a fair place or close, and... from the hill that was in that close he set right fiercely upon the end of the king's [army].

Somerset's attack threw Gloucester's division into disorder, and if supported by Wenlock might have decided the battle. No such support came and 'the king, full manly, set forth even upon them, entered and won the dyke and hedge upon them, into the close, and with great violence, put them up towards the hill'. Somerset's men were also attacked from the rear by the cavalry Edward had sent to the wooded hill and they broke, fleeing towards Lower Lode, to be massacred in the area known today as Bloody Meadow.

Although the anecdote dates from an account written many years later, it is believable Somerset should have made his way back to

Wenlock and brained him with his poleaxe. Whether true or not, panic spread and Wenlock's division dissolved, followed by Devon's. The fleeing men ran towards the bridges over the Swilgate, their flight covered by knots of men-at-arms who stood their ground. Wenlock, Devon, the Prince of Wales, Dorset and twenty-one named knights were killed on the battlefield.

Somerset and no few others did not stand, and rode to seek sanctuary in Tewkesbury Abbey. It was not an authorized place of sanctuary and despite the protestations of the clergy they were dragged out the next day. Tried by Norfolk as Earl Marshal and Gloucester as Constable of England, they were beheaded on a scaffold erected at the crossroads in the middle of the town. The first two to die were Somerset and Langstrother, who feature in an illustrated Burgundian copy of a briefer, more immediately written version of the *Arrival*, which shows a simpering Edward in the last place one would choose to stand when witnessing a beheading.

The third, Humphrey Tuchet, personified the divided loyalties and rivalries that ran below the surface of the Wars of the Roses like a neural map. He was the brother of Lord Audley, Edward's close friend since 1460, uncle of Lord Cobham and married to one of the Powderham Courtenays, one of whom Edward made a knight banneret for his company's service during the Tewkesbury campaign.

Hugh Courtenay of Bocconoc was among the fifteen others beheaded. The nine lives of Thomas Tresham, the oft-pardoned Speaker of the 1459 'Parliament of Devils' who had so narrowly escaped execution in 1468, finally ran out. Foresworn Nicholas Hervey, Recorder of Bristol, and John Delves, High Sheriff of Staffordshire, followed, but several of the others were men who never compromised with the Yorkist regime and whose only crime had been to accompany Marguerite and her son through the long years of exile.

Edward was also liberal in reward. As well as the nine bannerets, he knighted forty-five men after the battle – one, James Crowner of Tunstall in Staffordshire, was knighted on the battlefield, an indication that he had saved the king's life or performed some other notable act of valour at his side. Another of those knighted was George, heir to Edward Neville, Baron Bergavenny. George's minority had given Warwick the opportunity to dispossess Edward, his own uncle, when he seized every inch of land he could claim as his wife's inheritance.*

On 7 May Edward set out towards Worcester to deal with reported disturbances in the North. En route he learned that Marguerite and her now widowed daughter-in-law Anne Neville had been found in a 'poor religious house', probably Little Malvern, 10 miles north-west of Tewkesbury. They may have observed the battle from the abbey tower and escaped across the footbridge over the weir at the nearby water mill. The queen had been a thorn in Edward's side for ten years, and the news was most gratifying.

Still better news came at Coventry on the 13th, when Henry Percy arrived to inform him that the reports from the North were false, and that Lancastrians and Warwick retainers alike sought only the king's grace. This was as well, because even as he hunted Marguerite's army Edward received disquieting reports that he had not severed all the heads of the Neville hydra.

Not the least of the smiles bestowed on Edward by Lady Luck was that the Bastard of Fauconberg, in command of Warwick's squadron at Calais, only crossed the Channel to arrive at Sandwich on 2 May, eighteen days after Barnet. With him were 300 of Warwick's Calais retainers led by Geoffrey Gates, deputy lieutenant since Wenlock's departure. Undeterred by Warwick's defeat and death, the men of Kent rose up once more and the Mayor of Canterbury, Nicholas Faunt, threw the resources of the city behind the insurgency.

Joined by contingents from Surrey and Essex, by 8 May Neville was at Sittingbourne, whence he sent a letter to the mayor and aldermen of London demanding free passage through the city so

---

*Unsurprisingly, Edward Neville was a loyal Yorkist throughout 1469–71. The title was George's by right of his mother, who died in 1448, but he respected his father's right to it by marriage until his death in 1476.

that he could fight 'the usurper'. The city worthies replied denying his request and asking if he was aware that Warwick and Montagu were dead. It was a good question, and the only logical explanation for the timing of the uprising is if Neville and Gates believed Edward had drawn all the fighting men out of London before marching west.

He had not. He had entrusted the defence of the city to the Earl of Essex and the recuperating Earl Rivers and their retainers, and veteran Lord Dudley had command of the well-garrisoned Tower. It was as well Edward did take these precautions, because Neville's squadron sailed up the Thames and during the week 12–18 May the city was subjected to combined assaults of unprecedented ferocity. Convalescent Earl Rivers himself had to lead a mounted charge to disperse an attack on Aldgate that came close to breaking through into the city.

Eventually the rebels fell back to Blackheath, where Neville, the Calais contingent and the ships deserted them. Gates and his men returned to Calais, but Neville stayed at Sandwich to trade the squadron for a pardon on 26 May. It bought him four months. Ordered to serve in Yorkshire, in late September Richard of Gloucester had him executed on trumped-up charges, and his head went to join the hideous collection spiked on Tower Bridge.

On 21 May Edward arrived in London with almost the entire peerage in his train, and with Marguerite paraded like a captive in a Roman triumph. Only her Valois blood saved her when Edward closed the book on the House of Lancaster. The *Arrival* disingenuously states that Henry VI died that night of 'pure displeasure and melancholy'. When his bones were examined in 1910 the skull was found to be shattered, with residual scalp and dried blood suggestive of a heavy blow to the back of the head. Edward probably ordered it done as mercifully as possible, and somebody hit him with a club as he knelt, head bowed in prayer.

XX

GLOUCESTER

LITTLE MERCY WAS SHOWN TO THE MEN WHO HAD JOINED Thomas Neville when Edward followed Richard into Kent. Canterbury and the Cinque Ports were deprived of their civic rights and heavily fined. Mayor Faunt and one or two others were hanged, drawn and quartered, and many more were hanged, dispossessed or fined. 'Such as were rich were hanged by the purse, and the others that were needy were hanged by the necks', observed *The Great Chronicle*, 'by means whereof the country was greatly impoverished and the King's coffers some deal increased.'

The Earl of Essex was as harsh to the men of his namesake county. Men were hanged along the road from London to Stratford, and swingeing fines levelled on those rebels whom the Bourchiers chose to spare. Warkworth disapprovingly commented: 'Some men paid 200 marks, some 100 pounds, and some more and some less, so that it cost the poorest man 7 shillings which was not worth so much, but [forced them] to sell such clothing as they had, and borrowed the remnant, and laboured for it afterward.'

Added to which there was a virulent outbreak of the Black Death in August–October 1471, believed to have killed 10–15 per cent of the population, with East Anglia particularly hard hit. We cannot know whether this was seen as God's punishment for rebellion or for the murder of Henry VI; but a natural catastrophe of this magnitude must have had a chilling effect on political ardour.

The Calais garrison once more exploited its unique situation to obtain a pardon, and in July Hastings arrived with 1,500 men to reinforce its garrison and those of the outlying forts, dismissing the 500 men Warwick had sent in late 1470. Howard, Hastings's deputy, took over what had been Warwick's private navy. Geoffrey Gates and others who had played leading roles in the rebellions were, remarkably, left in place. Some months later Calais was attacked by Oxford and others who had escaped from Barnet, and the old garrison fought them off.

Jasper Tudor was still active in Wales and Edward commissioned Roger Vaughan of Tretower to deal with him. Instead, Jasper captured Roger and beheaded him at Chepstow in revenge for the execution of his father Owen after Mortimer's Cross in 1461. He then retreated with his nephew Henry to Pembroke Castle, where he was allegedly besieged by Morgan ap Thomas, who was in turn allegedly driven off by his brother David. The story was concocted by Morgan to discredit David, who was disputing his leadership of their locally powerful clan, and to conceal his own complicity in the unimpeded escape of the Tudors to Brittany.*

The most pressing political problem Edward had to resolve was not the South-East, Calais or Wales, but the perennial dilemma of what to do about the North. His solution brings 18-year-old Gloucester into the mainstream of our story, as he was entrusted with the delicate task of winning over the now leaderless Neville affinity. The purpose was to prevent both the resurgent Percy affinity and the untrustworthy Lord Stanley from filling the void of authority.

On 29 June Gloucester was given stewardship of Middleham, Sheriff Hutton and Penrith, and two weeks later Edward turned this into a grant of all the ex-Salisbury lands in Yorkshire and Cumberland entailed to male heirs. These should have passed to Montagu's 11-year-old son George, Duke of Bedford, but the king

*They were the sons of Thomas ap Gruffudd, killed fighting for Jasper at Mortimer's Cross. Edward did not believe Morgan's story and had him arrested.

and his brothers were to behave with total indifference to the property rights of the heirs, wives and mothers of the men they had lately defeated.

On 4 July Edward awarded Gloucester all the offices held by Warwick in the region. He became Warden of the West March, thus Constable of Carlisle Castle, Chief Steward of the duchy of Lancaster in the North – except for Knaresborough Castle, awarded to Henry Percy as complementary to his neighbouring lordship of Spofforth – and High Sheriff of Westmorland. The king also made him the Chief Steward of the duchy of York in the North and Constable of the family castles of Sandal and Conisbrough.

Warwick's retainers welcomed Gloucester. They had seen him grow up under Warwick's tutelage at Middleham from the age of 12 to 16, and appear to have liked him. It was their chance for redemption after many years of treasonous activity and they took it, serving him as faithfully as they had served Salisbury and Warwick. It was a warrior society, and his path was smoothed by his creditable performance at Barnet and Tewkesbury. To telescope the events of the following years, even as Gloucester was consolidating his new domain he set about extending it. The low-hanging fruit was picked first. The lands of Joan Fauconberg, widow of Warwick's uncle William Neville, Earl of Kent, were taken in exchange for an annuity. The Durham castles and manors of Raby and Brancepeth, held by the senior branch of the Neville family, were also ripe for plucking because Ralph Neville, 2nd Earl of Westmorland, had been incapacitated by dementia since the late 1450s.

The estates were managed by Westmorland's grandson and heir Ralph, Baron Neville, who was vulnerable for other reasons. His father had played a leading role in the ambush of Richard of York at Wakefield before being killed in turn, along with his cousin Thomas, Lord Clifford, at Dintingdale in 1461. Two more cousins, Humphrey and Charles Neville, had been executed for treason in 1469. All had been attainted.

Lord Ralph made a virtue of necessity and became not so much

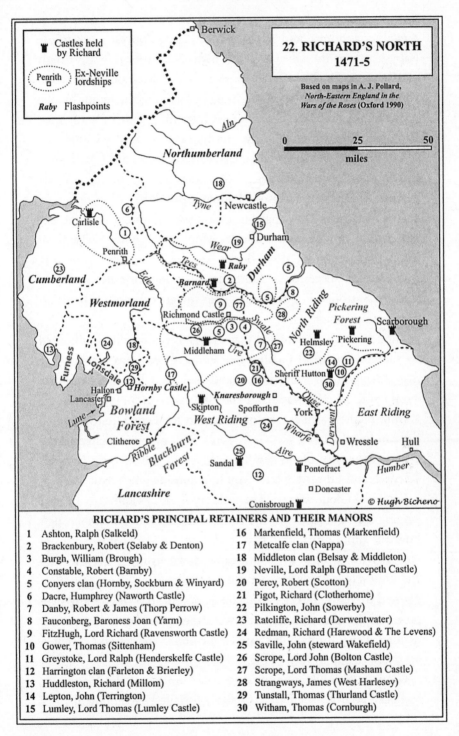

22. RICHARD'S NORTH 1471-5

Based on maps in A. J. Pollard, *North-Eastern England in the Wars of the Roses* (Oxford 1990)

Castles held by Richard

Penrith Ex-Neville lordships

Raby Flashpoints

0   25   50
miles

RICHARD'S PRINCIPAL RETAINERS AND THEIR MANORS

1	Ashton, Ralph (Salkeld)	16	Markenfield, Thomas (Markenfield)
2	Brackenbury, Robert (Selaby & Denton)	17	Metcalfe clan (Nappa)
3	Burgh, William (Brough)	18	Middleton clan (Belsay & Middleton)
4	Constable, Robert (Barnby)	19	Neville, Lord Ralph (Brancepeth Castle)
5	Conyers clan (Hornby, Sockburn & Winyard)	20	Percy, Robert (Scotton)
6	Dacre, Humphrey (Naworth Castle)	21	Pigot, Richard (Clotherhome)
7	Danby, Robert & James (Thorp Perrow)	22	Pilkington, John (Sowerby)
8	Fauconberg, Baroness Joan (Yarm)	23	Ratcliffe, Richard (Derwentwater)
9	FitzHugh, Lord Richard (Ravensworth Castle)	24	Redman, Richard (Harewood & The Levens)
10	Gower, Thomas (Sittenham)	25	Saville, John (steward Wakefield)
11	Greystoke, Lord Ralph (Henderskelfe Castle)	26	Scrope, Lord John (Bolton Castle)
12	Harrington clan (Farleton & Brierley)	27	Scrope, Lord Thomas (Masham Castle)
13	Huddleston, Richard (Millom)	28	Strangways, James (West Harlesey)
14	Lepton, John (Terrington)	29	Tunstall, Thomas (Thurland Castle)
15	Lumley, Lord Thomas (Lumley Castle)	30	Witham, Thomas (Cornburgh)

a retainer as a loyal and valued subject, and Gloucester was to use Raby Castle as though it were his own. No doubt this was deeply gratifying to Duchess Cecily, known as the 'Rose of Raby' in her youth, before the castle passed into the hands of the senior branch of the family. Gloucester also forced Edmund, heir to the attainted barony of Roos, to sell him the family seat of Helmsley Castle.

Edward had awarded the large lordship of Barnard Castle, long held by the Earls of Warwick but hotly disputed by the bishop's palatine of Durham, to Bishop Laurence Booth in 1470. Gloucester shared Warwick's view that possession was nine-tenths of the law and would not relinquish the lordship, and ignored subsequent injunctions to do so. After Booth was made Archbishop of York in 1476, his successor at Durham – the meteorically promoted William Sutton – all but handed over the governance of the palatinate to Gloucester.

Gloucester also calculated that Henry Percy would be inhibited by the same political fragility that emasculated Lord Neville. The first three earls of Northumberland had been killed backing the wrong side in civil wars, and the title twice attainted. With the erasure of the Nevilles, the main reason for Percy's restoration to the earldom in 1470 was gone. Percy had, however, delivered the crucial neutrality of his family's affinity in the struggle between Warwick and Edward, which won him considerable credit at court.

So, when Gloucester tried to undermine Percy's authority by challenging his stewardship of the castle and manor of Knaresborough, Edward summoned the two peers to appear before him at Nottingham in May 1473 and came down firmly on Percy's side. The king required his brother not to challenge or claim any office granted to Percy, and not to retain or accept into service any man previously retained by the earl. With their areas of authority now defined, Percy formally became Gloucester's retainer and accepted his overlordship in July 1474.

Gloucester's bullying tactics were not limited to the North. He had been awarded the Earl of Oxford's forfeited patrimony in 1471, but trustees for the dowager duchess held much of it. In response to her son's attacks on Calais, Edward put the lands in Gloucester's custody to prevent her sending any money to her son. In January 1473 Gloucester compelled the elderly lady to surrender her lands in exchange for an annuity. Six of her trustees, including the Bishop of Ely, refused to sign off on the agreement until compelled to do so by the king.*

Gloucester also clashed with Thomas, Lord Stanley, in Lancashire. Gloucester was the dominant lord of Lonsdale and Furness in the north of the county, in the centre lord of Clitheroe and Halton, and of the vast royal hunting grounds known as the 'forests' of Bowland, Amounderness and Blackburn. The feud he inherited between one of his new retainers and Lord Stanley over Hornby Castle and adjacent Farleton in Lonsdale, and of Brierley in the West Riding, was therefore a test of his local authority and good lordship.

The dispute began after Thomas Harrington and his eldest son John were killed fighting for the Yorkists at Wakefield. John left two daughters and after Edward assigned their wardship to others, their uncles James and Robert Harrington seized the girls and their lands, which they claimed were entailed in the male line. In 1468 Edward IV gave wardship of the girls to Lord Stanley, who married them to his sons, claimed the lands by right of primogeniture, and obtained a legal judgement against the Harringtons. Armed clashes, in which Richard may have been involved, followed in 1470.

The feud revived after Edward recovered the throne, with both parties believing they had earned royal favour. James Harrington had been among the first to join the king with a substantial following, but so had William, Lord Stanley's brother. Late in 1471 Edward made Lord Stanley steward of his household, and early in 1472 gave him permission to marry Margaret Beaufort, widowed for the second time when Henry Stafford was killed at Barnet. The balance of favours owed tipped towards the Harringtons.

*Richard assigned the stewardship of the Vere estates to John, Lord Howard, laying the basis for a strong working relationship between the two men.

In 1473 Edward paid it by appointing Gloucester to head a commission empowered to take possession of the castle and hand it over to the Stanleys. As he did in Durham, Gloucester simply ignored his brother's instructions and it was not until 1475 that the Privy Council agreed a compromise by which the Harringtons were granted Farleton and Brierley, and Hornby Castle was at last surrendered to the Stanleys.

The ex-Neville affinity would have been reassured to see their lord follow the principle of 'my retainer, right or wrong' in apparent defiance of his brother, but it was a charade. When Edward gave his brother an unequivocal order, he was obeyed – therefore he gave no such order. He probably felt he had done enough for Stanley, and the dubious value of his good will was not worth the certain cost of undermining Gloucester's good lordship.

Edward was inhibited from showing similar partiality when called upon to mediate between his brothers in their acrimonious dispute over the Warwick inheritance. In exchange for her loan he had promised Margaret that Clarence would be permitted to inherit Warwick's estate through his wife Isabel Neville. He had already reneged as much as he dared by awarding Gloucester lands in the North and in Wales dishonestly obtained by Warwick.

Blithely overlooking that Warwick would not have rebelled in 1469 without him, Clarence felt that Margaret's loan and his opportune coat-turning entitled him to as great or greater consideration than his younger brother. He was determined to take possession of the whole of the legitimate Warwick inheritance, to which end he claimed custody of Isabelle's 15-year-old sister Anne Neville, the other co-heiress and widow of the late Edward of Westminster.

Gloucester had grown up with Anne during his time at Middleham and liked her, but sentiment played no part in the tug-of-war that ensued when, not long after Tewkesbury, he obtained Edward's permission to marry her. In a repeat performance of the sordid squabble ninety years earlier between the sons of Edward III over the co-heiresses of the Bohun earldom of Hereford, Clarence planned to force Anne to become a nun and to renounce her inheritance, and in the meantime refused Gloucester access to her.

Gloucester returned from the North in the autumn of 1471 and allegedly spirited Anne away from the household where Clarence had tried to conceal her, and took her to sanctuary at St Martin's Le Grand. It is more likely that Anne escaped to sanctuary, perhaps in disguise, and then sought Gloucester's protection. The scandal became so notorious that Edward ordered his brothers to argue their case at a Council meeting. This they did, and impressed the councillors with their eloquence and legal sophistry.

All the eloquence in the world could not finesse the fact that Isabel and Anne were co-heiresses not so much of their Neville father as of their mother, Anne née Beauchamp, who was Countess of Warwick in her own right. She remained most inconveniently alive in sanctuary at Beaulieu Abbey, which she dared not leave because Edward refused to grant her safe conduct.

Gloucester went ahead and married Anne sometime in the spring of 1472, without waiting for the necessary papal dispensation to marry his cousin. Both brothers wanted to put their possession of ex-Warwick lands on a firmer legal footing than royal favour. Edward had made the original distribution in anticipation of an Act of Attainder, which would have put the whole Warwick inheritance in his hands, but his brothers were determined to pre-empt the issue.

With Burgundy such an uncertain ally Edward could not risk offending Margaret, who was Clarence's principal advocate – although we may depend on it that Duchess Cecily was also active in the background. At the same time Clarence could not be seen to have profited from his treachery, or permitted to achieve the regional dominance in the Midlands that adding the Warwick inheritance to his existing holdings would give him.

Edward's solution was to resume forty duchy of Lancaster and eight crown manors in the Midlands previously held by Clarence, including Tutbury Castle, the seat of what he had once imagined was his appanage. Although Clarence gained forty-four ex-Warwick estates in the Midlands and became the dominant lord in Warwickshire and Worcestershire, his lordship was eliminated from Derbyshire, Nottinghamshire and Staffordshire

In the final distribution Clarence got 105 ex-Warwick properties with revenues of about £3,450 [nearly £22 million], which was more than he had lost to resumption. The political price he paid was high, however, as the king could not have indicated his distrust more clearly. Adding to Clarence's uneasiness, when Edward had made him Earl of Warwick and of Salisbury in 1472 it had been as new creations and not by right of inheritance.

Gloucester made Edward's job easier in the matter of the Warwick inheritance by backing down from his original demand for parity, and was rewarded by being exempted from resumption. In addition to Barnard Castle, Glamorgan and Abergavenny, already in his possession, he settled for thirty-five properties scattered across sixteen counties. Not long afterwards he exchanged three of them for the castle and manor of Scarborough in Yorkshire, in a process of regional consolidation that also saw him exchange Chirk Castle (ex-Beaufort) in Denbigh for William Stanley's Skipton Castle (ex-Clifford) in the West Riding.

The final settlement, confirmed by Acts of Parliament in 1474–5, was shockingly cynical. Countess Anne was declared legally dead and her daughters' inheritances assigned to their husbands – *whether or not they were or remained legally married to them*. The legally dead countess was permitted to leave Beaulieu Abbey and was assigned to Gloucester's custody, which Clarence rightly saw as a threat: the settlement was a farce that could be unmade as easily as it was made. Should the countess's property rights be restored, Gloucester would be in a position to dictate the terms of their disposal.

To draw a line at 1475, Gloucester's achievements in the preceding four years paint a picture of a ruthless but sensible and charismatic young man. He had more than fulfilled Edward's hope that he would become the regime lock on the North, taming a region that had been a thorn in the side of every monarch since 1399. Although he was the beneficiary of a sea change among the northern lords and greater gentry, tired of being sacrificed to the national ambitions of the Nevilles, this alone does not explain how, in a relatively short period, he won the respect of a cohort of men as proud and hard-headed as any in England.

The discovery of Gloucester's bones has at least resolved one of the controversies that have swirled around him for so long. He did indeed carry one shoulder higher than the other as the result of a severe curvature of the spine (scoliosis), which may explain why contemporaries remarked on his habitual lip-chewing: he was probably in constant pain. The intense willpower required to overcome the handicap became his dominant character trait. As a result he was not greatly inhibited physically, proof of which was his performance as a commander and in battle during the Barnet and Tewkesbury campaigns.

Any king in history would have prayed to have such a sibling, and he was Constable of England and Lord Admiral for the duration of Edward's reign. As long as his elder brother drew breath Gloucester gave him no reason to doubt the sincerity of '*Loyaulte me lie*' (Loyalty binds me), the motto with which he signed every document.

XXI

ELIZABETH

THE GOOD THING/BAD THING SCHOOL OF HISTORY requires that Elizabeth should have exercised a malign influence over Edward, because otherwise the House of York was rotten to the core. That it undoubtedly was does not necessarily make her a 'good thing', although it should incline us to sympathy. All we really know about Elizabeth is that she was a conventional queen who administered her relatively modest estates competently, retained the affection of her philandering husband and gave him ten children in fourteen years.

There is no evidence that she tried to influence him to favour her family to the detriment of his authority, and it would have been foolish to try: he was not a biddable man, and with the sole exception of Jacquetta de Luxembourg he had little respect for women. He had slapped down his mother for presuming too much and would have done the same to his wife, his sisters or his mistresses. They could appeal for small favours in support of their own good ladyship, but it is highly unlikely any of them influenced him in matters of significance.

Warwick had struck at the Woodvilles to hurt Edward, but the spitefulness towards Jacquetta came from Duchess Cecily via Clarence. There can be no doubt about this: Clarence's will asked that compensation be made for the injuries and grievances he had inflicted on Earl Rivers and his parents, 'who had done him no harm'. The omission of Elizabeth is eloquent.

The queen did not name any of her daughters Jacquetta, but in addition to making the dowager duchess godmother to her own namesake firstborn, in 1469 she did name another daughter Cecily. This was the year Edward evicted his mother from Fotheringhay, and Elizabeth's gesture clearly did nothing to placate her mother-in-law. Hatred is often a projection onto another of deep personal unhappiness or even self-loathing, and Elizabeth had the misfortune to be the lightning rod for the sick relationship between Cecily and her eldest son.

Elizabeth's fourth daughter, born in 1472, was named for Edward's sister Margaret, and her third son, born in 1477, was named George in honour of Clarence.* It is difficult to see how this can be reconciled with the allegation by Mancini, repeated unquestioningly by later historians, that the queen nurtured deadly vengefulness towards Clarence. The king, who stood as godfather to Clarence's heir, Edward, born in 1475, would not have forced his wife to name the boy after a man she hated, least of all at a time when his own relationship with his brother had become frankly hostile.

The model for medieval queenship was set out in *The Treasure of the City of Ladies*, written in about 1405 by the Venetian-French Christine de Pisan. The book sought to buttress what she saw as an erosion of respect for the traditional role of women as mediators and peacemakers between their husbands and the rest of the world. Elizabeth's naming of her children should be seen as an attempt to build bridges between Edward and his family.

The worst that can be said of Elizabeth is that she did not win personal loyalty outside the circle of her own family, against which one can readily imagine what Edward's reaction would have been if her parents, her brothers or Elizabeth herself had tried to build a 'queen's party'. They were all totally dependent on the king's good will, as was almost everyone else in his court.

*Margaret died nine months later and George, a robust 2-year-old already made Duke of Bedford and Lord Lieutenant of Ireland, was carried off by the plague in 1479.

With regard to the alleged unpopularity of the queen and her kin, this was largely an artefact of Warwick's propaganda. We have seen the robust response of the City of London when he tried to get Jacquetta condemned for witchcraft, and she and her daughter won further admiration for their courage during their months in sanctuary during the Readeption, when Elizabeth gave birth to the long-awaited heir while enduring Spartan living conditions. They had also behaved courageously in the Tower during the Bastard of Fauconberg's desperate assault.

When the Commons were summoned in October 1472 the Speaker, William Alyngton, 'declared before the King and his noble and solemn Council the intent and desire of his Commons, especially in the commendation of the womanly behaviour and the great constancy of the Queen, he being beyond the sea'. Perhaps he would also have commended Jacquetta, but she had died five months earlier, aged 56. There is no record of her funeral, but we can be sure that it was befitting her high rank, and that her virtues were duly extolled.

Elizabeth and her mother had been exceptionally close, and Edward may have felt the loss of Jacquetta almost as keenly. Never a paragon of virtue, he became more dissolute after 1471 and it is not much of a stretch to speculate that the deaths of his respected parents-in-law released the brake on his self-indulgence. In this, as always, he was encouraged by Hastings, not simply because he had done so since Edward was a teenager, but also to undermine Elizabeth.

• ∽ •

Elizabeth's older brother Anthony, Earl Rivers, was poised to become a pillar of the regime in 1471 and spurned the opportunity. He had been a competent Keeper of the Seas for several years before Edward appointed him Lieutenant of Calais in 1470. Subsequently Rivers had organized the flight to Holland from Bishop's Lynn, where he had influence as lord of neighbouring Middleton, after which he played a leading role in assembling the invasion force and fought heroically at Barnet and against the Bastard of Fauconberg.

At the moment when he might have played a leading role in the post-war settlement, Rivers requested Edward's permission to go on a pilgrimage to fight the Moors in Portugal. In the preface to his 1477 translation of *The Dictes and Sayings of the Philosophers*, he wrote that during the recent turmoil he had sworn to devote his life to God's service.* Edward accused him of fleeing his obligations – although he had previously awarded the office of Constable of England, which should have been Anthony's in reversion from his father, to Gloucester. Now he did not reappoint him as Lieutenant of Calais and nominated Hastings instead.

Rivers went on pilgrimage in 1473 to Santiago de Compostela in Spain, and again in 1475 to Rome and other shrines in Italy, when the pope honoured him with the title of defender and director of papal causes in England. In Italy he travelled in sumptuous style, and was robbed of all his possessions when travelling in the Veneto. The notoriously tight-fisted Venetians made good his loss in deference to the English court, from which we can deduce that at least in 1475 Rivers was acting in an official capacity.

As well as being unusually cultured and learned, Rivers was an ascetic who wore a hair shirt next to his skin; but he was no better than the rest of his class with regard to worldly wealth. His father left him only three manors in Kent as well as Grafton in Northamptonshire, but he used legal chicanery to make himself the heir of his wife, whom he married not long after she became Baroness Scales in her own right in 1460. On her death in 1473 he retained fifteen manors in Norfolk and one in Cambridgeshire that should have reverted to the Scales family.

There was also something particularly unpleasant about the way Anthony extorted Maud Stanhope, dowager Lady Willoughby and

---

*Rivers was William Caxton's patron and the *Dictes* was the second book printed in England. Caxton also published Rivers's translation of the *Cordyal of the four last and final thinges* in 1479.

widow of Warwick's younger brother Thomas Neville, killed at Wakefield, into surrendering part of her Midlands inheritance to him in return for the pardon of Gervase Clifton, her third husband. This was a clear, if rare example of Anthony using his family's royal connection for personal profit. Clifton was to rebel again and was one of those beheaded after Tewkesbury.

After the death of Lady Scales Edward kept Anthony in reserve as a dynastic marriage counter for several years, but in 1480 granted him permission to marry Mary FitzLewis, granddaughter of Edmund Beaufort, the Duke of Somerset killed at St Albans in 1455. This was speculative, as although she was the sole heir of her recently deceased father, it was only a minor estate. However she was also the potential co-heiress of the attainted duchy of Beaufort, all legitimate male heirs being long dead. We may presume Rivers believed, and perhaps had been assured, that Edward would reverse the attainder so that he could inherit.

Edward's appreciation for his brother-in-law's talents preceded his marriage to Elizabeth. Anthony also won international renown for his skill in tournaments before he became the royal champion, and was elected to the Order of the Garter. Although exasperated by Anthony's unwillingness to play his part in the post-war settlement, on reflection he saw that Rivers's knightliness, erudition and lack of political ambition made him the ideal candidate to be entrusted with the education of the young Prince of Wales.

• ❦ •

The king lavished rewards on those who had looked after Elizabeth while she was in sanctuary and during her confinement. Thomas Myling, Abbot of Westminster, was made chancellor to baby Edward, and Elizabeth's midwife and doctor were given generous annuities. The boy was made Prince of Wales on 26 July 1471, and twelve days later the king appointed Elizabeth, Rivers, Clarence, Gloucester and the Archbishop of Canterbury to form his honorary Council, with day-to-day decisions taken by a cabinet run by the Queen.

So it remained until February 1473, when Edward decreed that the prince's household should move to the castle-palace of Ludlow in Shropshire. Along with Fotheringhay, Ludlow had been the principal administrative centre of the duchy of York, and the king had spent a carefree boyhood and adolescence there. This was not to be the prince's lot: the relocation was a political move of considerable significance designed to restore royal authority in Wales, and Edward intended it to be a working apprenticeship for his heir.

Gloucester was now fully taken up in the North, and Edward had no confidence in either of the two young magnates (both 18 years old in 1473) with large landholdings in Wales. William Herbert, Earl of Pembroke, had none of his father's ability. He was not allowed to enter his inheritance until 1475 and was to be deprived of it in 1479. Royal ward Henry Stafford, Duke of Buckingham, was allowed to enter his inheritance in June 1473, but he was another Clarence: a young man with an immense sense of entitlement unmatched by ability.

Edward made a progress through the north Midlands and the Welsh March, at the end of which Prince Edward and his Council were settled at Ludlow. The move diminished Elizabeth's role in her son's life, and while it was normal for aristocratic women to be separated from their sons, it was not usually done at such a young age. She remained at Ludlow until May and we know she accompanied Edward when he made his first progress with his son to deal with disorders in Shrewsbury, as that was where baby Richard was born on 17 August 1473.

The king's appointment of Earl Rivers as the Prince of Wales's guardian and head of his Council no doubt reassured Elizabeth that her son was in good hands, but the arrangement was misogynistic. He was to be brought up as far as possible without female influence, far away from his mother. To the degree that it recreated Edward's own childhood environment it may be taken as a sign of his vanity as well as his emotional immaturity.

• ☙ •

At about this time Edward and Hastings added an unsavoury twist to their revels by welcoming 21-year-old Thomas Grey, heir to the Ferrers of Groby barony and Earl of Huntingdon since August 1471, to join them. Grey was Elizabeth's eldest son from her first marriage, thus the king's stepson, and also his nephew-in-law through marriage to Anne Holland, the namesake daughter of the king's older sister and heir to the imprisoned Duke of Exeter.

There are indications that Thomas had already fallen under Hastings's influence when he fought under his command at Tewkesbury. Any doubt about it was removed when Anne died childless early in 1474. With no claim to the Holland lands, Thomas was more than compensated by marriage to one of the richest heiresses in England, Hastings's 13-year-old stepdaughter and ward Cecily, Baroness Bonville and Harington in her own right.

In theory Elizabeth had paid 4,000 marks [£848,000] for Grey's marriage to Anne Holland and now paid 2,500 marks [£530,000] for the Bonville marriage, which took place on 5 September 1474. In reality Edward discounted the bridal prices from money owed him by Exeter and Hastings: in other words, he arranged them both. Exeter, who was in exile at the time, had no say in the matter, but it is inconceivable that Edward should have arranged the Bonville marriage against Hastings's will.

Grey was granted possession of Cecily's inheritance on 23 April 1475 and three weeks later he was knighted and created Marquess of Dorset, renouncing the earldom of Huntingdon. With the Courtenay lands divided up among Clarence and others, the Bonville/Harington estates were the largest cohesive block in the West Country, and Edward may have entertained the idea of making Grey his regime lock on the region. He may also have hoped the marriage would bring about a reconciliation between Hastings and Elizabeth, whose detestation of his best friend remained a mystery to him until the day he died.

Her hatred, of course, stemmed from Hastings's sordid exploitation of her appeal for his good lordship in her dispute with her first mother-in-law, Baroness Ferrers of Groby by right, over Thomas Grey's inheritance from his father. The arrangement between them, promptly rendered null by her marriage to the king, had included a provision that Thomas should marry a daughter of Hastings's family; and so, in the end, he did.

Hastings may have hoped that by favouring Thomas so extravagantly he would detach him from loyalty to his mother. If so he failed, as in due course the tension between Thomas and Hastings became as notorious as it was, to the king, incomprehensible. The most likely explanation is that Elizabeth, disgusted by Hastings extending his corrupting influence from her husband to her son, told Thomas the reason for her animosity.

• ◌ •

Elizabeth's hatred of Hastings has been attributed to a competition for influence over the king, but there was no contest: Edward's attitude towards women precluded it. Hastings was the classic 'favourite' who normally served as a scapegoat for dissatisfaction with a medieval monarch. That neither at the time nor since does it seem to have occurred to anyone to blame him for Edward's policies is a tribute to Hastings's care to avoid incurring envy.

Elizabeth had no useful weapons to employ against such a man because she had no following at court, and the main reason appears to have been her personality. It is not unusual for mothers to resent their sons' wives. To overcome this requires a great deal of tact by the younger woman, and from the evidence of her poisonous relationships with both her mothers-in-law Elizabeth was lacking in that department. It cannot all be attributed to jealousy.

We may doubt that the Yorkists could ever have unequivocally accepted the daughter of a leading Lancastrian, or that the Lancastrians could ever forgive her family's outstandingly successful apostasy, or the Ferrers of Groby ever cease to hate her for marrying a man her first husband had died fighting against. But if she had exercised graciousness commensurate with her beauty she would have had no difficulty in winning devoted followers. Instead she invested all she had to offer in Edward, who would accept no less, and he was not worth it.

XXII

EDWARD

T HE TASK CONFRONTING EDWARD AFTER TEWKESBURY was even more daunting than it had been ten years earlier. Then, he had been invested with the hope of a nation tired of factionalism and disorder, and ready to give him the benefit of the doubt as he learned how to be king. How thoroughly he had disappointed that hope became apparent in 1469–71. He was shocked to learn how unpopular he had become, and knew very well that he had succeeded in recovering the throne only because his opponents did not combine against him.

For several years afterwards the *Paston Letters*, a useful source for informed gossip, paint a picture of widespread surliness and rumours of sedition, often tendentiously linked to Clarence. Edward was aware of it and of the need to win back the good will of his people. Not long after the pacification of Kent he, Elizabeth and their children made a well-choreographed pilgrimage to Canterbury, and he was to show himself to his people in more ceremonial progresses over the next three years than he had made in the first half of his reign.

Few potential sources of sedition remained after Barnet and Tewkesbury, but one of them was Archbishop Neville. Edward had a score to settle with him and went about it like a cat with a mouse. For ten months he behaved graciously towards Neville, to the point that in April 1472 the archbishop was preparing to receive Edward for a hunting party at More Palace. The best tapestries were hung, the gold dinner service unpacked and no expense spared. Instead of the king, however, on the 25th royal Household Controller William Parr and Treasurer of the Chamber Thomas Vaughan* arrived, arrested the archbishop and looted his palace.

The given reason was allegedly treasonous communication between Neville and the exiled Earl of Oxford, his brother-in-law. No evidence was ever produced to support the charge and there is no reason to believe it. It was a highly personal act of vengeance, underlined when Edward had the archbishop's opulent mitre broken up to create a new crown for himself. The palace and its contents added £20,000 [£12.7 million] to the royal coffers and Edward also enjoyed the revenues of the archbishopric for several years. Neville himself was imprisoned at Hammes Castle in the pale of Calais until released at the petition of the pope in November 1474.

There is likewise no evidence linking Clarence to any plot against his brother after 1470. How much of the gossip stemmed from pot-stirring by Louis XI is hard to say, but on at least one occasion, in July 1473, the Milanese ambassador reported some typical disinformation. The Earl of Oxford, Louis said, had sent him twenty-four 'original seals of knights and lords and one duke' who were ready to rise up against Edward if Oxford could provide the spark. The duke in question could only be Clarence.

The remark came apropos a landing by Oxford at St Osyth in Essex on 28 May 1473. Ten days earlier John Paston reported the confession of a captured courier that £1,000 had been sent to Oxford from England, and that 'a hundred gentlemen in Norfolk and Suffolk have agreed to assist the said earl at his coming thither… within eight days after St Dunstan [21 May]'. In fact Oxford found no response from his old affinity, and with the Earl of Essex and others on their way to crush him he quickly re-embarked.

After several months cruising off the English coast, permitted to resupply and sell pirated goods and ships in Scotland, on 30

*Of Monmouth: distantly if at all related to the Welsh Marcher Vaughans.

September Oxford, his brothers and Beaumont occupied St Michael's Mount, a rocky tidal island in the far west of Cornwall. It was a pointless operation that should have been dealt with by local levies, but was not. Finally Edward sent 600 men with cannon and ships commanded by his esquire of the body John Fortescue, a Hertfordshire knight, who blockaded the rock from 23 December 1472.

Fortescue was also empowered to offer pardons to all except Oxford and Beaumont, and with his followers deserting Oxford surrendered on 15 February 1473. He and Beaumont spent the next decade imprisoned at Hammes, where John Blount, the castle captain, was paid £50 [£31,800] per annum for their maintenance. This does not mean they were kept in luxury – the generous payment simply gave Blount a keen interest in making sure they did not escape.

In sum, tangible threats to Edward's throne were insignificant or imaginary, but the general malaise reported by John Paston was real. To counter it, Edward's big idea was to unite the kingdom behind him by invading France. Bishop John Alcock of Rochester, Chancellor Stillington's deputy and president of the Prince of Wales's Council, announced the king's intention when Parliament assembled on 6 October 1472. It was to remain in session until March 1475, by far the longest of Edward's six parliaments.

Unabashed by the fact that he was repeating Stillington's opening words to the 1467 Parliament almost word for word, Alcock spoke of the dastardliness of Louis XI, 'the principal ground, root and provoker of the King's let and trouble'. He needed to be punished, and how better than reasserting in arms Edward's rightful claim to the throne of France? Such an enterprise would channel the energies of the more unruly elements of society. Give war a chance was the message – it had worked for the most revered of England's kings.

More practically, Alcock continued, control of the Channel and Atlantic coasts of France would boost trade, reduce losses to French piracy and provide lands for the younger sons of noble and gentry families. The king had spent £100,000 [£63.6 million] to bring about alliances with Burgundy and Brittany, and other princes would join a league against Louis XI. Therefore, the message concluded, Edward looked to his loyal subjects to provide him with the means to carry his enterprise through to a glorious conclusion.

Edward had not brought about the boasted triple alliance against France, not least because £100,000 was wildly beyond his ability to pay. The exchequer was bare and, even trading at a steep discount, the accumulation of royal 'tallies' and other liabilities was unsustainable. Today's central bankers would applaud Edward's intuitive understanding of his situation: had such a device existed at the time, he might have compared kingship to riding a bicycle – the choice was between maintaining forward momentum or falling off.

The only alliance Edward had achieved at the time of his boast was with Brittany. In March 1472 Fransez had appealed for 6,000 archers to help him resist an imminent French attack. Edward sent Rivers and his brother Edward Woodville with 1,000 archers, and by August the French had withdrawn. A further 2,000 archers under Duras followed in September, and Rivers negotiated a treaty by which, in return for continuing English protection, Fransez would permit an English army to invade Normandy or Guyenne through his territory.

When the lord of Gruuthuse crossed to England in October 1472 he was lavishly entertained and made Earl of Winchester with £200 [£1.27 million] a year from the customs of Southampton for the indispensable services he had provided during Edward's exile. He also brought with him Duke Charles's arrogant conditions for an alliance. These were that if Edward became king of France, Charles was to have, by hereditary right, the duchies of Champagne and Bar, the counties of Picardy, Nevers, Rethel and Guise, the prince-bishopric of Tournai and also Louis of Luxembourg's lands of Saint-Pol, Brienne and Ligny.*

---

*A glance back at Map 7 will explain the rationale for this shopping list – it would have united the two halves of Burgundy and would have brought the recreation of Lotharingia a giant step closer.

Edward used Gruuthuse's presence to convince Parliament that he had achieved a triple alliance, but by the time they voted him money for the war even Brittany had dropped out. In return for an annual subsidy of 40,000 gold francs [£4.9 million], in October Frañsez agreed a truce with Louis XI and urged Charles and Edward to do likewise. In November Charles agreed a truce to end in April 1473, but before then Edward had agreed his own.

There were other obstacles to be overcome, chiefly a renewal of the naval war with the Hanseatic League provoked by Edward when he reneged on the promises made to the Hansards in return for their assistance in returning to England in 1471. He also renewed an exclusive arrangement with Cologne that had led to the city's expulsion from the League. The war was not only extremely damaging to English trade, but also made it a near certainty that the furious Hansards would make a full-scale attack on any invasion fleet.

After much toing and froing by delegations led by the king's private secretary William Hatcliffe, in February 1474 Edward signed a treaty conceding the Hansards' demands for the full reinstatement of their unilateral trading privileges, the return of their walled compounds with extra-territorial rights in London and Boston, and the grant of similar premises in Bishop's Lynn, all in perpetuity. He also agreed to pay an indemnity of £15,000 [£9.54 million] and repay a £484 forced loan extorted from their representatives in 1468.

It was a capitulation that did not endear Edward to his creditors in the City of London and the English merchant community. They were even required to submit their own exports to Hansard 'quality control' and consequently their trade with the Baltic and north Germany dwindled even as the League's trade with England boomed. As with other trade deals negotiated during Edward's reign, the terms were so one-sided that it is fair to suspect that Hatcliffe negotiated secret and lucrative exceptions for the king and his friends.

Another obstacle was Scotland, where Louis XI could be depended on to stir up trouble for England unless forestalled. The frontier remained as lawless as ever, and mutual recriminations about piracy continued to poison Anglo–Scots relations. Even so, the truce agreed in 1464 still held and in September 1473 Edward proposed a marriage alliance between James III's namesake heir, born in March, and his own 4-year-old daughter Cecily. On 26 October the formal betrothal took place and a treaty was signed, which included a forty-six-year truce. Edward was to pay a dowry of 20,000 crowns [£2.5 million] in instalments over seventeen years, and was delighted to have covered his back at so little cost.

His sister Margaret's dowry of 200,000 crowns, which should have been paid within three years of her marriage, was another matter. Still outstanding were 115,000 crowns, and although Charles agreed to annual payments of 10,000 crowns starting in 1475, Edward only ever paid 16,000. The entire sum was a bagatelle to Charles, who wore a diamond-encrusted mantle of about the same value to his meeting with Emperor Frederick III at Trier in September 1473; but it had serious implications for Margaret, as her Burgundian endowment was tied to the fulfilment of the marriage contract.

City of London merchants had underwritten the dowry, but took the view that since Edward owed them more and had failed to keep faith with them, their obligation was not binding. It would be hard to identify a better example of how honest dealing is not simply a question of morality. Edward's chicanery earned him the contempt of Duke Charles, Margaret's enmity, and the drying up of his principal domestic source of credit.

Charles no longer regarded war with France as a priority because his heart was set on becoming King of the Romans and successor to Frederick III, the first of the Habsburg emperors. He believed this was a reasonable quid pro quo should he agree to peace with the Holy Roman Empire and to lend military assistance against the Ottoman Empire, cemented by the marriage of Marie, his only child, to Archduke Maximilian of Austria, Frederick's heir.

The emperor did not agree. Faced with the duke's demand that his estates should be declared a kingdom to include the bishoprics of Liege, Utrecht, Toul and Verdun, and the duchies of Lorraine, Savoy and Cleves, after two months of fruitless negotiations Frederick fled from their summit meeting at Trier during the night of 24 November 1473. Charles's browbeating display of opulence and military might had spectacularly misfired.

Edward would have been informed about Charles's state of mind by Hatcliffe and Bishop John Russell of Rochester, his emissaries to the duke before the Trier summit, and subsequently by Dr John Morton and Duras, who tried to negotiate with him during the first half of 1474. Yet he went ahead with plans for a military expedition whose only hope for success depended on Charles turning away from what Edward knew was now his principal concern.

Edward was not stupid – but he was in too deep to abandon the expedition and now developed a fall-back plan, which was to cash out if Charles left him to face France alone. Getting to that point, however, took all his powers of persuasion because even – perhaps especially – those who knew him well suspected the expedition was a dishonest subterfuge. The money voted by the Commons and Lords at the end of 1472 came with the stipulation that he must have mustered his army before it was released to him.

In April 1473 the Lords yielded to Edward's request for funds to stockpile weapons and other equipment and released their supposed tenth. The sum collected was a derisory £2,461, even though the peers could look forward to recovering much more once they could claim indentures for their troops. The perfunctory amount in itself argues persuasively that the peers would believe it when they saw it, and not before.

Between 1472 and 1475 the Canterbury Convocation granted three and a half clerical tenths of about £13,000 each and the York Convocation two-tenths of about £1,400 each, for a total of about £48,000. The *Crowland Chronicle Continuations*, the only account of the period written by someone with first-hand knowledge, seldom states the author's opinion outright – save once. Writing many years later the Chronicler was still incandescent with rage over the way Edward had milked the clergy:

> [The king] did not hide his needs from the prelates, blandly demanding from them, in advance, the tenths which were shortly to be granted as if, once prelates and clergy had assembled in their Convocation, they were obliged to do whatever the king demanded. O what a servile and pernicious ruin for the Church!

When Morton and Duras returned from Luxembourg in mid-1474, only £31,411 of the income tax voted by the Commons in 1472 had been collected, and none at all of a further tenth and fifteenth granted in 1473. The king's blushes over the long delay in obtaining a treaty of 'perpetual amity and alliance' with Burgundy were spared by the Commons' embarrassment over their failure to keep their side of the bargain.

In principle the Commons had voted Edward more tax revenues than in all the preceding years of his reign. In practice he was caught in a chicken-and-egg situation where he lacked the means to pay the indentures for a muster, but unless he did so he could not draw on the Commons' money. He could have resorted to a forced loan, but that would simply have added to the mountain of unpaid tallies already outstanding. Instead he travelled the country to collect money himself, or through special commissioners, by means of 'benevolences'.

This was a nationwide arm-twisting exercise in which he summoned leading citizens to personal audiences, where they were persuaded to make voluntary contributions. He turned on the charm and the *Great Chronicle* reported an occasion when a wealthy Suffolk widow increased her donation from £10 to £20 [£12,700] in exchange for a royal kiss. Of course it would have been a brave man or woman who refused, but those who made the donations would have probably considered it money well spent to have their names recorded in a ledger prominently displayed in the audience chamber.

Records for benevolences raised in fifteen counties survive, total-ling £21,656; a pro-rata calculation for the other eleven would bring the amount up to a figure sufficient to pay the first quarter of inden-tures at the end of January 1475, thereby fulfilling the condition for releasing the first Commons disbursement. When Parliament met for its seventh and last session on 23 January 1475, the situation with regard to the 1472 grant had hardly improved at all. The rea-sons were set out in remarkably forthright terms:

> Some of the collectors have not delivered the sums by them received to the place limited and appointed by the commis-sioners, but have converted it to their own use, and some that have received it and not so delivered it are now dead, and some of the said tenth part delivered to the place limited have been converted to their own use by the governors of said places, and some of the commissioners who have received a part of the said tenth will not deliver it to the king's duly appointed receiver... and some persons with strong hands have taken part of the tenth out of the places where it was put by the collectors.

To make up the deficit, on 14 March the Commons voted a tra-ditional tenth and fifteenth payable in mid-April, and a further three-quarters on 11 November. The deadline for the expedition was reset for St John's Day (7 January) 1476, and the Commons voted to make good half the deficit by St John's Day 1475, and the other half by the following St Martin's Day (11 November).

Edward's great scheme to unite the country behind him had instead produced a vote of little or no confidence in his integrity. The cynicism and corruption that characterized the preparatory stage of the enterprise may not have been far beyond the norm for a government system in which all involved were expected to enrich themselves from the public purse – but it was more blatantly shameless than usual. As the old adage puts it, 'the fish rots from the head'.

XXIII

DISHONOUR

B Y HOOK OR BY CROOK EDWARD HAD COLLECTED ABOUT £120,000 [£76.3 million] with the expectation of a further £50,000, although much of it was spent before the expedition set out. The largest disbursements were two quarterly payments of indentures of about £45,000 each, but other advance costs included the acquisition of siege and field artillery, hiring an invasion fleet and hundreds of wagons to carry 10,000 sheaves of arrows, hard rations for the troops, fodder for the horses, cooking pots, anvils, tools, tents, etc.

The expected revenues would barely cover another quarter's indentures, and we may firmly reject the suspicion expressed by Philippe Commynes and others that the enterprise was fraudulent from its inception. Practically the entire peerage had signed up, and with so much money spent a cancellation had become unthinkable, not least because the Commons would undoubtedly conclude that the king had, once more, acted in premeditated bad faith. If Edward was to achieve anything at all he could delay no longer.

We are much better informed about the composition of this army than for any during the Wars of the Roses because it had to be paid for and, at least with regard to the fighting 'teeth', itemized royal accounts survive, set out in **Appendix E**. Payments made elsewhere than Canterbury and for the militia contingents sent by cities and boroughs are not included, and there was no separate accounting for mounted archers and the hobilars (light cavalry) who commonly rode with them. Their daily rate was ninepence and they were present in large numbers, yet the archers counted by the king's tellers were only paid sixpence.

The most likely explanation is that, as explained previously with reference to the Battle of Tewkesbury and in accordance with contemporary contracts for military service in Italy and Burgundy, a 'lance' (used interchangeably with 'spear' in the documents) meant a man-at-arms *and his mounted retinue*. This may be the reason why the 'lances' were paid sixpence more a day than usual for men-at-arms, and why knights and above were paid an additional lance's fee for themselves. Commynes personally observed that the English had more than 1,500 men-at-arms with 'many followers on horseback', and the same number of mounted archers.

In sum, nearly 12,000 units of account is likely to have meant actual combatants greatly in excess of the numbers tallied, if not quite the 20,000 men Edward claimed. It was a very large force indeed, perhaps double the size of the army with which Henry V had conquered Normandy sixty years earlier. However, the French now had a large standing army and had learned to avoid charging into arrow storms. There would be no new Agincourt unless Edward could force Louis to face him in battle, and he needed to do this before the money ran out. What he had in mind was a fast-moving *chevauchée* to which Louis must respond.

It was a reasonable plan, but it required Brittany and Burgundy to disperse French strength. Even bolstered by 2,000 archers under Lord Audley and Duras, Edward knew Frañsez would attack only if Louis XI suffered a severe defeat. Burgundy, however, was already at war with France, and after Charles let their truce lapse in May 1475 Louis sent columns to burn Burgundian towns in Picardy, to raid destructively as far as Arras and Hesdin in Artois, and also invaded the duchy of Burgundy

There is little doubt that Charles encouraged Edward to launch his expedition to relieve French pressure on his western flank, and never intended to join him. His relentless aggression had brought about an alliance between the Swiss and Sigismund of Austria that saw Upper Alsace lost to Charles in 1474–5, and Duke René II of Lorraine had made common cause against him with the Rhine cities and Emperor Frederick III. Defeating Louis would do little to resolve the wider strategic dilemma Charles had created for himself.

It is not clear when this finally dawned on Edward, but it must have been well before he launched the expedition. Instead of landing in Normandy, as Charles wished him to do and where Louis was waiting for him, he went to Calais, arriving on 4 July. Duchess Margaret was there to greet him, but Charles did not arrive until the 14th, and then with only a small retinue.

This came as an unpleasant surprise to much of the English army, but by now Edward and his inner circle knew to expect nothing more. Charles announced that he had abandoned the siege of Neuss and had sent his army to invade Lorraine, from where – he said – it would attack into Champagne while Edward advanced from the north. A glance back at Map 7 will reveal how little credibility could be attached to this alleged plan of action.

Indeed and as usual in military matters, maps speak louder than words. Map 23 illustrates that at no point did Edward venture into French territory. His strategic objective was Reims, where he hoped to be crowned king of France. He had spent vast amounts of money on jewellery and sumptuous clothing for himself and his household so that they should not look shabby when they met their Burgundian peers, and was accompanied by a panoply of prelates and heraldic officials to make the coronation ceremony sufficiently grand.

However the expedition could not become a self-sustaining *chevauchée* until it reached enemy lands. Even the peaceful passage of such a large army was destructive and Charles insisted it should avoid marching through Artois as far as possible. The first leg was through Boulogne to Fauquemberges, where Charles and Margaret met them again, after which they marched through Louis of Luxembourg's county of Saint-Pol. Charles met them at Doullens

Army returns
4-18 September

Calais
4-18 July

Guînes

Charles &
Margaret

FLANDERS

Saint-Omer

BOULOGNE

Fauquembergues
22-24 July

Agincourt
25-26 July

Blangy

Saint-Pol

ARTOIS

Hesdin

ARTOIS

Arras

Charles

Charles

CAMBRAI

Charles
15-18 August

Doullens
28 July

Edward IV

R. Somme

PONTHIEU

Éclusier

Péronne
6 August

Picquigny
29 August

11 August

P I C A R D Y

Saint-Christ
12 August

Saint-Quentin

Amiens
25-28 August

Reims
57 miles

EU

AMIÉNOIS

Lihons
15 August

VERMANDOIS

Roye
14 August

Beauvais
27 July

Louis XI

Compiègne
6 August

N O R M A N D Y

© Hugh Bicheno

23. EDWARD IV'S EXPEDITION
1475

0   5   10   15   20   25
miles

in northern Picardy and again at Péronne, neither of which opened their gates to the English. Charles could not have made it more clear that Edward could not count on him even for logistical support.

Louis XI had been frankly terrified at the prospect of a combined Anglo–Burgundian offensive and had spent many times more than Edward could dream of collecting to maintain large armies in the field and a fleet of warships patrolling the Normandy coast. His subjects were restless under the weight of taxation and he knew that some of his nobles would seize the opportunity to rebel should he suffer a military defeat. The last thing in the world he wanted was to face the fearsome English archers in battle.

Thus it was manna from heaven when, before the English even departed Dover, John Smert, Garter King of Arms, arrived at Louis's camp in Normandy to present Edward's formal challenge, and showed himself amenable to bribery. Commynes, who was present, says that Louis gave Smert a private message for his master that showed an accurate appreciation of the situation Edward was in. Duke Charles had tricked him, Louis of Luxembourg's word was valueless and little was left of the campaigning season.

> [Louis] also personally gave the Herald three hundred crowns and promised him another thousand if peace was agreed upon… The Herald replied that he would do all in his power to achieve this peace and that he believed his master would willingly entertain the suggestion; but nothing more should be said until the king of England had crossed the sea. When he had done so another herald should be sent to ask for safe conducts so that ambassadors could come to meet him; they should apply to Lord Howard or Lord Stanley and also to himself to help guide the herald.

In due course Edward learned the truth of Louis's warnings, the crowning disappointment coming on 11 August, when his Vanguard was fired on and attacked when approaching Saint-Quentin, which

Saint-Pol had promised in writing to deliver to him.* Even Charles's arrogance could not put a brave face on this and he departed the next day for Brabant to raise troops for the conquest of Lorraine. The English suffered a number of losses but came away with one prisoner, a valet, who was to play a crucial role in the events that followed.

The man was released with a gold noble pressed into his hand, along with a message from Lords Howard and Stanley urging Louis, by now at Compiègne, to propose negotiations. Louis realized that Garter King of Arms had not misled him and, as he scorned the traditional trappings of warfare, had a suitable tabard made for another valet to pose as a herald. The message he bore was that Louis had acted against Edward in the past only because of his alliance with Burgundy and, now that Duke Charles had made it clear how little he valued Edward's friendship, perhaps the time had come to talk.

On 15 August ambassadors from both sides met at Lihons-en-Santerre, about equidistant from Edward at Saint-Christ on the Somme and Louis, now camped outside Roye. After a perfunctory assertion, and rejection, of Edward's territorial demands, the English ambassadors spelled out their king's price. He required an immediate payment of 75,000 crowns [£9.54 million] to return home, and further annual payments of 50,000 crowns, guaranteed by the Medici and the pope, for the duration of a truce to last until the end of August 1482, renewable thereafter on the same terms.

Further conditions were for free trade between the two countries and a permanent treaty of amity to be sealed by the marriage of 5-year-old Dauphin Charles and 9-year-old Princess Elizabeth when they reached marriageable age, Louis to provide her with an endowment worth 50,000 crowns per annum. Should Elizabeth die before the marriage, her 8-year-old sister Mary would take her place. Both monarchs would undertake not to form alliances against each other, and would support each other if either faced armed rebellion. In

*A promise presumably made to dissuade Edward from running a *chevauchée* through his county evidence of the good faith of the last stipulation Edward offered to provide Louis proof of traitors in his service.

When Louis's ambassadors returned with these terms, they were relieved to find their king delighted with them. It was similar to the offer Louis had made through Warwick in 1466, although the payments were about one-third greater and on the earlier occasion there had been no possibility of a dynastic marriage because the dauphin was not yet born. All Louis had ever wanted was that Edward should not combine with Burgundy against him. As Edward was now prepared to renounce the Burgundian alliance, Louis was not going to quibble over the price.

Duke Charles returned to Péronne on 18 August and visited Edward the next day, but by that time the deal was done. Although he later poured scorn on what his brother-in-law had done, he did not so express himself at this, their last meeting. Edward had served his purpose; the French had fallen back across the river Somme and a month later Charles obtained a truce with the return of Saint-Quentin and other towns he had lost in Picardy. At no expense to himself he had covered his back and could now concentrate on his enemies along the Rhine.

The ambassadors agreed that their armies should march to Amiens on either side of the Somme. Louis wanted the English to pass through an area laid waste by his men so that they should be in no doubt about the hardship that would have awaited them had they marched on Reims. At the same time he wanted his own men to appreciate what a formidable army they would not now have to confront. The parallel march served its purpose and the two armies reached Amiens in a festive mood.*

Louis kept his own soldiers away and turned over Amiens to the English, with whores, tuns of wine and cartloads of meat pies brought in from many miles around. An epic three-day orgy ensued until Edward, embarrassed by their behaviour, posted armed guards

---

*Two thousand English soldiers, probably archers, were hired away by Duke Charles.

on the gates and ordered his men to sleep it off. On 29 August he rode at the head of his army to Picquigny, where he met Louis for the first time on a bridge divided by a trellis. Commynes, who was present, observed that Edward had become fat since he last saw him after he had fled England in 1470, when he did 'not recall ever having seen such a fine-looking man':

> When he was within four or five feet of the barrier he raised his hat and bowed to within six inches of the ground. The King, who was already leaning on the barrier, returned his greeting with much politeness. They began to embrace each other through the holes and... the King said to him 'My lord, my cousin, you are very welcome. There is nobody in the world whom I would want to meet more than you. And God be praised that we are here for this good purpose'.

Apart from the exaggerated depth of the bow this is probably an accurate description; but then Commynes gilded the lily by claiming to have heard words that would have been spoken in private – possibly Louis confided in him after the event. The words are consistent with Louis's view that Edward was too fond of creature comforts to have really wished to make war:

> Our King, who was never at a loss for words, jokingly said that [Edward] should come to Paris, that he would dine him with the ladies and that he would give him my lord the Cardinal of Bourbon as confessor, since [Bourbon] would very willingly absolve him from sin should he have committed any, because he knew the cardinal was a very merry fellow.

Once the treaty was signed and sworn, with 55,000 crowns in his saddlebags and the remaining 20,000 to follow once his army was back in England, Edward left Lord Howard and Master of Horse John Cheyne as hostages and marched to Calais. Before he left he told Louis that he would regard an attack on Duke Frañsez as a deal-breaker, as 'in his moment of need he had never found such a good friend'. It seems to have been a rather pathetic face-saving gesture at the moment when Edward was consigning the Burgundian alliance, for which he had laboured so long and at such great cost, to the diplomatic rubbish heap.

Edward did, however, avenge the treachery of his uncle by marriage Louis de Luxembourg. He handed over the letters he had received from him and Louis immediately sent Saint-Pol a letter saying 'he had need of a head such as his' to deal with some pending problems, commenting to his aides that the body did not need to be attached. Saint-Pol fled, but Duke Charles captured and handed him over. He was executed in Paris in December.

Edward dealt no less ruthlessly with Henry Holland, Duke of Exeter, thrown overboard during the journey back across the Channel. He had been held at the Tower since 1471 and in 1472 Edward's sister Anne divorced him, freeing her to marry her lover Thomas St Leger. Exeter had no lands, money or followers, and can only have been released from the Tower to join the expedition because Edward intended to have him killed under cover of a battle. That he disposed of him anyway argues that he no longer cared what people thought.

The army sailed back to England between 4 and 18 September, but Edward did not return to London until the 28th. Where he was we do not know, but there is little doubt that he was waiting to see if riots would greet the news of the inglorious outcome of the expedition. He did not dare – for many years – reveal the terms of the treaty of amity and marriage, and he also renounced the Commons' three-quarters of a subsidy due on 11 November. The moment is captured in an irony-studded commentary by the Crowland Continuator (my italics):

> The lord king returned to England with *honourable terms of*
> *peace: for they were so regarded by the upper ranks in the royal army*

though there is nothing so holy or proper that it cannot be distorted by ill report. Some, indeed, at once began to blame this action, for which they paid penalties befitting their presumption; others, once home, reverted to theft and pillage in consequence of which no road was safe for merchants or pilgrims throughout England. The lord king himself, therefore, was compelled to traverse his kingdom with his justices sparing no one, even of his own household, from being hanged if they were caught stealing or killing. This rigorous justice was put into operation wherever it was called for and daylight robberies were then checked for a long time afterwards. For, had the *farsighted prince* not vigorously resisted such evils from the beginning, the number of people complaining about the bad management of the country's wealth (after so much treasure had been snatched from the coffers of them all, and so uselessly consumed) would have grown so much that no-one would know whose heads were safe among the counsellors, *especially those who, moved by the friendship or by the gifts of the French king, had been influential in making peace on the terms described.*

He was right about the gifts: Louis lavished them on Edward's entourage and paid his closest advisers pensions totalling 16,000 crowns [£2 million], in accordance with how influential he believed them to be. Hastings received much the most, but Howard, Dorset, Stanley, Bishop Rotherham (who became Lord Chancellor on return to England), Master of the Rolls Dr John Morton, John Cheyne, the diplomat Thomas Montgomery and Edward's brother-in-law Thomas St Leger were all on Louis's annual payroll for substantial amounts.

We may reason that Edward made the best of a bad situation, even though it was one largely of his own making; but to the medieval mind what he had done was shameful. Worse, in the mirror held up by his fellow princes he had seen himself as of little account. He had set out proudly to be crowned king of France and returned furtively with sacksful of the real king's gold. The enterprise over which he had laboured for so long in the hope that it would rally his people behind him had instead undermined his prestige.

Perhaps worst of all, although probably a thought too bitter to be entertained, Warwick had been proved right about Duke Charles. Edward was now Louis's pensioner, a status which, had he been prepared to accept it in 1466, would have prevented the breach with Warwick and the deaths of countless brave and valued men. He returned from the expedition diminished in the eyes of his subjects – but perhaps also in his own.

XXIV

SEPTIC SIBLINGS

G LOUCESTER OPPOSED THE DEAL STRUCK WITH LOUIS, although he and Clarence were among those who paid their respects to him at Picquigny and came away with valuable gifts. Counting Northumberland's contingent the army contained enough northerners to have constituted a battle in their own right. They almost certainly formed the vanguard under Gloucester's command and suffered casualties at Saint-Quentin. They would have felt the disgrace of going home without a fight more keenly than anyone else.

Gloucester's disillusionment would have deepened in the years that followed as Edward devoted his attention to money-making at the expense of England's international standing, while spending freely to pose as a great king. I use the word 'pose' advisedly, as after 1475 cosmopolitan Englishmen knew their king was just a small fish in a big pond. Richard of York had believed passionately in England's greatness, and nobody in the country would have felt the humiliation of its diminished status more viscerally than his namesake youngest son.

Gloucester must also have been affected by the same guilty knowledge that convinced Clarence he was the legitimate king. Why, if not true, would their mother have diminished herself in their eyes by confessing that Edward was the product of her adultery? It goes to the heart of the tacit question posed by the Crowland Continuator:

'These three brothers, the king and the two dukes, were possessed of such surpassing talents that, if they had been able to
live without dissensions, such a threefold cord could never have
been broken without the utmost difficulty.'

But it was broken, repeatedly and without great difficulty, because
Edward was so evidently dissimilar in body and character to his
brothers and their father. Until quite recently there was no debate
about genetic determinism – all believed that 'blood will out'.
Edward's siblings would have perceived the coarseness of his appetites, his commercial dealings and even his affable approachability
as further proof that he could not be their father's son.

Gloucester was 8 years old when Richard of York was killed
and would have remembered him as a distant, god-like figure. He
would have grown up hearing how austere and noble he was, and
the contrast between how he believed a son of York should behave
and what he observed in Edward was stark. He did not keep away
from court because of the Woodvilles, far less favoured and powerful than he, but for fear his mask would slip.

Gloucester may have regarded Edward's profit-seeking as ignoble,
but in terms of affirming his authority at home it is hard to fault
the king's decision to do everything in his power to 'live of his own'
after 1475, 'his own' including the regularly sheared ecclesiastical
sheep. No doubt Lord Treasurer and royal uncle Henry Bourchier,
Earl of Essex, strongly urged him to pursue this course of action,
and also ensured compliance by his weak-willed younger brother
the Cardinal Archbishop of Canterbury.

It was therefore highly significant that Edward decided to make
the reinterment of Richard of York into one of the major political ceremonies of his reign. On one hand no expense was spared,
demonstrating that the monarchy was solvent and capable of gran-
deur; on the other it was an opportunity to draw the House of York
together and to indulge Gloucester's father-worship by permitting
him to make the ceremony as splendid as he could have wished.

The bodies of Richard and his second son Edmund, killed with him at Wakefield, had remained undisturbed where their enemies had buried them at Pontefract since April 1461, when they were reunited with their heads, previously adorning the Micklegate at York. On 24 July 1476 they were disinterred and laid in state in Pontefract church, Richard's remains in a coffin covered with cloth of gold, under a funerary image of him decked in ermine and purple velvet, surrounded by banners and by a life-sized silver angel holding a golden crown.

After a night's candlelit vigil the funerary procession set out for Fotheringhay, stopping for the night at churches in Doncaster, Blyth, Tuxford and the Yorkist boroughs of Grantham and Stamford. Laurence Booth, Archbishop of York, went ahead to ensure that the churches and clergy were appropriately prepared for the vigils, and funded so that everyone who came to pay their respects received a penny, and pregnant women twopence.

The funerary chariot, draped in black velvet embroidered with the royal arms of England and France, was preceded by a knight displaying the ducal arms and followed by Gloucester and the northern lords, with alms distributed to the crowds along the way. When the procession reached Fotheringhay on the 29th it was met by the king and queen, Clarence, Dorset, Rivers, Hastings, Ferrers and other lords. Edward embraced the effigy and made a show of weeping before the coffins were taken into the collegiate church, which he had refounded in 1461.*

Five thousand people received alms in the church, and many times more feasted afterwards in the castle and in tents around it. The catering was lavish in quality as well as quantity, with the bill for food and drink alone exceeding £300 [£191,000]. As public relations it was a complete success; but as an act of family solidarity it was marred by the conspicuous absence of Duchess Cecily. It may

---

*Gloucester was born at now destroyed Fotheringhay Castle, but the magnificent parish church built in Perpendicular style, the truncated remains of a far grander establishment, is a shrine for modern Ricardians.

be that widows were not normally included in such ceremonies, but had she wished to be present she would have been. On past form her boycott of the event was a barbed reminder to her other offspring that Edward was not Richard's son.

It was also a nail in Clarence's coffin. He had not been punished in 1471 because Edward was beholden to Margaret and hoped for her support to persuade Duke Charles to join him against France. This she had failed to do, and deceived him to boot. The king had also yielded to the entreaties of their mother, and she should have been grateful. Clearly she was not, any more than was Clarence himself. As Edward presided over the climax of his magnificent act of filial piety, it surely crossed his mind that he owed no loyalty to those who showed him none.

Another nail was that despite the 1473 resumptions Clarence still drew more wealth from land than anyone other than the king, and after 1475 Edward set about resuming royal and attainted lands wholesale. The outstanding exception was the estates held at the king's pleasure by Clarence, who incautiously confided in his servants that he believed the king intended to foreclose on him as well. Talking about it to people he should have known included royal informants went some distance towards making it a self-fulfilling prophecy.

Hammering on, Clarence attended court only when summoned and refused to eat anything prepared by the royal kitchens. Given that the court was populated with those he had wronged, not least the Woodvilles, it is understandable that he made no effort to win friends and allies. But to indicate that he feared poisoning in the king's household bordered on treason.

The problem was that Clarence's offences in 1469–70 had been unforgivable, and he knew it. There is an almost exact parallel in Louis XI's experience with his treacherous younger brother, who continued to conspire against him despite having been treated with outstanding generosity. The term 'catastrophizing' describes the common phenomenon of individuals driven by guilt to make the worst of an already bad situation, and it is a tenable hypothesis that Clarence was subconsciously courting the punishment he knew he deserved.

Matters came to a head when Isabel Neville, Duchess of Clarence, never recovered from the birth of their fourth child and second son in early October 1476 and died on 22 December, followed by baby Richard ten days later. The double tragedy appears to have unhinged Clarence, who in the months that followed cast aside what little circumspection he had previously shown. Projecting his mother-nurtured hatred, he convinced himself that Isabel and the baby had died because of the evil designs of the queen.

In all probability the action he took on the basis of this belief would have been sufficient to bring about his downfall, but Edward did not learn of it until other, more portentous events had already worsened relations between the two brothers. The first came after Duke Charles, already defeated heavily by the Swiss at Grandson and Morat in March and June 1476, was routed and killed at Nancy on 5 January 1477 by an army led by the Duke of Lorraine.

The northern Burgundian estates mutinied and, as there was no male heir, Louis XI declared the duchy of Burgundy and the counties of Picardy and Artois reversionary to France and invaded them. He also proposed a marriage between the 6-year-old Dauphin and 20-year-old Duchess Marie to get his hands on Flanders and Hainault, which had come to the dukes of Burgundy in the female line. It fell to dowager Duchess Margaret to salvage what she could for her stepdaughter Marie, with whom she had formed an exceptionally strong bond.

In the years that followed Margaret acted exclusively in the Burgundian interest. Some historians believe that England might have played a significant role in the struggle had Edward been willing to give up his French pension, but Edward could not have launched another expedition so soon after 1475 even if he had wished to. Margaret knew the duchy's salvation lay with the Empire, and bent all her efforts to getting Maximilian of Austria to marry Marie.

When she suggested in early 1477 that Marie might marry Clarence, it was simply a stratagem to get Maximilian and the emperor, his chronically indecisive father, to commit to the marriage and to the defence of Marie's patrimony. It was not seen as such by Clarence, but Edward showed he understood his sister's motives by flatly rejecting the suggestion and proposing that Marie should marry Earl Rivers instead. The idea that the greatest heiress in Europe might marry a mere English earl was ludicrous, and the proposal clearly not serious.

Louis XI dripped a little extra poison into the situation by sending Edward a warning that Margaret's proposal was intended to strengthen Duchess Marie's claim to the English throne in the Lancastrian line by uniting it with Clarence's claim to be the true Yorkist heir. Edward should have been well enough acquainted with Louis's inveterate pot-stirring to have dismissed this as ill-intentioned disinformation, but the seed fell on fertile ground.

Clarence's inflated idea of his own importance made it impossible for him to see how unrealistic it was for him to aspire to the hand of Duchess Marie. Edward also rejected a proposal by the Scots that Clarence might marry James III's sister Margaret, on the specious grounds that 'no honourable man' could contemplate remarriage within a year of his bereavement. There was definitely an ironic sting in the tail of that sentiment.

The final straw for Clarence and Edward alike was the trial for treason in May 1477 of the Oxford clerks John Stacy and Thomas Blake, and of Thomas Burdet, a member of Clarence's household. Blake and Burdet had been implicated in Stacy's tortured confession of necromancy in seeking to 'imagine and compass' the deaths of Edward and the Prince of Wales, and of telling others that they would die soon. Burdet was further charged with disseminating treasonable 'bills, writings, rhymes and ballads'.

This was so obviously an incandescently hot political potato that Edward appointed an extraordinarily powerful commission of five earls, twelve barons and six justices to hear the case. On 19 May they found the accused guilty and Stacy and Burdet were hanged the next day. Blake, whose role had been minor, was pardoned at the intercession of the Bishop of Norwich. Before he was executed Burdet made a long speech proclaiming his innocence.

On the same day the king sent a writ of judicial review to establish the facts of another capital case that had been tried under Clarence's authority at Warwick a month earlier. In mid-April two of Clarence's former servants, Ankarette Twynho and John Thursby, the former seized from her home in Somerset, were put on trial for having poisoned Duchess Isabel and baby Richard. Roger Tocotes, a Wiltshire knight banneret and a close associate of the duke, was accused of complicity but evaded arrest.

Clarence's justices of the peace and the Warwick jury found them guilty, even though the supposed evidence presented by Clarence was not even internally coherent – for example, Twynho was alleged to have poisoned Isabel at Warwick on 10 October, when the duchess was at that time resident at Tewkesbury. They were hanged and Clarence's later indictment stated that the verdict was obtained by the jury's 'fear and great menace and doubt of loss of their lives and goods', and that he had behaved 'as though he had used a king's power'.

It was the combination of the two that did for him. Intimidation by local magnates was commonplace in civil suits, but trials of capital offences were held to a higher standard. Edward had caused muted outrage by using his presence to obtain the judicial murders of Courtenay and Hungerford in 1469, but that is why the second point was so important. The king's word was legally unquestionable, and had he accused Courtenay and Hungerford himself their execution would not have been regarded as a perversion of justice.

By acting as he did Clarence had usurped the king's prerogative, in itself treason, and a day or two after the execution of Stacy and Burdet he compounded his offence by entering the Council chamber at Westminster and having Burdet's declaration of innocence read into the record. The most likely reason why he chose to insult the lords who had presided over the trial and to impugn the king's justice is that he knew Edward intended to proceed against him in the matter of Twynho and Thursby. By declaring his belief that Burdet was innocent he was saying that Edward was no better than he, and therefore unfit to judge him.

Edward returned from Windsor and in late June, equipped with full details of the Twynho and Thursby trial, summoned Clarence to appear before him at Westminster in the presence of the mayor and aldermen of London. According to the Crowland Continuator, who was there, the king himself accused him 'of contempt of the law of the land and a great threat to the judges and jurors of the kingdom'. Clarence was sent to the Tower to await trial.

Six months passed until Edward summoned Parliament on 19 January 1478 to arraign Clarence on a charge of high treason. The king himself presented the bill of attainder, which was long and detailed. Clarence had abused the king's trust and his own fraternal obligations, despite being the beneficiary of exceptional royal forbearance. He had repaid it with 'much higher, much more malicious, more unnatural and loathly treason than at any time hath been compassed [planned], purposed and conspired'.

The itemized indictments were a summary of the points made earlier about Clarence's growing paranoia, culminating in a plan to smuggle his son to Burgundy for safekeeping. In addition he had never ceased alleging that Edward was a bastard, and kept a copy of an agreement signed by Henry VI designating Clarence as the legitimate successor should Henry's line die out. The Crowland Continuator cut the long story short:

> No one argued against the duke except the king; no one answered the king except the duke. Some persons, however, were introduced concerning whom many people wondered whether they performed the offices of accusers or witnesses. It is not really fitting that both offices should be held at the same time, by the same persons, in the same case. The duke swept aside all charges with a disclaimer offering, if it were acceptable, to uphold his case by personal combat.

Parliament condemned him to death, the sentence pronounced on 7 February by Henry, Duke of Buckingham, newly created steward of England for the occasion. The Woodvilles are supposed to have influenced the king to execute his own brother, but there is no evidence that they did. Clarence doomed himself by making it clear that he did not regard Edward as his legitimate king, and no one apart from his mother made any effort to save him.

Edward still hesitated until William Alyngton, Speaker of the Commons, came to the Lords' chamber to ask that sentence be carried out. On 18 February Clarence was drowned in a wine barrel used as a bath, and permitted honourable burial next to Isabel behind the altar at Tewkesbury Abbey, where the remains of Edward of Westminster had been mouldering since 1471. The king paid his brother's debts, permitted his young son to inherit the earldom of Warwick, and paid for attendants to care for him and his older sister.

Edward possibly regretted the necessity of putting him to death, but the idea that he suffered from remorse is an invention by Polydore Vergil, who only came to England in 1502 and wrote his *Anglica Historia* at the invitation of Henry VII. Likewise we need place no credence in the story that Gloucester mourned his brother and blamed the Woodvilles for his death. He showed no hesitation in obtaining the earldom of Salisbury for his own son, in taking possession of Clarence's northern estates and in recovering the office of Great Chamberlain.

The main beneficiary was Edward himself, who took almost all Clarence's lands into the royal estate. For let us not forget the aphorism that it is not paranoia if they really are out to get you. Clarence was guilty as charged, but there was one important item that did not feature in the list of indictments: he had been holding lands worth £3,500 [£2.23 million] per annum, and Edward had better uses for this than to leave it in the hands of a dangerously erratic fool.

XXV

MONEY MATTERS

THE FINAL FIVE YEARS OF EDWARD'S REIGN ARE THE least commented of the period because, after years of headline events, nothing outstandingly dramatic happened. Rulers have a limited time to bring about changes in the way a country is governed. A standard X–Y graph would show a declining axis of energy, vision and popular good will crossing a rising axis of 'friction' – institutional inertia, fiscal constraints and indifference merging into sullen hostility.

Edward had won a second chance in 1471, so his X–Y axes crossed twice. His outstanding talent was for leading men in battle, but his effort to govern through the promotion of his comrades in arms was destroyed by Warwick in 1469. Then, after his heavy bet on the 1475 expedition came to an inglorious end, he was out of big ideas to unite the kingdom behind him and settled for repairing fences and not importuning his subjects for any more money.

The principal novelty in the later years of Edward's reign, therefore, is that he paid serious attention to the royal finances. They were in a deplorable state, with borrowing to pay for civil war campaigns piled on top of liabilities dating back to the years of Henry VI's personal rule. Royal tallies, bills and letters patent littered the country, with no clear idea of the total amount outstanding.

In February 1474 all creditors with claims predating December 1470 were ordered to present proofs to the exchequer for verification, to be settled by regular payments over twenty years. It is a measure of how rapidly the royal finances improved that in July 1478 Edward authorized Master of the Rolls Dr John Morton and William Essex, chief accountant of the exchequer, to settle – outright – all the verified debts called in by the 1474 proclamation.

Edward deserves considerable credit for recognizing Morton's exceptional ability. He went from principal adviser to Henry VI during the Readeption to becoming Edward's Master of the Rolls (keeper of the chancery records) in less than a year, and his advancement thereafter was extremely rapid. Between 1474 and 1478 he was awarded a succession of ecclesiastical sinecures, culminating in his appointment as Bishop of Ely. In terms of disposable income Ely was the richest diocese in England, and often a springboard to the archbishopric of Canterbury.

Morton was that rare being in public service – a man of principle. He took a potentially career-ending stand against Edward that might also have cost him his life, and came to terms with him only after Henry VI and his son were killed and the issue of usurpation became moot. Under him the Court of Chancery grew rapidly in importance and, although his relentless pursuit of efficiency made him no friends, he was incorruptible – and well paid to keep him that way. At the peak of his power, under Henry VII, he devised 'Morton's Fork' to pluck the feathers of the nobility: if a man lived well he was obviously rich, and if frugally he must have savings.

Also in mid-1478 Edward settled with the City of London, much the greatest of his domestic creditors. Arrears of £12,924 [£8.2 million] were cleared by granting the City the right to appoint a wide range of officials supervising commercial activity, as well as the office of Coroner for greater London. Royal appointees had been so corrupt and extortionate that the City judged it worth writing off the huge sum to be rid of them.

Edward continued to pay off international obligations, such as the loan raised by Margaret from the Flemish cities in 1471, by awarding trading privileges; but the irritation this caused English merchants was muted because the long recession in northern European trade came to an end. Greatly boosted by the opening up of French markets after 1475, exports and imports more than trebled in value between the nadir of 1469–71 and the end of Edward's reign, and complaints about systemic inequities are few when everyone is making money.

The southern and western regions were the principal beneficiaries of the trade bonanza, which dangerously accentuated the long relative decline of the North, exacerbated by the unilateral trade privileges enjoyed by the Hanseatic League. It is unlikely Edward gave this a moment's thought, because the normal signals of popular unrest were contained by his brother's good lordship. Gloucester put little effort into collecting the money voted by the Commons for the 1475 expedition, and a decline in royal revenue from the duchy of Lancaster estates entrusted to him suggests he took the same view of royal rents.

No doubt strongly influenced by his uncle the Lord Treasurer, and by Morton, Edward also tried to bring royal household expenditure under control. Detailed ordinances were issued concerning payments to suppliers, and the rules for catering were defined in minute detail to end wholesale abuse of the traditional 'perks' enjoyed by kitchen and serving staff. Condign punishment was also prescribed for staff who abused purveyance, the right of the sovereign to pay a lower than market price for goods and services. Originally introduced to prevent profiteering in time of war, it had become a commonly abused practice in peacetime as well.

With regard to revenue, Morton found such chaos in the king's accounts that he persuaded him to undertake a systematic review and enforcement of royal rights. Morton's own role was indirectly described by the Crowland Continuator: '[The king] also searches the registers and rolls of Chancery and exacts heavy fines from those who were found to have intruded into inheritances without following the procedure required by law, [the fines based on] what they had received in the meantime'.

We have already noted the Crowland Continuator's outrage at the king's regular demand for ecclesiastical tenths, added to which, 'the fruits of vacant prelacies, which according to Magna Carta cannot be sold, he lets out of his hands for a sum fixed by himself and on no other terms'. The conclusion nonetheless veered reluctantly towards admiration:

> These and similar kinds of snare, more numerous than anyone without special experience could imagine, together with the annual tribute of £10,000 due from the French... made him, within a few years, a very wealthy prince; so much so that in the collection of gold and silver vessels, tapestries and highly precious ornaments, both regal and religious, in the building of castles, colleges and other notable places and in the acquisition of new lands and possessions not one of his ancestors could match his remarkable achievements.

The annual payment from Louis XI was important, and the down payment of 85,000 crowns [£10.8 million] obtained at Picquigny – including 10,000 of 50,000 crowns Louis agreed to pay to ransom Marguerite d'Anjou – permitted Edward to begin the process of retrenchment with a healthy balance. But the ecclesiastical tenths, Clarence's estate, Morton's stricter financial oversight, the king's profit from trade and from his growing fleet of personally owned merchant ships would have permitted him to live comfortably 'of his own' without the French pension – so long as he could avoid ruinously costly wars.

It follows that the sole aim of Edward's diplomacy following the death of Duke Charles was to conceal the fact that he had no intention of going to war, because he could only continue to profit from the Franco-Burgundian war while the contestants believed he might come in on one side or the other. Two factors he did not control set a time limit on his balancing act. The first was that neither side should prevail militarily over the other; the second, of course, was his own credibility, which eroded the longer he played hard to get.

Perhaps the most remarkable feature of the Anglo–French nego-tiations in 1477–82 was that although Edward acted throughout in the belief that Louis would renege on the Treaty of Picquigny at the first opportunity, it was he who broke the terms repeatedly. The two kings had undertaken to support each other against enemies foreign and domestic, yet Edward continued to negotiate with Burgundy and Brittany against Louis's interests.

In the absence of military intervention it is doubtful whether any amount of English diplomatic skill could have influenced the outcome of the Franco–Burgundian conflict. Commynes smugly observed that 'there has never been a set of negotiations between the French and the English where the intelligence and cleverness of the French has failed to outshine that of the English'. Another way of looking at it is that Edward's ambassadors played a weak hand rather well.

Edward was a man of instincts and, with the exception of the trap he set for Warwick and Clarence in 1470 and the 1475 expedition, one looks in vain for evidence of the *furbizia* that characterized suc-cessful Renaissance princes. However, it would have availed him little in his dealings with the Universal Spider, who was the supreme practitioner of the dark art and whose network of informers kept him abreast of his opponents' machinations. Furthermore, with regard to Edward, Louis had the ace of trumps up his sleeve.

Edward himself put it there when he stipulated that the treaty of amity clause agreed at Picquigny should be kept secret, for fear of a violently adverse popular reaction in England. Even though the treaty was signed on holy relics, Louis had reneged on a similarly solemn undertaking with Charles of Burgundy and, as Thomas Hobbes put it in *Leviathan*, 'covenants, without the sword, are but words'. Worse, the treaty of amity would remain secret only until it suited Louis to reveal the terms.

The seemingly complex three-way diplomatic negotiations that took place in 1477–82 reflect the fact, evident since the loss of

Normandy and Guyenne, that England could be a player only if France and Burgundy remained at war with each other. The imperative of preventing the emergence of a single dominant power in Europe set the pattern for English diplomacy in peace and war for the next 500 years – to such good effect that the French, themselves past masters of negotiating in bad faith, still refer to England as 'Perfide Albion'.

Edward's alarm at Louis's proposal that the Dauphin should marry Duchess Marie was muted: it was clearly a bargaining ploy, like Margaret's proposed marriage with Clarence and Edward's own counter-proposal. Of greater concern was that Louis had not obtained the promised guarantee of the annual pension by the Medici and the pope. The instalments of Marguerite's ransom were also at risk, as she was of no further interest to Louis once he had forced her to sign over her rights of inheritance in Anjou, Bar and Lorraine.

Edward sensibly chose Lord Howard and Morton to lead the English delegations to France, as they had a strong personal interest in keeping the pensions coming. They were successful. Louis did pay Marguerite's ransom, and the last instalment of Edward's pension, as agreed at Picquigny, was paid in August 1482. By then Edward had received 475,000 crowns [£60.4 million] and the other pensioners 112,000 [£14.25 million], of which Howard alone received gifts to a value of 24,000 crowns in the two years following Picquigny.

Despite Louis's decrees, French merchants and port officials found many ways of obstructing English trade, while mutual piracy remained endemic. The main benefit of the treaty was the leverage it gave Edward in renegotiating the previously lopsided commercial treaty with Burgundy to abolish the tariff barriers to English textiles. Dowager Duchess Margaret promised further concessions during a state visit to England in 1480.

Louis believed the military cost of a renewed Anglo–Burgundian alliance against him would be greater then continuing to pay the burdensome English pensions. His moment of greatest weakness came after Archduke Maximilian smashed a French army at Guinegatte in Artois in August 1479. Even then, although he agreed to a 100-year extension of the Anglo–French treaty of amity, Louis continued to reject Edward's further demand to start paying Princess Elizabeth's dower after she reached the marriageable age of 12 in 1478.

The diplomatic quadrille came to an end after Duchess Marie was killed in a riding accident on 27 March 1482, with the title passing to her 3-year-old son Philippe. Despite Margaret's best efforts the Burgundian Netherlands distrusted Maximilian and refused to accept his authority as regent. His hope that England might be persuaded to enter the war on his side if he agreed to make good Edward's loss of the French pension was dashed when Louis finally played his ace of trumps by sending him the signed and sealed renewal of the Anglo–French treaty of amity.

The Franco–Burgundian Treaty of Arras, signed on 23 December 1482, marked the end of Edward's effort to keep himself profitably in the middle. It recognized Louis's right to the reversion of the duchy of Burgundy and the counties of Boulogne and Picardy. In addition Maximilian's not-yet 2-year-old daughter, named Margaret after her step-grandmother, was handed over to the French and betrothed to the Dauphin Charles, now 12 years old, with the imperial county of Burgundy (Franche-Comté) and Artois as her dowry.

Commynes suggests that Edward's furious chagrin at this outcome contributed to his death a few months later, but he had obtained all he could realistically have hoped for. He must have known that Elizabeth's marriage to the Dauphin had been unlikely to take place, and his demand for pre-payment of her marriage portion was transparently intended to extend the duration of his pension by other means. His disappointment would have been offset by the consideration that he was nineteen years younger than Louis, who had suffered two strokes during 1481, and could look forward to further opportunities to extort money during the minority of Louis's heir.

The release of Elizabeth from the French betrothal put her back in the pool for the more distasteful activity to which Edward also devoted considerable diplomatic effort, namely marrying his children for as much money as he could get. Cecily (born March 1469) was the only one offered with a traditional (and modest) dowry when she had been betrothed to the future James IV of Scotland in 1474. Margaret died in 1472 and George in 1479, while Catherine (born August 1479) and Bridget (born November 1480) were too young.

This left Mary (born August 1467), the 'spare' for Elizabeth agreed at Picquigny, Edward (born November 1470), Richard (born August 1473) and Anne (born November 1475). Mary was betrothed to the future Frederick I of Denmark in 1481, but she died the following year. Anne became a counter in her father's attempt to obtain a guarantee from Maximilian that he would make good the French pension if Louis ceased to pay it. She was affianced to baby Philippe of Burgundy in August 1480, when Maximilian also agreed not to seek any other contracts of marriage for three years. The betrothal, like Elizabeth's, was a casualty of the Treaty of Arras.

Edward hawked his namesake heir around the courts of Europe, first to Spain and then to Milan, before reaching agreement with Frañsez of Brittany in May 1480 that young Edward would wed the duke's 4-year-old daughter and heir Anne when she became marriageable in eight years' time. Her dowry was to be 100,000 crowns [£12.7 million] if she were still the heir at the time of their marriage, and double that amount if a son were born to the duke before then, the son to marry one of Edward's daughters. In breach of the Treaty of Picquigny Edward also undertook to provide 3,000 archers at his own expense to defend Brittany against an attack by France, and Frañsez to provide a like number if Edward were to invade France.

The validity of any contract with Frañsez was always tenuous, and in this case it was tacitly repudiated almost immediately. The duke's negotiator provided Louis with copies of all the secret correspondence, but did not live to enjoy the large bribe thus earned once

Louis revealed his knowledge of the exact terms of the agreement. Frañsez had the man killed, but quailed when Louis ominously reminded him that he held Brittany as a vassal of the French crown, and that his dealings with Edward were treasonous.*

Young Richard was the only one successfully married in his father's lifetime. In January 1476 John, the last Mowbray Duke of Norfolk, died very suddenly, his only child 4-year-old Anne. The Mowbray estate was vast but encumbered by two dowager duchesses, the doughty and much married Katherine née Neville and Anne's mother Elizabeth née Talbot, whom Edward pressured into surrendering most of her dower lands in exchange for an annuity.

The male Mowbray line had been thin for so long that should Anne die without issue, the legal heirs would be John, Lord Howard and William, Lord Berkeley, descendants of her father's great-aunts. Edward prevailed on Berkeley to surrender his succession rights in exchange for the cancellation of bonds totalling £34,000 [£21.6 million] extorted by the Lisle branch of the Talbots when they kidnapped the entire Berkeley family in the 1430s. In 1481 Edward also made him Viscount of Catherlough in Ireland.

In January 1477 Edward married Anne to his 4-year-old second son Richard, Duke of York, in the second no-expense-spared ceremony of state during the second half of his reign. Papal dispensation for consanguinity had been obtained, also at great expense, and the two infants became the centrepiece of a magnificent display. Anthony, Earl Rivers, and John de la Pole, Earl of Lincoln, led the young bride to St Stephen's Chapel, and the Dukes of Gloucester and Buckingham escorted her to the wedding feast for the massed nobility of England.

The prominence given to the Woodvilles during and after the marriage was a further signal that Edward had the utmost confidence in them. Rivers played a leading role in the wedding and

---

*Frañsez did not produce a male heir before he died in 1488. Brittany was finally annexed by France after Duchess Anne was forced to marry Charles VIII in 1491 and Louis XII in 1499.

the following tournament, where other contestants included his nephews Thomas and Richard Grey, his brother Edward, and Richard Haute, the son of the queen's aunt Joan.

Anne Mowbray died in November 1481 but before then, as he had done with the Countess of Warwick, Edward had set aside Howard's rights by an Act of Parliament that gave his son Richard a life interest in the estate, after which it would revert to the crown. Howard was paid nothing, on the face of it base ingratitude to a loyal servant. Possibly Edward judged that Howard's vastly profitable role as lead ambassador to Louis XI was compensation enough.

XXVI

THE MARCHES

THE LATER YEARS OF EDWARD'S REIGN WERE NOT SOLELY devoted to the shameless pursuit of money: he also tried to resolve the problem of endemic lawlessness in the Welsh and Scots Marches. The policy he pursued for the first was innovative, economical and was copied by his successors. His approach to the second was the opposite – brutally traditional, ruinously expensive and counter-productive.

We have seen how Edward began to develop an alternative to the regime lock on Wales lost with the elder William Herbert by moving the Prince of Wales's Council to Ludlow in early 1473. The king did not push the project at first, as he was fully taken up with preparing the invasion of France. Also, it was prudent not to invest too much political capital in Prince Edward until he had survived the dangerous early years.

From 1476 onwards the project rapidly gathered pace. The two greatest non-royal Welsh landowners, Herbert's 25-year-old namesake heir and 21-year-old Henry Stafford, Duke of Buckingham, had not shown the capacity and dependability Edward looked for, and were excluded. The Council became a Woodville-dominated enterprise, grist to the mill of historians anxious to attribute the sordid failure of the Yorkist dynasty to their evil influence.

The idea that Rivers, his brothers and his nephews worked to a plan concerted by Elizabeth to increase their power and influence is manifest nonsense. To the contrary and as we saw in the case of Calais, Rivers spurned opportunities to make himself a magnate. He was a highly intelligent and cultivated individual, and the presumption must be that he knew to do so would risk the good will of his royal brother-in-law. The Woodvilles knew they owed everything to the king and repaid him by loyally performing the tasks he delegated to them.

Chief among them was the project nearest to Edward's heart – the rearing of his heir and preparing him for kingship. It is not remotely likely that a medieval king would have entrusted such a sensitive responsibility to men who showed any sign of independent ambition. Perhaps even more to the point, is it also not the slightest bit remarkable that the queen should have wished for her sons to be in the care of men she trusted.

As befits any experiment in governance, Edward increased the power of the prince's Council incrementally. Between 1473 and 1476 he still hoped that it could work in coordination with the Marcher lords, but the division of judicial authority sabotaged efforts to bring wrongdoers to justice. Local courts would pre-emptively acquit men indicted by the Council, with the Herbert affinity in south Wales among the most prominent offenders.

In January 1476 Edward increased the Council's judicial powers and summoned the Marcher lords to a meeting with the Council at Ludlow on 24 March, but before then he had decided to abandon the established structure. On 16 March he granted the Council power to intervene in all Welsh and Marcher lordships, and in June the Council pointedly met at Buckingham's lordship of Newport. Seventy-three individuals, three Herbert bastards and two sons of the late Roger Vaughan among them, were required to post bonds of good behaviour.

In December Edward completed the process of delegating to the Council most of the judicial and executive powers of the ancestral Mortimer earldom of March in Herefordshire, Shropshire, Radnor, Brecknock and Monmouth. Towards the end of 1477 he persuaded

Richard of Gloucester to exchange his sparsely populated lordship of Elfael (about a third of Radnor) for the duchy of Lancaster estate around the port of Ogmore in Gloucester's lordship of Glamorgan. In December 1477 Prince Edward was granted possession of almost all the March earldom's castles, lordships and manors, to which Elfael was added in March 1478.

The writing was on the wall for the younger William Herbert from the time of the Council sessions at Newport. In 1479 he was forced to surrender the earldom of Pembroke and all the lands once controlled by his father except the lordship of Raglan, including Caerleon and Usk. He was fobbed off with the title of Earl of Huntingdon vacated by Thomas Grey when made Marquess of Dorset, and with duchy of Cornwall lands in Dorset and Somerset, which complemented his existing Somerset holdings as Baron Dunster.

Prince Edward was made Earl of Pembroke on 8 July 1479, and ten days later Earl of March. Usk and Caerleon were transferred to him in February 1483, leaving Herbert with his father's magnificent castle at Raglan and little else in Wales and the March. Herbert's uncle Walter Devereux, Lord Ferrers of Chartley, remained a Council member and lord of Weobley and of Richard's Castle in Herefordshire, but surrendered the ex-Talbot manors of Archenfield and Goodrich in the south of the county.

The Talbots had been the only serious rivals of the House of York on the English side of the middle March. They never recovered from the loss of the 1st Earl of Shrewsbury and his son, Viscount Lisle, at Castillon in 1453, and of the 2nd earl at Northampton in 1460. When the 3rd earl died in 1473, his heir George Talbot was only 5 years old. His remaining, mainly Shropshire lands were put in the custody of the queen and administered by the Council.

Clerical members of the Council were promoted to the bishoprics of Hereford (Thomas Myling, the prince's chancellor, in 1474), Worcester (John Alcock, ex-Lord Chancellor, co-tutor and co-president of the Council with Rivers, in 1476) and St David's (Richard

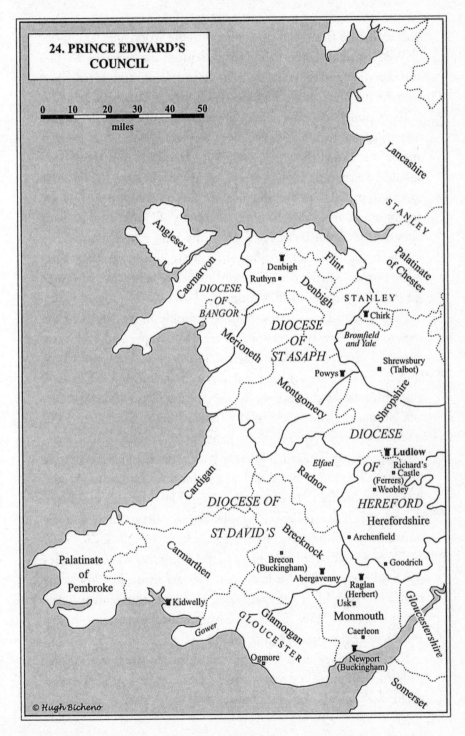

24. PRINCE EDWARD'S COUNCIL

0 10 20 30 40 50
miles

Lancashire

STANLEY

Palatinate
of Chester

Anglesey

Caernarvon

DIOCESE
OF
BANGOR

Flint

Denbigh
Ruthyn

Denbigh

STANLEY

Chirk

DIOCESE
OF
ST ASAPH

Bromfield
and Yale

Merioneth

Shrewsbury
(Talbot)

Montgomery

Powys

Shropshire

DIOCESE

Ludlow

Elfael

Radnor

Richard's
Castle
(Ferrers)
Weobley

OF

HEREFORD

Cardigan

DIOCESE OF

ST DAVID'S

Brecknock

Herefordshire

Archenfield

Carmarthen

Brecon
(Buckingham)

Goodrich

Palatinate
of
Pembroke

Abergavenny

Raglan
(Herbert)

Usk

Kidwelly

Monmouth

Gower

Glamorgan

GLOUCESTER

Caerleon

Gloucestershire

Ogmore

Newport
(Buckingham)

Somerset

© Hugh Bicheno

Martin, in 1482). All had close links with the Woodvilles – as Abbot of Westminster Myling had given the queen sanctuary in 1470–1 and stood as godfather to the new-born prince, and Martin had served with Rivers in his embassy to Charles of Burgundy in 1475.

The Council exercised direct government over a far larger proportion of the region than the older William Herbert had enjoyed, and it was clearly Edward's intention that Wales and the March should be a training ground where his heir could learn the business of kingship. The queen's influence was further strengthened by the appointment of her sons Thomas, Marquess of Dorset, and Richard Grey to the Council. In April 1482 the king gave Richard Grey the duchy of Lancaster lordship of Kidwelly, and in February 1483 made him co-equal with Rivers and Alcock as supervisor of Prince Edward's deportment and finances.

The Council shared territorial control only in the north of the region. Lord Stanley's areas of influence in Chester and Flint were respected, as were William Stanley's lordships of Holt and Chirk. William was also steward of the duchy of York lordship of Denbigh and administered the lands of the minor John Grey in Montgomery and Shropshire on behalf of the Council until November 1482, when John entered into his inheritance as Baron Grey of Powys.

When young Richard, Duke of York, married Countess Anne Mowbray his estate included half the lordship of Bromfield and Yale on the border of Denbigh and Shropshire. The king purchased the other half from George Neville, Baron Abergavenny, and the lordship was administered by the Council: which, since Bromfield and Yale was adjacent to Chirk, probably means William Stanley was made responsible for it as well. He was made steward of the prince's household in 1481 and both his active involvement in the Council and the lands put under his administration were to have a considerable bearing on future events.

The Woodvilles established an excellent working relationship with the Stanleys. They were trustees of each other's properties elsewhere in England, and the queen made Lord Stanley steward of her dower lands in Cheshire. In return, Thomas married his heir George to the land-poor widow Joan, Baroness Strange of Knockyn and daughter of the queen's sister Jacquetta. He had been steward of Edward's household since 1471 and would have been a member of a 'queen's party' if Elizabeth had ever dared to form one.

Prince Edward's Council did not have time to resolve the chronic problems of governance in Wales and the March. However it is notable as the one major institutional innovation made by Edward, and the prototype of the councils with which the Tudors and early Stuarts sought to bring a semblance of order and justice to a once ungovernable region.

• ᴄʌ •

The contrast between Edward's policy in Wales and his attempt to impose his authority on the Scots Marches could not have been more stark. Not only did it waste the financial surplus he had built up since 1475, it also tied up the military resources that were his principal bargaining chip with Louis XI and Maximilian. At great expense he recovered the border fortress of Berwick; but it was an entirely self-inflicted strategic debacle.

After defeat at Guinegatte in 1479 Louis XI needed to distract Edward, who gave him an opening by tearing up the truce signed with James III of Scotland in 1473. It would have been more logical if James had done so, as the truce and the betrothal of his heir to Edward's daughter Cecily was highly unpopular with the Scots nobility. Unfortunately contemporary sources are negligible when not also wildly fanciful, and a rational explanation for Edward's decision to kick over the table is hard to identify.

It is fair to assume that Richard of Gloucester had a great deal to do with it. Scots raids were a reproach to his good lordship, particularly in the West March, for which he was personally responsible, but also in the East March, where Henry Percy, Earl of Northumberland and his chief retainer, was briefly captured in a border skirmish. Gloucester may also have calculated that a war against their ancestral enemy would cement the northmen's loyalty to him as their tribal leader.

The proximate cause of the escalation was that James III's sister Margaret, betrothed to Earl Rivers in 1478, became pregnant by her lover William, Lord Crichton. When news of this reached London in January 1479, Edward declared that England's honour had been insulted and demanded repayment of the dowry instalments he had made for Princess Cecily's future marriage. He seized Scots property in London, and Scots residents in England began to petition for denizenship to protect their assets.

During 1479 the rancorous Scots royal family fell apart. This was believed to be the work of James's low-born favourites led by his physician William Sheves, made Archbishop of St Andrews in 1478 when his predecessor was deposed for corruption and insanity. James's sister Mary was already in prison consequent on the attainder of her husband Thomas Boyd, Earl of Arran; his brothers John, Earl of Mar, and Alexander, Duke of Albany, suffered forfeiture and imprisonment. Mar died in mysterious circumstances and James gave the earldom to Robert Cochrane, his architect. Albany escaped from prison and fled to France.

Edward then funded Gloucester and Northumberland to prepare for war before Easter of 1480. He also sent an embassy to tell the Scots that they must surrender Berwick, Coldingham and Roxburgh as reparation and hand over Prince James to ensure that he married Cecily in May 1481, or else face 'rigorous and cruel war'. In May Gloucester was appointed lieutenant-general in the North and commissions of array were issued for all the northern counties.

In September 1480 Archibald 'Bell-the-Cat' Douglas, Earl of Angus, raided Northumberland and burned the town supposedly guarded by Bamburgh Castle. Gloucester and Percy chased him back into Scotland, but he had achieved the objective of preventing the negotiated settlement sought by James III. Angus was a 'Red' Douglas and knew that Edward had demanded the reinstatement of

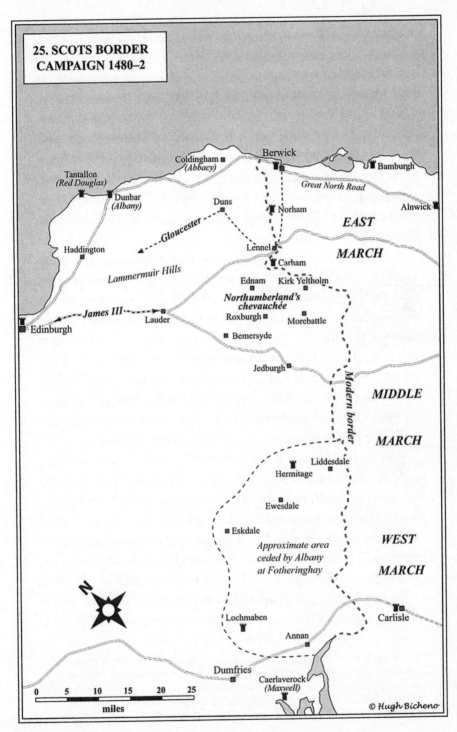

25. SCOTS BORDER CAMPAIGN 1480–2

Coldingham
(Abbacy)

Berwick

Bamburgh

Tantallon
(Red Douglas)

Dunbar
(Albany)

Duns

Norham

Great North Road

Alnwick

EAST

Gloucester

Lennel

MARCH

Haddington

Lammermuir Hills

Carham

Ednam

Kirk Yeltholm

*Northumberland's
chevauchée*

James III

Lauder

Roxburgh

Morebattle

Edinburgh

Bemersyde

Jedburgh

Modern border

MIDDLE

MARCH

Liddesdale

Hermitage

Ewesdale

Eskdale

WEST

*Approximate area
ceded by Albany
at Fotheringhay*

MARCH

N

Lochmaben

Carlisle

Annan

Dumfries

Caerlaverock
(Maxwell)

0   5   10   15   20   25

miles

© Hugh Bicheno

the attainted and exiled James, last of the 'Black' Earls of Douglas, who had been a Garter knight since 1463.

So far Edward had paid for military preparations entirely 'of his own', testimony to how successful he had been in transforming royal finances. During the winter of 1480–1, still loth to summon Parliament, he embarked on a new round of 'benevolences' and also claimed the three-quarters of a subsidy voted by the Commons in 1475, worth about £24,000 [£15.3 million], which he had renounced on return from France with his saddlebags full of Louis's gold. He also extracted another tenth from the Canterbury Convocation.

The York Convocation was not immediately called upon to make a similar contribution and the northern counties were exempted from the king's exactions in recognition of their payment in kind. This was burdensome: although there had been a poor harvest, supplies for the army were gathered by purveyance. Against which service in the forthcoming campaign was by paid indenture. Lord Stanley brought 3,000 archers from Lancashire, Rivers indented for 3,000 more from the Welsh March, and Dorset brought 600 from the West Country, but the main body of the army was naturally and profitably provided by the Gloucester and Percy affinities.

The plan for 1481 was for Lord Howard to make a naval *chevauchée* into the Firth of Forth while Edward led a land invasion. Only the naval assault, accompanied by a devastating attack on Scots trade by private ship-owners granted letters of marque, went ahead.* Howard seized the larger ships and burned the rest at Leith (Edinburgh's port), at Blackness, 17 miles further up the Firth of Forth, and at Kinghorn, opposite Leith on the northern side of the Firth.

Edward did not ride north to lead the army, and in a letter to the pope he explained this was because of unrest in England. We know

---

*The use of 'letters of marque and reprisal', traditionally issued to merchants who could not recover losses to pirates operating from foreign jurisdictions, became a scheme of licensed piracy in which the Crown took a share of the profits without necessarily risking a penny of investment. See my book *Elizabeth's Sea Dogs*.

nothing more, although it may have been prompted by the combination of a poor harvest and renewed demands for taxes. However it is also the case that Edward's continental diplomacy was at a particularly crucial stage that summer, and he would not have wanted to absent himself from London for long.

The situation changed in 1482 because Louis sent the Duke of Albany to England. Albany had been a strident opponent of the Anglo–Scots truce, but when he met Edward and Gloucester at Fotheringhay on 11 July he signed a treaty by which, if Edward made him king, he would surrender Berwick and, in the West March, cede Lochmaben and Hermitage Castles and the nests of border bandits in Annandale, Liddesdale, Eskdale and Ewesdale. Albany would also recognize that he held Scotland as Edward's vassal, would revoke the French alliance and, once extracted from a recent marriage arranged by Louis, he would marry Princess Cecily.

The treaty of Fotheringhay delayed and added a layer of political over-elaboration to what had been until then a straightforward campaign devised by Gloucester. In 1482 Edward had already spent, on indentures alone, about £4,300 [£2.7 million] on naval forces, £4,500 on English troops, and £2,200 on professional mercenaries. This was overkill against a penurious opponent who could command only feudal levies led by unruly lords who hated the court party. The intention was clearly to destroy Scots resistance utterly, but the two months' delay caused by Edward's dalliance with Albany ate up the campaigning season, supplies and money.

Gloucester and Albany rode north to join Northumberland and Stanley at Berwick. The town surrendered without a fight, but the fortress held out. Leaving Stanley to conduct the siege, Gloucester sent Northumberland to ravage the triangle between the Lennel and Jedburgh highways into England. Following with the main army, Gloucester waited until he knew the *chevauchée* had drawn the Scots army, then crossed the Tweed at Lennel and marched towards Duns before turning north-west. The aim was to go around the Lammermuir Hills and get between James's army and Edinburgh, trapping him against Northumberland's force and culminating in a battle of annihilation.

Oblivious to the fate Gloucester had planned for him and buoyed up a minor triumph in his first experience of battle in 1481, James marched at the head of a large feudal host towards Lauder, where the Jedburgh and Lennel highways divide. On 22 July his nobles, realizing that James was leading them to destruction, mutinied. They hanged Cochrane and other royal favourites from the bridge at Lauder and hustled James back to the capital, where they imprisoned him in Edinburgh Castle, an impregnable and well-supplied fortress.

With no one to fight and James out of reach, when Gloucester reached Edinburgh soon afterwards he found himself facing a strategic conundrum. He could not sack the city because of the commitment to Albany, and he could not besiege the castle because time and money were running out. The citizens of Edinburgh undertook to repay Edward's dowry payments if he did not want the marriage to take place, but that was the only return on investment Gloucester obtained before setting off back to England on 4 August.

Two days earlier he and Albany had signed an agreement with representatives of all the Scots noble factions that promised a pardon for Albany and the restoration of his lands and offices. When details of what Albany had agreed at Fotheringhay became known his situation became precarious once more, but he claimed that he had only signed to moderate the English plan to devastate the Lowlands. In his letter to the Pope Edward acknowledged that Albany did indeed save Scotland from severe consequences, which opens the door to suspicion that the Scot played him for a fool. The only English gain was Berwick Castle, which capitulated on 24 August. The Crowland Continuator was not impressed:

> This trifling, I really know not whether to call it 'gain' or 'loss' (for the safe keeping of Berwick each year swallows up ten thousand marks [£9.5 million]) at this period diminished the resources of

king and kingdom by more than a hundred thousand pounds
[£63.6 million]. King Edward was vexed at this frivolous outlay
of so much money, although the recovery of Berwick in some
degree alleviated his sorrow.

Gloucester must have been consumed with rage that Edward
had once more denied him the opportunity to win martial glory.
Presumably aware of this, the king tried to appease him by making
Gloucester's friend Lord Lovell a viscount, by declaring all his
brother's offices in the West March hereditary, and by awarding
him as an appanage the territory ceded in principle by Albany at
Fotheringhay as well as any other he might conquer.

But nothing could conceal the fact that in 1481–2, as in 1475,
the nation had provided Edward with a mighty sledgehammer to
shatter his enemies, and he had just gone through the motions.
When 1482 ended with the diplomatic humiliation of the Franco-
Burgundian Treaty of Arras, the full extent of Edward's failure was
revealed.

XXVII

DAGGERS IN MEN'S SMILES*

THE SIREN SONG OF 'AFTER WHICH THEREFORE BECAUSE of which' must be resisted during the last months of Edward's reign. We know he had little time to live – but *he* did not, although there are hints he had intimations of mortality before the fatal illness took him. He made a new will, but it was ignored and destroyed so we do not know what provisions it made for the succession. Not enough, certainly, but it is hardly surprising that he did not anticipate what was to come.

Despite his austere distaste for the king's morals and bitter condemnation of his regular shearing of the clerical sheep, our eye-witness the Crowland Continuator paints a glowing picture of the last great festivity of Edward's reign:

> King Edward kept the following feast of the Nativity at his palace of Westminster, frequently appearing clad in a great variety of most costly garments, of quite a different cut to those which had been usually seen hitherto in our kingdom... as to give that prince a new and distinguished air to beholders, he being a person of most elegant appearance, and remarkable beyond all others for the attractions of his person. You might have seen, in those days, the royal court presenting no other appearance than such as fully befits a most mighty kingdom, filled with riches

---

*'There is daggers in men's smiles: the near in blood,/The nearer bloody': *Macbeth*, Act III, Scene 3.

and with people of almost all nations, and (a point in which it excelled all others) boasting of those most sweet and beautiful children, the issue of his marriage... with queen Elizabeth.

Edward's gargantuan appetites had barely moderated. According to the invaluable testimony of the Augustinian friar Dominic Mancini, who was in England during the crucial period as an envoy of the Archbishop of Vienne (Poitiers) and whose principal informant was the Italian-speaking John Argentine, one of the Prince of Wales's physicians, Edward had become 'fat in the loins'. The king remained 'most immoderate' in food and drink, and 'it was his habit... to take an emetic for the delight of gorging his stomach once more'.

However, it appears he had become less sexually promiscuous. For the last years of his life he had what the French would have called a *maîtresse en titre* in Elizabeth née Lambert, better known as Jane Shore, the name given to her by the dramatist Thomas Heywood in 1599, which I will use to avoid confusion with the queen. Jane had been married to a London merchant called Shore, but the marriage was annulled in 1476 on grounds of his impotence. Since her liaison with Edward began that year, it is fair to suspect that her husband preferred to accept the private stigma of impotence than to be a very public cuckold.

Thomas More knew Jane in old age and his *The History of Richard III* is our main source of information about her. From others More learned that in her prime, 'a proper wit had she, and could both read well and write, merry in company, ready and quick of answer, neither mute nor full of babble, sometimes taunting without displeasure, and not without playfulness'. In other words, a charming flirt. Nobody had a bad word to say about her because:

For many [Edward] had, but her he loved, whose favour, to speak truth, she never abused to any man's hurt, but to many a man's comfort and relief: where the King took displeasure, she would mitigate and appease his mind; where men were out of favour, she would bring them in his grace; for many who had highly offended, she obtained pardon; of great forfeitures she got men remission; and finally, in many weighty suits, she stood many men in great stead either for none or very small rewards, and those rather gay than rich – either because she was content with the deed itself well done, or because she delighted in being asked for favours and to show what she was able to do with the King.

Intriguingly, Jane told More that the king spoke of only three long-term lovers, 'in whom three diverse qualities differently excelled: one [Jane] the merriest; another the wiliest; the third the holiest harlot in his realm'. The other two 'were somewhat greater personages' but either Jane or More chose not to name them. The 'holiest harlot' may have been Lady Eleanor Boteler née Talbot, on whom more later. The 'wiliest' was probably Elizabeth Lucy née Wayte, Edward's mistress from the early 1460s, who bore the king two recognized bastards and may have died giving birth to the second in 1476.

There is every reason to believe More's suggestion that Jane and the queen were friends. Elizabeth was almost constantly pregnant during the marriage (the last of ten children, Bridget, was born in November 1480), and would have welcomed some relief from the corpulent king's attentions. Jane posed no threat, could serve as a conduit for favours the queen hesitated to ask for in person, and one can readily imagine them discreetly comparing notes and having a giggle about the man whose bed they shared.

Early 1483 was a time of heightened international tension for England. Smarting at having been outwitted by Louis XI, and believing the Scots had contributed to his humiliation, Edward went through the motions of preparing for war against both. He summoned Parliament, which assembled on 20 January, and before it adjourned a month later it had voted him the necessary funds.

Having failed to become the power behind the Scottish throne, the Duke of Albany sent ambassadors to London to meet Edward, Gloucester, Northumberland, Lord Scrope of Bolton and Lord Parr, and they signed another treasonous treaty on Albany's behalf.

After Parliament voted him the funds, on 20 February Edward offered Duke Frañsez 4,000 archers for three months' service at Edward's expense, and to have them ready at Plymouth or Dartmouth within a month of the duke requesting them. On the same day Parliament voted Gloucester the hereditary grants described in the last chapter and adjourned. Gloucester departed London not long afterwards and never saw his brother again.

Giving Gloucester an appanage and an incentive to keep busy making war on Scotland is one indication that Edward's mind was turning to what might happen when he died. Another is that on 8 March Anthony Woodville sent his lawyer a copy of royal patents appointing him sole governor of the Prince of Wales, and empowering him to raise troops in the Welsh Marches. Taken together, the two measures are suggestive of a monarch seeking to ward off possible threats to his son's succession.

Some time between 25 March and 2 April Edward became ill and took to bed after a fishing trip on the Thames. It may have been malaria but pneumonia seems more likely, as he was lucid to the end. He had been blessed by good luck all his life, but there was none left for his posterity. The first and probably definitive domino to fall in the sequence that doomed his dynasty was that his uncle Henry Bourchier, Earl of Essex, Lord Treasurer and mainstay of the regime, died on 4 April, leaving no one else of his stature within the government.*

News of Bourchier's death appears to have become garbled with the king's illness and on 6 April a false report of Edward's death reached York, where a dirge was sung in the cathedral. On the 7th Edward summoned Elizabeth and their children, her son Dorset

---

*His interim replacement was under-treasurer John Wood, who had been responsible for the day-to-day running of the treasury since 1480.

and his old friend Hastings to his bedside. He begged them to sink their differences and work together to ensure his son's succession, and they tearfully assured him that they would. On the 9th he died.

Hastings immediately wrote to Gloucester at Middleham and possibly also to Buckingham at Brecon, telling them that the Woodvilles intended to seize power. It was 1469 all over again, and once more his fear of Elizabeth's vengeance for the wrong he had done her led him to put at risk the dynasty to which he owed everything. For all the fulsome posthumous praise of the chroniclers he had never been much more than chief panderer to the late king, and made the fatal error of believing he could continue to play a leading role.

The Woodvilles also owed their eminence entirely to the late king, and the idea that they might have thought they could impose their will on the Privy Council and on Gloucester is laughable. Although the Council in London proclaimed the Prince of Wales King Edward V on 11 April, and his coronation date set for 4 May, news of his father's death did not reach Ludlow until the 14th. If Rivers had been intent on seizing power he would have set out for London with the king at once; instead, he waited for orders from the Council.

The new king could easily have been in London in time for his father's funeral on 18–19 April. He was not because Hastings started the hare of a Woodville *coup d'état* by telling the Privy Council that if Rivers came to London with an army he would retreat to Calais. There is no indication that Rivers, although legally empowered to do so, had any such intention. Hastings prevailed on the Council to instruct Rivers to come with 'only' 2,000 men and to arrive in London on 1 May, and the royal party did not set out until 24 April.

In the evening of the 11th Hastings invited Lord Howard to dine. It is a safe assumption that Hastings was seeking to win him to an anti-Woodville alliance, and told him about his correspondence with Gloucester and Buckingham. It would have been prudent for Howard to have written to Gloucester immediately, both to confirm the truth of Hastings's assertions and to establish an independent line of communication to the most powerful man in the country.

On receipt of Hastings's and Howard's letters Gloucester wrote to Rivers, saying he wished to join the royal party before it entered London, to Elizabeth declaring his intention – according to the Crowland Continuator – 'to come and offer submission, fealty, and all that was due from him to his lord and King, Edward V', and to Hastings, Buckingham and Howard stating that he feared dire consequences from the Woodvilles having possession of the king.

Gloucester summoned his affinity to meet him at York and on 20 April set out from Middleham with 300 men-at-arms. On the 21st, at a heavily attended funeral service for his brother at York Minster, he led the northern nobility in swearing an oath of loyalty to Edward V. While in York, he received a reply from Buckingham, expressing a wish to rendezvous with him at Northampton.

During this time the Council met every day. The Crowland Continuator, who was present at these sessions, wrote of 'the most urgent desire of all present that the Prince should succeed his father in all his glory'. Discussions centred on the type of government to be established during the king's minority, but the emphasis was on how to counter foreign aggression aiming to exploit the interregnum. It was a given that Gloucester would become Protector, but the Council members do not appear to have doubted that the precedent of Henry VI's minority Council, in which no one lord predominated, would be followed. The Council also commissioned Edward Woodville to assemble a fleet to combat an expected surge of French and Breton piracy.

To avoid arousing suspicion Gloucester did not add to his retinue when set out from York on 23 April. The next day he stopped at Pontefract after receiving a reply from Rivers agreeing to meet at Northampton on the 29th. The town lay north of the royal party's itinerary along Watling Street, the high road from Ludlow to London. It was also where Gloucester had agreed to rendezvous with Buckingham, who had marched across country from Brecon with a likewise unremarkable retinue of 300 men-at-arms.

The trap was set and Rivers walked into it, accompanied only by his nephew Richard Grey, newly come from London. Men planning to seize power would not have left the security of the 2,000 men who remained with the new king at Stony Stratford, 15 miles south of Northampton, to put themselves at the mercy of the man they were allegedly conspiring against. After an apparently convivial dinner with Gloucester and Buckingham, they were put under arrest.

On the 30th Gloucester and Buckingham rode to Stony Stafford, dismissed the king's escort and arrested two members of the Prince of Wales's household: his chamberlain Thomas Vaughan and his household comptroller Richard Haute, son of Joan Woodville, Rivers's aunt. On the same day Gloucester sent a letter to the Council declaring that he had acted to pre-empt a Woodville *coup d'état*. The young king angrily rejected Gloucester's allegations but was powerless to influence events.

On 1 May Elizabeth, along with 9-year-old Richard, Duke of York, the five princesses, her son Dorset and brother Lionel, Bishop of Salisbury, fled to sanctuary at Westminster Abbey. In an act of panicked abdication the Lord Chancellor, Archbishop Rotherham of York, gave her the Great Seal. When the Council met to consider Gloucester's letter Hastings once again played a crucial role by assuring the councillors that Gloucester's loyalty to Edward V was unquestionable, that he would not make such allegations without substance, and that the arrested men would be granted the opportunity to defend themselves.

Giving the Woodvilles their day in court was the last thing either Hastings or Gloucester were going to permit. Instead of bringing them to London, Gloucester sent Rivers to Sheriff Hutton, Grey to Middleham and Vaughan to Pontefract. Haute did not share their fate, for reasons unknown. Gloucester also showed his hand by sending the Council an order he was not legally entitled to give, declaring that Rotherham had abdicated his responsibility, as indeed he had, but permitting him to remain a Council member. The royal party, now consisting entirely of men loyal to Gloucester and Buckingham, spent the night of 3 May at St Albans. Presumably this was where they were joined by Duchess Cecily from Berkhamsted, 10 miles away, as she was with them when they rode into London the next day.

There was an arms depot along the road and Gloucester had its contents loaded into wagons and sent ahead of the royal party, having it announced that this was proof of the Woodvilles' plan to seize power. Some people may have believed this, but every member of the royal party knew it to be false and presumably it failed to convince anyone else of substance, as no more was said about this supposed evidence.

The king was taken to the Bishop of London's palace and Gloucester went with Cecily to her palace of Baynard's Castle. We may be certain that she stilled whatever doubts Gloucester may still have entertained. She had waited nearly twenty years for revenge on Elizabeth and threw discretion to the wind when Gloucester summoned the late king's executors to Baynard's Castle sometime between 5 and 7 May.

Elizabeth had surrendered the Great Seal and Gloucester gave it to Cardinal Bourchier to bestow as he wished, in itself probably enough to win over a man whose vanity had been wounded by Edward IV's accurate assessment of his worth. The executors, Bourchier chief among them, then took the extraordinary step of agreeing that the late king's will should not be executed. The given excuse was that Edward's bequests to his children could not be honoured while they were in sanctuary.

The truth was that Cecily told the gathering that Edward had been conceived in adultery, and Bourchier and the others were convinced it must be true, because why would a distinguished lady admit to such a thing if it were not? This unsavoury fact has been glossed over to a remarkable degree, yet it was widely known at the time, and not forgotten for many years.

In a letter of 23 May 1535 to Emperor Charles V, his ambassador Eustace Chapuys reported a representation made to Thomas Cromwell, Henry VIII's chief minister, about Henry's having set aside Catherine, his first wife and the emperor's aunt, to marry Anne Boleyn. Chapuys was scornful of Cromwell's attempts to justify the king's action (my italics):

> The King ought not to attach so much weight in such a case to the judicial proceedings, or to the statutes of this realm, which only depended on the prince's wish, as might be seen by the Acts of King Richard, who, not content with having declared by sentence that the sons and daughters of King Edward were illegitimate, *caused King Edward himself to be declared a bastard, and, to prove it, called his own mother to bear witness to it, and caused it to be continually preached so. [Cromwell] confessed that was true of King Richard*; but the said King was a tyrant and a bad man, and he had paid for it accordingly.

Note the feline subtlety of Chapuys's thrust. If Edward was indeed a bastard and his children doubly so, then his eldest daughter Elizabeth, Henry VIII's mother, brought not the slightest legitimacy to the Tudor dynasty. Cromwell did not dispute the facts as stated by Chapuys and could only concur in the convenient fiction that her son forced 'proud Cis' to humiliate herself. Improbable, to put it mildly, especially in the light of a letter she sent Richard in 1474, imperiously summoning him to answer for a wrong done by his servants to one of hers.

Oceans of ink have been spilled debating when Gloucester decided to usurp the throne, the prevalent theory being that events inexorably forced him to do so. This is to dismiss abundant evidence of Cecily's deranged malice. Whether she lied about Edward's conception or not is immaterial: her other sons believed Edward was not the son of Richard of York, therefore Gloucester's decision was made as soon as he learned of his half-brother's death.

When Chapuys wrote 'caused it to be continually preached' he was referring to a sermon delivered on 22 June by Dr Ralph Shaw in the presence of Gloucester, Buckingham and many other lords at the open-air pulpit outside St Paul's Cathedral, and by others elsewhere in London. Shaw was the brother of Edmund, the Mayor of London, who was by now fully on board with the conspiracy. According to Mancini his topic was 'bastard slips should not take deep root', and he declared (my italics) that the 'progeny of King Edward *should be instantly eradicated*, for neither had he been a legitimate King, nor could his issue be so'.

Buckingham and others spoke in support of Shaw's assertions. They appear to have been oblivious to the discredit this brought on the entire House of York, but once it became apparent that the allegation reflected ill on him Gloucester changed tack, as he had with the wagons of arms. Even so, when in 1484 his tame Parliament passed *Titulus Regius*, the Act supposedly establishing his right to the throne (**Appendix F**), the words (my italics) 'Over this we consider how that ye be *the undoubted son and heir* of Richard late Duke of York' after a litany of accusations against Edward and Elizabeth.

'Over this' – that is to say *greater than* the preceding charges, which included 'sorcery and witchcraft' by Elizabeth and her mother, and Edward's 'sensuality and concupiscence' leading to recidivist bigamy. It is impossible to finesse this blunt statement by Gloucester himself that he believed his undoubted parentage was the principal plank of his right to the throne.

NAKED VILLAINY*

BETWEEN THAT FIRST SECRET MEETING AT BAYNARD'S Castle and the overt usurpation beginning on 22 June, Gloucester conducted a rolling *coup d'état* in which he deceived, divided and ultimately destroyed the minority Council. The Crowland Continuator judged that he enjoyed power 'just like another King', after the Council appointed him Protector on 10 May and gave him 'the tutelage and oversight of the King's most royal person', but in fact sovereignty was still vested in the Council. For the next month Gloucester showed friendly respect for Hastings, Stanley and Bishops Rotherham, Stillington and Morton, and even invited the young king's former tutor John Alcock, Bishop of Rochester, to join the Council.

With the Council's approval Edward V was moved to the royal apartments in the Tower and the neutral figures of Bishop John Russell, Rotherham's successor at Lincoln, and the cleric John Gunthorpe were made Lord Chancellor and Lord Privy Seal, both at Cardinal Bourchier's recommendation. These reassuring appointments were window-dressing: Bourchier became a co-conspirator from the moment he agreed not to implement or publish Edward IV's will and ordered the sequestration of the late king's goods, jewels and seals.

The Council concurred with Gloucester's condemnation of Edward

---

*'And thus I clothe my naked villainy/With odd old ends stol'n out of holy writ,/And seem a saint, when most I play the devil': *King Richard the Third*, Act I, Scene 3.

Woodville, who had sailed from Southampton on 29 April, having first robbed a vessel in port of £10,250 [£6.5 million] in gold coins. However the councillors rejected his attempt to extend the condemnation to Rivers, Grey and Vaughan, all supposedly part of the same treasonous plot. Since a charge of treason must mean they had planned the destruction of Edward V, it was a manifest absurdity. They also rebuked Gloucester for speaking disrespectfully of the dowager queen and on 13 May they rejected his request to declare that his Protectorate should last until Edward V's majority, saying this was a matter for Parliament to decide.

Irked by these legal niceties, Gloucester claimed that the queen, Dorset and Edward Woodville had looted the treasury. Records survive to prove this yet another false allegation. The Scottish campaign had depleted the hoard built up by Edward IV, but the loss was being made good by his enhanced revenue collection. Furthermore Richard was to spend lavishly in 1483–4 without recourse to taxation. The accusation stemmed from his fury when, although his agents persuaded the Genoese captains of most of the fleet to desert Woodville, he got away to Brittany with two ships and the looted money, leaving the crown liable for the loss.

Duke Frañsez publicly welcomed Woodville and gave him a pension. This was the first indication that opposition to Gloucester's rule might coalesce around the exiled Henry Tudor, another pensioner of the Breton court. Also, the withdrawal of the Channel fleet left English shipping defenceless against French and Breton pirates, and the new Protector was obliged to send the prominent London wool merchant Thomas Grafton to bribe the leading French raider, known to the English as 'Lord Cordes', for a truce.

Despite the Council's unwillingness to endorse his charge of treason against the Woodvilles, Gloucester never ceased to proclaim it and arbitrarily declared their lands forfeit. He did not again summon the whole Council but instead divided it into committees meeting separately, purportedly to plan different aspects of the coronation, now scheduled for 22 June. Meanwhile he appointed

Howard Chief Steward of the duchy of Lancaster, and Buckingham Constable of England and Chief Justice and Lord Chamberlain of Wales for life, also granting him the stewardship of all the lordships previously governed by the Prince of Wales's Council.

Hastings was allowed to continue as Lord Chamberlain and Governor of Calais, and was appointed Master of the Mint, but received no other reward for his treachery. He would have had to be a very dull man not to perceive that there was writing on the wall, but appears to have had no suspicion that it was his death sentence. He sent his lawyer William Catesby to attend the meetings of Gloucester's separate committee of co-conspirators, but Gloucester turned Catesby and used him to feed soothing disinformation to the loyalist councillors.

Catesby warned Gloucester of growing suspicion among Hastings, Stanley, Morton and Rotherham that he intended to seize the throne, but according to the Crowland Continuator this had not yet hardened into certainty before Gloucester moved against them. As Mancini observed, he would have done so anyway because he 'considered that his prospects were not sufficiently secure without the removal or imprisonment of those who had been the closest friends of his brother and were expected to be loyal to his brother's offspring'.

Realizing he had gained all he could by consent, on 10 June Gloucester wrote to the civic council of York requesting it to send as many men as possible 'to aid and assist us against the Queen, her blood adherents and affinity,' who of course by now posed no threat whatever. On the 11th, by hand of his retainer Richard Ratcliffe, he sent illegal warrants to the Earl of Northumberland and Ralph, Lord Neville, for the execution of Rivers, Grey and Vaughan.

On 12 June he summoned Buckingham, Howard, Hastings, Morton, Rotherham and Stanley to a full Council meeting at the Tower the next day. Howard's son Thomas played the role of Judas goat by ensuring that Hastings came to the meeting. Gloucester greeted them with smiles and then withdrew, only to return feigning a thunderous rage. Hastings was dragged out into the Tower yard and beheaded on a log, and Stanley was wounded in the scuffle.

With his own affinity marching south, Gloucester dared not risk an uprising by the powerful Stanley affinity in Lancashire and Cheshire, led by Stanley's capable brother William and his son George, Lord Strange. Accordingly Stanley was released, no doubt with apologies and a promise of compensation. Bishop Rotherham was committed to the Tower in the custody of Gloucester's knight of the body James Tyrell, and Bishop Morton was assigned to Buckingham, who eventually sent him under guard to his castle at Brecon. Even Gloucester did not dare murder princes of the Church.

A proclamation justifying Hastings's murder was read out to the people of London, details of which need not trouble us other than to observe the first appearance of a puritanical theme that appears to have been as sincerely felt as it was hypocritical from a man who had himself fathered two bastards. Gloucester ordered the imprisonment of Jane Shore, whom he believed had been acting as a conduit between the loyalist councillors and the queen, and she was condemned to a prostitute's public penance of being paraded through the streets in her underclothes 'for the life that she led with the said Lord Hastings and other great estates'.

The gambit backfired. Witnesses told Thomas More that 'she went in countenance and pace demure so womanly, and albeit she were out of all array save her kyrtle [petticoat] only yet went she so fair and lovely that her great shame won her much praise'.* We know from an undated letter written to Chancellor Russell by Gloucester after he had made himself king that Thomas Lynom, the royal solicitor, expressed a wish to marry Jane when she was still in Ludgate prison. The letter asked Russell to try to talk Lynom out of his infatuation, but failing that she was to be released. The two were married and Lynom prospered under Henry VII.

---

*Vide the public shaming of Cersei Lannister in George R. R. Martin's *A Dance with Dragons*. A Freudian would argue that Richard's vindictiveness was a displacement activity for his ambivalent feelings about his mother.

Others now openly identified with the rolling coup, chief among them Gloucester's childhood friend Francis, Viscount Lovell, former Chancellor Bishop Stillington, and two magnates disesteemed by Edward IV: Gloucester's nephew John de la Pole, Duke of Suffolk, and William Herbert, Earl of Huntingdon. Richard later married his illegitimate daughter Katherine to Herbert, with an annuity of £600 [£381,600] as her dowry. So reduced were Herbert's circumstances that the annuity nearly doubled his income.

At about this time Dorset fled from Westminster Abbey, seemingly with the complicity of the abbot, and got away to join his uncle Edward with Henry Tudor in Brittany. Bishop Lionel Woodville was permitted to leave sanctuary to return to his diocese. He should have remained with his sister and her children, to stand with them against the baseness to come, but perhaps shared Elizabeth's belief that she would again be protected by the Church.

Instead, on 16 June Gloucester sent Cardinal Bourchier to prevail on her to give up Richard, her remaining son, failing which Howard and his son Thomas, who had surrounded the abbey with men-at-arms, were to seize him by force. Thomas More quotes Bourchier angrily telling her the Church would not protect her. Mancini wrote that 'when the Queen saw herself besieged and preparation for violence, she surrendered her son, trusting in the word of the Archbishop of Canterbury that the boy should be restored after the coronation'.

Not long after young Richard joined his brother in the Tower the young king's attendants were dismissed and later paid off for their services to 'Edward, bastard' and the boys were moved from the state apartments to close confinement within the fortress. Writs were issued cancelling the Parliament scheduled for 15 June and preparations for the coronation of Edward V halted. Gloucester ceased to wear mourning and rode through London dressed in purple with a large retinue of men-at-arms wearing royal livery.

A letter of 21 June in *The Stonor Letters and Papers* from Simon Stallworth, a servant of Bishop Russell, told William Stonor that he was lucky to be away from London, for there was 'much trouble, and every man doubts the other', precisely what Gloucester sought to achieve. Stallworth reported that Hastings's men had entered Buckingham's service and that Edward Grey, the dowager queen's brother-in-law from her first marriage, who had taken part in the arrest prior to murder of her father and brother Thomas in 1469, had come to curry favour with Gloucester. His reward was to be recognized as Viscount Lisle by marriage.

On 23 June Anthony Woodville, Earl Rivers, was told he was to be taken to Pontefract Castle for execution. The poem he wrote knowing he was soon to die has survived, set to music by Robert Fayrfax (1464–1521), to remind us what a shining exception Rivers was to the dull aristocratic norm:

Somewhat musing/And more mourning
In remembering/Th'unsteadfastness;
This world being/Of such wheeling,
Me contrarying,/What may I guess?

I fear, doubtless,/Remediless
Is now to seize/My woeful chance;
For unkindness,/Withoutenless,*
And no redress,/Me doth advance.

With displeasure,/To my grievance,
And no surance/Of remedy;
Lo, in this trance,/Now in substance,
Such is my dance,/Willing to die.

Methinks truly/Bounden am I,
And that greatly,/To be content;

*Withoutenless = to speak plainly

Seeing plainly/Fortune doth wry*
All contrary/From mine intent.

My life was lent/Me to one intent.
It is nigh spent./Welcome Fortune!
But I ne'er went†/Thus to be shent‡
But so she meant:/Such is her won.§

On 25 June Rivers, Richard Grey and Thomas Vaughan were beheaded in the presence of Northumberland, Neville, Ratcliffe and other members of Gloucester's northern affinity. They were not allowed to make final speeches and were buried in an unmarked common grave. Rous reported that Rivers was found to be wearing a hair shirt 'which was long after displayed in the church of the Carmelite friars in Doncaster as a holy object'. Vaughan was later reburied at Westminster Abbey, where his marble tomb survives in the Chapel of St John the Baptist.

Mancini and the Crowland Continuator concur that when Gloucester issued a new summons to the lords on 13 May, the day of Hastings's murder, Buckingham went to the key figures bearing a first draft of what was eventually to be published as *Titulus Regius*. Bishop Stillington had come up with an alternative to trumpeting Duchess Cecily's adultery and perjured himself by declaring that Edward IV, prior to his marriage with Elizabeth Woodville, had married Eleanor Boteler née Talbot. Therefore Edward's children by Elizabeth were illegitimate.

Because Edward was a notorious womanizer and his marriage to Elizabeth had been informal, the allegation that he might have made a habit of seducing women by going through a form of marriage was believable. However, the Boteler 'pre-contract' (which in the context means marriage, not betrothal) has been researched in great depth, without finding corroborative evidence. It was, anyway,

---

*Wry = turn aside; †Went = thought; ‡Shent = cut off; §Won[t] = custom.

a matter for the Church to decide, and no clerical ruling was sought. Even if Stillington's statement had been true both the princes in the Tower were born after Eleanor died in 1468, so they were free of the taint of bigamy. The claim did, however, shame the Talbots. Fifteen-year-old George, Earl of Shrewsbury, was a royal ward, but the Talbot Marcher affinity was led by his uncle Gilbert, who did not forget the insult.

On 25 June Gloucester's handpicked Parliament declared that Edward V was not the king although, as it had been summoned in his name, it had no legal standing to do so. The following day a delegation of tame lords led by Buckingham assembled at Baynard's Castle and petitioned Gloucester to take the throne, permitting Gloucester to claim that he had been ordained king 'by the concord assent of the Lords and Commons'.

He assumed the title of Richard III and confirmed Bishop Russell, John Gunthrope and John Wood, now also Speaker of the Commons, as Lord Chancellor, Lord Privy Seal and Lord Treasurer respectively. Lord Stanley was appointed to the honorary office of Steward of the Household, but real power was vested in the functional members, the new king's cabinet. Lovell took over Hastings's role as Lord Chamberlain, Hastings's betrayer William Catesby was made Chancellor of the Exchequer, Robert Percy of Scotton became Comptroller and John Kendall was appointed the king's private secretary.

Gloucester, Lovell and Percy had become friends as fatherless boys in the Kingmaker's household in the late 1460s, and Kendall had been Gloucester's private secretary during the years when he made himself lord of the North. Richard Ratcliffe, the other key figure in the regime, became hereditary Sheriff of Westmorland when his uncle Lord Parr of Kendal died in August 1483, but his informal power was far greater. The Prior of Durham commented on 'the great rule that [Ratcliffe] beareth under the king's grace in our country'.

On 28 June Buckingham was granted the ceremonial office of

Great Chamberlain of England and Lord Howard declared Duke of Norfolk and hereditary Earl Marshal of England, while his son Thomas was made Earl of Surrey. The Mowbray estates were divided between Howard and Lord Berkeley, who was made Earl of Nottingham. This reversed the award of the estates to Prince Richard by Acts of Parliament in 1478 and 1483, which were not formally repealed. By now Gloucester had shed any pretence of respect for the law.

In preparation for his coronation alongside his wife, Gloucester announced a curfew and prohibited the bearing of arms by anyone not in his livery. On 5 July all the nobles who had been summoned were required to join an imposing procession from the Tower to Westminster, with the route lined what by what Mancini estimated to be 6,000 of Richard's armed retainers.

Among the lords was William Hastings's younger brother Richard, Lord Welles. Edward IV had made him a contentious grant of the title and lands of the baronies of Welles and Willoughby by right of his wife, Joan Welles, after her father and brother were executed in 1470. The grant could be as easily erased by the new king, and Hastings could not afford to stand on principle. Like Gilbert Talbot, he was to eat the dish of revenge cold.

On the following day, 6 July, Richard III and Anne were crowned. There were two notable absentees. It is entirely understandable that Catherine Woodville, Duchess of Buckingham, should have refused to attend the coronation of her brother's murderer. It is, however, highly remarkable that Duchess Cecily was not present. Perhaps she was ashamed to show her face after being publicly branded an adulteress; but possibly it had dawned on her, much too late, that she had put her grandsons in mortal peril. The ostentatious piety of her later life suggests belated repentance for the great evil she had wrought, and when she died her will mentioned her husband and Edward IV, but not her youngest son.

Mancini left England in mid-July and reported that before his departure the princes had 'ceased to appear altogether', something corroborated by other sources. 'I have seen many men burst forth into tears and lamentations when mention was made of [Edward V] after his removal from men's sight, and already there was a suspicion that he had been done away with. Whether, however, he has been done away with and by what manner of death, so far I have not at all discovered'.

There is no reasonable doubt that Richard was responsible for the murder of his nephews: he had made them defenceless, and they were in the custody of his men. It would not diminish his culpability if, as some have suggested, either Buckingham or Norfolk pre-empted the issue, because he had created a situation where it was possible for them to do so. The sentence of death was pronounced when Dr Shaw declared in his approving presence that the progeny of King Edward must be eradicated.

Thomas More wrote that Richard ordered them killed after a failed attempt to spring them from the Tower in early August. When Robert Brackenbury, Constable of the Tower, refused to sully his hands with innocent blood, Richard sent his knight of the body, James Tyrell, previously Bishop Rotherham's jailer and so familiar with the Tower and its staff, to do the deed. The most minutely researched study of the question has identified 3 September, the day before Tyrell left London to re-join his master at York, as the most likely date.*

Tyrell certainly did something highly meritorious in Richard's eyes, as he subsequently received a cascade of rewards. Thomas More falsely accused Richard of earlier crimes, but he was in a position to verify that Tyrell confessed to murdering the princes during his trial for treason in 1502. As to why he should have admitted his guilt, he was doomed anyway and had nothing to lose, and men did not go to their deaths with mortal sins unconfessed. David Starkey has also uncovered evidence suggesting Henry VII and his queen, sister to the murdered boys, may have attended Tyrell's trial, which would have been a highly unusual occurrence.

---

*Alison Weir's admirable *The Princes in the Tower*, first published in 1992.

Wicked though the murder of the princes was, the greater crime was committed against the kingdom. Richard III trampled on the laws and the unwritten constitution of England, and in the process completed the destruction of the 300-year-old Plantagenet dynasty It may be argued that he was not a great deal more evil than some of his predecessors, but if so this would simply confirm that they were also psychopaths.

NEMESIS*

ITIS NOT SURPRISING THAT THERE WAS LITTLE OPPOSITION to the usurpation. The senior peerage had been hollowed out during Edward IV's reign and the simultaneous minorities of the three Bourchier lords – the Earl of Essex and Barons FitzWarin and Berners – disempowered the only clan that might have been able to restrain Richard. Once the nobles of the court party were neutralized the remaining magnates either supported the coup or kept their heads down. Those whose titles and lands depended on royal favour as usual rushed to jump on the bandwagon.

On 20 July 1483, a mere two weeks after his coronation, Richard embarked on a grand progress through the kingdom, initially accompanied by Buckingham and throughout by his 21-year-old nephew John de la Pole, Earl of Lincoln, leaving Howard in charge of the capital. This was a signal mark of trust in a man twice his age (Richard was thirty, Howard about sixty) who had been one of Edward IV's henchmen. Howard's enthusiastic participation in the usurpation testifies to how deeply betrayed he had felt when Edward cheated him of his right of succession to the dukedom of Norfolk.

At Reading Richard issued a posthumous pardon to William Hastings and granted his widow Katherine née Neville custody of

---

*'Nemesis, winged balancer of life,/dark-faced goddess, daughter of Justice.': Mesomedes of Crete.

his estates and the wardship and marriage of their son. He also thought it magnanimous to assure Rivers's widow that the lands she had brought into the marriage were safe, which should have been unquestionable. She received nothing from Rivers's estate, all of which went to Howard over the coming days, without a shred of legal justification.

The royal party was at Viscount Lovell's grand manor house at Minster Lovell when the fateful news arrived of the bungled plot to liberate the princes from the Tower. The next stop was Gloucester, where Buckingham departed for Brecon to assume his new role as Richard's regime lock on Wales. Even after being awarded the half of the historic Bohun estate stolen by Henry IV, Buckingham must have known that he lacked the personal following to make a success of the appointment. He was riding for a fall, and according to Thomas More he knew the king had ordered the murder of his nephews before they parted company.

Richard was joined by Queen Anne at Warwick, and by their sickly 9-year-old son Edward at Pontefract, where Richard's northern affinity gathered to honour the boy and to ride with their leader in a state entry to York at the end of August. This was the culmination of the progress, and Richard was to spend most of September in the city or in nearby Sheriff Hutton. On the 8th young Edward, already declared Earl of Salisbury, Duke of Cornwall and Lord Lieutenant of Ireland, was invested as Prince of Wales and Earl of Chester in a ceremony so grand that it was described as a second coronation.

Richard declared Sheriff Hutton a royal residence for his sister's son the Earl of Lincoln and for Clarence's 8-year-old son Edward, Earl of Warwick. They were the next in line to the throne should Richard's heir die before him, and it was probably an error to make such obvious preparation for the eventuality, however sensible it may have seemed to one obsessed with the purity of the York bloodline. It drew attention to the fact that the royal succession now rested with a single boy who could not even ride a horse for any great distance, instead of with Edward IV's robust 'heir and a spare'.

26. RICHARD III'S PROGRESS
1483

20 July	Windsor
22 July	Reading
24 July	Oxford
25 July	Woodstock
26-29 July	Minster Lovell
31 July	Gloucester
4 August	Tewkesbury
8-14 August	Warwick
15 August	Coventry
18 August	Leicester
22-23 August	Nottingham
25-27 August	Pontefract
30 August to late September	York and Sheriff Hutton
End September	Pontefract
10 October	Gainsborough
11 October	Lincoln
19-22 October	Grantham
23-25 October	Leicester
27-28 October	Oxford
29 October	Hungerford
30 October	Tidworth
31 October to 4 November	Salisbury
8-14 November	Exeter
25 November	London

© Hugh Bicheno

0   25   50   75   100
miles

There was a religious sub-plot to the progress. At Tewkesbury Richard made a donation to the abbey as atonement for Edward IV's breach of sanctuary, and at Pontefract he restored the landed endowment of the priory, rebuking his late brother for having taken it when it should have remained to support masses for the soul of Richard of York, buried there until 1476. He also ordered the construction of a chapel at Towton, where his father's death had been avenged.

Strangely uncommented until Michael Jones joined up the dots in *Bosworth 1485: Psychology of a Battle* (2002), Richard also undertook to fund a massive chantry of 100 priests at York Minster. Chantries were often established to pray for the souls of the founders, and the size of Richard's foundation meant that Masses for his soul would be conducted almost continuously. The coincidence of the foundation and the date of his nephews' murder suggests that Richard wished to reduce the amount of time his soul would be spending in Purgatory.

Not the least of Richard's early errors was to have sent a disrespectful reply on 18 August to a tentatively welcoming letter from King Louis XI. Louis died on the 30th, leaving the regency for his 13-year-old son Charles in the hands of his 22-year-old eldest daughter, Anne de Beaujeu. Richard's letter would have been among the first she read and confirmed in her mind her dying father's belief that Richard intended to reopen hostilities. In March 1484 she sent Bernard Stewart, Seigneur d'Aubigny and commander of the royal *Garde Écossaise*, to sign a treaty with the Scots renewing the 'Auld Alliance'.

According to the Rolls of Parliament the leaders of the October 1483 rebellion 'launched their enterprise' on 24 September, as this was the day Buckingham joined them by writing to Henry Tudor with regard to an invasion on 18 October. However Buckingham was in no way an initiator or leader of the revolt. He was a Johnny-come-lately to a conspiracy among former servants of Edward IV, including but not led by the surviving Woodvilles.

The crucial point is that the conspirators chose to make the exiled Tudor their candidate for the throne, although Edward IV had regarded him as a threat to his dynasty and had tried to eliminate him. The rebels therefore were certain that Richard III had murdered his nephews, which opened the door for Henry Tudor's mother Margaret Beaufort, Lady Stanley, to initiate contact with Elizabeth, and through her to a wider constituency united by hatred of the usurper.

While it is likely that Lady Margaret (through her confidential emissary Reginald Bray) and Buckingham's Woodville wife played some considerable part in persuading him to turn his coat, another agent was Bishop Morton, his prisoner at Brecon. Given that Morton was Thomas More's mentor, the subtly nuanced dialogue at the end of *The History of Richard III*, in which Morton turns Buckingham's head by suggesting he might claim the throne himself, probably came from the episcopal horse's mouth.

Of course this requires us to believe that Buckingham was a vain fool, a fair assumption in the light of his less than stellar career. Revulsion at the murder of the princes is not likely to have played any part in his decision to turn against the man whose willing accomplice he had been. More likely is that he belatedly realized that John Howard, not he, was going to be Richard's right-hand man, and was galled that once more he was not going to play the role corresponding to his royal blood, high rank and even higher opinion of himself.

The most regime-threatening part of the conspiracy was among the Yeomen of the Crown, royal household servants and a key component of the London garrison, led by George Brown, Sheriff of Kent and stepson of the lately murdered Thomas Vaughan, who had carried the flag of St George at Edward IV's funeral. Yeomen occupied a uniquely English place between esquires and commoners. The origin of the term may be 'yewmen', referring to the wood from which the longbow was made, and *Holinshed's Chronicles* (1577) described them as:

They that in times past made all France afraid, and albeit they be not called Master, as gentlemen are, or Sir, as to Knights appertaineth but onlie John and Thomas etc., yet have they beene found to have done verie good service, and the Kings of England in foughten battles were wont to remaine among them (who were their footmen) as the French Kings did amongst their horsemen, the Prince thereby showing where his cheefe strength did consist.

Henry Tudor was to recognize a very particular debt to them and in 1485 named them 'Yeomen of the Guard' with responsibility for guarding the Tower of London, a duty they perform to this day. The debt stemmed from their leading role in the 1483 revolt, for which Brown and five Yeomen of the Crown were put to death. The rest of the rebels in the South-East, including John Fogge, Richard Haute, the Earl of Essex's younger son Thomas Bourchier, and Thomas Fiennes, grandson and heir to Joan, Baroness Dacre by right, either fled to join Henry Tudor in Brittany or accepted an offer of pardon.

One of the yeomen, William Bracher, betrayed his comrades to Howard and the ringleaders were rounded up on or about 10 October. Bracher also revealed that uprisings were planned in the South-West and the West Country to coincide with Henry Tudor's arrival on 18 October with an invasion force of 5,000 mercenaries, replicating the Kingmaker's 1470 invasion and paid for by Edward Woodville's loot and 10,000 crowns [£1.3 million] from Duke Fransez. The bombshell was that Buckingham intended to lead an army from Brecon to join them.

The astounding news reached Richard at Lincoln on the 11th, and the following day he wrote to Chancellor Russell calling Buckingham 'the most untrue creature living'. Although he summoned troops to join him at Leicester on 21 October, for the time being Richard remained at Lincoln. On the 10th he had stayed with Thomas Burgh at Gainsborough Hall, when his host warned him there might by a local uprising.* The 1470 Lincolnshire rebellion began with an assault on Burgh's manor, and he would have been alert to unrest among the Welles affinity. Richard would also have known that the broader Hastings affinity would move against him if the rebellion looked like succeeding.

As an experienced military commander Richard knew to remain in one place while intelligence reports came in, so his sojourn at Lincoln served a double purpose. Even after he set out, when he learned on the 20th that Lord Strange had departed Lathom in Lancashire at the head of a large force, he paused at Grantham until it was confirmed that Strange was not marching to join the rebels in the South-West. While he waited, nature took care of the rebellion for him.

On 15 October Richard proclaimed Buckingham a traitor and a prolonged storm of unusual violence struck south-western England. The storm kept Tudor's fleet in port during the crucial week he was supposed to have crossed the Channel and also caused the river Severn to flood, preventing Buckingham from using the lower river crossings, while Humphrey Stafford of Grafton destroyed the bridges across the upper river. Bombarded by rain, Buckingham's army, described by Polydore Vergil as Welshmen 'whom he, as a sore and hard dealing man, had brought to the field against their wills, and without any lust to fight for him', dissolved.

On 19 October Richard issued a further proclamation denouncing Dorset and Bishop Morton as traitors and putting a £1,000 [£636,000] price on Buckingham's head. Bizarrely, Richard issued another denunciation of Dorset a few days later, accusing him of immorality and adultery with 'Shore's wife', as though this would have meant anything to the general public. Richard obviously thought it would, although it is hard to imagine what constituency in bawdy England might have shared his obsessive prudery.

Buckingham marched his diminishing band to Weobley in

---

*There is no other obvious reason why Richard III made him a Garter knight later in 1483, in the select company of Lovell, Ratcliffe, Lord Stanley and John Howard's son Thomas, newly made Earl of Surrey.

Herefordshire in the hope of raising the Marches. Weobley belonged to Lord Ferrers of Chartley, and lay at the heart of the ancestral Yorkist domain that had turned out in force to defeat Jasper Tudor at Mortimer's Cross in 1461. Far from joining the rebellion, any doubts the Yorkist Marchers had about Richard were resolved. Led by Thomas Vaughan of Tretower, whose father had been beheaded by Jasper Tudor in 1470, they marched into Brecknock and captured Brecon Castle.

Buckingham went on to Shrewsbury, where he failed to enlist Gilbert Talbot, and then donned a disguise and rode north, perhaps hoping to find refuge with Lord Stanley in Lancashire. He stopped for the night at Wem, 10 miles north of Shrewsbury, at the home of his servant Ralph Banastre, who promptly betrayed him to Thomas Mytton, Sheriff of Shropshire.

The leaders of the rebellion in the South-West were Giles Daubeney and John Cheyne, later to be the only followers for whom Henry VII created new titles of nobility. Daubeney was a considerable landowner in Dorset and Somerset and was the first person in the area contacted by Reginald Bray, Lady Stanley's emissary. The giant (6ft 8ins) Cheyne held lands in Wiltshire and Hampshire. He had been Edward IV's Master of the Horse, and some of his men had been involved in the failed attempt to spring the princes from the Tower in early August.

Lionel Woodville, Bishop of Salisbury, was among those who fled to France when the rebellion collapsed, and Richard Woodville, who became Earl Rivers after Anthony's murder, was attainted. Given that the king would not have given any Woodville the benefit of the doubt, it is highly indicative of Richard Woodville's innocence that he did not flee and was later pardoned. Lionel's flight simply confirms that he was a coward, something already indicated when he needlessly joined Elizabeth in sanctuary and then abandoned her. He died the following year.

The Woodville influence made itself felt through the female line. Elizabeth's sisters were the mothers of the new Duke of Buckingham (aged 5 in 1483) and the future Earls of Essex (11), Kent (2) and Arundel (7). Finally, Lord Stanley's heir George was Lord Strange through marriage to the dowager queen's niece. Women could go where men dared not, and this was the network Lady Stanley tapped into when she made contact with Elizabeth in sanctuary and they agreed what became the unifying theme of opposition to Richard III: the marriage of her son Henry Tudor to Elizabeth's namesake eldest daughter.

The rebellion in the South-West collapsed and the main conspirators fled to France before Richard, at the head of a considerable army, marched into the region. He arrived at Salisbury on 31 October, but found nobody to execute except Buckingham, brought from Shropshire and beheaded on 2 November. Richard could not stand to see him, perhaps as well because the duke's heir later alleged that his father had a concealed dagger and meant to kill him.

It is not unusual for partners in crime to turn on each other, but Buckingham's motivation remains a tantalizing mystery. He appears to have been mourned by none, and one cannot dismiss the suspicion that Bishop Morton and Lady Stanley wound him up principally to refute Richard's claim that the 'old blood' of the English aristocracy supported his right to the throne.

There remained the rebellion in the West Country, whose principal movers were leading members of the Courtenay clan, notably Edward Courtenay of Bocconoc in Cornwall, heir to the attainted earldom of Devon, and Peter, Bishop of Exeter. Their allies the Luttrells of Somerset rose up on 2 November, the day that Henry Tudor arrived off Plymouth with two ships but found the port was in the hands of Richard's men. Thomas Grey, Marquess of Dorset, appears to have returned from exile to play some role, and Richard's brother-in-law Thomas St Leger was one of the few who did not flee opportunely. He was executed on 13 November.

There was a subtext to the West Country rebellion that must have concerned Richard deeply. Among the rebels now in exile were Thomas Arundel, his brother-in-law Richard Nanfan, Sheriff of Cornwall, and Robert Willoughby of Broke, Sheriff of Devon. In 1460–1 Nanfan and John, Lord Dynham, had been comrades-in-arms, Arundel was Dynham's brother-in-law, Willoughby his father-in-law – and Dynham himself was Lieutenant of Calais, whose garrison had all been members of murdered Lord Hastings's affinity.

As he rode back from Exeter to London, Richard had much to think about. He had needed a cathartic Towton, but circumstances had denied him the opportunity. Overly fixated on the nobility, he must have been shocked to discover how deeply he was loathed by the essential cogs in the machinery of government – royal servants and the sheriffs and commissioners of array of southern England, none of whom had suffered by his usurpation.

Perhaps most of all he would have been profoundly shaken to learn that men like Nicholas Latimer, who had once followed his brother Clarence and who by Richard's reckoning should have celebrated his overthrow of the bastard Edward's line, were now making common cause against him with the followers of Clarence's executioner, with unreconciled Lancastrians and even with the demonized Woodvilles. He had redeemed the House of York – how was it possible that so many once loyal Yorkists now supported Henry Tudor?

Psychopaths are polarizing individuals, mesmerizing to weak personalities but repulsive to those who can see them as they are. Richard commanded a loyalty from his northern retainers that went far beyond hope of gain, and clearly expected the same alchemy to work for him as king. It did not, and one of the reasons may have been that the personalities of his northern followers were pre-shaped by submission to the will of the no less psychopathic Kingmaker.

Nor should we overlook the fact that Richard was physically unimpressive, especially by comparison with his half-brother. Edward had also oozed charm – he was a seducer whose appeal was not limited to women, most clearly demonstrated by the manner in which he personally collected benevolences before the 1475 expedition. Richard had none of the easy self-confidence and common touch that had inclined people to be indulgent of Edward's many but very human failings.

Like the father whose memory he worshipped, Richard thought he could command by divine right; and so he could, but only among those persuaded he had right on his side. There can have been few who genuinely believed that God could possibly endorse a man who shamed his mother, terrorized a recently widowed queen and climbed to the throne over the murdered bodies of well-regarded lords and innocent children.

HEARTS AND MINDS

RICHARD REALIZED IT HAD BEEN FOOLISHLY HUBRISTIC to embark on a grand progress so soon after his coronation. The rebellion had blind-sided him, and he spent the rest of his short reign ensuring that he would not again be caught unprepared. There is, however, an iron rule of political and military momentum: you do not get a second chance to make a first impression. Damaging civil strife had returned to England after twelve years of political stability and rising prosperity.

As soon as he returned to London Richard installed his knight of the body Marmaduke Constable at Buckingham's forfeited Penshurst palace in Kent and flooded the troublesome county with commissioners to administer an oath of allegiance. This was followed by a proclamation inviting any Kentishman with a grievance to submit a complaint for his personal attention, 'for his grace is utterly determined that all his subjects shall live in rest and quiet, and peaceably enjoy their lands, livelihoods and goods, according to the laws of this his land, which they were naturally born to inherit'.

With regard to the laws, Richard's sole Parliament assembled on 23 January 1484, with Catesby as Speaker of the Commons. Over the next five weeks eighteen private and fifteen public statutes were enacted and published. I cannot resist quoting a comment published online by a Yorkshire Ricardian: 'Richard's reforms, aimed at making England a more equal society, show him to have been a remarkably liberal King, with ideas on social justice that were far ahead of his time'. So there we have it: Richard III was 'progressive', and as we all know that means he must have been 'a good thing'.

Foremost of the private statutes was *Titulus Regius*, whose 'progressive' nature readers can judge for themselves. The rest showed Richard's commitment to social justice in acts of attainder against 104 rebels – which is to say declaring them guilty of treason without trial and legally non-persons, thus without right to life, titles of nobility or of property, thereby disinheriting their heirs. Irony aside, this was the normal consequence of failed rebellion and, as his brother had done, Richard pardoned those who stayed in England and petitioned for reversal of attainder, in the hope that they would be grateful.

The public statutes were another matter. They addressed chronic abuses of the legal system in considerable detail and were to be singled out for praise by generations of legal scholars. Three statutes condemned common fraudulent practices in property transfers and required those made in the Court of Common Pleas to be made public – what we call 'transparency', the most effective weapon in the unending struggle against government corruption. Other statutes condemned Edward IV's 'benevolences' and his abusive collection of ecclesiastical tenths.

Richard also attempted to pose as a restorer of legality. A statute prohibiting the confiscation of an accused's property before conviction harked back to Edward's theft from London Alderman Thomas Cooke in 1468. Another recalled Edward's (and Clarence's) intimidation of jurors by requiring that they should be men of independent means. This was cosmetic: the law already specified that they should be men of substance. The problem was that 'good lordship' trumped justice, and would continue to do so for centuries.

Five acts were in response to lobbying by the City of London and revoked some of the privileges corruptly awarded to foreign merchants by Edward IV – although notably not those enjoyed by the Hanseatic League. Richard was already at war with French and Breton raiders, and it would have been insane to antagonize the masters of the most powerful fleet in north European waters. There was one specific exception made to the new tariff barriers: printing presses and books were exempt. This was a spiteful attack on William Caxton, who had been printing books in England since 1476 thanks to the patronage of murdered Earl Rivers.

Thankful that the king had not asked for the usual tenth and fifteenth, before adjourning on 1 March Parliament voted Richard tunnage and poundage (customs revenues) for life. On the same day Richard brought an end to the shameful stand-off at Westminster Abbey, from which Elizabeth and her daughters refused to emerge without ironclad guarantees. Humiliating though it was, Richard accepted a document worked out with Elizabeth's legal advisors:

> I Richard by the grace of God King of England and of France, and lord of Ireland, in the presence of you my lords spiritual and temporal, of you aldermen and mayor of my city of London, promise and swear on my word as king and upon these Holy Evangiles of God by me personally touched, that if the daughters of Dame Elizabeth Gray, late calling herself Queen of England, that is to wit Elizabeth, Cecily, Anne, Katherine and Bridget, will come unto me out of the sanctuary of Westminster, and be guided, ruled and demeaned* after me, I shall see that they be in surety of their lives, and also not suffer any manner of hurt, by any manner of person or persons to them or any one of them in their bodies and persons to be done by way of ravishment or defouling contrary to their wills, nor any of them imprison within the Tower of London or other prison, but that I shall put them in honest places of good name and fame, and there honestly and courteously shall see to be found and treated, and to have all things requisite and necessary for their exhibition and finding as my kinswomen.

*Anglo-French *demener* = to lead or to conduct.

Other clauses undertook to provide modest dowries for the girls and an annuity for Elizabeth in three annual payments to be brought to her by one of Richard's esquires of the body, and a promise not to act against her or her daughters on the basis of any accusation against them without first hearing 'their legal defence and answer'.

There are some wicked barbs in this document, including the imputation of intent to rape, the fact that the princes were not mentioned and the pointed reference to the Tower of London where they had disappeared; but above all it impugned Richard's honour. Elizabeth could not have made it clearer that she did not trust him to behave decently or even respect the law unless bound by an exceptional and sacred oath, witnessed by the highest in the land.

Richard had to swallow the insult because nobody believed his siege of the abbey was anything other than unmanly bullying of a defenceless woman, who had made common cause with other dissidents out of desperation. Clearly he hoped that a show of magnanimity would persuade Elizabeth to abandon her agreement with Lady Margaret Stanley, but he was also playing to the gallery, as he continued to do for the rest of his reign.

The irreversible political fact was that Lady Margaret's initiative had made Elizabeth's namesake eldest daughter a political player, something confirmed when Henry Tudor declared himself betrothed to her at Rennes cathedral on Christmas Day 1483. Marguerite d'Anjou had died in August 1482, but the witnesses to Henry's declaration included veteran Lancastrians led by his uncle Jasper as well as the new Yorkist exiles.

Henry's Lancastrian credentials were thin: on his father's side he was the grandson of Henry V's French widow, and on his mother's the great-grandson of John of Gaunt, both through illegitimate lines. Having tried and failed to get Duke Fransez to hand him over, Edward IV had been negotiating an accommodation with Lady Margaret by which Henry would be restored as Earl of Richmond, his security guaranteed by marriage to one of Edward's daughters.

Even if Richard had been inclined to seek reconciliation with Henry, there was no credible guarantee a man who had murdered his nephews could offer. It was worse than a crime – it was a political blunder of the first order. Nothing less could have brought about the coalition that Lady Margaret formed against him with such astonishing rapidity. She had never ceased to lobby for her only child to be permitted to take his place in English society: Richard had created a situation where only one such place remained.

It is not clear where the dowager queen and her other daughters went after they left sanctuary, but Richard and Queen Anne welcomed 18-year-old Elizabeth into the royal household and treated her with honour and even affection. Tudor historians alleged that Richard intended to marry her to his heir, but to have done so would have called into question the bastardy of Edward's children. This said, it was thought highly suspicious that he married off her younger sister Cecily but not Elizabeth, when to do so would have annulled the Tudor betrothal.

Once Richard switched his propaganda effort to emphasizing his intention to rule justly and with respect for the law, it reassured those of his subjects who had not already made up their minds about him. The failure of the rebellion also invested him with the 'inevitability factor', the tendency of the undecided to support a winner, or at least conform to what they believe is a new status quo. If Richard could see off the Tudor challenge, he had a reasonable expectation of a relatively untroubled reign.

Accordingly and unsurprisingly, for the next eighteen months Richard devoted himself first to prevention and then to preparing for the inevitable invasion. Poignantly, one of his first acts of prevention was to require the rest of the nobility to swear the public oath of allegiance to his son that the northern lords had sworn at Pontefract in September 1483. When young Edward died on 9 April 1484, the Crowland Continuator permitted himself an uncharitable gloat about the vanity 'of a man who desires to establish his interests without the aid of God':

This only son of his, in whom all the hopes of the royal succession, fortified with so many oaths, were centred, was seized with an illness of but short duration, and died at Middleham Castle. On hearing the news of this, at Nottingham, where they were then residing, you might have seen his father and mother in a state almost bordering on madness, by reason of their sudden grief.

Richard had continued to rule the North through his son's ducal council at Middleham. Now he buried the boy at Sheriff Hutton, which became the location of a new Council of the North akin to the one Edward IV had established for Wales at Ludlow ten years earlier. He appointed the Earl of Lincoln as president of the Council, which tacitly nominated him as his heir. The Council maintained the balance between the Percy, Neville and related affinities that had been Richard's greatest political achievement.

He was obliged to base the post-rebellion settlement on that achievement for lack of dependable supporters in the south, a measure of which was his appointment of the 67-year-old Earl of Arundel to replace Hastings as Warden of the Cinque Ports. Arundel was at best neutral, but he had collaborated with Marmaduke Constable in the relatively bloodless pacification of Kent and it was vitally important not to offend him.

The Bourchiers were a problem. At some point 14-year-old John, Baron Fitzwarin, crossed the Channel to join Henry Tudor, a defection made more ominous by the fact that his mother was the daughter and co-heir of Lord Dynham. The widowed mother of 12-year-old Henry, 2nd Earl of Essex, was Anne née Woodville, who had remarried George Grey, heir to the earldom of Kent, and had borne him a son. Against which the widowed mother of 17-year-old John Bourchier, 2nd Baron Berners, had remarried Howard's heir Thomas, now Earl of Surrey.

Cardinal Bourchier, the last of the older generation, had been conspicuous by his absence from Richard's coronation feast, and did not collaborate with him in the matter of the rebel Bishops of Ely, Salisbury and Exeter. Lionel Woodville's death in July 1484 permitted the king to appoint his man Thomas Langton to the see of Salisbury, but the Canterbury Convocation refused to deprive Morton (who had escaped to Flanders) and Courtenay (with Henry Tudor in Brittany) for rebellion. Furthermore both Pope Sixtus IV and his successor Innocent VIII openly received Bishop Morton as Henry Tudor's ambassador.

One does not look for genuine contrition in a psychopath, and Richard's most notable act of apparent atonement was yet another attempt to make himself look virtuous by contrast with his brother. This was the solemn transfer of the remains of Henry VI from Chertsey Abbey, where they had become an object of veneration, to a splendid new tomb in St George's Chapel, Windsor, Edward IV's magnificent creation. Henry was reburied on the other side of the altar from Edward's tomb, thus giving the last Lancastrian king parity of honour with his murderer.

Apart from the North, the regime was only really secure in East Anglia, thanks to Howard. Even there, however, there was residual sympathy for the imprisoned Earl of Oxford, and the rebellion and defection to Tudor of William Brandon, scion of a leading gentry family that achieved local prominence as Mowbray retainers, shows that acceptance of the new Duke of Norfolk was not universal. The only obvious reason was that his elevation was tainted by the murder of young Prince Richard, his predecessor and widower of the last direct Mowbray heir.

Richard was more worried by the Midlands than any other region. His frequent visits and the large sums spent to upgrade his castle-palace at Nottingham testify to his belief that it was an unexploded bomb. The Midlands had once been strongly Lancastrian, more recently Hastings had built up a strong affinity in the area, and Hastings's brother was the dominant lord in Lincolnshire. A layer below the Hastings affinity was the ancient barony of Roos and other Lancastrian lordships attainted after Towton.

Richard could count on John, Baron de la Zouche, a 25-year-old Northamptonshire lord, but he had more ambition than affinity.* Ferrers of Chartley had estates in Leicestershire and Shropshire as well as Herefordshire, but although he was rewarded for his actions against Buckingham he had been one of Edward V's councillors and did not wish for a role in the new regime. Richard's close friend Viscount Lovell had suffered the humiliation of learning that William Stonor, his chief Oxfordshire retainer, had been one of the leading rebels, and his extensive Midlands estates could not be regarded as an assured regime asset.

The 1484 attainders permitted Richard to redistribute the duchy of Buckingham estates, the most extensive after Lancaster and York, and to impose men he trusted across the South-West and the West Country. The Crowland Chronicler observed that the forfeited estates were 'distributed among his northern adherents whom he planted in every spot throughout his dominions, to the disgrace and lasting and loudly expressed sorrow of all the people in the south'. Perhaps, but that did not necessarily make them supporters of Henry Tudor.

In much of the country the strength of land-based affinities had been eroded by frequent changes of lordship. This was why propaganda became increasingly significant. The Kingmaker had been the first to appeal to the general public and Richard's effort to win hearts and minds drew on the accusations made against Edward in 1469–70, sometimes word for word. He controlled 'the media' – proclamations posted in public places, loyal addresses and sermons by roving preachers – but as many another dictator has discovered, rumour-mongering is a potent weapon of the opposition.

As maddened by subversive murmuring as Edward had been in 1468 when he judicially murdered Hungerford and Courtenay, in July 1484 Richard had William Collynsbourne, once one of his mother's servants but now a Tudor partisan, arrested, convicted of

*Zouche was, however, married to Lord Dynham's other daughter and co-heir, and Richard envisaged a leading role for him in an eventual settlement of the West Country.

treason, hanged, drawn and quartered for nailing a subversive couplet to the door of St Paul's Cathedral. Consequently the couplet became known across the country and survives to this day:

The Cat, the Rat, and Lovell our Dog
Ruleth all England under the Hogge.*

Another example was the canard spread by Richard's enemies when Queen Anne died following a long illness (probably tuberculosis) in March 1485. He was alleged to have poisoned her in order to marry young Elizabeth, and the rumour troubled his followers so greatly that Catesby and Ratcliffe warned him that the North would not stand for it. The outcome was that Richard found himself obliged to make a humiliating denial of any such intention at a gathering of notables in the great hall at St John's Hospital in London.

One of the strongest modern Ricardian arguments against the guilt of their hero is that Henry Tudor never specifically accused Richard of having murdered his nephews, even though he was widely believed to have done so. But that, surely, is the explanation: suspicion and rumour were already doing all the damage that could be hoped for, and an open accusation risked the possibility that Richard might produce the princes like a rabbit out of a hat. Later, having won the throne by conquest, Henry had nothing to gain by reopening the issue of legitimacy.

It is doubtful whether propaganda does more than reinforce opinions people already hold. The fact that Richard was a treacherous and murdering non-bastard was fully discounted by 1485. He had the advantage of incumbency, he was saying and doing the right things, there was rising prosperity and in such circumstances people are averse to change. The kingdom was his to lose.

---

*The cat being William Catesby and Richard Ratcliffe the rat. The hog referred to Richard's white boar badge.

XXXI

OPENING MOVES

ICHARD WAS JUSTIFIABLY CONFIDENT OF HIS MILITARY skill. He was an experienced, competent and respected commander who had understudied Edward IV, one of the most successful generals in English history, and had led his half-brother's vanguard to victory at Barnet and Tewkesbury. During the 1475 expedition he had commanded the largest and most active contingent, and in 1480–2 he had occupied the Scots capital and recovered Berwick.

Soldiers do not care whether their leaders are good or bad men: their only criterion is whether they can deliver victory and the rewards that follow. The same consideration applies to political affiliation – stripped of the fig leaves of ideology with which they seek to camouflage their ambition, most people who enter politics do so in the hope of living well at public expense, and they will usually support whoever offers them the best chance of achieving their goal.

Henry Tudor was not an attractive leader under either heading. He had no combat experience, his Lancastrian uncle Jasper had been routed in every battle he had fought, as had the Earl of Oxford, who joined them in October 1484 under circumstances explained below. The Lancastrian cause died at Tewkesbury and the red and white rose narrative invented by Victorian historians caused them to cram events into a conceptual straightjacket from which they have been struggling to escape ever since. If it had been that simple, it is doubtful whether Henry could ever have mounted a believable challenge.

The whole of Henry's appeal was that he was not Richard III. Thanks to his remarkable mother he became the figurehead for those outraged by Richard's *coup d'état*, but the abject failure of the 1483 counter-coup exhausted the financial windfall brought by Edward Woodville and the subvention from deeply disappointed Duke Frañsez, while wasting key assets like the Yeomen of the Crown. Henry's standing should not have been able to recover from such a setback – and with regard to being able to inspire a broadly based rebellion, it did not.

The irreconcilable Edwardians who joined Henry in exile did not change his basic situation: he was totally dependent on support from England's enemies. Those still in England who hated Richard would join Henry if he could mount a credible invasion; but as in the case of the Kingmaker's invasion in 1470 and to a lesser degree Edward's in 1471, this would have to be provided by foreign money and troops. It was this consideration that made Richard's arrogant reply to Louis XI's last letter so profoundly unwise.

In fairness he had more pressing diplomatic problems. Among the offices he passed to Howard was that of Lord High Admiral, a role Howard had been performing as his nominal subordinate for many years and with considerable success, most recently in the Scots campaign. After the hiatus caused by Edward Woodville's defection Howard rapidly regrouped to wage a naval war against Brittany and Scotland – for trying to force Richard to do what he would have done unforced. It was all very Renaissance.

Contemporary princes laughed at the idea that the shortest route between two points might be a straight line. James III wanted Richard to resume the Anglo–Scots marriage alliance of 1473–80, which was opposed by his pro-French nobles, and Frañsez wanted an assurance of English support should he be attacked by France. Both thought the best way to achieve their objectives was to show

Richard how much trouble they could cause him. He wanted peace in the North and for Frañsez to stop supporting Henry Tudor, but could not afford to show weakness. So, after bloodying Scots and Breton noses, Richard gave them what they – and he – wanted.

James III, by renewing the 'auld alliance' with Anne of Beaujeu's emissary Bernard Stewart in March 1484 (and no doubt pocketing a financial inducement), and by besieging English-held Dunbar, appeased the nobles who had kidnapped him at Lauder, who were bitterly opposed to his pro-English policy. Thus when his brother the Duke of Albany and the long-exiled Earl of Douglas invaded in July, nobody rallied to them. Richard did not support them either, signalling his willingness to abandon Edward's aggressive policy.

The naval war and a display of force by land led by Richard himself served to discredit the pro-French faction and make it easier for James to sue for peace on his terms. The deal was done between 12 and 21 September 1484 at Nottingham Castle, where a Scottish delegation led by James's Chancellor the Earl of Argyll met with Richard. The proceedings began with a flowery oration by James's private secretary Archibald Whitelaw, Archdeacon of Lothian, who laid it on with a trowel:

> In you, most serene Prince, all the excellent qualities of a good king and great commander are happily united, such that to the perfection of your accomplishments nothing could be added by the highest rhetorical flights of a most consummate orator... I look for the first time upon your face [and see] a countenance worthy of the highest power and kingliness, illuminated by moral and heroic virtue... To you may not be unfitly applied what was said by the poet Statius of a most renowned Prince of the Thebans, that Nature never united to a small frame a greater soul or a more powerful mind.

Two treaties were signed on the 21st, a three-year truce and an agreement that James's namesake heir would marry Richard's niece,

Anne de la Pole, sister of his heir presumptive the Earl of Lincoln. Remarkably, both parties included Duke Frañsez among the foreign monarchs nominated to act as guarantors of the treaties, which shows that Richard was confident he had resolved his differences with Brittany.

In 1483 Duke Frañsez's chief minister Pierre Landais survived an effort by Breton nobles to overthrow him with support from France. Having facilitated Henry Tudor's expedition in the hope of putting an ally on the English throne, in September 1484 Landais offered to hand him and his uncle Jasper over to Richard in exchange for 4,000 archers on standby to combat a second incursion by French-backed rebels. Richard readily agreed and in early October Landais sent troops from Rennes to arrest the Tudors at Vannes, the port on the south-west coast of Brittany where they and about 300 exiles were now based.

Bishop Morton, at this stage still in Flanders, got wind of the negotiations and sent a warning that enabled Henry and Jasper to flee across the border into Anjou ahead of Landais's men. Frañsez denounced – but did not dismiss – Landais for his initiative and ordered the release from custody of other exiles arrested at Vannes. They were permitted to join Henry, now with the French court at Langeais in the Loire valley. Frañsez's aim, transparently, was to preserve Richard's military guarantee while hedging his bet with Henry, but for the time being Richard judged it politic to go along with the charade.

The French Regency Council required Henry and his followers to move to Montargis, 68 miles south of Paris, while they decided what to do with them. A trickle of voluntary exiles continued to arrive, as well as English residents in Paris including the cleric Richard Foxe, who was to become Henry's principal private secretary, Lord Privy Seal and successively Bishop of Exeter, Bath and Wells, Durham and Winchester.

Between October 1484 and January 1485 they were joined by part of the Calais garrison, England's only standing army. The back story was complex: Hastings had been Captain of Calais since 1471 and had appointed the entire garrison of the Pale, including John Blount, Baron Mountjoy, who was lieutenant of the fort at Hammes and well paid to keep the Earl of Oxford and Viscount Beaumont incarcerated. After Richard III murdered Hastings he appointed Lord Dynham as Lieutenant of Calais, promoted Mountjoy to Constable of the castle at Guînes, while Blount's younger brother James took over as Lieutenant of Hammes.

Mountjoy was ill and absent on 28 October when Richard ordered the return of Oxford and Beaumont to England. James Blount released them to Thomas Montgomery, Mountjoy's deputy at Guînes and once Edward's key diplomat in dealings with Louis XI; and Montgomery along with John Fortescue, to whom Oxford and Beaumont had surrendered in 1473, took them to join Henry Tudor, while Hammes held out against a half-hearted siege by Dynham.

In January 1485 Oxford and Montgomery returned at the head of a small French army, hoping the garrison at Guînes would defect. It is remarkable that any of the well-paid garrison in the Calais pale opted for the uncertainty of joining Tudor, but some did. Not enough to deliver Guînes, however, and Oxford could only relieve the desultory siege of Hammes and evacuate the garrison.

Convinced that Dynham had been complicit in Oxford's escape but anxious to avoid an open breach, Richard appointed his young bastard son John of Gloucester as Captain of Calais over Dynham's head, under the tutelage of his trusted assassin James Tyrell, whom he appointed Lieutenant of Guînes.* The defections permitted him to man Guînes and Hammes with his own men, but the main garrison remained as before. It was paid by the Company of the Staple, which had a long-established relationship with Hastings's men and

---

*The two pardons later issued to Tyrell by Henry VII have been grist to the mill of conspiracy theorists, but they were in keeping with pardons previously extorted by an ousted regime's officers – like Geoffrey Gates in 1471 – who could credibly threaten to sell Guînes or Hammes to the French or Burgundians.

did not want them replaced. This was a situation Richard had to live with for the time being.

There would have been many more defections and even greater success at Calais if the French had not imposed conditions on their support that came close to destroying Henry's credibility. In November the Council required him to claim the throne as the legitimate Lancastrian successor, supposedly as the younger son of Henry VI. It is not clear why they made this absurd stipulation and it may have been simply a requirement for a fig leaf of legality by the clerical members of the Council, with an eye to approval by the pope.

However it played in Paris and Rome, it went over like a lead balloon in England. Although he did not stress his alleged royal paternity, Henry sent letters to England claiming to be the legitimate Lancastrian successor, signed with the regnal initial H. He must have told the Yorkist exiles that he had been forced to do this by the French, as otherwise they would not have stayed. Richard alleged that Henry had bought French support by promising them Calais, and we cannot dismiss this as propaganda: Oxford's expedition into the Pale certainly lent itself to just such an interpretation.

When a copy of Henry's letter came into Richard's possession in early December he must have thought Christmas had come early. He promptly issued a proclamation published across the kingdom pouring scorn on Henry's double illegitimacy: the Beauforts were illegitimate offspring of John of Gaunt, specifically excluded from royal succession by Henry IV, and the Tudors were the product of dowager Queen Catherine de Valois's cohabitation with her major-domo Owen Tudor without benefit of clergy.

The proclamation was an own goal. Richard's father had claimed the throne by superior right of succession over the House of Lancaster, which made any claim by Henry Tudor immaterial. Richard himself had claimed the throne as the legitimate heir of his father, which undermined his argument that a Lancastrian restoration would undo the Yorkist settlement – because if Edward had not been the true heir, then the Yorkist settlement was legally questionable.

The contradictions finally compelled Richard to recognize what a pit he had dug for his own feet, and to seek reconciliation with Elizabeth Woodville. Historians of the greedy-and-grasping-parvenu Woodvilles persuasion have portrayed her coming to terms with her sons' murderer in the worst possible light, blithely ignoring her situation. She was at Richard's mercy, and what we now call the 'Stockholm syndrome' was a compelling survival strategy.

It may be that Henry Tudor's claim to the Lancastrian succession caused her to doubt that he would eventually deliver on his promise to marry her eldest daughter, but her more pressing concern was the likely result if she did not submit to Richard's will. The Crowland Continuator was a disapproving witness of the outcome during the Christmas celebrations at court:

> Oh God! why should we any longer dwell on this subject, multiplying our recital of things so distasteful, so numerous that they can hardly be reckoned, and so pernicious in their example, that we ought not so much as suggest them to the minds of the perfidious. So too, with many other things which are not written in this book, and of which I grieve to speak; although the fact ought not to be concealed that, during this feast of the Nativity, far too much attention was given to dancing and gaiety, and vain changes of apparel presented to queen Anne and the lady Elizabeth, the eldest daughter of the late king, being of similar colour and shape; a thing that caused the people to murmur and the nobles and prelates greatly to wonder thereat; while it was said by many that the king was bent, either on the anticipated death of the queen taking place, or else, by means of divorce, for which he supposed he had quite sufficient grounds, on contracting a marriage with the said Elizabeth. For it appeared that in no other way could his kingly power be established, or the hopes of his rival be put an end to.

Whether or not Richard had any such intention, well-informed people believed him capable of it. When news of the Christmas festivities reached Henry, Polydore Vergil says he felt 'pinched to his stomach' and the pain increased when in January 1485 Richard Woodville, and in February John Fogge, swore fealty to Richard and had their lands restored. In March even Richard Haute, who had somehow avoided being murdered in June 1483 along with the others arrested by Richard, also made submission and was pardoned.

It must have been at this time that Elizabeth's son Thomas Grey, Marquess of Dorset, tried to slip away from Henry's court, intending to return to England, but he was intercepted and brought back by John Cheyne's brother Humphrey. Presumably Dorset acted at the entreaty of his mother and with an assurance that Richard would reverse his attainder. Although Elizabeth's brother Edward remained steadfast, the final balance of Henry's claim to the Lancastrian succession was the loss of the extensive Woodville family network, minimally offset by the gain of the few Lancastrians who remained in England.

· ☙ ·

To mix metaphors, the wild cards in the endgame were the Stanleys. Other peers, notably Arundel but by this time the great majority, survived the *Sturm und Drang* of the Wars of the Roses by masterly inaction. Lord Stanley alone had been an active player in every phase of the struggle, professing loyalty to whomever seemed to be winning at a given moment. Frequently demonstrating his ability to raise impressive numbers of troops at short notice, he displayed a no less impressive talent for arriving a little too late to take part in any fighting.

Stanley was supposed to be the hammer that smashed his father-in-law Richard Neville, Earl of Salisbury, against the anvil of Queen Marguerite's Cheshire army at Blore Heath in 1459, but his brother William rode with Salisbury and Thomas contrived not to arrive in time. Barely escaping attainder, he rode with Henry VI against Richard of York and the Nevilles during the subsequent Ludford Bridge campaign, but could not quite manage to join him at Northampton in 1460. Later that year he organized a civic reception for Richard of York at Chester when he returned from exile in Ireland, but refrained from further involvement while brother William joined Edward IV to fight at Towton.

Thomas joined his brother-in-law Warwick in the suppression of Lancastrian resistance in the North in the early 1460s and may have conspired with him prior to his 1469 rebellion. When Edward turned the tables on Warwick and Clarence in 1470 they marched to Manchester expecting Stanley to join them – in vain. When they returned later that year he marched at the head of a substantial body of retainers to greet them at Bristol, but having made it plain that he was best left alone he went home and took no part in the Readeption. Once again it was William who took the risk of openly joining Edward on his return.

Both Edward IV and Richard III made Lord Stanley steward of their households for the same reason: they wanted him at court, where they could keep an eye on him, and not back in Lancashire and Cheshire, where he could do as he pleased. He brought a force of retainers as large as Hastings's on the 1475 expedition and together they brokered the Treaty of Picquigny. It is unlikely that Stanley ever did anything without an ulterior motive, so when we read of him leading 3,000 archers to join Gloucester's Scottish campaign in 1480, we can be tolerably sure it was a show of force to remind the lord of the North why his remit ended in mid-Lancashire.

If Lord Stanley had been fatally wounded on 13 June 1483, Richard would not have become king. William Stanley and Thomas's heir Lord Strange would have marched south at the head of a combined affinity numbering many thousands, and would have been joined by Rivers's and Hastings's affinities. Without popular support Richard's northern retainers could not have stood against them. He never forgot that, and we have seen how he paused at Grantham to be sure that Strange was marching to join him at Leicester and not to join the 1483 rebellion.

Richard had no choice: he had to appease the Stanleys. Consequently he did not dare arrest Lady Stanley for organizing the rebellion, and although he declared her estate forfeit she was entrusted to the custody of her husband, who was to enjoy the income from her lands during her lifetime. Richard also felt obliged to reward the Stanleys for their military support, even though it had not been forthcoming until it was apparent the rebellion had failed, and made Lord Stanley a Garter knight.

Richard awarded the Stanley brothers additional offices in north Wales and the northern March, because they were the de facto rulers of the region anyway. He had every reason to believe that when Henry Tudor finally landed, Stanley would back the winning side. Having no doubt that it would be his, and since Stanley had made no move to support his stepson in 1483, Richard discounted the possibility that he might break the habit of a lifetime and commit to a risky adventure with no guarantee of success. It was to prove a fatal error of appreciation.

XXXII

ENDGAME

RICHARD REMAINED AT NOTTINGHAM CASTLE UNTIL the end of the 1484 campaigning season and returned in late May or early June 1485, after spending a week with his mother at Berkhamsted. It is not difficult to imagine what passed between them. He had prepared thoroughly: beacons were built on headlands along the coast from East Anglia to south Wales, and he issued commissions of array to his supporters across the kingdom, requiring them to rehearse a general mobilization by mustering and drilling their men.

Richard's strategic deployment shows that while any landing near London was to be met with overwhelming force, elsewhere the role of his subordinates was to delay the invaders' advance to give him time to come up with the main royal army. There can be little doubt that he had in mind a battle of annihilation, as he had in Scotland. He wanted Henry to land far from London and to draw malcontents into the open – so that he could kill them all.

Howard was at Framlingham Castle in Suffolk, ready to counter a landing on the east coast or to march in support of Brackenbury's London garrison if it were made in the South-East. Lovell was at Southampton to supervise the fleet and to prepare the South-West to contain an invasion of the West Country. Should that occur, Lovell supposedly could count on support from the South March by Lord Ferrers and Thomas Vaughan, and by the Herberts of Raglan.

The Vaughans had a blood feud with the Tudors, but despite the marriage of Lord Herbert to Richard's bastard daughter, Henry made contact with Herbert's younger and more vigorous brother Walter after the Woodville affinity submitted to Richard. Henry mooted a possible marriage with one of the Herbert sisters, in the hope of also drawing in Henry Percy, who was married to the eldest. The matter was not pursued after Richard disavowed any intention of marrying Elizabeth of York, but the line of communication with Walter remained open.

In Wales, Richard's well-paid man on the spot was Rhys ap Thomas, head of a locally dominant Carmarthen clan that had fought for Lancaster and suffered for it, to whom Richard promised to restore offices held by his family before 1461. Rhys's father had died for Jasper Tudor at Mortimer's Cross in 1460 and his older brothers had played dangerous games in 1470–1, but Rhys had submitted to Edward IV to recover his lands, and supported Richard against Buckingham. Their reciprocal killings in 1460 and 1471, however, had left a legacy of latent blood feud between Rhys's clan and the Vaughans.

The brutal pacification of the Principality in 1468 had left deep scars, and Richard's obsession with blood right should have alerted him to the deep loyalty commanded by the Tudors, not only in Jasper's attainted earldom of Pembroke but also as descendants of one of Owain Glyn Dŵr's loyal nephews in the last Welsh rebellion. Henry enjoyed the unanimous support of the Welsh bards, who proclaimed the coming of *y mab darogan* (the man of destiny), and he was to march through Wales under the red dragon banner of Cadwaladr.*

Richard appointed his esquire of the body Richard Williams constable and steward for life of the castles and lordships of Pembroke, Tenby, and other fortified places, but Williams failed to win local support. In May 1485 he arrested John Savage, namesake son of

---

*A seventh-century king of Gwynedd made legendary as the last of the ancient kings of Britain in Geoffrey of Monmouth's twelfth-century *Historia Regum Britanniae*.

Lord Stanley's brother-in-law, who had come from France with messages for Jasper's supporters. Richard ordered him sent to London as a hostage for his father's good behaviour, but the young man escaped from Pembroke Castle dungeon with the connivance of the garrison.

Historians have generally accepted the Tudor narrative about how difficult it was to obtain significant support from the French court, and the supposedly low quality of the French troops who provided the bulk of Henry's invasion force. As to the first, supposedly Henry was required to leave Thomas Grey, Marquess of Dorset, and Thomas Bourchier, Lord FitzWarin, as surety for a loan of 20,000 *livres* [£3,000]. Nonsense. He received far more than that in cash and kind, and the 'hostages' were Yorkist lords he could do without. Dorset had already tried to desert and FitzWarin was too young to play a military role commensurate with his rank.

The French troops were professional soldiers, members of the standing army whose salaries were paid by the French court, and their commander was the Savoyard knight Philibert de Chandée, lord of Montfalcon and later a marshal of France. According to *The Ballad of Bosworth Field*, written by a participant and the only roll-call we have, Bernard Stewart, commander of the royal French *Garde Écossaise*, also took part in the expedition and would have led a contingent of his own men. There may have been only 2,000 of them, but that was four times as many as the English exiles, including the professionals from Calais.

The army that embarked at Harfleur, on ships also paid for by the French court, was therefore of far greater military weight than numbers suggest. Chandée and Stewart would have equipped and drilled the English to bring them nearer the standard of their own men. This would have included instruction in the combined use of the long pike and the shorter halberd in rectangular or wedge-shaped infantry formations, now the norm in continental warfare. The English still enjoyed the advantage of the deadly longbow, but about a fifth of the French and Scots would have been arquebusiers, with a smaller number of crossbowmen. They intended to conduct a fast-moving campaign over rough terrain, so brought only light field artillery.

The invasion fleet sailed on 1 August with a steady easterly wind and six days later made landfall at the mouth of Milford Haven, near the town of Dale. With no possibility of offering resistance Richard Williams fled Pembroke Castle to warn Rhys ap Thomas at Carmarthen. He then rode 200 miles to Nottingham to bring the news personally to Richard on the 11th.

Messengers were immediately dispatched across the country. A letter survives from the king to Henry Vernon of Haddon, Derbyshire, which demanded that he come at once with the men-at-arms he had promised, properly horsed and harnessed, on pain of forfeiture. Haddon had ignored a similar summons by the Kingmaker in 1471, and did so again.

John Howard summoned his men to rendezvous with him at Bury St Edmunds by the evening of 16 August. His letter to John Paston survives, requesting him to meet him with 'such a company of tall men as you can easily make up at my expense, as well as what you have promised the king'. Richard's reaction to the news from Wales was prompt and decisive, but it appears the machinery of general mobilization was not as well oiled as he had hoped.

Henry Percy had more ground to cover than Howard and could not have got from the far north to the rendezvous any faster than he did. On 19 August Richard moved from Nottingham to Leicester, a day's march nearer Howard and away from Percy, yet they arrived within twenty-four hours of each other. Richard's key retainers were already with him, but Percy had many lords and knights under his command who would have killed him at the slightest hint of trea-sonable intent, and it is absurd to suspect that he was laggard either in his response to the king's summons or during the battle.

The invading army blitzed up the west coast of Wales, bypassing the royal castle at Aberystwyth and turning inland at Machynlleth to avoid strongly garrisoned Harlech. Marching parallel to the

HENRY TUDOR'S INVASION, AUGUST 1485

invaders, Thomas and Herbert reported to Richard that they had prevented it from marching into England. In fact they had sent Richard Griffith and John Morgan to join Henry at Cardigan, bringing word that they had accepted his offer of the chamberlain-ship of south Wales for Thomas and immunity for his older brother for Herbert.

At Welshpool Henry was joined by fierce Rhys ap Maredudd from the Denbigh moors and other clan leaders from the hard uplands of Snowdonia. Thomas and Herbert finally joined him 6 miles east of Welshpool at Cefn Digoll (Long Mountain), which spans the border between Montgomery and Shropshire. The Welsh more than doubled the size of the army, but arguably as important was the food freely provided in its passage through Wales, which permitted Henry to dispense with foraging and to advance more rapidly than Richard expected.

Henry arrived outside Shrewsbury on 16 August, and the next day Thomas Mytton, the bailiff, opened the gates and lay down so that Henry should symbolically ride over him. Although he had arrested Buckingham in 1483, he suffered no further indig-nity. Richard had to assume that Henry's aim was to race down Watling Street, the main road from the north March to London, and his own move to Leicester suggests he intended to march down the Fosse Way, which crosses Watling Street 25 miles south-east of Leicester, to block his advance.

Instead, Henry marched away from Watling Street to Newport, where he was joined by Gilbert Talbot with 500 men, and thence to Stafford, where he finally made contact with his stepfather, Lord Stanley, camped 7 miles to the north at Stone. Stanley must have planned the whole campaign, as otherwise Henry's march into his area of hegemony makes no sense. Stanley did not join Henry but left John Savage to act as coordinator, working with Oxford and Chandée to direct the rebel army. Uncle Jasper was left in Wales, perhaps to act as governor but probably because he was unwilling to take orders from younger and abler men.

Some months before the invasion Richard had reluctantly permitted Thomas, Lord Stanley to leave the court, allegedly to attend to pressing business in Lancashire, but he had required him to leave his heir, Lord Strange, as a hostage. After failing to secure John Savage's heir he had instructed Brackenbury to arrest Thomas Bourchier, Walter Hungerford, John Fogge and others pardoned after the 1483 rebellion, and now ordered them brought to him. On the way, according to *The Great Chronicle of London*:

> Many gentlemen that held good countenance with master Brackenbury then lieutenant of the Tower, and had for many of them done right kindly, took their leave of him, in giving him thanks for his kindness before showed, and exhorted him to go with them, for they feared not to show him that they would go unto that other party, and so departed leaving him almost alone.*

Strange played a lonely and heroic part in his father's deception. Before departing for Leicester Richard had Strange 'put to the question' and extracted a confession that he, his uncle William and John Savage had indeed conspired against him. However, he insisted that his father remained loyal. Since he knew with absolute certainty that this was not the case, he resigned himself to death but had the wit to sustain the lie in letters to his father and wife.

With regard to the likely numbers who joined Henry, the *Ballad* roll-call must be handled with care. It is distorted by an over-representation of the exiles, who would have had small retinues and who may not have been joined by many from those of their affinity who had remained behind in England. It also grossly understates the numbers led by the Stanleys, perhaps because the author was a Stanley retainer and thought it unnecessary.

By sorting them into side-by-side columns arranged by region,

---

*Robert Brackenbury was a tragic character, torn between his tribal loyalty to Richard and the innate decency he showed in refusing to murder the princes or to deliver hostages for almost certain execution.

NAMED IN THE BALLAD OF *BOSWORTH FIELD* AND OTHER CREDIBLE SOURCES

(leading families in parentheses)

HENRY (122)		RICHARD (132)	
WEST COUNTRY / SOUTH-WEST (27)		**THE NORTH (72)**	
Devon (Courteney)	7	Yorkshire/Richmondshire*	40
Wiltshire (Hungerford, Cheyne)	6	Durham (Lord Lumley, Brackenbury)	8
Cornwall (Courtenay, Nanfan, Arundel)	5	Cumberland (Lords Dacre & Greystoke)	7
Somerset (Daubeney)	4	Northumberland (Earl of, Middleton)	7
Dorset (remnant Beaufort affinity)	3	Westmorland (Earl of, Radcliffe)	6
Gloucestershire (Berkeley)	2	Lancashire (Ashton, Harrington)	5
WALES (26)		**MIDLANDS (23)**	
Monmouth/Glamorgan (Herbert)	7	Derbyshire (Lord Audley)	5
Carmarthen (Thomas)	6	Warwickshire (Kendall)	3
Flint/Denbigh (Maredudd, Wm. Stanley)	6	Northamptonshire (Lord Zouche)	3
Pembroke/Cardigan (Jasper Tudor)	4	Worcestershire (Staffords of Grafton)	2
Caernarvon/Conwy (Eyri chieftains)	3	Staffordshire (Lord Ferrers)	2
HOME COUNTIES (23)		Oxfordshire (Lord Lovell)	2
Kent (Woodville, Fogge)	5	Leicestershire	2
Sussex	3	Rutland	1
Buckinghamshire	3	**HOME COUNTIES (14)**	
Essex (Vere)	3	London/Middlesex	3
Bedfordshire (Digby)	2	Essex (Howard)	3
Berkshire	2	Berkshire	3
Oxfordshire (Stonor, Harcourt)	2	Buckinghamshire	2
Surrey (Poynings, Bourchier)	2	Kent/Surrey	2
Hertfordshire (Fortescue)	1	Hertfordshire	1
MIDLANDS (22)		**EAST ANGLIA (11)†**	
Staffordshire (Blount)	7	Norfolk (Duke of)	6
Lincolnshire (Beaumont, Welles, Hastings)	3	Cambridgeshire	2

*Includes Lord Scrope of Bolton, the Conyers clan and most of Richard's other chief retainers.

†The small number of named individuals is misleading: this was the second largest regional contingent.

Northamptonshire (Hastings affinity)	3	Huntingdon	2
Warwickshire (Mountfort)	2	Suffolk (Duke of)	1
Gloucestershire (Berkeley)	2	WEST COUNTRY / SOUTH- WEST (7)	
Leicestershire (Hastings affinity)	2	Devon (Courtenays of Powderham)	4
Nottinghamshire, Rutland, Worcestershire	3	Cornwall (Bodrugan)	1
THE MARCHES (13)		Hampshire	1
Shropshire (Talbot)	9	Gloucestershire	1
Cheshire (Wm. Stanley/Savage)	4	THE MARCHES (5)	
THE NORTH (8)		Herefordshire (Lord Ferrers)	3
Lancashire (Lord Stanley)	5	Shropshire	2
Yorkshire	3		
EAST ANGLIA (3)			
Suffolk, Norfolk	2		
Cambridgeshire (Brandon)	1		

we can see that the great value of the *Ballad* roll-call lies in contrasting Henry's wide if shallow geographical support with the overwhelming preponderance (54 per cent of those named) of northerners in Richard's army. Also, while Richard's presence at Nottingham may have deterred a separate uprising in the east Midlands, it did not prevent the Welles brothers and members of the Hastings affinity from making their way to join Henry's army.

As one would expect, the main additions came along the line of march through Shropshire and Staffordshire, which contributed perhaps another 1,500 men. Contingents from elsewhere would have built up a total of about 8,000, not counting the Stanleys. Lord Stanley indented for 3,000 archers during the Scottish campaign and a full call-out of his Lancashire affinity plus levies under commissions of array could have doubled that number in 1485. Brother William and Savage may have assembled another 1,500 from north-east Wales and western Cheshire.

The Crowland Continuator believed Richard's was the largest army ever assembled in England, and a full turnout by the North cannot have produced much fewer than 10,000 men, pointing to a total in the region of 20,000. While it is unlikely to have been so tidy, a working hypothesis is that Howard's battle numbered about 10,000 and Percy's about 8,000, with the cream of the northerners forming a largely mounted reserve of 2,000 men under Richard's command. As we shall see, battlefield circumstances put most of the guns with Percy's battle.

Stanley repeated the tactic used by Thomas and Herbert. He marched parallel to Henry, reporting to Richard that he was blocking a rebel advance towards London but actually screening Henry's movements. Richard's scouts kept him well informed about the Stanleys' movements but do not appear to have been able to track Henry's. The invaders regained Watling Way at Tamworth and marched down it to Atherton, where Henry spent the night of 21 August at nearby Merevale Abbey.

Finally Stanley reported the startling intelligence that Henry's vanguard had turned along another Roman road called Fenn Lane running from Watling Street towards Leicester, and had camped at Fenny Drayton. There may have been a skirmish with Richard's scouts at Atterton, which would have given credence to Stanley's disinformation that the main enemy force was advancing north of Fenn Lane.

The aim of operational deception is to confuse the enemy commander with regard to where and in what strength the attack will come. Lord Stanley's performance before Bosworth marks him as one of the greatest but least recognized masters of medieval warfare. Richard was confused, and marched north of Fenn Lane to rendezvous with Stanley, who was camped at Shenton professing to be ready to form the right wing of the royal army.

Richard may have believed he held the trump card in Lord Strange, but he had to be ready for Stanley to jump either way. If loyal, the battle was a foregone conclusion. If not, Richard had to cover him at Shenton or risk being outflanked. Accordingly he advanced through Sutton Cheney, where Percy and the main artillery park remained, to Ambion Hill, which gave a commanding view of the broad valley in which Shenton nestles.

The outcome of Stanley's deception was that Richard gave battle at a location that neutralized his numerical advantage. Now we know where the battle was fought there can be no doubt that Chandée and Vere came forward on the 21st to confer with Stanley, to review the ground and to agree tactics. After seizing power Henry restored Vere as Earl of Oxford, richly endowed from Howard's forfeited estates, and also created and endowed Lord Stanley as Earl of Derby and Philibert de Chandée as Earl of Bath.

XXXIII

CHECKMATE

THANKS TO A MULTI-YEAR SURVEY OF THE SITE CON-
ducted by the Battlefields Trust and Leicestershire County
Council we now know where Bosworth was fought. Better
than that, the survey also established where there would have been
marshland in 1485, and among other significant battle debris found
more lead shot than in all other fifteenth- and sixteenth-century
European battlefields put together. The findings argue that highly
skilled battlefield tactics decided the battle.

The following is a wider interpretation than the authors of the
survey's findings permitted themselves, but rests entirely on their
admirable research.* In particular, the fall of shot points to a non-
treasonous explanation for Henry Percy's inaction. When John
Milton ended the sonnet 'On His Blindness' with the words 'They
also serve who only stand and wait' he had something else in mind
– but they apply with rare precision to the decisive role played by
Thomas, Lord Stanley.

The deception continued until the hour of battle. Early on 22
August Stanley marched from Shenton to Dadlington, located on
high ground overlooking Fenn Lane, almost certainly explaining
it as a response to learning that the rebel army was not, after all,
marching north of the road. Salazar, a Spanish professional soldier

*The new information is comprehensively set out in Glenn Foard and Anne Curry's
invaluable *Bosworth 1485: A Battlefield Rediscovered* (Oxford, 2013).

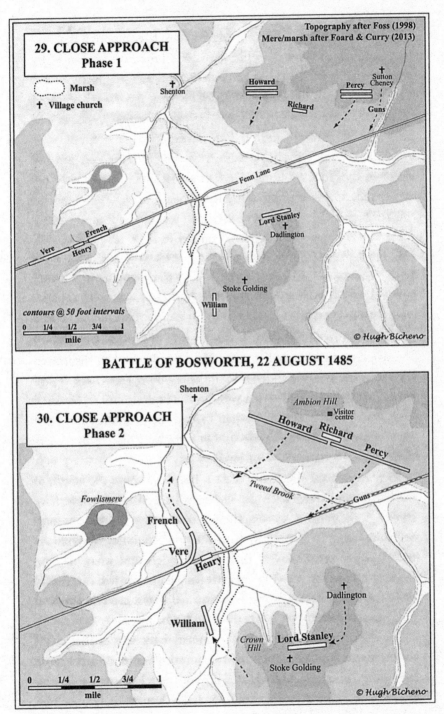

29. CLOSE APPROACH
Phase 1

Topography after Foss (1998)
Mere/marsh after Foard & Curry (2013)

⋯ Marsh
+ Village church

Shenton

Howard

Percy

Sutton
Cheney

Richard

Guns

Fenn Lane

Lord Stanley
+ Dadlington

French
Vere
Henry

+ Stoke Golding

William

contours @ 50 foot intervals

0   1/4   1/2   3/4   1
mile

© Hugh Bicheno

BATTLE OF BOSWORTH, 22 AUGUST 1485

30. CLOSE APPROACH
Phase 2

Shenton
+

Ambion Hill
■ Visitor
centre

Howard   Richard
Percy

Tweed Brook

Guns

Fowlismere

French

Vere
Henry

Dadlington
+

William

Crown
Hill

Lord Stanley

+ Stoke Golding

0   1/4   1/2   3/4   1
mile

© Hugh Bicheno

sent as an observer by Emperor Maximilian, later reported that 'my lord Tamerlant [Thomas would have been pronounced 'Tamas' by northerners] with King Richard's left wing left his position and passed in front of the king's vanguard'. Salazar incorrectly reported that 'Tamerlant' began to fight for Henry immediately, but he did not – and the move by itself did not reveal Stanley's intentions.

William Stanley probably concealed his battle behind the hill crowned by Stoke Golding. He had about 3,000 men under his command, so his brother must have lent him 1,500, to remain himself with about 4,500. Map 29 shows just how clever the deployment was. Lord Stanley appeared poised to form up on Richard's left, but equally he now held the high ground overlooking Fenn Lane, making any advance along it perilous. Since the heavy artillery must necessarily follow the road, Richard could only send his guns forward strongly escorted.

Richard formed his host in a long line overlooking the valley. The display was intended to intimidate Stanley and to dishearten Henry's army as it descended into the valley along Fenn Lane. Vergil wrote that it 'stretched forth a wondrous length, so full replenished both with footmen and horsemen that to the beholders afar off it gave a terror for the multitude, and in front were placed his archers, like a most strong trench and bulwark'.

Richard donned the crown of St Edward and rode the length of the battle line, drawing dutiful cheers as he went, and would have spoken some rousing words. The performance is unlikely to have been the boost to morale Richard intended. Soldiers have always taken an irreverent view of their commanders and what his men made of a tiny man on a big horse wearing a huge crown can readily be imagined. The state crown was returned to the camp at Ambion Hill, to be replaced by a gold circlet on his helmet.

The display precipitated a new manoeuvre by Stanley that could not be seen as anything other than a commitment to the rebel cause. He withdrew from Dadlington Hill and marched west to a new position in front of Stoke Golding, today known as Crown Hill, positioning himself as the flank guard for the approaching rebel army. At the same time William Stanley emerged from behind the hill and marched to join Henry on Fenn Lane. Furious, Richard ordered Strange beheaded, but his guards prudently opted to await the outcome of the battle.

At this point the position and extent of the marsh that used to be crossed by Fenn Lane in front of Crown Hill becomes extraordinarily important, and the key to understanding why Henry's forces suffered so few casualties. Richard had to divide his army, with Percy and the northerners marching down to Fenn Lane to escort the guns and to confront the Stanleys, while Howard's massive battle, formed deeper than usual because the terrain constricted his front, headed north of the marsh.

Without a doubt the marsh was the reason why the rebel leaders chose the location, knowing that Richard must attack. His authority rested on force of arms, and his army might not hold together if he backed down. Also, the trickle of volunteers joining Henry would have become a flood, and rebellions would have broken out in unguarded parts of the country. Salazar did not understand how fragile Richard's political situation was and advised him to pull back:

> Now when your little vassal, who was there in King Richard's service, saw the treason of the king's people, he approached him and said: 'Sire, take steps to put your person in safety, without expecting to have the victory today, owing to the manifest treason in your following'. But the king replied: 'Salazar, God forbid I yield one step. This day I shall die like a king or triumph'.

Chandée's vanguard peeled off from Fenn Lane to march behind the marsh along a ridge running between two brooks. After 500 years of cultivation, drainage and erosion, this is now an insignificant topographical feature, but there is a confused observation in the *Chroniques* of the Burgundian Jean Molinet that gives a hint why it was crucial in 1485: 'the French, knowing by the king's shot

31. ADVANCE TO CONTACT

Marsh

Ambion Hill

French

Ferrers

Savage

Tweed Brook

Howard

Richard

Vere

Talbot

Henry

Guns

Percy

William S

Dadlington

Lord Stanley

Crown Hill

Stoke Golding

contours @ 50 foot intervals

© Hugh Bicheno

1,000 yards

32. DEATH RIDE

the lie of the land and the order of his battle, resolved, in order to avoid the fire, to mass their troops against the flank rather than the front of the king's battle'.

Henry's commanders knew exactly what they were up against before a shot was fired. With their right flank secured by Stanley on Crown Hill and the centre protected by the marsh, the elite of the rebel army marched to secure the left at the confluence of two brooks. The best thing about the ridge between the brooks was that it permitted them to deploy out of sight, protected from artillery fire on the reverse slope. The Duke of Wellington employed the same tactic during his Iberian campaign in the early nineteenth century, and for the same reason: he too was usually outnumbered and outgunned.

Vere's battle followed the French, led by Savage's Cheshiremen and with Gilbert's Marchers bringing up the rear. They formed a curving line behind the ridgeline from Chandée's position back to a point opposite the start of the marsh. Henry was behind the marsh with a small entourage, and finally William Stanley's men formed up with the army's guns across Fenn Lane opposite the marsh crossing, a gravelled ford across the narrowest point.

The greatest concentration of shot discovered by the archaeological survey is well to the west of where the battle was fought, consistent with counter-battery fire to silence Stanley's guns on the ridge. The undershoots that must have pockmarked the ridge itself would have been dug up soon after the battle. Lead was valuable, and the cannon balls that lay undisturbed for 500 years were overshoots in distant places where scavengers did not think to look.

The hypothesis portrayed in Map 31 shows Percy's men formed in columns along Fenn Lane in the hope of being able to charge across the marsh bottleneck once the enemy guns were silenced, but also ready to repel an attack by Lord Stanley. The concentration of shot found by the survey beyond Crown Hill would have been overshoots from guns fired beyond effective range at Lord Stanley's men, perhaps hoping to provoke them to charge.

Unless they did, Percy's tactical situation was unenviable: he did not know how many men were waiting behind the ridge to his front, and if he attempted to charge across the marsh regardless, Lord Stanley could either march to support William or, more probably, attack Percy's battle in the flank. Nobody killed the Earl of Northumberland because all under his command could see they were stymied.

The curving configuration of the enemy line along the ridge caused Howard to dispose his battle with a strong right wing, angled back in a manoeuvre known as 'refusing the flank'. It is likely he entrusted this vital duty to his senior subordinate, Lord Ferrers, with his own and other Marchers and Midlanders.

Polydore Vergil's history was commissioned by Henry VII, who would have spoken to him about Bosworth. One section, the only detailed description of combat tactics in any account of the Wars of the Roses, reads like eyewitness testimony. The action portrayed on the north flank in Maps 31 and 32 is based on the following:

> The king, as soon he saw the enemy advance past the marsh, ordered his men to charge… the Earl of Oxford, afraid that in the fighting his men would be surrounded by the multitude, gave out the order… that no soldier should go more than ten feet from the standards. When in response to the command all the men massed together and drew back a little from the fray, their opponents, suspecting a trick, took fright and broke off from the fighting for a while… Then the Earl of Oxford in the one part, with tightly grouped units, attacked the enemy afresh, and the others in the other part pressing together in wedge formation renewed the battle.

I read this as Vere's men making a short charge downhill to check Howard's battle after it crossed the stream and then, outnumbered and under intense pressure, at an agreed signal falling back to regroup into defensive squares. There was a lull, but then it was

Howard's, not Vere's men who surged forward again.

Meanwhile the better drilled French and Scots formed attacking wedges and drove into Howard's refused right flank. Billmen facing this formation for the first time would not have stood for long, leaving their men-at-arms fighting for their lives. If my assumption is correct, this was where Ferrers and fourteen of the thirty-six royal Marchers and Midlanders named in the *Ballad* were killed.

Winston Churchill's aphorism that in war everything is going on all the time applies even more exactly to battlefield developments. By this stage Richard would have known that Percy and the northerners had not been able to achieve the breakthrough at the marsh crossing that would have split the enemy army; but it seems unlikely that the crumbling of his right wing had already begun, as otherwise he would have committed the reserve to shore it up. All he knew was that his battle plan was not producing the battle of annihilation he craved.

However, Howard's renewed push opened a gap at Vere's right wing, through which Richard caught a clear sight of Henry and his entourage, who may have moved to support Talbot. Richard's motives for what followed are not hard to deduce: mounting frustration and rage, the provocation of Henry's royal banners, confidence in his military judgement, perhaps a desire to prove the will of God in single combat with his rival. He assembled his household knights and launched the only all-out heavy cavalry charge of the Wars of the Roses.

The move achieved total tactical surprise. The brook emerging from the marsh and the slope beyond would have slowed its impetus, but when Talbot and some of his men tried to intercept the charge they were smashed aside, leaving Talbot himself severely wounded. Vergil's account again reads as though from Henry himself:

> In the first charge Richard killed several men, toppled Henry's standard along with the standard bearer William Brandon [actually Charles, the only notable fatality among Henry's followers],

contended with John Cheyne, a man of surpassing bravery who stood in his way, and thrust him to the ground with great force, and made a path for himself through the press of steel.

Tradition has it that Henry's Welsh bodyguard halted the charge, rallied by Rhys ap Maredudd, thereafter known as Rhys Fawr (Rhys the Mighty), who picked up Henry's red dragon banner and held it aloft for the remainder of the battle. 'Then, behold, William Stanley came in support with 3,000 men. Indeed it was at this point, with the rest of his men taking to their heels, Richard was killed fighting in the thickest of the press.' Molinet tells it differently:

> The king bore himself valiantly according to his destiny... but when he saw this discomfiture and found himself alone on the field he thought to run after the others. His horse leapt into the marsh from which it could not retrieve itself. One of the Welshmen then came after him and struck him dead with a halberd.

We cannot place much confidence in Molinet, whose estimates of the numbers involved are wildly exaggerated and whose account is a thinly disguised morality tale about Richard's deserved fate. However, examination of Richard's bones revealed that the death blow was indeed a skull-penetrating blow, probably by a halberd, to the back of his head. The remains eloquently confirm that once down he vanished under a hacking and stabbing mob.

There may have been a pause in the fighting, as the soldiers became spectators of the drama unfolding on the ridge at the centre of the battlefield. Once they saw Richard fall, Vere's men charged down the hill into Howard's demoralized men, the duke himself being killed and Surrey badly wounded, probably fighting to defend his fallen father. Vergil says 1,000 were killed, nearly all of them Richard's men, which seems about right.

The casualties deny the allegation that Richard was abandoned by his household: Robert Brackenbury, William Conyers, Ralph Danby, Alan Fulthorpe (Constable of Middleham), Thomas Gower, Thomas Markenfield, Robert Percy, Thomas Pilkington and Richard Ratcliffe all died with him.

The Crowland Continuator, who was not there, reported some words spoken by Richard on the morning of the battle that read like a textbook example of a psychopathic mirroring:

> 'He asserted that the issue of this day's battle, to whichever side the victory might be granted, would prove the utter destruction of the kingdom of England. He also declared that it was his intention, if he should prove the conqueror, to crush all the supporters of the opposite faction; while at the same time he predicted that his adversary would do the same towards well wishers to his own party, in case the victory should fall to his lot.'

Contrary to Richard's prediction the victors did not even indulge in the wholesale slaughter that almost invariably followed a medieval battle – the wounded Earl of Surrey was not killed though he refused quarter. It is likely the defeated men did not trigger the usual feral hunting response among their foes because instead of fleeing they dropped their weapons and surrendered in place; but Richard's death may well have been catharsis enough.

Nor did Henry indulge in a post-battle purge. The only executions were of William Bracher and his son for having betrayed their Yeomen of the Crown comrades, and of William Catesby for his treachery to Lord Hastings. Only twenty-eight men, ten of them killed at Bosworth, were attainted: five lords (Norfolk, Surrey, Lovell, Ferrers and de la Zouche), eight knights and fifteen others. Apart from Lovell and the Staffords of Grafton, who fled to sanctuary and remained adamant, the survivors made submission and most eventually recovered their family estates.

It was as though the spell cast over so many by the fierce will that had driven Richard in life had suddenly dissipated, and there was to be none of the lasting loyalty to the deposed king's cause that had bedevilled Edward IV and Richard himself. Once dead it was as though he had never been anything except Shakespeare's panto-mime villain – until the emergence of a passionate fan club many centuries later.

SOMEWHAT MUSING

I**T WOULD BE ANTICLIMACTIC TO EXTEND THE WARS OF**
the Roses narrative beyond Bosworth. There were several rebellions against the Tudor succession, including one by Thomas
Vaughan in 1486, crushed with relish by Rhys ap Thomas, and two
in 1487 and 1497 led by Yorkist impostors sponsored by Margaret
of York, dowager Duchess of Burgundy. During the first John de la
Pole, Earl of Lincoln and Richard III's heir presumptive, was killed.

Although Henry VII claimed the throne by right of conquest,
he was finally provoked into crushing the Yorkist seed. He executed Clarence's feeble-minded and blameless son Edward, Earl
of Warwick, in 1499. Emperor Maximilian surrendered John de
la Pole's rebellious brother Edmund to Henry, under oath not to
harm him. Previously demoted from duke to earl of Suffolk and
then deprived of the earldom, Edmund was executed by Henry VIII
in 1513. Richard de la Pole, the last Yorkist pretender, was killed in
1525 fighting for France in Italy.

Edward Gibbon observed that history is 'little more than the reg-
ister of the crimes, follies, and misfortunes of mankind', hardly the
stuff of comedy. Although the doings of our ancestors were often
farcically inept, an awareness of our own on-going stupidities generally constrains our urge to laugh at them. Happily we need feel
less inhibited when – to bowdlerize T. H. Huxley – a fanatically
held belief is slain by an ugly fact.

Just such a moment occurred when, thanks to the persistence and brilliant deduction from sparse facts of Philippa Langley, a devoted Ricardian, the remains of Richard III were discovered and their identity confirmed by mitochondrial DNA. Unfortunately the bones revealed that he was, after all, the deformed individual portrayed by Shakespeare in *The Tragedy of King Richard the Third*.

The discovery undermines the defining purpose of the Richard III Foundation, which is 'to challenge the popular view of King Richard III by demonstrating through rigorous scholarship that the facts of Richard's life and reign are in stark contrast to the Shakespearian caricature'. It is going to be harder to defend that thesis now we know that the most salient characteristic of Shakespeare's Richard III was not, in fact, a caricature.

The modern Ricardian movement is the historiographical oak that sprang up from the acorn planted by Josephine Tey's 1951 detective story *The Daughter of Time* and a sixteenth-century portrait of Richard that portrays him as a sensitive soul. I could not have written these books without the vast amount of excellent scholarship the movement has generated. However the defining Ricardian dogma – that Richard III's black villainy was an invention of Tudor propagandists – was always skating on thin ice.

The key contemporary sources for the events of 1483, by which Richard III is rightly judged, are the Crowland Continuator and Mancini. The first was unknown to a wider audience until the end of the Tudor period, and the second not until 1934. As the editors of the *Crowland Chronicle Continuations* judiciously observe, this helps 'to explain why Tudor propaganda was so successful: like all good propaganda it offered an interpretation which even informed people, in independent possession of the facts, could accept'.

No serious historian doubts that Richard was directly responsible for the murder of his nephews, and that it was the defining act of his life and reign. Despite this, we saw the strength of the Ricardian cult in the veneration surrounding the reburial of his remains in March 2015. As Thomas Cromwell said to Ambassador

Chapuys, Richard was a bad man who met the end he deserved; that Cromwell's master Henry VIII was also loathsome does not alter the justice of that verdict. It is far more debatable whether Richard deserved a handsome tomb monument in Leicester Cathedral with '*Loyaulte me lie*' inscribed without irony on the plinth.

It was, however, perfectly expressive of the Zeitgeist. If a latter-day Richard III were put on trial today for murdering his nephews in order to steal their inheritance, well-paid apologists would be lining up to argue in mitigation not only that his intentions were good, but also that he was not responsible for his actions because of his congenital deformity and malignant upbringing. They would also, of course, assert that society, not he, was to blame.

It should go without saying that Richard's personality was shaped by his genetic endowment, his dysfunctional family and the violent social environment in which he grew up. But while such influences predispose to psychopathy, they are not predictive. He was also immensely privileged and raised in the Christian chivalric tradition, which did not constrain him in the slightest. Only his elevated social status differentiates him from common criminals.

If the Tudor 'big lie' turns out not to be so big after all, the same cannot be said for other black holes in the historiography of the Wars of the Roses. In *Battle Royal* it was the demonization of Marguerite d'Anjou for having fought for her son's birthright, and in *Blood Royal* it has been the greedy-and-grasping-parvenu Woodvilles trope. These influential interpretations have scant basis in fact and are little more than manifestations of the universal human tendency to 'blame the foreigner', of a startling amount of misogyny, and of petty bourgeois snobbery.

In Darwinian terms the final verdict on the Houses of York and Neville, who have dominated our narrative, is that even their mitochondrial DNA will be extinguished upon the death of the childless donor who provided the sample that permitted the identification of Richard's remains. By contrast, a fair proportion of the native English population, including the monarchy and much of the old aristocracy, carries the mitochondrial DNA of Jacquetta de Luxembourg, wife of murdered Richard Woodville, mother of Queen Elizabeth and of murdered Anthony and John, and grandmother of the little boys murdered in the Tower of London.

If, as Darwinian absolutists argue, human beings are simply DNA's means of reproduction, then the winner's rosette in the competition among the bloodlines of senior titles of aristocracy goes to John Howard. Despite vicissitudes including two subsequent attainders under Henry VIII and Elizabeth I and a genetic bottleneck in 1975, his linear descendant is Edward William Fitzalan-Howard, since 2002 not merely the 18th Duke of Norfolk and Earl Marshal of England, but also Earl of Arundel (with Jacquetta's DNA along for the ride), of Surrey and of Norfolk, and Baron Maltravers, Beaumont and Howard of Glossop.

Neck and neck with Howard in the DNA stakes is Charles Somerset, illegitimate son of Charles the Bold's heartthrob Henry Beaufort, 3rd Duke of Somerset. Charles married Elizabeth, daughter and sole heiress of the younger William Herbert and Margaret Woodville, and through her became Lord Herbert. From them descend the line of earls and marquesses of Worcester, finally made dukes of Beaufort in 1692. The current duke is the only member of the aristocracy descended in the male line from the Plantagenets.

Battle Royal and *Blood Royal* were inspired by George R. R. Martin's *A Song of Ice and Fire* saga, for which he in turn drew inspiration from the Wars of the Roses. Martin's genius lies not only in his multi-layered and compelling narrative, but also in the interwoven motives of his vividly developed characters. Within the constraints of non-fiction I have tried to do the same.

Sadly, a lack of personally illuminating sources prevented me writing the story as the true-life sex'n'violence soap opera that it undoubtedly was, more akin to the florid 1980s American TV series *Dallas* and *Dynasty* than to the fastidious observation of aristocratic families not doing very much at which the BBC excels. I wonder, though, whether anyone would dare to broadcast a saga in which adultery, cuckoldry, homo-eroticism, incest and satyriasis punctuate a narrative of unchecked aristocratic greed and criminality, illuminated by savage blood feuds, spectacular battles, brutal beheadings and the ever-popular ritual disembowelments.

Alison Weir, Susan Higginbotham, Philippa Gregory and Sarah Gristwood have done sterling work in print and on TV to give a voice to the women of the Wars of the Roses, but all any of us can do is to reason that Catherine de Valois, Marguerite d'Anjou, Elizabeth Woodville, Jacquetta de Luxembourg, Cecily Neville, Margaret Beaufort and others filled many of the holes in the historical record. It is enormously frustrating that precisely how they did it is lost to us, because there was no other period in English history during which women were more influential. That it was also one of the bloodiest does not necessarily support the contention that the female of the species is more deadly than the male.

On a personal level, researching and writing these two books have brought to life so many of what Lawrence Durrell called 'spirits of place'. I live in a small market town that was once Richard of York's, not far from twice fought-over St Albans. My family lived near or in Cambridge for centuries but I was the first to attend the university, architecturally dominated by breathtaking King's College Chapel, Henry VI's foundation, and where several other famous colleges were founded by leading characters in *Battle Royal* and *Blood Royal*.

By any measure of comfort and physical well-being we enjoy standards beyond the imagination of Renaissance princes, and if a cause and effect could be shown, the loss of the creative highs of the past would be considered a fair price to pay for the elimination of the squalid lows of endemic disease and violence. But it cannot, and therein lies the attraction of reading about a far less humane but more effervescent time, when some at least of the tax burden that rulers imposed on their subjects went to decorate the world with works of lasting beauty.

I have revisited with new eyes the tomb monuments in Westminster Abbey, St George's Chapel at Windsor and the spectacular Beauchamp sarcophagus at St Mary's, Warwick. But most of all I have been enormously privileged to walk the sites of the battles that provide the climaxes of the two books in the wake of meticulous archaeological research that at last permits an educated guess about how they were fought. For, like it or not, war has defined human history, and nothing better illustrates the definitive importance of *fortuna* – blind chance – than properly understood battles.

A hair's breadth of *fortuna* separated victory from defeat at Towton and Bosworth. Had either gone the other way the flow of history might have followed fundamentally divergent channels. Despite this, battles still tend to be presented in unnatural isolation from political and social history, I suspect largely because people do not want to be reminded of the irreducible element of often unmerited good or bad luck that governs human existence.

Readers will draw as much or as little deeper meaning from the events I have described as they choose, and it is not for me to say what it might be. I set out to tell a tale of families riven by ambition, greed, lust and folly and I hope to have done it justice. History is the mistress of life, and I have tried to make love to her as she deserves.

ENGLISH PEERAGE
1462–85
by Seniority

KG = Knight of the Garter   KIA = killed in battle; senior titles in italics

Under Edward IV the duchy of York and earldoms of March and Cambridge in England and Ulster in Ireland were added to the crown's existing merged titles, which included the Principality of Wales (conjoined with the earldom of Chester), the dukedoms of Cornwall, Lancaster and Hereford, the earldoms of Leicester, Lancaster, Derby and Northampton, and the barony of Halton.

Since 1422 the heir to the throne has been Prince of Wales, Duke of Cornwall and Earl of Chester.

DUKES

Date created	Name	Dates	Comments
Norfolk (1397)[1]	John Mowbray, KG, 4th duke	1461–76	Extinct in the male line
Exeter (1416)	Henry Holland, 3rd duke	1447–61	Attainted. Murdered 1475
Buckingham (1444)	Henry Stafford KG, 2nd duke	1460–83	Executed, attainted
	Edward Stafford, 3rd duke	1485–1521	Restored
Somerset (1448	Henry Beaufort, 2nd duke	1455–64	Attainted 1461–3, restored. Executed, attainted 1464
	Edmund Beaufort, 3rd duke	1470–1	KIA Tewkesbury, extinct
Suffolk (1448)	John de la Pole KG, 2nd duke	1463–91	Restored
Clarence (1461)	George Plantagenet KG	1461–78	Executed, attainted
Gloucester (1461)	Richard Plantagenet KG	1461–83	Merged to crown
Bedford (1470)	George Neville[2]	1470–8	Degraded for poverty
York (1474)	Richard (Edward IV's second son)	1474–83	Murdered
Norfolk (1477)	Richard (Edward IV's second son)	1477–83	Murdered
Bedford (1478)	George (Edward IV's third son)	1478–9	Died an infant
Norfolk (1483)	John Howard KG	1483–5	KIA Bosworth, forfeit
Bedford (1485)	Jasper Tudor KG	1485–95	Extinct

1. Also Earl of Nottingham, Earl Warenne, Baron Mowbray and Baron Segrave.
2. Son of John Neville, created Marquess Montagu in 1470, previously Earl of Northumberland.

MARQUESSES

Montague (1470)	John Neville KG	1470–1	KIA Barnet, forfeit
Dorset (1475)	Thomas Grey KG	1475–1501	

EARLS

Warwick (1088)	Anne Beauchamp, 16th countess	1448–92	
	Richard Neville KG, 16th earl	1449–71	KIA Barnet
	George Plantagenet KG	1472–8	*Duke of Clarence*
	Edward Plantagenet	1478–99	
Arundel (1138)	William FitzAlan KG, 16th earl	1438–87	
Devon (1141) (see 1469)	John Courtenay, 15th earl	1471	KIA Tewksesbury, attainted
	Edward Courtenay, 16th earl	1485–1509	Restored
Oxford (1142)	John Vere, 12th earl	1417–62	Executed
	John Vere KG, 13th earl	1462–75	Attainted, restored 1485
Salisbury (1337)	Richard Neville KG, 6th earl	1460–71	*Earl of Warwick*
Stafford (1351)	Henry Stafford, 7th earl	1460–77	*Duke of Buckingham*
	Edward Stafford, 8th earl	1477–1523	
Suffolk (1385)	John de la Pole, 5th earl	1463–92	*Duke of Suffolk*
Westmorland (1397)	Ralph Neville, 2nd earl	1425–84	Dementia from *c.* 1458
	Ralph Neville, 3rd earl	1484–99	Nephew
Northumberland (1416)	Henry Percy KG, 3rd earl	1470–89	Restored
Shrewsbury (1442)	John Talbot, 3rd earl	1465–73	Attainted 1461, restored
	George Talbot, 4th earl	1473–1538	
Worcester (1449)	John Tiptoft KG	1449–70	Executed
	Edward Tiptoft, 2nd earl	1470–85	Extinct
Surrey & Warenne (1451)	John Mowbray	1451–76	*Duke of Norfolk*
Richmond (1452)	Henry Tudor, 2nd earl (Henry VII)	1461	Attainted
		1485	Restored, merged to crown
Pembroke (1452)	Jasper Tudor KG	1452–61	Attainted
		1471	Restored, attainted
		1485–94	Restored

EARLS

Essex (1461)	Henry Bourchier KG	1461–83	
	Henry Bourchier, 2nd earl	1483–1540	
Kent (1461)	William Neville KG	1461–3	Extinct
Richmond (1461)	George Plantagenet KG	1461–78	*Duke of Clarence*
Northumberland (1465)	John Neville KG	1465–70	*Marquess Montagu*
Rivers (1465)	Richard Woodville KG	1465–9	Murdered
	Anthony Woodville KG, 2nd earl	1469–83	Murdered
	Richard Woodville, 3rd earl	1483–91	
Kent (1465)	Edmund Grey of Ruthyn	1465–98	
Lincoln (1467)	John de la Pole	1467–87	Son of Duke of Suffolk
Pembroke (1468)	William Herbert KG	1468–9	Executed
	William Herbert, 2nd earl	1469–79	Surrendered
Devon (1469) (see 1141)	Humphrey Stafford of Southwyck	1469	Murdered, extinct
Wiltshire (1470)	John Stafford KG	1470–3	
	Edward Stafford, 2nd earl	1473–99	
Huntingdon (1471)	Thomas Grey KG	1471–5	*Marquess of Dorset*
Winchester (1472)	Louis de Gruuthuse	1472–92	*Stadtholder of Holland*
Salisbury (1472)	George Plantagenet KG	1472–8	*Earl of Warwick*
Nottingham (1476)	Richard (Edward IV's second son)	1476–83	*Duke of York*
Surrey & Warenne (1477)	Richard (Edward IV's second son)	1477–83	*Duke of York*
Richmond (1478)	Richard Plantagenet	1478–83	*Duke of Gloucester*
Salisbury (1478)	Edward (Richard III's only son)	1478–84	Died, extinct
March (1479)	Edward (Richard III's only son)	1479–84	Died, merged to crown
Pembroke (1479)	Edward (Richard III's only son)	1479–84	Died, merged to crown
Huntingdon (1479)	William Herbert (son)	1479–91	
Nottingham (1483)	William Berkeley	1483–92	
Surrey & Warenne (1483)	Thomas Howard	1483–5	
Derby (1485)	Thomas Stanley KG	1485–1504	
Bath (1485)	Philibert de Chandée	Unknown	

VISCOUNTS

Beaumont (1440)	William Beaumont, 2nd viscount	1460–70	Attainted
		1470–1	Restored, attainted
		1484–1507	Restored
Bourchier (1446)	William Bourchier	1461–72	On promotion of his father
	Henry Bourchier, 2nd viscount	1472–1540	*Earl of Essex*
Lisle (1451)	Thomas Talbot, 2nd viscount	1453–70	KIA Nibley Green
Berkeley (1481)	William Berkeley	1481–92	*Earl of Nottingham*
Lisle (1483)	Edward Grey of Groby	1483–92	
Lovell (1483)	Francis Lovell KG	1483–7	Forfeit 1485

MARCHER LORDSHIPS

Glamorgan (1449)	Richard Neville KG	1449–71	*Earl of Warwick*
Crickhowell/Tretower (1463)	William Herbert KG	1463–9	
	William Herbert (son)	1469–79	*Earl of Pembroke*
Raglan/Caerleon/Usk (1465)	William Herbert KG	1465–9	
	William Herbert (son)	1469–79	

BARONS

Roos (1264)	Edmund Roos, 11th baron	1485–1508	Restored
Neville (1295)	Ralph Neville, 6th baron	1472–99	Restored
Fauconberg (1295)	Joan Fauconberg, 6th baroness	1429–90	Abeyant
	William Neville KG, 6th baron	1429–63	*Earl of Kent*
Fitzwalter (1295)	Elizabeth Radcliffe, 8th baroness	1431–85	
	John Radcliffe, 9th baron	1485–96	
FitzWarin (1295)	William Bourchier, 9th baron	1433–70	
	Fulk Bourchier, 10th baron	1470–9	
	John Bourchier, 11th baron	1479–1539	
Grey of Wilton (1295)	Reginald Grey, 7th baron	1442–93	
Clinton (1299)	John Clinton, 6th baron	1464–88	
de la Warr (1299)	Richard West, 7th baron	1451–75	
	Thomas West, 8th baron	1475–1525	

Ferrers of Chartley (1299)	Anne Ferrers, 7th baroness	1450–68	
	Walter Devereux KG, 7th baron[3]	1461–85	KIA Bosworth
Lovell (1299)[4]	John Lovell, 8th baron	1455–65	
	Francis Lovell, 9th baron	1465–87	*Viscount Lovell*
Fitzwalter (1295)	Elizabeth Radcliffe, 8th baroness	1431–85	
	John Radcliffe, 9th baron	1485–96	
FitzWarin (1295)	William Bourchier, 9th baron	1433–70	
	Fulk Bourchier, 10th baron	1470–9	
	John Bourchier, 11th baron	1479–1539	
Scales (1299)	Elizabeth Scales, 8th baroness	1460–73	
	Anthony Woodville KG, 8th baron	1460–83	By marriage. *Earl Rivers*
	Edward Woodville, 9th baron	1483–8	
Welles (1299)	Richard Welles, 7th baron	1468–70	Restored, executed[5]
	Joan Welles, 9th baroness	1470–5	Also Willoughby
	Richard Hastings, 9th baron[6]	1470–1503	Created again 1487
Clifford (1299)	Henry Clifford, 10th baron	1485–1523	Restored
Ferrers of Groby (1299) *Grandson of Lady Ferrers*	Elizabeth Ferrers, 6th baroness	1445–83	
	John Bourchier, 6th baron	1462–83	By marriage
	Thomas Grey, 7th baron	1483–1501	*Marquess of Dorset*
Morley (1299)	Alianore Morley, 7th baroness	1442–76	
	William Lovell, 7th baron[7]	1442–76	Son of Lord Lovell
	Henry Lovell, 8th baron	1476–89	
Strange of Knockyn (1299)	John Strange, 8th baron	1449–77	
	Joan Strange, 9th baroness	1477–1514	
	George Stanley KG, 9th baron	1477–1503	
Zouche (1308)	William Zouche, 6th baron	1462–8	
	John Zouche, 7th baron	1468–85	Attainted, restored 1495
Beaumont (1309)	John Beaumont, 6th baron	1417–69	*Viscount Beaumont*
	William Beaumont, 7th baron	1469–1507	
Audley (1313)	John Tuchet, 6th baron	1459–90	
Cobham (1313)	John Brooke, 7th baron	1464–1512	

3. By marriage, confirmed in his own right by Edward IV in 1461.
4. Also Baron Holland, Deincort, Bedale and Grey of Rotherfield.
5. His son Robert, 8th baron, executed a few days later.
6. Younger brother of Baron Hastings. The Welles/Willoughby succession is too complex to unravel here.
7. By marriage. Confirmed in his own right by Edward IV in 1461.

Willoughby (1313)	Richard Welles, 8th baron	1455–69	Also Welles. Executed
	Robert Welles (informally)	1469	Executed
	Joan Welles, 9th baroness	1470–5	Also Welles
	Richard Hastings, 9th baron	1470–1503	By marriage
Dacre (1321)	Joan Dacre, 7th baroness	1458–86	
	Richard Fiennes, 7th baron	1458–83	
FitzHugh (1321)	Henry FitzHugh, 5th baron	1452–72	
	Richard FitzHugh, 6th baron	1472–87	
Greystoke (1321)	Ralph Greystoke, 5th baron	1436–87	
Grey of Ruthyn (1325)	Edmund Grey, 4th baron	1441–90	*Earl of Kent*
Harington (1326)	Cicely Bonville, 7th baroness	1460–1530	Also Bonville
	Thomas Grey, 7th baron	1474–1501	*Marquess of Dorset*
Maltravers (1330)	William FitzAlan KG, 3rd baron[8]	1417–61	*Earl of Arundel*
	Thomas FitzAlan KG, 4th baron	1461–1524	
Talbot (1331)	John Talbot, 9th baron	1460–73	*Earl of Shrewsbury*
	George Talbot, 10th baron	1473–1538	
Poynings (1337)	Eleanor Poynings, 6th baroness	1446–82	
	Henry Percy, 7th baron	1482–9	*Earl of Northumberland*
Bourchier (1342)	Henry Bourchier, 5th baron	1433–83	*Earl of Essex*
	Henry Bourchier, 6th baron	1483–1540	
Scrope of Masham (1350)	Thomas Scrope, 5th baron	1455–75	
	Thomas Scrope, 6th baron	1475–93	
Botreaux (1368)	Margaret Hungerford, 4th baroness	1462–77	
	Mary Hungerford, 5th baroness	1477–1529	Also Hungerford
Scrope of Bolton (1371)	John Scrope KG, 5th baron	1459–98	
Beauchamp of Bletsoe (1379)	Margaret Beauchamp, 4th baroness	1429–82	Grandmother of Henry VII
Lumley (1384/1461)	Thomas Lumley, 2nd baron[9]	1461–85	
Bergavenny (1392)	Edward Neville, 1st baron (de jure)	1450–76	By marriage 3rd baron
	Governed by Richard Neville KG	1450–71	*Earl of Warwick*
	George Neville, 2nd/4th baron	1476–92	
Grey of Codnor (1397)	Henry Grey, 4th baron	1444–96	
Berkeley (1421)	William Berkeley, 2nd baron	1463–92	*Earl of Nottingham*

8. Edward IV permitted Arundel's 11-year-old son Thomas to assume the Maltravers title in 1461.
9. First baron attainted in 1399. Attainder reversed for his grandson Thomas in 1461.

Hungerford (1426)	Robert Hungerford, 3rd baron	1459–61	Attainted, executed 1464
	Mary Hungerford, 4th baroness	1485–7	Restored. Also Botreaux
Tiptoft (1426)	John Tiptoft KG, 2nd baron	1443–70	*Earl of Worcester*
	Edward Tiptoft, 3rd baron	1475–85	Extinct
Latimer (1432)	George Neville (disputed)	1432–69	Declared incompetent 1447
	Richard Neville, 2nd baron	1469–1530	
Dudley (1440)	John Sutton KG	1440–87	
Sudeley (1299/1441)	Ralph Boteler KG, 6th/1st baron	1441–73	Abeyant
Lisle (1444)	Thomas Talbot, 2nd baron	1453–70	*Viscount Lisle*
	Elizabeth Talbot, 3rd baroness	1475–87	
	Edward Grey of Groby, 3rd baron	1483–92	
Say and Sele (1447)	William Fiennes, 2nd baron	1450–71	KIA Barnet, dormant
Beauchamp of Powick (1447)	John Beauchamp	1447–75	
	Richard Beauchamp, 2nd baron	1475–1503	
Rivers (1448)	Richard Woodville KG	1448–69	*Earl Rivers*
	Anthony Woodville, 2nd baron	1469–83	As above. Also Scales
	Richard Woodville, 3rd baron	1483–91	As above
Stourton (1448)	William Stourton, 2nd baron	1462–79	
	John Stourton, 3rd baron	1479–85	
Bonville (1449)	Cicely Bonville, 2nd baroness	1461–1530	Also Harington
	Thomas Grey, 2nd baron	1474–1501	*Marquess of Dorset*
Vescy (1449)	Henry Bromflete	1449–69	
	Margaret Bromflete, 2nd baroness	1469–93	
Berners (1455)	John Bourchier KG	1455–74	
	John Bourchier, 2nd baron	1474–1533	
Stanley (1456)	Thomas Stanley KG, 2nd baron	1459–1504	*Earl of Derby*
Neville (1459)	Ralph Neville	1472–99	*Earl of Westmorland*
Montagu (1460)	John Neville KG	1460–71	*Marquess Montagu*
Cromwell (1461)	Humphrey Bourchier	1461–71	Extinct
Hastings (1461)	William Hastings KG	1461–83	Executed
	Edward Hastings, 2nd baron	1483–1506	See Botreaux, Hungerford
Ogle (1461)	Robert Ogle	1461–9	KIA Edgecote
	Owen Ogle, 2nd baron	1469–86	
Wenlock (1461)	John Wenlock KG	1461–71	KIA Tewkesbury, extinct

Herbert of Raglan (1461)	William Herbert	1461–9	*Earl of Pembroke*
	William Herbert, 2nd baron	1469–91	
Stafford of Southwyck (1461)	Humphrey Stafford	1461–9	*Earl of Devon*
Lumley (1461)	Thomas Lumley	1461–85	
Mountjoy (1465)	Walter Blount KG	1465–74	
	Edward Blount, 2nd baron	1474–5	
	John Blount, 3rd baron	1475–85	
Dunster (1466)	William Herbert (son)	1466–85[10]	*Earl of Pembroke*
Dynham (1467)	John Dynham	1467–1501	
Howard (1470)	John Howard KG	1470–85	*Duke of Norfolk*
Dacre of Gilsland (1473)	Humphrey Dacre	1473–85	
	Thomas Dacre, 2nd baron	1485–1525	
Parr of Kendal (1474)	William Parr KG	1474–83	
	Thomas Parr, 2nd baron	1483–1517	
Grey of Powys (1482)	John Grey	1482–97	
Daubeney (1486)	Giles Daubeney KG	1486–1508	
Cheyne (1487)	John Cheyne KG	1487–99	

10. Lands restored to the Luttrell family.

Appendix B

ARCHBISHOPS AND BISHOPS
1462–85

Diocese	Incumbent	Dates	Offices
CANTERBURY	Thomas Bourchier	1454–86	*Created cardinal 1467*
Bath and Wells	Thomas Beckington	1443–65	
	Robert Stillington	1465–91	Lord Privy Seal 1460–7 Lord Chancellor 1467–70, 1471–3
Chichester	John Arundel	1459–77	
	Edward Story	1478–1503	Queen Elizabeth's confessor
Exeter	George Neville	1455–65	Lord Chancellor 1460–67, 1471 *Translated to York*
	John Booth	1465–78	
	Peter Courtenay	1478–87	Fought at Bosworth
Ely	William Grey	1454–78	Lord Treasurer 1469
	John Morton	1479–86	*Translated to Canterbury*
Hereford	John Stanberry	1453–74	
	Thomas Myling	1474–92	*Previously Abbot of Westminster*
Lichfield/Coventry	John	1459–90	Lord Privy Seal 1470–1
Lincoln/Dorchester	John	1452–71	
	Thomas Rotherham	1472–80	Lord Privy Seal 1467–70,1471–4; Lord Chancellor 1475–83; *Translated to York*
	John Russell	1480–94	Lord Chancellor 1483–5
London	Thomas Kemp	1448–89	
Norwich	Walter	1446–72	
	James Goldwell	1472–99	
Rochester	John Lowe	1444–67	
	Thomas Rotherham	1468–72	*Translated to Lincoln*
	John Alcock	1472–6	Lord Chancellor 1475 *Translated to Worcester*
	John Russell	1476–80	Lord Privy Seal 1474 *Translated to Worcester*
	Edmund Audley	1480–92	

	Richard Beauchamp	1450–81	
Salisbury	Lionel Woodville	1482–4	*Brother of Queen Elizabeth*
	Thomas Langton	1485–93	
Winchester	William Wainflete	1447–86	
Worcester	John Carpenter	1443–76	
	John Alcock	1476–86	Lord Chancellor 1485 *Translated to Ely*
Bangor	James Blakedon	1453–64	*Dominican monk*
	Richard Edenham	1464–94	*Franciscan monk*
Llandaff	John Hunden	1458–76	*Resigned*
	John Smith	1476–8	
	John Marshall	1478–96	
St Asaph	Thomas Bird	1450–63	*Deprived for rebellion; see vacant*
	Richard Redman	1471–95	
St David's	Robert Tully	1460–81	*Benedictine monk*
	Richard Martin	1482–3	
	Thomas Langton	1483–5	Edward IV's chaplain *Translated to Salisbury*
YORK	William Booth	1452–64	*Half-brother of Laurence*
	George Neville	1465–76	
	Laurence Booth	1476–80	
	Thomas Rotherham	1480–1500	Lord Chancellor 1485
Carlisle	William Percy	1452–62	*Brother of the Earl of Northumberland*
	John Kingscote	1462–3	
	Richard Scroope	1464–8	
	Edward Story	1468–78	Queen Elizabeth's confessor *Translated to Chichester*
	Richard Bell	1478–95	
Durham	Laurence Booth	1457–76	Lord Chancellor 1473 *Translated to York*
	William Dudley	1476–83	
	John Sherwood	1484–94	

CHIEF OFFICE HOLDERS
1460–85

Lords Treasurer	Lords Chancellor
EDWARD IV	
1460–2 Henry Bourchier, Earl of Essex	1460–7 George Neville, Bishop of Exeter Archbishop of York 1465
1462–3 John Tiptoft, Earl of Worcester	
1463–4 Edmund, Baron Grey of Ruthyn[1]	
1464–6 Walter Blount[2]	
1466–9 Richard Woodville, Earl Rivers	1467–70 Robert Stillington, Bishop of Bath
WARWICK	
1469 John Langstrother, Prior of St John	Stillington
EDWARD IV	
1469–70 William Grey, Bishop of Ely	Stillington
WARWICK	
1470–1 John Langstrother	1470–1 George Neville, Archbishop of York
EDWARD IV	
1471–83 Henry Bourchier, Earl of Essex	1471–3 Stillington
	1473–5 Laurence Booth, Bishop of Durham
	1475 John Alcock, Bishop of Rochester
	1475–83 Thomas Rotherham, Bishop of Lincoln[3]
RICHARD III	
1483–4 John Wood[4]	1483–5 John Russell, Bishop of Lincoln
1484–5 John Tuchet, Baron Audley	

1. Earl of Kent 1466.
2. Baron Mountjoy 1466.
3. Archbishop of York 1480.
4. Under-treasurer of the exchequer 1480–3 and Speaker of the Commons in 1483

TITLES, LANDS, HONOURS
and OFFICES of RICHARD
'THE KINGMAKER' NEVILLE*

BY MARRIAGE TO ANNE BEAUCHAMP

1449   16th Earl of Warwick (senior earldom). The Beauchamp (including part Bergavenny) and Despenser (including barony of Burghersh) estates in Glamorgan, Powys, Warwickshire, Worcestershire, Gloucestershire, Staffordshire and Barnard Castle, Durham. *All disputed.*

ROYAL APPOINTMENT OR ASSENT (HENRY VI)

c. 1449   Marcher Lordship of Glamorgan, including the lands, and apparently with the consent of his uncle Edward Neville, Baron Bergavenny by marriage.

1450   Hereditary Chamberlain of the Exchequer. *Disputed.*

1452   Co-Warden of the West March (North) with his father.

1454   Rulings in his favour over the Beauchamp inheritance, including the Chamberlainship of the Exchequer.

Dec 1455 Captain of Calais.

1457   Keeper of the Seas, with the right to collect customs dues at all ports except Sandwich and Southampton.

c. 1458   Made custodian of his uncle George Neville (dementia), Baron Latimer in Buckinghamshire, with seat at Snape Castle in Richmondshire.

1459   Attainder and forfeiture of all titles and honours.

1460   Reversal of attainder.

BY INHERITANCE FROM HIS FATHER AND MOTHER

1460-2   6th Earl of Salisbury and 7th Baron Montacute. Heads of Lordship at Penrith (Cumberland), Sheriff Hutton (Yorkshire), Middleham (Richmondshire), with seat at Bisham (Berkshire).

* From A. J. Pollard, *Warwick the Kingmaker* (London, 2007)

Estates in Dorset, Wiltshire, Somerset, Hampshire, Norfolk and Nottinghamshire.

ROYAL APPOINTMENT (EDWARD IV)

1461   Lands of the barony of Bergavenny legally transferred to Warwick and all disputes relating to the Despenser inheritance resolved in his favour.

1461   Brother George, Bishop of Exeter, made Lord Chancellor.

1461–2 Great Chamberlain of England, Master of the King's Mews, Warden of the Cinque Ports and Constable of Dover Castle and Carlisle, all for life. Captaincy of Calais renewed and made Admiral of England for five years. Wardenship of the East March added to his wardenship of the West March. Steward of the entire duchy of Lancaster. Awarded Newport Pagnell (Bucks) from the attainted Earl of Wiltshire's estates.

1463–4 Awarded some of the Percy and all the Clifford estates in Yorkshire and, for two years, the temporalities of the Bishop of Durham, whose claim to Barnard Castle was dismissed in Warwick's favour.

1463   Wardenship of the East March transferred to brother John, Baron Montagu.

1464   Montagu made Earl of Northumberland, endowed with the Percy estates not previously awarded to Warwick or Clarence, the king's brother.

1465   Warwick awarded Percy and Clifford estates in Cumberland and Westmorland, and the shrievalty of Westmorland.

1465   Brother George, Lord Chancellor, made Archbishop of York.

MARRIAGE

1469   Eldest daughter Isabel married George, Duke of Clarence, heir presumptive to the throne, defying Edward IV's prohibition.

ROYAL APPOINTMENT (HENRY VI)

1470   Lieutenant of England.

ACQUISITIONS

1461–70 Many – notably around Little Snoring in Norfolk, Collyweston in Northamptonshire and Erdington in Warwickshire.

1475 EXPEDITION: INDENTURES

Duke – 13s. 8d. | Marquis – 10s. | Earl – 6s. 8d. | Baron/Banneret – 4s.
Knight – 2s. | Lance (man-at-arms) – 1s. 6d. | Archer – 6d.

Principals	Lances	Per diem	Archers	Per diem
Relatives and Household				
11 Peers & heirs	516	£38 14s. 0d.	4,080	£102 10s. 0d.
7 Bannerets	69	£5 3s. 6d.	720	£18 0s. 0d.
5 Knights	39	£2 18s. 6d.	370	£9 5s. 0d.
28 Esquires	107	£8 0s. 6d.	910	£22 15s. 0d.
3 Gentlemen (a)	45	£3 7s. 6d.	323	£8 1s. 6d.
9 Officials	29	£2 3s. 6d.	134	£3 7s. 0d.
7 Others	10	15s. 0d.	80	£2 0s. 0d.
King's archers			184	£4 12s. 0d.
Sub-total	**815**	**£61 2s. 6d.**	**6,801**	**£170 10s. 6d.**
Non-Household				
12 Peers & heirs	231	£17 6s. 6d.	1,619	£40 9s. 6d.
2 Scots Peers	8	12s. 0d.	60	£1 10s. 0d.
5 Bannerets	32	£2 8s. 0d.	272	£6 16s. 0d.
13 Knights	52	£3 18s. 0d.	449	£11 4s. 6d.
52 Esquires	91	£6 16s. 6d.	672	£16 16s. 0d.
6 Gentlemen	5	7s. 6d.	32	16s. 0d.
32 Others	40	£3 0s. 0d.	268	£6 14s. 0d.
Sub-total	**463**	**£34 8s. 6d.**	**3,372**	**£84 6s. 0d.**
Specialists (b)			387	£9 13s. 6d.
TOTAL	**1,278**	**£95 11s. 0d.**	**10,560**	**£264 10s. 0d.**

The cost of combat troops alone for the main expedition was therefore no less than **£32,760** per quarter. There were also 2,000 archers (£50 p.d.) deployed to Brittany under Lords Audley and Duras, and 3,000 men (£75 p.d.) serving on Lord Dinham's fleet, a minimum additional quarterly cost of **£11,375**.

NOTES: Roll taken in Canterbury by Teller of the King's Money John FitzHerbert in June 1475. From Jack Lander, 'The Hundred Years War and Edward IV's Campaign in France', in Arthur Slavin (ed.), *Tudor Men and Institutions* (Louisiana State University, 1972).
The per diems are my calculations. The quarterly calculation is per diems x 91.
(a) Includes 43 'Gentlemen of the House of the Lord King' under Sir John Elrington.
(b) Non-combatant but essential support personnel such as armourers, blacksmiths, coopers, farriers, fletchers, saddlers, sawyers, plumbers, turners, wheelwrights, etc.

PARTIAL LIST OF JUNE 1475 INDENTURES

KG = Garter Knight

Principals	Knights	Lances	Archers
5 DUKES			
Clarence KG	10	100	1000
Gloucester KG (a)	10	100	1000
Buckingham KG (b)	4	40	400
Norfolk KG	2	40	300
Suffolk KG	2	40	300
Sub-total	28	320	3000
1 MARQUESS			
Dorset	*Not listed – separately reported to have brought 600 archers*		
5 EARLS			
Northumberland KG	10	40	200
Rivers KG	2	40	200
Pembroke		40	200
Douglas KG (Scots)		4	40
Ormond (Irish)		2	16
Sub-total	12	126	656
11 BARONS			
Hastings KG		40	300
Stanley		40	300
Scrope of Bolton KG		20	200
Howard KG		20	200
Ferrers of Chartley KG		20	200
Grey of Codnor		10	155
Grey of Ruthyn (c)		10	140
FitzWarine		10	50
Lisle		7	50
Cobham		5	50
Boyd (Scots)		2	20
Clinton	*Not listed*		
Sub-total		184	1665

11 KNIGHTS BANNERET			
William Parr KG		16	140
Thomas Burgh		16	140?
Thomas Montgomery		10	100
Humphrey Talbot (d)		10	100
Richard Tunstall		10	100
Ralph Hastings (e)		8	100
Robert Tailboys		12	80
John Grey (f)		8	80
John Ratcliffe		6	70
Thomas Howard (g)		6	40
John Fiennes (h)		4	40
William Stanley (i)		2	20
John FitzAlan (j)		2	20
John Astley KG		2	12
Sub-total		112	942
15 KNIGHTS			
James Harington		12	100
Robert Chamberlain		12	100
William Norris		12	100
Laurence Rainford		12	60
Nicholas Langford		8	60
William Trussell		6	60
John Croker		6	60?
John Harlewin		3	50
John Mauleverer		3	30
John Savage		3	30
Richard Corbet		3	30?
John Ferrers		2	15
James Radcliffe		1	12
Richard Brandon		1	12?
Simon Mountfort		1	12?
Sub-total		85	731
TOTAL (k)	74	827	6994

NOTES: From Francis Barnard (ed.), *Edward IV's French Expedition of 1475* (1925), facsimile of a manuscript in the College of Arms by John Sorell and John FitzHerbert, Tellers of the King's Money, of indentures submitted by those entitled to heraldic arms. An additional list of mainly non-combattant and non-armigerous royal officials omitted here. Question marks indicate extrapolations for missing entries.

(a) Gloucester was paid an extra £666 13s. 4d. for the next quarter because he took a larger-than-indented-for retinue to France. This was probably because some of his knightly retainers (Parr, Burgh, Tunstall, Harington, Mauleverer and Mountfort) subsumed their indentures to his.

(b) The manuscript notes that Buckingham 'went home' before embarkation.

(c) Lord Grey of Ruthyn was heir to the Earl of Kent.

(d) Humphrey Talbot was the uncle of the Earl of Shrewsbury.

(e) Ralph Hastings was the younger brother of Lord Hastings.

(f) John Grey was heir to Lord Grey of Wilton.

(g) Thomas Howard was heir to Lord Howard.

(h) John Fiennes was heir to Lord Dacre of the South.

(i) William Stanley was the younger brother of Lord Stanley.

(j) John FitzAlan was a younger son of the Earl of Arundel.

(k) The total financial disbursement differed from the first list by only £265, despite considerable divergence in the numbers tallied. Creative accounting, perhaps?

TITULUS REGIUS

Key passages italicized

To the High and Mighty Prince Richard, Duke of Gloucester

Please it your Noble Grace to understand the consideration, election, and petition of us the lords spiritual and temporal and commons of this realm of England, and thereunto agreeably to give your assent, to the common and public weal of this land, to the comforts and gladness of all the people of the same.

First, we consider how that heretofore in time passed this land many years stood in great prosperity, honour, and tranquillity, which was caused, forasmuch as the kings then reigning used and followed the advice and counsel of certain lords spiritual and temporal, and other persons of approved wisdom, prudence, policy, and experience, dreading God, and having tender zeal and affection to indifferent ministration of justice, and to the common and politic weal of the land; then our Lord God was feared, loved, and honoured; then within the land was peace and tranquillity, and among neighbours concord and charity; then the malice of outward enemies was mightily repressed and resisted, and the land honourably defended with many great and glorious victories; then the intercourse of merchandises was largely used and exercised; by which things above remembered, the land was greatly enriched so that as well the merchants and artificers as other poor people, labouring for their living in diverse occupations, had competent gain to the sustenance of them and their households, living without miserable and intolerable poverty.

But afterward, when that such as had the rule and governance of this land, delighting in adulation and flattery and *led by sensuality and concupiscence*, followed the council of persons insolent, vicious, and of inordinate avarice, despising the council of good, virtuous, and prudent persons such as above be remembered, the prosperity of this land daily decreased so that felicity was turned into misery, and prosperity into adversity, and the order of policy, and of the law of God and man, confounded; whereby it is likely this realm to fall into extreme misery and desolation – which God defend – without due provision of convenable remedy be had in this behalf in all godly haste.

Over this, amongst other things, more specifically we consider how that the time of the reign of King Edward IV, late deceased, *after the ungracious pretence of marriage, as all England hath cause to say, made between the said King Edward IV and Elizabeth, sometime wife to Sir John Grey, Knight, late naming herself and many years heretofore Queen of England,* the order of all politic rule was perverted, the laws of God and of God's church, and also the laws of nature, and of England, and also the laudable customs and liberties of the same, wherein every Englishman is inheritor, broken, subverted, and slighted, against all reason and justice, so that this land was ruled by self-will and pleasure, fear and dread, all manner of equity and laws laid apart and despised, whereof ensued many inconveniences and mischiefs, as murders, extortions, and oppressions, namely of poor and impotent people, so that no man was sure of his life, land, nor livelihood, nor of his wife, daughter, no servant, every good maiden and woman standing in dread to be ravished and befouled.

And besides this, what discords, inward battles, effusion of Christian men's blood, and namely, by the destruction of the noble blood of this land, was had and committed within the same, it is evident and notorious through all this realm unto the great sorrow and heaviness of all true Englishmen. *And here also we consider how the said pretended marriage, between the above named King Edward and Elizabeth Grey, was made of great presumption, without the knowing or assent of the lords of this land, and also by sorcery and witchcraft, committed by the said Elizabeth and her mother, Jacquetta Duchess of Bedford, as the common opinion of the people and the public voice and fame is through all this land;* and hereafter, if and as the case shall require, shall be proved sufficiently in time and place convenient. And here also we consider how that the said pretended marriage was made privately and secretly, with edition of banns, in a private chamber, a profane place, and not openly in the face of the church, after the laws of God's church, but contrary thereunto, and the laudable custom of the Church of England.

And how also, that at the time of the contract of the same pretended marriage, and before and long time after, the said King Edward was and stood married and troth plighted to one Dame Eleanor Butler, daughter of the old Earl of Shrewsbury, with whom the said King Edward had made a precontract of matrimony, long time before he made the said pretended marriage with the said Elizabeth Grey in manner and form aforesaid. Which premises being true, as in very truth they are true, it appears and follows evidently, that the said King Edward during his life and the said Elizabeth lived together sinfully and damnably in adultery, against the law of God and his church; and therefore no marvel that the sovereign lord and head of this land, being of such ungodly disposition, and provoking the ire and indignation of our Lord God, such heinous mischiefs and inconveniences as is above remembered, were used and committed in the realm amongst the subjects. *Also it appears evidently and follows that all the issue and children of the said king are bastards, and unable to inherit or to claim anything by inheritance, by the law and custom of England.*

Moreover we consider how that afterward, by the estates of this realm assembled in a Parliament held at Westminster the 17th year of the reign of the said King Edward IV, he then being in possession of the crown and royal estate, by an act made in the same Parliament, George Duke of Clarence, brother to the said King Edward now deceased, was convicted and attainted of high treason; as in the same act is contained more at large. *Because and by reason whereof all the issue of the said George was and is disabled and barred of all right and claim that in any wise they might have or challenge by inheritance to the crown and royal dignity of this realm, by the ancient law and custom of this same realm.*

Over this we consider how that ye be the undoubted son and heir of Richard late Duke of York very inheritor to the said crown and royal dignity as in right King of England by way to inheritance and that at this time the premises duly considered there is no other person living but ye only, that by right may claim the said crown and royal dignity, by way of inheritance, and how that ye be born within this land, by reason whereof, as we deem in our minds, ye be more naturally inclined to the prosperity and common weal of the same: and all the three estates of the land have, and may have more certain knowledge of your birth and filiation above said. We consider also, the great wit, prudence, justice, princely courage, and the memorable and laudable acts in diverse battles which we by experience know ye heretofore have done for the salvation and defence of this same realm, and also the great nobleness and excellence of your birth and blood as of him that is descended of the three most royal houses in Christendom, that is to say, England, France, and Spain.

Wherefore these premises by us diligently considered, we desiring affectuously the peace, tranquillity and public weal of this land, and the reduction of the same to the ancient honourable estate, and prosperity, and having in your great prudence, justice, princely courage and excellent virtue, singular confidence, have chosen in all that is in us nd by this our writing choose you, high and mighty Prince unto our King and sovereign lord &c., to whom we know for certain it appertains of inheritance so to be chosen. And hereupon we humbly desire, pray, and require your said noble grace, that according to this election of us the three estates of this land, as by your true inheritance ye will accept and take upon you the said crown and royal dignity with all things thereunto annexed and appertaining as to you of right belonging as well by inheritance as by lawful election, and in case ye do so we promise to serve and to assist your highness, as true and faithful subjects and liegemen and to live and die with you in this matter and every other just quarrel.

For certainly we are determined rather to adventure and commit us to the peril of our lives and jeopardy of death, than to live in such thraldom and bondage as we have lived long time heretofore, oppressed and injured by new extortions and impositions, against the laws of God and man, and the liberty, old policy and laws of this realm wherein every Englishman is inherited. Our Lord God King of all Kings by whose infinite goodness and eternal providence all things have been principally governed in this world lighten your soul, and grant you grace to do, as well in this matter as in all other, all that may be according to his will and pleasure, and to the common and public weal of this land, so that after great clouds, troubles, storms, and tempests, the son of justice and of grace may shine upon us, to the comfort and gladness of all true Englishmen.

Albeit that the right, title, and estate, which our sovereign lord the King Richard III hath to and in the crown and royal dignity of this realm of England, with all things thereunto annexed and appertaining, have been just and lawful, as grounded upon the laws of God and of nature and also upon the ancient laws and laudable customs of this said realm, and so taken and reputed by all such persons as are learned in the above-said laws and customs. Yet, nevertheless, forasmuch as it is considered that the most parte of the people of this land is not sufficiently learned in the above said laws and customs whereby the truth and right in this behalf of likelihood may be hid, and not clearly known to all the people and thereupon put in doubt and question: And over this how that the court of Parliament is of such authority, and the people of this land of such nature and disposition, as experience teaches that manifestation and declaration of any truth or right made by the three estates of this realm assembled in Parliament, and by authority of the same makes before all other thing, most faith and certainty; and quieting men's minds, removes the occasion of all doubts and seditious language:

Therefore at the request, and by the assent of the three estates of this realm, that is to say, the lords spiritual and temporal and commons of this land, assembled in this present Parliament by authority of the same, be it pronounced, decreed and declared, that our said sovereign lord the king was and is very and undoubted king of this realm of England; with all things thereunto within this same realm, and without it annexed unite and appertaining, as well by right of consanguinity and inheritance as by lawful election, consecration and coronation. And over this, that at the request, and by the assent and authority above said be it ordained, enacted and established that the said crown and royal dignity of this realm, and the inheritance of the same, and other things thereunto within the same realm or without it annexed, unite, and now appertaining, rest and abide in the person of our said sovereign lord the king during his life, and after his decease in his heirs of his body begotten. And especially, at the request and by the assent and authority above said, be it ordained, enacted, established, pronounced, decreed and declared that the high and excellent Prince Edward, son of our said sovereign lord the King, be heir apparent of our said sovereign lord the king, to succeed him in the above said crown and royal dignity, with all things as is aforesaid thereunto unite annexed and appertaining, to have them after the decease of our said sovereign lord the king to him and to his heirs of his body lawfully begotten.

FURTHER READING

Dates are of the most recent, usually paperback editions
Published in London unless otherwise specified

As it appears I did not make it clear enough the last time, this is not an academic bibliography. It is a guide for readers who may wish to pursue their own investigations online, or by daisy-chaining citations in hard copy. I have cited one or two particularly valuable sources in the text, and recommend below, by category, only other books and articles I found informative or stimulating, rather than make an undifferentiated list of all the works consulted.

Nearly all the primary sources are online, along with an enormous amount of genealogical research. Fascinating nuggets can appear if you simply input a name and date. Wikipedia is often useful, but should be cross-checked where possible against the online *Oxford Dictionary of National Biography*, available to anyone with a public library card, or failing that on sites like *Tudor Place* and *Geni*. The *Dictionary of Welsh Biography* is open access.

The Ricardian is partially online, with more back catalogue being added, and is a cornucopia for the period covered in *Blood Royal*. An online index identifies earlier articles that can be downloaded as PDFs. Some articles in other journals are also open access, the rest can be accessed via JSTOR. Those I found useful are listed below.

Second-hand books are easy to find online and I have got into the habit of buying those I need for regular reference that cost less than the price of a round trip to the Cambridge University Library, my home from home. Definitely not in that category is Cora Scofield's two-volume biography of Edward IV published in 1923, an ex-library copy of the 1967 edition of which was wincingly expensive but worth every penny for her unrivalled international research.

More recent biographies of Edward IV, Richard III, Clarence and Warwick the Kingmaker are listed below, also valiant efforts to weave the stories of Elizabeth Woodville and Margaret Beaufort from barely adequate facts. Sources beyond the dreams of historians writing about contemporary English subjects illuminate the standard biographies of Louis XI, Charles the Bold and his father Philippe, and Margaret of York.

Robert Stansfield's prohibitively priced study of the South-West and the West Country fills a gaping hole in the historiography of English regional trouble-spots. Howell Thomas Evans's classic account of Wales has aged well thanks to his bardic sources, but is best checked against Ralph Griffiths's more recent study. The North has been well served by Anthony Pollard and others. No specifically regional studies have been written about the Midlands, East Anglia, the Home Counties or the South-East, but some partial accounts are listed below.

ONLINE PRIMARY SOURCES (search by title)

Anglica Historia (Polydore Vergil).
Battlefields Resource Centre (Battlefields Trust).
Bosworth Contemporary and Tudor Accounts (by permission of Michael Bennett *q.v.*).
Calendar of documents relating to Scotland 1357–1509.
Calendar of Patent Rolls (1461–67; 1467–77; 1476–85).
Calendar of state papers and manuscripts in the archives and collections of Milan.
Calendar of state papers and manuscripts relating to English affairs, existing in the archives and collections of Venice, and in other libraries of northern Italy.
Cely Letters 1472–88.
Chronicle of the Rebellion in Lincolnshire.
Chronicles of London.
Chronicles of the White Rose of York, contains:
   Hearne's Fragment of an Old Chronicle from 1460 to 1470.
   Doctor John Warkworth's Chronicle of the first thirteen years of King Edward the Fourth.
   History of the Arrivall of Edward IV in England and the final recovery of his kingdoms from Henry VI A.D. 1471.
   The Manner and Guiding of the Earl of Warwick at Angiers.

Chroniques (Jean Molinet).

Collection of the chronicles and ancient histories of Great Britain (Jehan de Wavrin).

Complete peerage of England, Scotland, Ireland, Great Britain, and the United Kingdom (lead editor George Cockayne).

Crowland Chronicle Continuations (the hard copy 1986 edition by Nicholas Pronay and John Cox is better).

Excerpta Historica (contains confession of Robert Welles).

Fabyan's 'The new chronicles of England and France', in two parts.

Gerhard von Wesel's Newsletter from England, 17 April 1471 (Hannes Kleineke).

Gregory's Chronicle.

Hall's Chronicle.

History of King Richard the Third (Thomas More).

Letters and Papers, Foreign and Domestic, Henry VIII, Vol. 8, January–July 1535 (contains Chapuys-Cromwell conversation).

Memoirs (Philippe de Commynes).

Oeuvres de Georges Chastellain.

Parliament Rolls of Medieval England 1275–1504.

Paston Letters.

Stonor Letters and Papers 1290–1483.

Usurpation of Richard the Third (Dominic Mancini).

Warwick Roll (John Rous).

SECONDARY SOURCES

BOOKS

Biographical

Armstrong, Charles, 'The Piety of Cecily Duchess of York', in Douglas Woodruff (ed.), *For Hilaire Belloc: Essays in Honour of his 72nd Birthday* (1942).

Baldwin, David, *Elizabeth Woodville: Mother of the Princes in the Tower* (2012).

Breverton, Terry, *Jasper Tudor: Dynasty Maker* (2014).

Castor, Helen, *Blood & Roses: the Paston Family and the Wars of the Roses* (2005).

Dockray, Keith, *William Shakespeare: The Wars of the Roses and the Historians* (Stroud, 2002).

Dockray, Keith, *Richard III: from Contemporary Chronicles, Letters and Records* (2013).

Dockray, Keith, *Edward IV: from Contemporary Chronicles, Letters and Records* (2015).

Field, Peter, *The Life and Times of Sir Thomas Malory* (1993).

Gregory, Philippa, David Baldwin & Michael Jones, *The Women of the Cousins' War* (2013).

Gristwood, Sarah, *Blood Sisters: The Women behind the Wars of the Roses* (2013).

Hicks, Michael, *False, Fleeting, Perjur'd Clarence: George, Duke of Clarence* (1992).

Hicks, Michael, *Warwick the Kingmaker* (2002).

Horrox, Rosemary, *Richard III: A Study of Service* (2010).

Jones, Michael & Malcolm Underwood, *The King's Mother: Lady Margaret Beaufort* (1993).

Kendall, Paul, *Louis XI* (1974).

Kendall, Paul, *Warwick the Kingmaker* (2002).

Mitchell, Rosamund, *John Tiptoft 1427–1470* (1938).

Rawcliffe, Carol, *The Staffords 1394–1512* (Cambridge, 1978).

Ross, Charles, *Edward IV* (1997).

Scofield, Cora, *The Life and Reign of Edward the Fourth, King of England and of France and Lord of Ireland*, 2 vols. (New York, 1967).

Vaughan, Richard, *Charles the Bold: The Last Valois Duke of Burgundy* (2014).

Vaughan, Richard, *Philip the Good: The Apogee of Burgundy* (2014).

Weightman, Christine, *Margaret of York, the Diabolical Duchess* (Stroud, 2012).

Weir, Alison, *The Princes in the Tower* (2011).

Regional

Carpenter, Christine, *Locality and Polity: a Study of Warwickshire Landed Society* (1992).

Evans, Howell Thomas, *Wales and the Wars of the Roses* (1998 – 1915 edition online).

Griffiths, Ralph (ed.), *Patronage, the Crown and the Provinces in Later Medieval England* (Stroud, 1981).

Griffiths, Ralph, *King and Country: England and Wales in the Fifteenth Century* (1991).

Horrox, Rosemary (ed.), *Richard III and the North* (Hull, 1986).

Pollard, Anthony, *North-Eastern England during the Wars of the Roses* (Oxford, 1990).

Pugh, Thomas (ed.), *The Marcher Lordships of South Wales 1415–1536* (1963).

Stansfield, Robert, *Political Elites in South-West England, 1450–1500: Politics, Governance, and the Wars of the Roses* (2009).

Military

Barnard, Francis (ed.), *Edward IV's French expedition of 1475: the Leaders and their Badges* (1975).

Bell, Adrian, Anne Curry, Andy King & David Simpkin (eds.), *The Soldier in later Medieval England* (2013).

Bicheno, Hugh, *Vendetta: High Art and Low Cunning at the Birth of the Renaissance* (2008).

Bicheno, Hugh, *Elizabeth's Sea Dogs: How the English became the Scourge of the Seas* (2012).

Clark, David, *Barnet 1471: Death of a Kingmaker* (2007).

Cunningham, Sean, 'The Yorkists at War: Military Leadership in the English War with Scotland 1480–82', in Kleineke, Hannes & Christian Slater (eds.), *The Yorkist Age* (2014).

Foard, Glenn & Anne Curry, *Bosworth 1485: a Battlefield Rediscovered* (Oxford, 2013).

Foss, Peter, *The Field of Redemore: the Battle of Bosworth* (1998).

Gill, Louise, *Richard III and Buckingham's Rebellion* (1999).

Goodchild, Steven, *Tewkesbury: Eclipse of the House of Lancaster 1471* (2005).

Goodman, Anthony, *The Wars of the Roses: the Soldiers' Experience* (2005).

Haigh, Philip, '...*Where both the hosts fought...*': the Rebellions of 1469–70 and the Battles of Edgecote and Lose-Cote Field* (1997).

Hammond, Peter, *The Battles of Barnet and Tewkesbury* (Stroud, 1990).

Ingram, Mike, *Bosworth 1485* (2012).

Jones, Michael, *Bosworth 1485: Psychology of a Battle* (2002).

Lander, Jack, 'The Hundred Years War and Edward IV's Campaign in France', in Arthur Slavin (ed.), *Tudor Men and Institutions* (Louisiana State University, 1972)

Matthews, Rupert, *The Battle of Losecoat Field 1470* (2013).

Rodger, Nicholas, *The Safeguard of the Sea: a Naval History of Britain 660–1649* (2004).

General

Bellamy, John, *Crime and Public Order in England during the later Middle Ages* (1973).

Bramley, Peter, *A Companion and Guide to the Wars of the Roses* (2011).

Kekewich, Margaret, Colin Richmond, Anne Sutton, Livia Visser-Fuchs & John Watts (eds.), *The Politics of Fifteenth-Century England: John Vale's Book* (1995).

Lander, Jack, *The Limitations of English Monarchy in the Later Middle Ages* (1989).

Pisan, Christine de (trans. Sarah Lawson), *The Treasure of the City of Ladies, or, The Book of the Three Virtues* (2003).
Power, Eileen, *The Wool Trade in English Medieval History* (1941) – online.
Ross, Charles (ed.), *Patronage, Pedigree, and Power in Later Medieval England* (1979).
Wagner, John, *Encyclopedia of the Wars of the Roses* (2011).

ARTICLES
(alphabetical by journal and chronological)

Archaeologia Aeliana
> Charlesworth, D., 'Northumberland in the early years of Edward IV' (1952).

Bulletin of the Board of Celtic Studies
> Lowe, D., 'The Council of the Prince of Wales and the decline of the Herbert family during the second reign of Edward IV' (1976–78).
> Lowe, D., 'Patronage and Politics: Edward IV, the Wydevilles and the Council of the Prince of Wales' (1981).

Bulletin of the Institute of Historical Research
> Peake, M., 'London and the Wars of the Roses' (1926–7).
> Lander, J., 'Council, administration and councillors' (1959).
Lander, J., 'Marriage and politics in the fifteenth century: the Nevills and the Wydevills' (1963).
> Hicks, M., 'Descent, partition and extinction: the Warwick inheritance' (1979).
> Hicks, M., 'The Beauchamp Trust, 1439–87' (1981).
> Orme, N., 'The education of Edward V' (1984).
> Allan, A., 'Royal propaganda and the proclamations of Edward IV' (1986).

Bulletin of the John Rylands Library
> Myers, A., 'The household of Queen Elizabeth Woodville 1466–7' (1967–8).

Economic History Review
> Payling, S., 'Social mobility, demographic change, and landed society in late-medieval England' (1992).
> Payling, S., 'The economics of marriage in late medieval England: the marriage of heiresses' (2001).

English Historical Review
> Storey, R., 'The wardens of the marches of England towards Scotland 1377–1489' (1957).

Lander, J.,'The Yorkist council and administration' (1968).

Richmond, C., 'Fauconberg's Kentish rising of May 1471' (1970).

Holland, P., 'The Lincolnshire rebellion of March 1470' (1988).

Virgoe, R., 'The benevolence of 1481' (1989).

Historical Journal

Lander, J., 'Attainder and forfeiture 1453–1509' (1961).

History

Richmond, C., 'English naval power in the fifteenth century' (1967).

Rosenthal, Joel, 'Other victims: peeresses as war widows, 1450–1500' (1987).

Journal of Medieval Military History

Curry, A. & A. Bell, 'Soldiers, weapons & armies in the fifteenth century' (2011).

Nottingham Medieval Studies

Ballard, M., 'An expedition of English archers to Liège in 1467 and the Anglo-Burgundian marriage alliance' (1990).

Northern History

Hicks, M., 'The Duke of Somerset and Lancastrian localism in the North' (1986).

Parliamentary History

Jurkowski, M., 'Parliamentary and prerogative taxation in the reign of Edward IV' (1999).

The Ricardian

Hillier, K., 'The Rebellion of 1483: Part 1', PDF (September 1982).

Hillier, K., 'The Rebellion of 1483: Part 2', PDF (March 1983).

Dockray, K., 'The Yorkshire Rebellions of 1469' PDF (December 1983).

Visser-Fuchs, L., 'The Casualty List of the Battle of Barnet', PDF (March 1988).

Transactions of the Royal Historical Society

Armstrong, C., 'The Inauguration ceremonies of Yorkist Kings and their title to the throne' (1948).

Brown, A., 'The King's councillors in fifteenth-century England' (1969).

Morgan, D., 'The King's affinity in the polity of Yorkist England' (1973).

University of Birmingham Historical Journal

Knecht, R., 'The Episcopate and the Wars of the Roses' (1957).

ACKNOWLEDGEMENTS

With many thanks to Ian Drury, Literary Agent *extraordinaire*, Lyn McMeekin, for her invaluable beta reading and Georgina Blackwell, for her excellent production.

IMAGE CREDITS

Stained glass window of Edward IV and Elizabeth Woodville (Topham / Woodmanstern)

King Edward IV (Royal Collection Trust © Her Majesty Queen Elizabeth II, 2016 / Bridgeman Images)

Elizabeth Woodville (Queen's College, Cambridge)

Richard Neville, Earl of Warwick (Wikimedia Commons)

Louis XI of France (Wikimedia Commons)

Charles the Bold, Duke of Burgundy (Wikimedia Commons)

King Richard III (Wikimedia Commons)

An early portrait of King Richard III (Society of Antiquaries of London / Bridgeman Images)

Bust of Henry VII (Wikimedia Commons)

INDEX

'n' after a page number refers to a footnote

Alcock, John, Bishop of Rochester 165, 223, 263
Alnwick, sieges of 14, 17, 18
Alyngton, William 214, 249
Angus, Earl of *see* Douglas, George; Douglas, James
Anjou, Marguerite d', Queen of
  army of 45
  character 76, 167
  and Charles Burgundy 25
  death of 307
  and Edward IV 190
  and Louis XI 15, 36, 40, 158, 253, 255
  and Richard Neville, Earl of Warwick 4, 159–60, 193
  at Tewkesbury 200
Anjou, René d', Duke 37, 38, 72–3
Arundel, Earl of *see* FitzAlan, William
Arundel, Thomas 302
Audley, Baron *see* Tuchet, John
Austria, Archduke Maximilian of 246–7, 256, 336, 346

Balue, Cardinal Jean 147, 149
Bamburgh, sieges of 14, 17, 22, 130
Barnard Castle 88, 156, 206
Barnet, Battle of (1471) 185–90
Baynard's Castle 141, 279, 289
Beauchamp, Anne, Countess of Warwick 8, 55, 192, 209, 210
Beaufort, Edmund, Duke of Somerset 13, 27, 44, 170, 192, 198–9, 239
Beaufort, Henry, Duke of Somerset 18, 24, 34, 183, 188, 192, 199
Beaufort, John, Marquess of Dorset 170, 183
Beaufort, Margaret, Countess of Richmond 8, 167, 297
Beaujeu, Anne of 89, 296
Beaumont, William, Viscount 13, 58–9, 168, 175, 179, 182, 223, 317
Beaune, Jean de 173
Bedford, Duke of *see* Neville, George
Bellingham, Henry 28, 58, 104
Bergavenny, Baron *see* Neville, Edward
Berkeley, Baron William, later Earl of

Nottingham 153, 258, 290
Berkhamsted Castle 114
Berners, Baron *see* Bourchier, John
Berry, Charles, Duke of 71, 72–3, 147, 148, 149
Berwick-upon-Tweed 15, 17, 36, 265, 269, 270, 313
Bishop's Lynn 225
Blore Heath, Battle of (1459) 179, 320
Blount, James 317
Blount, John, Baron Mountjoy 223, 317
Blount, Walter, Baron Mountjoy 51, 166, 189
Bonville and Harington, Baroness Cecily 62, 218
Booth, Laurence, Prince-Bishop of Durham 156, 206, 243
Booth, William, Archbishop of York 23
Bosworth, Battle of (1485) 334–44
Boteler, Lady Eleanor 274, 288–9
Boteler, Ralph 183
Bourchier, Edward, Baron FitzWarin 293
Bourchier, Henry, Viscount, later Earl of Essex 91, 165, 201, 202, 222, 242, 275, 293
Bourchier, Humphrey, Baron Cromwell 51, 166, 185, 188
Bourchier, Humphrey, son of Baron Berners 185, 189
Bourchier, John, Baron Berners 293
Bourchier, John, Baron Ferrers of Groby 46
Bourchier, Thomas 46, 298, 325, 329
Bourchier, Thomas, Cardinal Archbishop of Canterbury 94, 96, 112, 127, 133, 165, 175, 242, 279, 282, 286, 309–10,
Bourchier, William, Baron FitzWarin 154, 293
Bourchier, William, Viscount Bourchier 46, 51, 62, 96
Bracher, William 298, 344
Brackenbury, Robert 291, 323, 329, 344
Bray, Reginald 297
Brecon Castle 300
Breton pirates 283
Brézé, Pierre de 15, 17, 18, 71, 73, 98
Brittany, Fransez, Duke of
  and Edward IV 92, 173, 224, 231, 238, 275
  and Edward Woodville 283, 298

and Henry VI 314
and Jasper Tudor 57
and John Stafford 35
and Louis XI 30, 39, 72, 73, 102, 145, 225, 257–8
and Pierre Landais 316
Brooke, John, Baron Cobham 62, 194
Brown, George 297
Brugge, Lodewijk van, lord of Gruuthuse 164, 170, 172, 174, 224
Buckingham, Duke of see Stafford, Henry
Burgh, Thomas, lord of Gainsborough 137, 138, 298
Burgundy, Anthony, Grand Bastard of 80, 90, 93
Burgundy, Charles 'the Bold,' Duke of and alliance conditions 224
  Anglo-Burgundian offensive 231–7
  character 150–1
  death of 245
  and Edward IV 129, 161, 170, 174
  and Frederick III 226–7
  and Henry Beaufort 21, 34–5
  and Louis XI 30, 39, 41, 72–5, 144, 146–8, 158, 193
  and Marguerite d'Anjou 25
  marriage 104
  and Philippe de Commynes 171–2
  and Richard Neville, Earl of Warwick 89
Burgundy, Marie, Duchess of 94, 227, 245, 256
Burgundy, Philippe, Duke of 34–6, 38, 40, 41, 72, 80, 81, 92
Butler, John, Earl of Ormond 13, 168

Caernarvon Castle 57
Caister, siege of (1470) 129
Calais 4, 15, 112, 154–6, 203, 316–17
Canterbury 202
Carlisle 23
Castille see Isabella, Queen of Castille
Catesby, William 284, 289, 304, 312, 344
Chandée, Philibert de, lord of Montfalcon 325, 333, 337, 340
Chapuys, Eustace 280–1, 348
Charles VII of France 15, 31, 34, 36, 39, 72
Charolais, Count of see Burgundy, Charles
Chaucer, Alice, dowager Duchess of Suffolk 60
Chaucer, Geoffrey 60

Chester 70, 264, 321
Chirk Castle 24, 210, 264
Cinque Ports 120, 202
Cirencester 194
Clapham, John 121, 126, 127
Clarence, George, Duke of 64–75
  Battle of Barnet 181–2
  character 5
  and Duchess Cecily Neville 212
  and Edward IV 119–20, 136, 141–3, 152, 208, 210
  loss of estates 168
  marriage 94, 113, 119, 246
  and Robert Welles 137
  sibling rivalry 87, 244–5
  treason 115, 170, 248–9
Clifton, Gervase 216
Cobham, Baron see Brooke, John
Collynsbourne, William 311–12
Commons, House of 14, 214, 228–9, 268
Commynes, Philippe de
  and Charles Burgundy 74, 171–2
  and Edward IV 230, 231, 237, 256
  Franco-Burgundian war 254
  and Louis XI 145, 146–7
Conisbrough 204
Constable, Marmaduke 301, 309
Conyers, John 114, 128, 152, 179
Cooke, Thomas 104–5, 120, 183, 305
Corbet, Richard 99
Council, Great 41, 48, 50, 94, 128, 133, 134–6
Council, Privy 46, 208, 276–7, 278, 282–3
Courtenay of Bocconoc, Edward 301
Courtenay of Bocconoc, Hugh 154, 193, 199
Courtenay, Elizabeth 154
Courtenay, Henry 105, 106, 153, 310
Courtenay, Peter, Bishop of Exeter 301
Courtenays of Powderham, Humphrey, Walter and William 153–4, 193
Coventry 97, 121, 128, 142, 180–1, 200
Cromwell, Baron see Bourchier, Humphrey
Cromwell, Thomas 280, 347
Crowland Chronicle Continuations
  (Crowland Continuator) 227, 238–9, 241, 248, 252–3, 270–1, 272–3, 277, 288, 311, 319, 331, 344, 347

Dacre, Humphrey, Baron Dacre of the North 13, 135

Daubeney, Giles 300
Dempsey, Jack 181
Denbigh Castle 57
Devereux, Walter, Baron Ferrers of Chartley
53–7, 161, 185, 262, 300, 311, 341, 344
Devon, Earl of *see* Stafford of Southwyck
Dorset, Marquess of *see* Beaufort, John; Grey,
Thomas
Douglas, Archibald, Red Earl of Angus 267
Douglas, George, Red Earl of Angus 17, 18
Douglas, James, Black Earl of Angus 79, 268,
315
Dover 191, 234
Dudley, Baron *see* Sutton, John
Dunstanburgh, sieges of 14, 17
Duras, Gaillard, lord of 79, 154, 172, 224,
227, 231
Durrell, Lawrence 350
Dynham, Baron John 62, 154, 302, 317

East Anglia 58, 60, 61, 113, 175, 310
Edgcote, Battle of (1469) 122–7, 156
Edinburgh 270
Edward IV 10–19, 53–63, 76–83, 93–101,
102–10, 221–9
Anglo-Burgundian offensive 231–7
Battle of Barnet 179–81, 185–90
Battle of Edgcote 124–7
Battle of Losecote Field 142–3
Battle of Tewkesbury 194–201
Battle of Towton 10–11
children 257–8
estates of the crown 65–8
finances 174, 250–2
Franco-Burgundian Treaty of Arras 256
and Henry Percy 175
and Henry VI 1
and Laurence Booth 23
and Louis XI 30
and the Nevilles 84–92, 133–4, 213–16
and Northumbria 28
and property rights 203–4
reign of 6, 8, 272–6
and Richard Neville 3–4, 111–15, 127,
130, 131, 155, 163, 175
and the Scots 25, 28
siblings 132, 181–2, 203–4, 208, 241–9,
302
and the Woodvilles 42, 44–9, 52–3,
212–13, 218, 288–9

Edward of Middleham, Prince of Wales 309,
346
Edward of Westminster, Prince of Wales 160,
190, 192, 249
Edward, Prince of Wales (Edward V)
birth 87, 170
childhood 216, 217, 262
protection of 275, 286
reign of 276, 278, 282–3, 291
Egmond, Arnold, Duke of 150
Essex, Earl of *see* Bourchier, Henry
Exeter 122, 153, 154, 193–4
Exeter, Duke of *see* Holland, Henry
Eynon, David ap 58, 104

Fauconberg, Baron *see* Neville, William
Fauconberg, 'Bastard of' *see* Neville, Thomas
Faunt, Nicholas 200, 202
Ferrers of Chartley, Baron *see* Devereux,
Walter
Ferrers of Groby, Baroness Elizabeth 46, 219
Fiennes, William, Baron Saye and Sele 185,
189
FitzAlan, Thomas, Baron Maltravers 185
FitzAlan, William, Earl of Arundel 48, 91,
107, 157, 161
FitzHugh, Baron Henry 18, 20, 86, 114, 161,
162
FitzLewis, Mary 216
Fitzwarin, Baron *see* Bourchier, Edward;
Bourchier, William
Fogge, John 105, 120, 298, 320, 329
Fortescue, Dr John 165, 166–7, 191
Fortescue, John (knight) 223, 317
Fotheringhay 113, 114, 213, 243, 269
Frederick III, Emperor 232
French pirates 156, 224

Gates, Geoffrey 77n, 121, 165, 200, 201, 203
Gaunt, John of 3, 9, 68, 318
Gloucester 195–6
Gloucester, John of 317
Gloucester, Richard, Duke of 203–11
Battle of Barnet 185, 189
coup d'état 282–9
and Edward IV 25, 86, 132, 241–9, 302
lord of Elfael 262
and Margaret of York 173
and Richard Neville 88
Scots raids 265–6

and the Woodvilles 276–7, 278–81
see also Richard III
Glyn Dŵr, Owain 54, 57, 324
Grantham 321
Great Chronicle of London 183, 184, 202,
229, 329
Grey, Edward, Viscount Lisle 127, 287
Grey, Richard 58, 264, 278
Grey of Ruthyn, Baron Henry, later Earl of
Kent 20
Grey, Thomas, Marquess of Dorset, 77,
218–19, 264, 278, 283, 286, 299, 301,
320, 325
Grey, William, Bishop of Ely 132, 165, 207
Greystoke, Baron Ralph 20, 86
Gruuthuse, lord of see Brugge, Lodewijk van
Guelders, Mary of 22
Guînes 317

Hammes 222, 223, 317
Hanseatic League (Hansards) 99, 164, 172,
174, 225, 305
Harcourt, Robert 79, 169
Harlech Castle 57, 102–3, 166, 326
Harrington, James 179, 207
Hastings, Baron William, 6, 46, 50, 53, 59,
87, 90, 115, 118–19, 157, 185, 188, 203,
218–9, 276–7, 284–5, 293–4
Hastings, Richard, Baron Welles 142n, 290,
310
Hatcliffe, William 225, 227
Haute, Richard 259, 278, 298, 320
Hedgeley Moor, Battle of (1464) 27
Hedingham 175
Henry VI, King of England
and Archbishop Neville 183
Battle of Towton 1
childhood friends 58
death of 201
and Edward IV 184
exiled 15, 27, 28, 85
reign of 3, 165, 169
and Richard Neville 192
virtues of 79
Henry VII, King of England 291, 318, 344,
346, 333
see also Tudor, Henry
Herbert of Raglan, Baron William, later Earl
of Pembroke 6, 54–8, 92, 101, 103, 104,
122–7

Herbert, Richard 54, 77
Herbert, William, Baron Dunster 135, 217,
260, 262, 286, 324, 326, 328
Hervey, Nicholas 195, 199
Hexham, Battle of (1464) 27
Hildyard, Robert, 'Robin of Holderness' 109,
112, 153
Holland, Henry, Duke of Exeter 13, 57, 170,
179, 189, 238
Home Counties 88
Hornby Castle 207
Howard, Baron John, later Duke of Norfolk,
25, 53, 61, 156, 166, 182, 203, 239, 255,
259, 268, 276–7, 284, 289, 293, 297, 314,
326, 341–2, 344, 349
Howard, Thomas, Earl of Surrey 284, 290,
309, 344
Hungerford, Baron Robert 2, 13, 22, 27, 193
Hungerford, Thomas 105, 193
Hungerford, Walter 194
Huntingdon, Earl of see Herbert, William

Isabella, Queen of Castille 26

James III, King of Scotland 22, 265, 266,
270, 314–15
Jones, Michael 296

Kendall, John 289
Kennedy, James, Bishop of St Andrews 5, 40
Kent, Earl of see Grey of Ruthyn; Neville,
William
Knaresborough 204, 206

Landais, Pierre 316
Langley, Philippa 347
Langstrother, John 129, 132, 174, 191, 199
Latimer, Baron see Neville, George
Latimer, Nicholas 302
Leconfield 109, 178
Leicester 24, 180, 182, 326, 334, 348
Liège 37, 80, 145–8
Lincoln, Earl of see Pole, John de la
Lisle, Viscount see Talbot, Thomas
London, City of 24, 214, 225, 226, 251, 305
Lords, House of 227, 249, 288
Lorraine, René II, Duke of 232, 245
Losecote Field, Battle of (1470) 142, 156
Lotharingia 150, 224n
Louis XI of France 30–41

Anglo-Burgundian offensive 144, 231–7, 234–5
character 5
and Charles, Duke of Berry 71–3
and Clarence 222
death of 296
and Duke Berry 149
and Duke Charles 74
and Edward IV 163, 223–4, 231, 239, 246
and enemies 102–3, 172
Franco-Burgundian war 156, 245, 253, 254
health 256
and Liège revolts 145–8
and Marguerite d'Anjou 15
and Richard Neville 85–6, 91, 93, 158–9, 173, 193
Lovell, Baron Francis, later Viscount, 18, 86, 88, 97, 271, 286, 289, 294, 311, 323, 344
Ludford campaign (1459) 321
Ludlow Castle 64, 217, 260, 309
Lumley, Baron Thomas 86
Luttrell family 54, 58, 154, 193, 301
Luxembourg, Jacques de 50
Luxembourg, Jacquetta de 7, 44–5, 47, 76, 77, 128, 212, 214
Luxembourg, Louis de 35, 71, 80, 146, 158, 173, 234–5, 238
Lynom, Thomas 285

Mackerell, Dr Ralph 165, 166
Maletta, Alberico 41
Maltravers, Baron see FitzAlan, Thomas
Mancini, Dominic 77–8, 213, 273, 281, 284, 288, 290, 347
Marches, Scots 260, 265–70
Marches, Welsh 88, 101, 103, 217, 260–5, 268, 275
Maredudd, Rhys ap 328, 343
Markham, Dr John 105
Martin, George R. R. 285, 349
Michelson, Robert 175
Middleham 27, 88, 128, 161
Midlands, the 68, 88, 217, 310–11
Milan, Duke of see Sforza, Francesco; Sforza, Galeazzo Maria
Minster Lovell 294
Molinet, Jean 337, 340, 343
Montagu, Marquess see Neville, John
Montgomery, Thomas 239, 317
More Palace 113, 221–2, 279

More, Thomas 273–4, 285, 291, 294, 297
Mortimer's Cross, Battle of (1461) 35, 123, 203
Morton, Dr John, 165–6, 227, 239, 251–3, 255, 285, 297, 299, 310, 316
Mountjoy, Baron see Blount, Walter
Mowbray, Anne, Countess of Norfolk 258, 259
Mowbray, John, Duke of Norfolk 60, 129, 165, 197, 199, 258
Myling, Thomas, Abbot of Westminster 216, 263–4
Mytton, Thomas 300, 328

Nanfan, Richard 3, 302
Neville, Anne, Duchess of Gloucester 160, 167, 192, 200, 208–9, 290, 294, 312
Neville, Cecily, dowager Duchess of York
absence from state events 243–4, 290
'adulteress' 3, 64, 279–80
and Edward IV 8, 207, 209
and Elizabeth Woodville 44, 51, 65, 70, 78, 184, 279
'Rose of Raby' 206
Neville, Edward, Baron Bergavenny 55, 61
Neville, George, Baron Bergavenny 200, 264
Neville, George, Baron Latimer 124, 135
Neville, George, Bishop of Exeter/
Archbishop of York, 23, 45, 86–7, 90, 92, 96–7, 109, 119, 127, 129, 165, 174, 183–4, 221–3
Neville, George, Duke of Bedford 7, 133, 166
Neville, Isabel, Duchess of Clarence 94, 112, 119, 154, 155, 208, 209, 245, 247
Neville, John, Baron Montagu, 20–2, 23, 27–8, 107–8, 110, 133–4, 153, 163, 179
Neville, Katherine, dowager Duchess of Norfolk 48, 58, 60, 61, 258, 293–4
Neville, Katherine, Lady Harington 62
Neville, Ralph, Earl of Westmorland 28, 130, 204, 206
Neville, Richard 'the Kingmaker,' Earl of Warwick and Salisbury 20–9, 84–92
Battle of Barnet 180, 185–90
and the Bonville succession 62–3
and Charles Burgundy 240
and Clarence, Duke of York 141–2, 182
and Edward IV 3–5, 43–4, 51, 53, 57, 93–4, 97–9, 142–3, 152

and France 93, 155, 168–9, 174
government personnel 132
and Henry VI 165
and John Tiptoft 166
and Marguerite d'Anjou 159–60, 191, 193
military leader 17–19, 111–21, 129, 130, 157, 163
sieges in the North-East 15–17
Neville, Thomas, 'Bastard of Fauconberg' 156, 200–1
Neville, William, Baron Fauconberg 17, 20, 174, 188
Nibley Green, Battle of (1470) 153
Noreys, William 180
Norfolk, Duke of (d.1476) see Mowbray, John
Norfolk, Duke of (k.1485) see Howard, Baron John
Normandy 86, 93, 156, 159, 162, 231–2, 234
North, the 22, 57, 97, 161, 203, 266, 321
Northampton 121, 126, 277
Northampton, Battle of (1460) 4, 20, 35, 51, 59, 94, 107, 187
Northumberland, Earl of see Percy, Henry
Northumberland, Earl of (k.1471) see Neville, John
Nottingham 206, 309, 315, 331

Ogle, Baron Robert 17, 23, 86, 114, 120–1, 122, 123, 125
Oxford, Earl of see Vere, John

Parliament
Acts of 210, 259, 290
postponements 26, 129, 130, 287
Rolls of 296
sessions 223, 229, 274–5
statutes 306
Titulus Regius 281, 288, 304–5
Parr of Kendal, William, lord (Baron Kendal) 121, 152, 179, 222, 289
Paston, John 26, 131, 222
Paston Letters, The 26, 129, 221
Pembroke Castle 57, 70, 203, 325, 326
Pembroke, Earl of see Herbert, William; Tudor, Jasper
Penshurst Palace 304
Percy, Henry, Earl of Northumberland 17, 104, 123, 127, 133, 135, 153, 161, 175, 200, 204, 206, 265, 326, 332, 334, 337,

340–1
Percy, Ralph 14, 15, 18, 22, 27
Percy of Scotton, Robert 289, 344
Péronne 146, 156, 158, 163, 172
Picquigny 6, 253, 254, 257, 321
Pisan, Christine de 213
Pole, John de la, Duke of Suffolk 60, 86, 107, 286
Pole, John de la, Earl of Lincoln 107, 293, 294, 309, 346
Pontefract Castle 179, 287, 294, 296
Portugal, Isabella of, Duchess of Burgundy 150–1, 173
Purbeck peninsula 192

Raglan Castle 57, 262
Ratcliffe, Richard 284, 289, 312, 344
Ravenspur 178
Richard, Duke of York (k. 1459) 60, 107, 243–4, 264, 296
Richard, Duke of York (x. 1483) 3, 64
Richard III 289–92, 293–303, 304–12
Battle of Bosworth 8, 326, 328–33, 336–7, 342, 343
character 347–8
and Henry Tudor 318–19
and James III 315–16
military leader 313
and the Stanleys 320–2
strategic planning 323
and Wales 324
see also Gloucester, Richard
Richard III Foundation 296, 347
Richmond, Countess of see Beaufort, Margaret
Richmond, Earl of see Henry VII; Tudor, Henry
Rivers, Baron/Earl see Woodville, Richard
Rivers, Earl see Woodville, Anthony
Robin of Holderness see Hildyard, Robert
Robin of Redesdale 108, 113, 115, 119
Roos, Edmund 168, 206
Roos, Baron Thomas 13, 18, 27, 59
Russell, John, Bishop of Lincoln 227, 282, 287, 289, 298

Saint-Pol, Count of see Luxembourg, Louis de
Salisbury 105
Salisbury, Earl of see Neville, Richard
Salkeld, Richard 114, 156

Sandal Castle 204
Sandwich 112
Savage, John 324–5, 328, 340
Savoy, Bona of, Princess 40, 41, 43
Saye and Sele, Baron see Fiennes, William
Scales, Baron see Woodville, Anthony
Scrope of Bolton, Baron John 79, 86, 114, 152, 179
Severn, River 195, 196, 299
Sforza, Francesco, Duke of Milan 79, 158
Sforza, Galeazzo Maria, Duke of Milan 90
Shakespeare, William 1–2, 42, 345, 347
Shaw, Dr Ralph 281, 291
Sheriff Hutton 203, 278, 294, 309
Shore, Jane 273–4, 285
Shrewsbury 86, 217, 300, 328
Shrewsbury, Earl of (d.1473) see Talbot, John
Shrewsbury, Earl of (d.1538) see Talbot, George
Sigismund of Austria, Archduke 150, 232
Smert, John 234
Somerset, Charles 349
Somerset, Duke of see Beaufort, Henry
South-East, the 114, 161, 163, 185, 191, 298
South-West, the 88, 301
Southampton 154, 155, 224, 283, 323
St Albans, First Battle of (1455) 4n
St Albans, Second Battle of (1461) 36, 45, 46, 122
St John's Hospital (London) 129, 312
St Leger, Thomas 164, 238, 239, 301
St Martin's Le Grand 165, 184, 209
St Michael's Mount 223
St Paul's Cathedral 184, 189, 281, 312
Stafford, Henry (k.1471) 185, 188
Stafford, Henry (x.1483), Duke of Buckingham 217, 249, 261, 277–8, 288, 289, 294, 296–9
Stafford, John, Earl of Wiltshire 35, 54, 58, 59, 107, 122–4, 166, 167
Stafford of Grafton, Humphrey 299, 344
Stafford of Southwyck, Baron Humphrey, later Earl of Devon 13, 44, 53, 62, 63, 106, 134
Stanley, George, Baron Strange 265, 285, 299, 301, 321–2, 329, 331–3
Stanley, Lady Margaret see Beaufort, Margaret
Stanley, Baron Thomas, later Earl of Derby 25, 91, 203, 207, 239, 264–5, 289, 320–2,

328–9, 334, 337, 340–1
Stanley, William 180, 264, 285, 320–2, 336, 337, 340–1, 343
Stewart, Bernard, Seigneur d'Aubigny 296, 315, 325
Stillington, Richard, Bishop of Bath and Wells 96, 100, 165, 194, 286, 288
Stockholm syndrome 319
Stonor Letters and Papers 287–8
Strange, Baron see Stanley, George
Sudeley, Ralph, Baron see Boteler, Ralph
Suffolk, Duke of see Pole, John de la
Surrey, Earl of see Howard, Thomas
Sutton, John, Baron Dudley 179
Sutton, William, Bishop of Durham 179, 206

Tailboys, William 14, 27
Talbot, George, Earl of Shrewsbury 262
Talbot, Gilbert 289, 300, 328, 340, 342
Talbot, John, Earl of Shrewsbury 13, 54, 86, 94, 152, 182, 289
Talbot, Thomas, Viscount Lisle 153, 258
Tewkesbury Abbey and town 199, 249, 296
Tewkesbury, Battle of (1471) 194–201, 313
Tey, Josephine 347
Thames, River 201, 275
Thomas, Morgan and David ap 203
Thomas, Rhys ap 324, 326, 328, 346
Tiptoft, John, Earl of Worcester 17, 21, 26, 27, 51, 77, 157, 166
Titulus Regius 281, 288, 305
Towton, Battle of (1461) 1, 2, 3, 10–11, 18, 53, 101, 125
Trent, River 97
Tresham, Thomas 106, 199
Tuchet, Humphrey 199
Tuchet, John, Baron Audley 44, 120, 231
Tuddenham, Thomas 21
Tudor, Henry, Earl of Richmond and Henry VII, King of England
    Battle of Bosworth 328–33, 340, 342–3
    character 313–14
    exiled 283
    and Jasper Tudor 167
    marriage 301, 307, 324
    and William Herbert 57, 104
    'Yeomen of the Guard' 298
Tudor, Jasper, Earl of Pembroke
    Battle of Edgcote 126
    and Edward IV 194, 203

and Henry Tudor 167, 328
and Louis XI 93, 102–3
military leader 313
Mortimer's Cross 13, 35, 300
and Pierre Landais 316
and Richard III 312, 324
and Richard Neville 164
and William Herbert 54, 57
Tudor, Owen 203
Tunstall, Richard 28, 58, 104, 166
Tutbury Castle 69, 209
Twt Hill, Battle of (1461) 57
Tyrell, James 285, 291, 317

Valois, Catherine de 318
Vaughan of Monmouth, Thomas 222, 278,
  283, 288, 297, 346
Vaughan of Tretower, Roger 54, 203
Vaughan of Tretower, Thomas 54, 278, 300
Veere, lord of 174
Veere, port 172
Vere, John, Earl of Oxford 21, 51, 60–1, 106,
  109–10, 114, 134–5, 166, 175, 179, 182,
  188–9, 222–3, 249, 299, 313, 317, 320,
  333, 336, 340–3
Vernon, Henry 326

Wakefield 2
Wakefield, Battle of (1460) 3, 36, 62, 64,
  204, 207, 216, 243
Warkworth's Chronicle 106, 114, 202
Warren, Brian 188
Warwick, Countess of see Beauchamp, Anne
Warwick, Earl of see Neville, Richard
Welles, Baron Richard 86, 142, 331
Welles, Robert, Baron Willoughby 18, 86,
  137, 141–2, 302, 331
Wenlock, Baron John 40, 89, 105, 154, 172,
  191, 198, 199
Wesel, Gerhard von 186–7, 189
West Country, the 62–3, 106, 157, 163, 218,
  268, 301–2
Westminster Abbey 50, 137, 165, 170, 184,
  278, 288, 306
Westminster, Palace of 135, 165, 247, 248,
  272, 371
Williams, Richard 324–5, 326
Willoughby, Baron see Welles, Robert
Windsor Castle 310
Woodville, Anne, Countess Bourchier,

Countess of Kent 96, 309
Woodville, Anthony, Baron Scales/Earl Rivers
Battle of Barnet 189
character 214–16
and Edward IV 127
execution 287–8
military leader 77, 79, 154, 173, 201, 224,
  275
treason 283
and William Hastings 276–8
Woodville, Catherine, Duchess of
Buckingham 51, 52, 290
Woodville, Edward 77, 224, 277, 283, 298,
  314
Woodville, Eleanor, Countess of Kent 289
Woodville, Elizabeth, Queen of England
  42–52, 212–20
children 65, 87–8, 170, 264, 274, 278
and Margaret Stanley 301
marriage 7, 41
and Richard III 306–7, 319
at Westminster Abbey 165
Woodville, Jacquetta, Lady Strange of
Knockyn 47, 265, 301
Woodville, Joan 265, 278
Woodville, John 48, 50, 51, 60, 127
Woodville, Lionel, Bishop of Salisbury 77,
  278, 286, 300, 310
Woodville, Margaret, Lady Maltravers 349
Woodville, Mary, Lady Dunster/Countess of
Pembroke/Countess of Huntingdon 135
Woodville, Richard, Baron and Earl Rivers 7,
  44–5, 50, 51, 166
Woodville, Richard (son) 50, 300, 320
Worcester, Earl of see Tiptoft, John
Worcester, William of 182

York 162, 284, 296
York, Anne of, Duchess of Exeter 238
York, Archbishop of see Booth, William;
  Neville, George, Bishop of Exeter
York, Cecily, dowager Duchess of see Neville,
  Cecily
York, Elizabeth of, Princess 136, 235, 256,
  257, 280, 291, 308, 324
York, Margaret of, Duchess of Burgundy 89,
  90, 92, 104–5, 145, 170, 173, 208, 209,
  226, 232, 245, 255, 346

Zouche, Baron John de la 62, 63, 311, 344